VIOLENCE AND SUICIDALITY

Clinical and Experimental Psychiatry

Monograph Series of the Department of Psychiatry
Albert Einstein College of Medicine of Yeshiva University/
Montefiore Medical Center
New York, N.Y.

1. ***Contemporary Approaches to Psychological Assessment***
SCOTT WETZLER, Ph.D., & MARTIN M. KATZ, Ph.D.; Eds.

2. ***Computer Applications in Psychiatry and Psychology***
DAVID BASKIN, Ph.D.; Ed.

3. ***Violence and Suicidality: Perspectives in Clinical and Psychobiological Research***
HERMAN M. van PRAAG, M.D., Ph.D., ROBERT PLUTCHIK, Ph.D., & ALAN APTER, M.D.; Eds.

Clinical & Experimental Psychiatry Monograph No. 3

VIOLENCE AND SUICIDALITY

Perspectives in Clinical and Psychobiological Research

Edited by

HERMAN M. VAN PRAAG, M.D., Ph.D.
ROBERT PLUTCHIK, Ph.D.
ALAN APTER, M.D.

Routledge
Taylor & Francis Group
LONDON AND NEW YORK

First published 1990 by
BRUNNER/MAZEL, INC.

Published 2013 by Routledge
2 Park Square, Milton Park, Abingdon, Oxfordshire OX14 4RN
711 Third Avenue, New York, NY 10017

First issued in paperback 2015

Routledge is an imprint of the Taylor & Francis Group an informa business

Library of Congress Cataloging-in-Publication Data

Violence and suicidality : perspectives in clinical and psychobiological research / edited by Herman M. van Praag, Robert Plutchik, Alan Apter.
p. cm. — (Clinical and experimental psychiatry ; 3)
Includes bibliographical references.
ISBN 978-0-876-30551-5 (hbk)
1. Violence—Physiological aspects. 2. Suicidal behavior—Physiological aspects. 3. Monoamine oxidase—Therapeutic use. 4. Biological psychiatry. I. Praag, Herman M. van (Herman Meir), 1929– . II. Plutchik, Robert. III. Apter, Alan.
[DNLM: 1. Monoamine Oxidase—therapy use. 2. Receptors, Sensory—physiology. 3. Suicide. 4. Violence. W1 CL664EH v. 3 / BF 575.A3 V7946]
RC569.5.V55V55 1990
616.85'82—dc20
DNLM/DLC
for Library of Congress 90–1309
CIP

ISBN 13: 978-1-138-88443-4 (pbk)
ISBN 13: 978-0-87630-551-5 (hbk)

A Note on the Series

Psychiatry is in a state of flux. The excitement springs in part from internal changes, such as the development and official acceptance (at least in the U.S.A.) of an operationalized, multiaxial classification system of behavioral disorders (the DSM-III), the increasing sophistication of methods to measure abnormal human behavior and the impressive expansion of biological and psychological treatment modalities. Exciting developments are also taking place in fields relating to psychiatry; in molecular (brain) biology, genetics, brain imaging, drug development, epidemiology, experimental psychology, to mention only a few striking examples.

More generally speaking, psychiatry is moving, still relatively slowly, but irresistibly, from a more philosophical, contemplative orientation, to that of an empirical science. From the fifties on, biological psychiatry has been a major catalyst of that process. It provided the mother discipline with a third cornerstone, i.e., neurobiology, the other two being psychology and medical sociology. In addition, it forced the profession in the direction of standardization of diagnoses and assessment of abnormal behavior. Biological psychiatry provided psychiatry not only with a new basic science and with new treatment modalities, but also with the tools, the methodology and the mentality to operate within the confines of an empirical science, the only framework in which a medical discipline can survive.

In other fields of psychiatry, too, one discerns a gradual trend towards scientification. Psychological treatment techniques are standardized and manuals developed to make these skills more easily transferrable. Methods registering treatment outcome—traditionally used in the behavioral/cognitive field—are now more and more requested and, hence, developed for dynamic forms of psychotherapy as well. Social and community psychiatry, until the sixties more firmly rooted in humanitarian ideals and social awareness than in empirical studies, profited greatly from its liaison with the social sciences and the expansion of psychiatric epidemiology.

Let there be no misunderstanding. Empiricism does *not imply* that it is only the measurable that counts. Psychiatry would be mutilated if it would neglect that which is not yet capturable in numbers and probably never will be. It *does imply* that what is measurable should be measured. Progress in psychiatry is dependent on ideas and on experiment. Their linkage is inseparable.

This monograph series, published under the auspices of the Department of Psychiatry of the Albert Einstein College of Medicine/Montefiore Medical Center, is meant to keep track of important developments in our profession, to summarize what has been achieved in particular fields, and to bring together the viewpoints obtained from disparate vantage points—in short, to capture some of the excitement ongoing in modern psychiatry, both in its clinical and experimental dimensions. Our Department hosts the Series, but naturally welcomes contributions from others.

Brunner/Mazel is not only the publisher of this series, but it was Bernie Mazel who generated the idea—an ambitious plan which, however, we all feel is worthy of pursuit. The edifice of psychiatry is impressive, but still somewhat flawed in its foundations. May this Series contribute to consolidation of its infrastructure.

—HERMAN M. VAN PRAAG, M.D., PH.D.
Silverman Professor and Chairman
Department of Psychiatry
Albert Einstein College of Medicine
Montefiore Medical Center
Bronx, New York

Contents

Contributors

Alan Apter, M.D.
Associate Professor, Department of Psychiatry, Tel Aviv University, Israel

J. C. Bizot, M.D.
Departement de Pharmacologie, Faculte de Medecine, Pietie-Salpetriere, Paris, France

Gerald L. Brown, M.D.
Chief, Division of Family Studies, National Institute of Alcohol Abuse and Alcoholism, Bethesda, Maryland

Sajaak den Daas, Ph.D.
Department of Pharmacy, State University of Groningen, The Netherlands

Robert E. Feinstein, M.D.
Assistant Professor, Columbia University College of Physicians and Surgeons; Assistant Unit Chief–Research Unit, New York State Psychiatric Institute, New York, New York

Menek Goldstein, Ph.D.
Professor of Neurochemistry, Department of Psychiatry, New York University Medical Center, New York, New York

Frederick K. Goodwin, M.D.
Administrator of the Alcohol, Drug Abuse and Mental Health Administration, Rockville, Maryland

Maria Hadjiconstantinou, M.D.
Associate Professor, Department of Psychiatry and Pharmacology, Ohio State University, College of Medicine, Columbus, Ohio

J. D. Higley, Ph.D.
Research Fellow, National Institute of Alcohol Abuse and Alcoholism, Poolesville, Maryland

Robert A. Hinde, D. Phil.
Royal Society, Research Professor; Honorary Director, Medical Research Council Unit on the Development and Integration of Behavior, Cambridge, United Kingdom

Markku Linnoila, M.D., Ph.D.
Clinical Director, Division of Intramural Clinical Biological Research, NIAAA DICBR, LCS, Bethesda, Maryland

Dr. Jan Mos
Department of Pharmacology, DUPHAR BV, Weesp, The Netherlands

Norton H. Neff, Ph.D.
Professor and Chairman, Department of Pharmacology, Ohio State University, College of Medicine, Columbus, Ohio

Berend Olivier, Ph.D.
Head CNS Section, Department of Pharmacology, DUPHAR BV, Weesp, The Netherlands

Stephen J. Peroutka, M.D.
Assistant Professor of Neurology, Stanford University Medical Center, Stanford, California

Robert Plutchik, Ph.D.
Professor of Psychiatry (Psychology), Albert Einstein College of Medicine/Montefiore Medical Center, Bronx, New York

William Z. Potter, M.D., Ph.D.
Chief, Section on Clinical Pharmacology, NIMH, Bethesda, Maryland

Stephen Rachlin, M.D.
Associate Professor, Clinical Psychiatry, State University of New York, Stony Brook; Chairman, Department of Psychiatry and Psychology, Nassau County Medical Center, East Meadow, New York

Alec Roy, M.B.
Professor of Psychiatry, Albert Einstein College of Medicine/Long Island Jewish Hospital Center, New Hyde Park, New York

Dr. Jacques Schipper
Department of Pharmacology, DUPHAR BV, Weesp, The Netherlands

Phillipe Soubrie, M.D.
Departement de Pharmacologie, Faculte de Medecine, Pietie-Salpetriere, Paris, France

Stephen J. Suomi, Ph.D.
Chief, Laboratory of Comparative Ethology, Bethesda, Maryland

Dr. Martin Tulp
Department of Pharmacology, DUPHAR BV, Weesp, The Netherlands

Herman M. van Praag, M.D., Ph.D.
Professor and Chairman, Department of Psychiatry, Albert Einstein College of Medicine/Montefiore Medical Center, Bronx, New York

Matti Virkkunen, M.D.
Senior Lecturer, University of Helsinki, Helsinki, Finland

Dr. G. A. van Oortmerssen
Department of Biological Centrum, State University of Groningen, Haran, The Netherlands

Introduction

Violence and suicidality have always been major public health issues, but it is only fairly recently that they have become the focus of some major clinical and biological research efforts. This is due partly to a large increase in suicide and homicide rates in the young and partly to a realization that effective management of psychiatric patients cannot be based on categorical diagnosis alone, but requires an understanding of the patient's entire behavioral profile.

This volume attempts to describe some of the most important advances in the psychobiological understanding of the behavioral dimensions of suicide and violence that have been made over the last 10 years. It is comprised of papers presented at two symposia held under the auspices of the department of psychiatry of Albert Einstein College of Medicine that were devoted to the topics of violence and suicide. The first was held as part of the American College of Neuropsychopharmacology meeting in Washington, DC; the second, one of the Einstein Symposia, was held at the New York Academy of Sciences. Both were largely devoted to biological issues which have previously been somewhat neglected. However, some clinical and psychometric research was also presented in the belief that only collaboration among basic scientists, clinical psychobiologists, psychometricians and clinicians can bring about advances in this complex area.

In bringing together these papers, the monograph represents the state of the art in research dealing with both inwardly and outwardly directed aggression in a number of different fields. Perspectives that are represented are: the clinical; the ethological; the human neurochemical; the animal neurochemical and basic "bench lab" science.

CLINICAL ISSUES

The clinical section of the monograph consists of two papers. The first, by Feinstein, represents his research and experience as an emergency room psychiatrist, evaluating patients for imminent violence. The author first gives an idea of the complexity and magnitude of the problem. Violent behavior in clinical situations does not have a low base rate as does suicide, and in fact is rather common. He believes that in most psychiatric patients short-term predictions are quite possible if systematic guidelines for assessment are adhered to. These guidelines include evaluation of: violent ideation; behavior during the interview; recent history of violence; past history of violence; the presence or absence of a supportive social network; the ability of the patient to cooperate with treatment; substance abuse, and neurological and medical illnesses associated with violence. Some clinical illustrations of how these principles are used in practice are given.

The second paper in the clinical section, by Rachlin, also deals with assessment and management. The approach in this paper however, is from the point of view of psychiatric liability for patient violence. Rachlin notes that "since the law is not an empirical science, it can impose accountability even in the absence of our ability to predict or control what others do." Having said this, Rachlin then provides us with some basic information on which we can build rational approaches to the assessment of the violence potential of psychiatric patients so as to diminish the danger of litigation while improving patient care. This information includes an outline of some basic and relevant medicolegal concepts such as "special relationship" (between doctor and patient), "direct causation," and "foreseeability." There is a discussion of the controversial Tarasoff decision and its implications for the care of potentially dangerous patients, as well as some other legal decisions in this area.

ETHOLOGICAL ISSUES

The ethological section of the monograph begins with a chapter by Plutchik and van Praag which describes an evolutionary approach to violence and suicide. This hypothesis is based on the view that the same aggressive impulse underlies both suicidal and violent behavior. The literature review focuses on the frequency with which violence and suicide are associated with one another. Based on this literature and on a series of psychometric studies, Plutchik and van Praag have isolated groups of variables which act on the aggressive impulse to either attenuate or augment it. At a second stage, other groups of factors act to turn the aggression either inward (suicidal behavior) or outward (violent behavior). The eventual fate of the aggressive impulse is thus determined by the resultant of competing vectorial forces. Since the behavior evinced acts on the environmental stimulus, feedback mechanisms which influence natural selection are set up.

The next chapter in this section, by Robert Hinde, who received the 1987 Einstein Award for his outstanding contributions to the understanding of behavior, points the way to an integration of biological data with social science. Biological data is not only biochemistry and physiology but ethology as well. The author reviews the concept of agonistic behavior—the complex of aggressive behavior, threat, fleeing, and submission. He then tackles the thorny problem of the classification of human behavior, including aggression, giving examples of how this might be attempted. He describes his own work on preschool children and suggests an hypothesis to explain how biological development, determined by naturally selected genes, and child-rearing practices might interact to produce an aggressive person. He concludes with some ideas as to how we might better understand some social institutions, such as international war, in the light of these considerations.

The paper by Olivier et al. can be regarded as a particular example of Hinde's proposal that ethology has bearing on psychiatric research. Olivier has pioneered the concept of "ethopharmacology" wherein the influence of drugs on social behavior of animals and human is studied. In this article, the effect on aggression in rats of a new group of drugs called the "serenics" is discussed. Many psychotropic compounds will eventually cause a diminution of aggressive behavior, but the serenics have a specific action not involving effects on other behavioral systems such as motor activity, defensive capability, social interest and exploration. Using ethological methodologies it becomes possible to measure several aspects of agonistic behavior together and to tease out differential effects of specific drugs.

The authors classify aggressive behaviors in animals using an ethological perspective. For instance, they divide aggression into offensive aggression and defensive aggression. Examples of offensive aggression include: isolation induced aggression; intermale aggression; territorial aggression; aggression induced by electrical stimulation of the hypothalamus; and maternal aggression aimed at protecting pups. Defensive aggression includes pain-induced aggression and resident-intruder aggression. Predatory aggression is placed into a separate category. They hypothesize that these different kinds of aggression are related to different biological mechanisms involving different types of serotonin receptors. Different serenics have different actions on each type of aggression, and this differential action on aggressive behaviors is somehow thought to be based on the in-vitro profiles of these serenic drugs.

CLINICAL NEUROCHEMICAL ISSUES

The section on clinical neurochemical and metabolic perspectives consists of three papers which attempt to review the relationship among biochemical, psychometric and clinical variables associated with suicidality and violence. The additional psychological variable of impulsivity is looked at in this and other sections, since there is a great deal of evidence that impulsivity is an integral part of both suicidal and violent behavior.

The contribution by Roy and Linnoila concentrates on suicide. They initially outline some of the important demographic and public health issues that make suicidal behavior such an important topic for psychiatric research. This is followed by a review of their own work as well as that of others on the role of the monoamines (serotonin, dopamine, and norepinephrine) in suicidality. They suggest that biological abnormalities such as dysregulations of monoamine metabolism may influence enduring behavioral patterns by their effect on personality and thus may increase vulnerability to self-destructive behavior. After reviewing postmortem and genetic studies of suicide, they then discuss some peripheral endocrine markers. These are of particular importance, as these tests may be valuable in routine clinical assessments of suicidal patients. These tests include: urinary 17-hydroxycorticosteroids; hypercortisolemia; DST non-suppression; cortisol response to 5-hydroxytryptophan; thyroid-stimulating hormone response to thyroid-releasing hormone stimulation, and habituation of skin conductance responses. There is also a discussion of platelet markers such as serotonin uptake and 3(H) imipramine binding to platelet membranes.

The authors then go on to the subject of prediction of suicide, and this part of the paper will probably be of special interest to clinicians. Their feeling is that "most suicides are probably preventable." This statement is supported by an assessment of clinical, CSF and peripheral biological predictors of suicide that are potentially available to the clinician. They propose that these predictor variables may be of particular interest in three at-risk groups: patients with affective disorders, patients with a past history of suicidal behavior, and patients with a family history of suicide.

The second contribution in this section, by Brown, Linnoila and Goodwin, deals with the interface of clinical and biological data as they pertain to human aggression and impulsivity. As in the previous paper, the focus is on monoamine metabolism. The literature on human studies is first reviewed, followed by an attempt to delineate some different kinds of aggressive behavior in animals and man. Aggression in animals is divided into predatory aggression, affective aggression, and "other" aggression. The discussion on human aggression points out that most studies to date have addressed culturally defined "antisocial" behaviors and not aggression in its clinical context. State and trait aggression are also differentiated. The relationship between psychiatric conditions, both in adults and children, and violence is then discussed in detail, followed by a similar section on medical and neurological illnesses as they relate to aggression.

An important part of this paper is a critical assessment of the psychometrics of aggression, especially in the context of biological research. The authors point out some of the difficulties associated with trying to measure aggression such as lack of cooperation and dissimulation by the patients and the need to control for contextual variables such as physical environment, diet and length of observations. Data from cross-sectional measures such as the Overt Aggression Scale may differ from historical, longitudinal measures such as the Brown-Goodwin Questionnaire. With the above material as contextual background, the authors then review their own and some other studies on human aggression and CSF neurotransmitter metabolites. This includes studies correlating MMPI, Buss-Durkee, and historical measures with monoamine CSF levels. The findings are detailed, as are the relative merits of the different psychometric measures.

The final paper in this section, by Linnoila, Virkunnen, Roy and Potter, deals with the issue of impulse control. They attempt to relate biochemical findings to some of the clinical manifestations of this basic psychological dimension. These include patients with personality disorders, violent offenders, arsonists, and alcoholics. As in the previous studies, much of the discussion is focused on monoamine neurotransmitter metabolites, although dysregulation of glucose metabolism is also discussed. The literature on animal and human studies is first reviewed, and the authors point out that there is a great deal of evidence to support the hypothesis that impulsivity is a discrete psychological dimension with an inherited biological basis. It is improbable that only one biological system would underlie such a trait and it seems that at the very least impulse control is determined by the interaction of the serotonergic and dopaminergic systems. Empirical evidence for such an hypothesis is described and a mathematical model representing this interaction is proposed.

ANIMAL NEUROCHEMICAL STUDIES

The section on animal studies and the biochemistry of aggression and impulsivity is composed of two articles. The work by Higley and his colleagues uses a developmental model to study the parallel between aggression and serotonin metabolism. Monkeys and humans both show different levels of aggression at different stages of development. Thus a prepubertal child and an adolescent will not show the same aggressive patterns. In addition, the way a monkey or a child is reared will also affect his propensity for aggression. Both the above variables interact with sex to produce their effects on aggression. Their study on monkeys attempts to longitudinally follow CSF 5HIAA levels as development unfolds under different rearing conditions. The results indicate that reduced serotonin metabolism parallels changes in aggressive behavior.

The paper by Soubrie and Bizot is also directed to the biological underpinnings of impulsivity, an area which seems to be so important in the understanding of suicide and violence. The authors have designed some animal testing procedures which appear to simulate various aspects of impulse control such as waiting capacity and the tolerance for reward delay. They then tested the sensitivity of these dimensions to a variety of psychotropic drugs in order to gain insight into the neurochemical correlates of impulse control. They conclude that both serotonergic and noradrenergic systems are involved, most probably in an interactive way. Finally they describe a model which involves control of information processing and response emission that allows the organism to tolerate and/or arrange a delay before it acts.

BASIC NEURORECEPTOR FUNCTIONS

The section on neurotransmitter receptors concludes the monograph. This section is designed to bring the reader up to date on the two receptor systems that have been most associated with suicide and violence research, the serotonergic and the dopaminergic. The chapter on central serotonin receptors by Peroutka describes in detail some of the basic functional correlates of these receptors. The history of the classification of these receptors is reviewed. Radioligand binding studies initially differentiated between 5-HT1 and 5-HT2 receptors. Then 5-HT1 receptors were shown to be heterogeneous. 5-HT1a, 5-HT1b, 5-HT1c and

5-HT1d receptors were distinguished from one another. Finally 5-HT3 receptors were isolated. Each receptor binding site is labelled by different ligands and is concentrated in different areas of the brain. Different drugs have different affinities for the different receptors and each different receptor has different functional correlates. These differences are detailed and catalogued in the text and in tables and will be of great reference value to the reader trying to follow research into the biochemistry of suicide and aggression since the identification and characterization of these 5-HT receptor subtypes has, and will continue to have, multiple clinical applications.

The paper by Neff and Hadjiconstantinou describes the same parameters for central dopamine receptors. The D-1 and D-2 receptor types are distinguished and characterized. The relationship of these receptors to different neuropsychiatric conditions is described. Some of the basic neurophysiological functional activity associated with the two receptor subtypes is then detailed.

Goldstein's paper further examines some of the functional activities related to the dopamine receptor. Of especial interest for this volume is his discussion of a possible dopaminergic influence in self-biting behavior in monkeys and how this might relate to Lesch-Nyhan syndrome. This syndrome is of particular interest to investigators of suicide and violence as it is probably the best characterized neuropsychiatric illness involving self-destructive behavior in humans.

SUMMARY

The papers in this volume thus cover a wide range of questions connected with an understanding of suicide and violence. Clinical and legal issues are connected with experimental and clinical studies of suicidal or violent populations of humans. Studies of animals are also presented from both an ethological and a laboratory perspective. Basic biochemical and neuroanatomical studies are given to complete the picture. The overall presentation thus represents the state of the art concerning the understanding of the complex nature of suicide and violence.

PART I

Clinical Issues

1

Clinical Guidelines for the Assessment of Imminent Violence

ROBERT E. FEINSTEIN

Almost daily, psychiatric clinicians must evaluate the imminent risk of violence posed by their patients. Their decisions are frequently guided by nonspecific impressions or intuitive clinical judgments. Many psychiatric professionals feel discouraged when making assessments about violence because of an overly pessimistic reading of early studies on violence prediction. These studies (Cohen et al., 1978; Kozol & Boucher, 1972; Monahan, 1982) suggest that there are no valid or reliable predictors of long-term violence. Long-term violence is defined as violence occurring within periods of years. While it may be true that we will never be able to predict the specific timing or nature of the violence, it seems likely that we can greatly improve our ability to make reliable probability estimates of the risk of imminent violence. Imminent violence is defined as violence that occurs within a three-week period after an initial evaluation. This paper will attempt to outline specific clinical guidelines which may improve our ability to make short-term probability estimates of imminent violence. A brief review of some of the relevant literature will be presented from which specific clinical guidelines will be derived. Three short clinical cases will then be presented to illustrate the use of these guidelines.

REVIEW OF THE LITERATURE

The combined wisdom of authors such as Cohen et al. (1978), Kozol and Boucher (1972), Monahan (1981, 1982) and Steadman et al. (1978) suggests that we are poorly equipped to make reliable long-term predictions about violence. A simplified summary is that these studies showed that approximately two-thirds of predictions of future violence were inaccurate. In other words, the prisoners, violent sex offenders, and psychiatric patients whom they predicted would again become violent did not do so in two-thirds of the cases. These early studies, however, may not be directly applicable to the probability estimates of imminent violence. As Monahan states in his classic work (1981, 1982), these studies were examining long-term predictions of the behavior of institutionalized clients after discharge. These studies did not assess the reliability of short-term probability estimates of imminent violence in a psychiatric population.

Pokorny (1983) pointed out that suicide predictions may be unsuccessful because suicides are rare events and, as such, cannot be easily predicted without creating false positives. This same logic has been applied to homicide and violence prediction. However, Skodal and Karasu's paper (1978) and extrapolation from Silver and Yudofsky's Overt Aggression Scale (1987) seems to contradict this common viewpoint. If violence is defined broadly to include homicide, physical assault, destruction of property, and verbal violence, then violence is not a rare event at all. Violence, broadly defined, is quite common in the psychiatric and general population.

Despite the continuing controversies about our ability to predict violence over the long term, there are other authors who are more optimistic about making probability estimates of imminent violence. These authors (Warner, 1961; Werner, 1983; Baxter, 1968; Bengelsdorf, 1984) have moved away from trying to predict the occurrence of a specific violent episode at a specific time. Instead, they have tried to find variables that will aid in assessing the probability of violence, broadly defined, over a short time span of days or weeks. Warner (1961) showed significant evidence that the ability to care for oneself, the presence of family supports, danger potential, and treatment prognosis were reliable variables that correlate with the probability of imminent violence in psychiatric patients. Baxter et al. (1968) showed that the duration of the illness, previous psychiatric illness, the ability to communicate, and personal appearance may also be factors to help in our assessment of the short-term risk of violence. Monahan (1981, 1982) added past history of violence, family relations, and coexisting medical conditions to a growing list of relevant factors. Bengelsdorf et al. (1984) developed a "Crisis Triage Rating Scale" which was based on three factors: dangerousness (which was an assessment of suicide and violence potential); support systems; and the patient's ability to cooperate with treatment. These three factors were shown to be significant determinants of clinicians' decisions as to which patients needed to be committed to a hospital and which could be released and treated in the community. The work of Bleuler (1930), Fish (1967), and Yesavage (1983) suggests that a patient's ideation offers valuable clues as to the potential for imminent violence. Plutchik et al. (1985) proposed that poor impulse control, feelings of hostility, the triad of enuresis, firesetting and cruelty to animals in childhood, menstrual problems, young age, limited education, past history of violence, and repeated automobile infractions are variables which may help us in our short-term assessments of the potential for violence. Tinklenberg and Woodrow (1974) and Elliot (1987) added substance abuse to the list of relevant factors. Silver and Yudofsky (1987) remind us of the importance of neuropsychiatric disorders as risk factors for imminent violence. Finally, McNeil and Binder (1987) showed that emergency commitment did permit judgments of dangerousness with a high degree of short-term predictive reliability.

CLINICAL GUIDELINES IN ASSESSING THE RISK OF IMMINENT VIOLENCE

Based on the above literature review, it is possible to propose the use of eight broad variables to assist clinicians in making probability estimates of imminent violence. These variables can be used as a guide when making clinical decisions about short-term violence potential. These variables are: (1) violent ideation; (2) behavior during the interview; (3) recent history of violence; (4) past history of violence; (5) support network; (6) cooperation with treatment; (7) substance abuse; and (8) neurological or medical illnesses associated with violence. It is unlikely that any single variable, by itself, will be significantly useful in making probability estimates of imminent violence. The literature suggests that the complex interactions of the constellation of these eight variables may be the most useful approach to the clinical assessment of the potential for violence in the immediate future. Clinical application and assessment of imminent violence using these variables will therefore be described.

Violent Ideation

The literature suggests that patients' violent thought or homicidal ideation can probably be put in a spectrum, from a higher to a lower probability of violence risk. The highest-risk thoughts on this continuum suggesting a high probability of imminent violence are those involving an intense desire to kill a specific person. Other work (Goodwin et al., 1971; Hellerstein et al., 1987) suggests that command hallucinations and/or delusions to hurt or kill are also the highest-risk ideation for imminent violence. A nonspecific wish to hurt or kill a member of a group (i.e., a wish to kill blacks or homosexuals) probably carries a slightly more modest risk for short-term violence potential. Ambivalent wishes to hurt others or damage objects, or nonspecific feelings of hostility, may carry lesser risks. Patients who have few thoughts of violence or homicide have the least risk of short-term violence potential.

Behavior During the Interview

My earlier work (Feinstein, 1986) suggests that there is a natural progression of behaviors that signal increasing risk of violence during the interview. Patients progress from a calm phase to an increase in psychomotor movements followed by an "early verbal phase" where they question authority. Increasing risk is signaled by a "late verbal phase" where patients may challenge authority, use profanity, or display approach-avoidance behaviors which frequently lead to a violent assault. By observing these behaviors as patients progress through them, it is possible to anticipate the immediate risk of violence and take preventative measures.

Recent History of Violence

There may be a similar spectrum of recent events or recent behaviors which may correlate with the degree of imminent violence potential. Violence risk, from the highest to the lowest probability for potential violence, includes: (a) impulsive or deliberate assaultive behavior with weapons (e.g., assaults with a gun, knife, club, or bottle); (b) impulsive or deliberate physical assaults (e.g., beatings or an attempt at strangulation which have caused either fractures or the need for hospital assessment); (c) recent violence without serious sequellae (e.g., a slap, punch, or push); (d) other impulsive or unpredictable behaviors indicating a moderate risk potential for violence; (e) destruction of property or isolated objects, which may indicate a lower risk potential for violence; (f) no recent behavior associated with violence and clinical evidence that a patient's impulses are well regulated, indicating only minimal risk for imminent violence.

Past History of Violence

The past history of violence is still considered by many to be the best indicator of the probability of short-term risk for violence. A detailed history about a patient's past pattern of violence is essential for the assessment of imminent violence potential, as well as for planning interventions which may help prevent violence. Special attention should be paid to previous precipitants that initiated violence, the severity of past violence, the frequency of the violence, and the countervailing forces (Plutchik et al., 1985) which may inhibit or attenuate violence. Psychiatric patients who repeatedly become violent generally show repetitive patterns to their violence. As part of this assessment, clinicians should inquire about a patient's knowledge of weapons and their availability.

It is also useful to obtain a history of past arrests, automobile infractions, criminal records, or involvement in frequent legal proceedings. A childhood history of frequent disruptive changes in caretakers (Rockwell, 1972), frequent childhood abuse or punishment (Bryer et al., 1987), and the triad of enuresis, firesetting and cruelty to animals (Plutchik et al., 1985; Felthous et al., 1987) may also be associated with an increased potential for imminent violence. Also, adolescent histories of chronic problems with authority (as evidenced by truancy, running away, losing one's temper easily, sexual promiscuity, and overeating) (Plutchik et al., 1985) may also carry a greater risk in the short term for future violence.

There is little convincing evidence as to the relative significance of such past history regarding the probability of imminent violence potential.

Support Systems

Bengelsdorf et al. (1984), Schoenfeld (1986), Schnur et al. (1986) and new research (Feinstein et al., 1988) indicate that the social network or support system may be the main variable used by emergency psychiatric clinicians when determining which violent patients need commitment and which ones can be released. Support systems such as family, friends, mental health care providers, religious groups, etc. should be evaluated according to their interest, availability and competence. There is probably a spectrum of quality among support networks. A competent support system that is disinterested or unavailable will increase the likelihood of imminent violence. Similarly, an interested and available support system which is not competent (i.e. children) increases the likelihood for short-term violence potential. Patients who are discharged to support systems that demonstrate competence, interest and availability are at only slight risk for imminent violence.

Ability to Cooperate with Treatment

This variable is widely used by clinicians in deciding if a potentially violent patient can be released. The research of Feinstein,

Plutchik, and van Praag (1988) on 95 patients evaluated at the Bronx Municipal Hospital /Albert Einstein College of Medicine confirms the earlier work of Bengelsdorf (1984). It demonstrated a high correlation between a patient's ability to cooperate with treatment and clinicians' judgments about admitting a potentially violent patient. Patients who refused to cooperate with their treatment or who were unable to do so in the past were likely to be admitted. Patients who had weak motivation for treatment or who showed limited capacity to *participate* were less frequently admitted. Patients who actually sought treatment or who demonstrated a willingness or ability to participate in their treatment were more typically treated in outpatient settings.

Substance Abuse History

The literature correlating acute alcohol intoxication and an acute risk of imminent violence is extensive. The correlation between other forms of intoxication and an acute risk of violence is also well established. The correlation between substance abuse history and the potential for imminent violence is less clear, though likely (Tinklenberg & Woodrow, 1974, Elliot, 1987). The research of Feinstein et al. (1988) indicates that clinicians widely regard a substance abuse history as a guiding variable in their decision-making about the short-term potential for violence. However, these results showed that there was no relationship between substance abuse history and short-term violence when patients were also admitted to an inpatient service and followed over the next three weeks. This issue, however, remains unresolved for patients who have risk variables for imminent violence, a substance abuse history, and who are discharged into the community.

Because of this and with an extensive literature showing an association between violence and substance abuse, the wise clinician considers substance abuse a major factor when trying to assess the imminent risks of violence. Patients who are either intoxicated or who are in withdrawal have a very high risk for violence. Patients who are long-term substance abusers or compulsive users probably also have a significant risk for violence. The recreational user, or the intermittent user may have less risk. The absence of a substance abuse history is reassuring to most experienced clinicians. It may also be true that there are different risks associated with different substances of abuse.

Neurological and Medical Histories

There is ample evidence in the literature that demonstrates a clearcut association between some neurological disorders and an increased risk for imminent violence. Silver and Yudofsky have done a recent review (1987). Neurological disorders that are associated with a risk of imminent violence potential include disorders involving damage to the frontal lobes or other deep brain structures. A partial list would include head trauma, cerebrovascular accidents, Alzheimer's Disease, multi-infarct dementia, mental retardation seizures or kindling, or organic personality disorders. If there is a high index of suspicion for imminent violence, patients should be assessed for behavioral, social, affective, and intellectual changes. Part of this assessment includes a detailed neurological exam looking for frontal release signs or other evidence of "soft" neurological signs. When indicated, detailed neuropsychological testing may be helpful. Further testing such as EEGs, CT scans, etc. should also be pursued vigorously if there are any clinical indications for a more extensive evaluation.

There are many medical causes for violence that may also require further evaluation. Certainly, any drug intoxication or signs of drug withdrawal must be carefully evaluated. Organic delirium and premenstrual syndrome in women (Plutchik et al., 1985; Dalton, 1979) are other disorders that probably have a higher risk for imminent violence. This is especially so in patients who have other risk variables as previously mentioned.

USE OF THE CLINICAL GUIDELINES: CLINICAL EXAMPLES

The following clinical illustrations attempt to show how these eight variables can serve as a guide to clinicians assessing the risk of imminent violence. As there is still no consensus as to which of these eight variables are most important, clinicians must still exercise individual judgment on a case-by-case basis when deciding on an overall probability estimate of imminent violence potential.

Case I

Mr. B. was a 20-year-old Italian man, employed in the furniture-moving business, who referred himself to the psychiatric outpatient clinic after having a fistfight with his boss and assaulting a man in a candy store. The outpatient clinic referred this patient to the psychiatric emergency room to assess his violence potential.

Mr. B. had no previous psychiatric history or contacts. Over the past two years he had worked for a furniture-moving company. He had been fired and rehired at least three times over these two years. Each violent episode would begin when the patient felt he was harshly criticized in front of his coworkers. He would get into a verbal argument with his boss and follow this with a physical assault, typically involving several blows to his employer's face. He would be fired, but after two weeks he would be rehired because he is a "good worker." Three days prior to this visit, Mr. B. had again assaulted his employer under the same circumstances. Moreover, two days prior to his visit, Mr. B. had also assaulted a man in a candy store who was unknown to him. This assault was unprovoked and occurred after he had had two beers. While he held the man on the ground, he scraped the man's knuckles on the cement and began banging his head on the ground. The assault was halted by other customers. There was no police involvement, nor were there any charges filed against Mr. B.

During the interview, Mr. B. was calm and cooperative, and showed no behavioral signs of immediate violence risk. He denied violent ideation, had no clinical signs of psychosis except that he occasionally heard a solitary voice that would say "kill" during times when he was angry. He described no other auditory hallucinations, nor was this voice commanding him. He had no delusions. The patient had a past history that included multiple physical assaults on men in positions of authority. He had no criminal record but as a child he was frequently beaten by his father and had a history of some truancy from school. He never used any weapons.

Mr. B. lived with his wife of two years and he never abused nor threatened her. It was his wife who referred him to psychiatry. She was three years older than the patient, and was eager, available, willing and interested in participating in the treatment of her husband's violence. Mr. B's father had died two years earlier around the same time of year as this most recent assault on his employer. His mother and siblings were alive and well, living in the area. Mr. B. was cooperative and eager for treatment, saying "This can't go on. . . . I just don't know how to stop myself." Mr. B. drank two beers a day, especially as a refreshment at work. He denied use of any other substances and any drinking other than beer. Neurologic assessment revealed no new behavioral, affective, nor cognitive changes. He did, however, show signs of left-right confusion, and some reading difficulties which were consistent with a mild learning disability. He had, however, completed high school.

Mr. B's risk for violence can be summarized as follows: He was expressive of mild-risk violent ideation, since he heard a solitary voice saying "kill" when he was angry. During the interview, he was calm and cooperative, though quite unaware of the seriousness of his assault on the man in the candy store. There was no acute risk of violence during the interview. He showed high risk regarding recent-event-behavior in his two impulsive assaults. He had a past history of severe assaults in specific situations. As a child, he had been physically assaulted by his father and also had been truant from school. He had an excellent support network (his wife), who was eager and competent in her assistance with his treatment. Mr. B. was cooperative with planning specific temporary interventions in order to prevent a recurrence, and he was eager to be in treatment. He had a mild alcohol abuse problem, but was willing to stop drinking entirely. He had some "soft" neurological signs consistent with a long-standing mild learning disability. In summary, his risk potential for violence over the next several weeks was assessed as mild to moderate.

Follow-up at three weeks revealed no recurrent violence. Mr. B. was attending brief treatment at the crisis intervention service. His EEG was pending, and a trial of Inderal was begun for the pharmacotherapy of this patient's violence.

Case II

Mr. C. was a 42-year-old white, unemployed male, living in a shelter. He was brought to the emergency room by police after he had brutally assaulted a shelter resident, believing that this resident was a homosexual who was trying to infect him with AIDS.

This patient was a very poor historian, but he did reveal that he had been in a state psychiatric hospital many times. He was last hospitalized two years ago for six months, and had received no follow-up treatment. A past history of violence could not be elicited. He had family members living "somewhere locally," although he did not know their address nor how they could be contacted. He lived mostly on the street, except on cold nights, when he would stay at a shelter. He had been living at his current shelter for two days. While living there, he became fearful that the man in the next bed was a homosexual with AIDS. The police were called, and when they discovered that he was speaking illogically, they brought him to the psychiatric emergency room. Mr. C. denied any drug use, although a shelter caseworker had seen him drunk on at least one occasion.

Mr. C. was evaluated three times for the risk of imminent violence. The first assessment of his presenting symptomatology can be summarized as follows: Mr. C. expressed high-risk violent ideation; he was psychotic, with delusions about AIDS and the destruction of the world by homosexuals; he had command hallucinations demanding that he "defend all heterosexuals"; he showed psychomotor agitation throughout the interview; he revealed high-risk recent-event-behaviors in his impulsive and unpredictable assault on a sleeping shelter resident; his past history of violence could not be determined; he had no support system, and was only minimally cooperative with his treatment; it is likely that he had an alcohol abuse problem; he had no medical or neurological findings. This initial assessment was of an extremely high risk of imminent violence. Because of this high risk and concern that he might develop an alcohol withdrawal syndrome, Mr. C. was held in the emergency room. Over the next three days he was treated with neuroleptics and observed for signs of withdrawal, which never materialized.

On the fourth day, a second risk-potential assessment was performed and the patient was released from the hospital. This decision was based on the report that his command hallucinations had disappeared and his delusions were less prominent, though persistent. He was pleasant, calm and cooperative with staff and other patients in the emergency room. There were no legal charges pending for the assault on the shelter resident. There was no additional information about any past history of violence. The staff discovered he had a caseworker at the shelter who could see him upon his return there. No family or friends could be located. Mr. C. agreed to take a neuroleptic and to arrange follow-up treatment at an outpatient clinic. He had no neurological or medical illness. His risk of imminent violence was assessed, at that time, as mild.

Three days after his release, Mr. C. was returned to the psychiatric emergency room by police. He again had brutally assaulted another man, believing he was trying to infect him with AIDS. The third violence assessment was identical to his initial presentation. However, prior to the patient's initial release from the emergency room, the clinicians had unfortunately been in error in their assessment of his violence potential. In retrospect, the second assessment revealed a moderate-to-high risk of violence potential. Mr. C., in fact, had demonstrated high-risk violent ideation, since his delusional system persisted, even though his command hallucinations had subsided. Behaviorally, he showed little risk of violence while in the emergency room setting, a much more structured environment than the shelter. His recent-event history was unchanged and high-risk. The inability to clarify any past history of violence should alert the prudent clinician to potential hidden risks. Significantly, he had a poor support system. The caseworker was interested and probably competent; however, nobody asked about this caseworker's availability. In fact, he only saw Mr. C. once for five minutes shortly after he returned to the shelter. While superficially cooperative with outpatient treatment plans, Mr. C. had a known past history of poor compliance. In addition, Mr. C. had abused alcohol on at least one occasion. The absence of an alcohol withdrawal syndrome in the emergency room indicates that he probably had a mild to moderate alcohol abuse problem. He had no medical or neurological factors associated with violence risk. Overall, his risk for imminent violence was moderately high. The second assault, in retrospect, confirmed this assertion, indicating that the patient, his second victim and the community might have been better served had he been committed to the hospital.

Case III

Ms. A. was a 65-year-old Black female who was brought to the emergency room after she struck her private male attendant at a nursing home.

Ms. A. had a 40-year history of manic-depressive illness, which had been well controlled on lithium. Over the course of her illness, she had been hospitalized four times, followed by complete remissions lasting years. She had no past history of violence prior to three years ago, when she began to show behavioral, affective and cognitive changes, including lewdness, poor social interactions and dyscontrol leading to assaults on her husband. This was initially diagnosed as a recurrent manic episode. However, when she also developed new difficulties with language, decreased arithmetic skills and poor logical skills, she was diagnosed as having Alzheimer's Disease. Ms. A. stayed at home with her husband on lithium and low doses of haldol. Approximately six months previously, she had slapped her husband while he was feeding her, and was thereafter placed in a nursing home. While in the home, she continued to have verbal outbursts and minor assaults, though able to function in many activities. During this most recent assault, she struck her attendant while he was helping her eat. He injured his knee and had a possible hairline jaw fracture.

Her initial assessment revealed that she had mild-risk violent ideation. She was hostile and verbally abusive toward men, whom she confused with her husband. She had no delusions or hallucinations. Her behavior during the interview was assessed to be of the highest risk. She was demanding, swearing and minimally responsive to verbal intervention. This is the kind of verbal behavior signifying high violence risk. Her recent-event behavior indicated a high risk, since she had struck her attendant. Her past history of violence showed progressive worsening of violence risk. Her support system at the nursing home subsequent to the assault remained good, since the home was willing to continue to provide attendants (preferably female) as long as the hospital stabilized her condition.

The patient was mildly cooperative with her treatment in the emergency room. While hostile, she was willing to take required medication. She had no substance abuse problem. Medical evaluation revealed a mild organic delirium that was caused by a urinary tract infection. Lithium level was normal, and there were no signs of lithium toxicity.

Ms. A. was assessed as having a moderate to high risk for imminent violence potential. She was held in the emergency room for the next 24 hours. She was treated with IV fluids and oral antibiotics, and her delirium resolved. At this point, a second violence risk assessment revealed mild-risk violent ideation, in that she was angry at being in the emergency room, but was no longer hostile to males or her husband. Her behavior during the interview showed mild-risk psychomotor agitation. Her recent-event behavior was assessed as high. Her past history of violence was assessed as mild to moderate, with the likelihood of becoming severe as her Alzheimer's disease progressed. Her support system was very good, and the home was accepting her back. Ms. A. was cooperative with taking her medication, which could be continued in the home. She had no substance abuse risk. Her delirium, presumably precipitated by a urinary tract infection, had resolved significantly. Though her bipolar disorder was stable, her Alzheimer's Disease appeared to be worsening. However, after medical stabilization, her imminent violence risk was assessed as mild to moderate. She was released to the nursing home on antibiotics, lithium and an increased dose of haldol. One week later, the patient threw her breakfast on the floor, and a course of tegretol was begun to control her outbursts. Six weeks later, there were no further reports of any violence. The patient was attending the nursing home activities and doing well.

REFERENCES

Baxter S., et al. (1968). Psychiatric emergencies: Dispositional and the validity of the decision to admit. *Amer. J. of Psychiatry*, 124, 1542–1548.

Bengelsdorf, H., et al. (1984). A crisis triage rating scale: A brief dispositional assessment of patients at risk for hospitalization. *J. Nerv. and Mental Disease, 172* (7), 424–429.

Bleuler, E. (1930). *Textbook of Psychiatry*. Translated by Brill AA. New York: Macmillan, p 62.

Bryer, J., et al. (1987). Childhood sexual and physical abuse as factors in adult psychiatric illness. *Amer. J. of Psychiatry, 144* (11), 1426–1430.

Cohen, M., Groth, A., & Seigel R. (1978). The clinical prediction of dangerousness. *Crime and Deliquency, 1,* 28–39.

Dalton, K. (1979). *Once a Month: The Premenstrual Syndrome*. Pomona, California: Hunter House.

Elliot, F. (1987). Neuroanatomy and neurology of aggression. *Psychiatric Annals, 17* (6), 385–388.

Feinstein, R. (April 1986). Managing violent episodes in the emergency room. *Resident and Staff Physician, Problems in Primary Care:* 3Pc–6Pc.

Feinstein, R., Plutchik, R., & van Praag, H. (Prepublication 1990). *Violence and Suicide Risk Assessment in the Psychiatric Emergency Room.*

Felthous, A., & Kellert, S. R. (1987). Childhood cruelty to animals and later aggression against people: A review. *Amer. J. of Psychiatry, 144* (6), 710–717.

Fish, F. (1967). *Clinical Psychopathology: Signs and Symptoms in Psychiatry*. Bristol, England: John Wright & Sons, 19–33.

Goodwin, D. W., et al. (1971). Clinical significance of hallucinations in psychiatric disorders. *Arch. Gen. Psychiatry, 24,* 76–80.

Hellerstein, D., et al. Clinical significance of command hallucinations. *Amer. J. of Psychiatry, 144* (2), 219–221, February 1987.

Kozol, H., & Boucher, R. (1972). The diagnosis and treatment of dangerousness. *Crime and Delinquency, 18,* 371–392.

McNeil, D., & Binder, R. (1987). Predictive validity of judgments of dangerousness in emergency civil commitment. *Amer. J. of Psychiatry, 144* (2), 197–200.

Monahan, J. (1981). *The Clinical Prediction of Violent Behavior.* U.S. Dept. of Health and Human Services, ADAMHA Washington, D.C.

Monahan, J. (1982). The clinical prediction of violent behavior. *Psych. Annals, 5,* 509–513.

Plutchik, R., van Praag, H., & Conte, H. Suicide and violence risk in psychiatric patients. *Biological Psychiatry,* C. Shagass et. al., Editors, 1985.

Pokorny, A. Prediction of suicide in psychiatric patients. *Arch. Gen. Psychiatry, 40,* 249, March 1983.

Rockwell, D. Can you spot potential violence in a patient? *Hospital Physician, 10,* 52–56, 1972.

Schnur, D., et al. Assessing the family environment of schizophrenic patients with multiple hospital admissions. *Hospital and Community Psychiatry, 37* (3), 249–252, March 1986.

Schoenfeld, P. Long-term outcome of network therapy. *Hospital and Community Psychiatry, 37* (4), 373–376, April 1986.

Silver, J., & Yudofsky, S. Aggressive behavior in patients with neuropsychiatric disorders. *Psychiatric Annals, 17* (6), 367–370, June 1987.

Silver, J., & Yudofsky, S. Documentation of aggression in the assessment of the violent patient. *Psychiatric Annals, 17* (6), 385–388, June 1987.

Skodal, A. E., Karasu, T.B. Emergency psychiatry and the assaultive patient. *Amer. J. of Psychiatry, 135,* 202, 1978.

Steadman, H., et al. Explaining the increased crime rate of mental patients: The changing clientele of State Hospital. *Amer. J. of Psychiatry, 135,* 816–820, 1978.

Tinklenberg, J. R., Woodrow K. M. Drug use among youthful assaultive and sexual offenders. *Association for Research in Nerv. and Mental Disorders. 52,* 209–224, 1974.

Warner, S. L. Criteria for involuntary hospitalization of psychiatric patients in a public hospital. *Mental Hygiene, 45,* 122–128, 1961.

Werner, P., et al. Reliability, accuracy, and decision-making strategy in clinical predictions of imminent dangerousness. *J. of Consulting and Clinical Psychology, 51* (6), 815–825, 1983.

Yesavage, J. A. Inpatient violence and the schizophrenic patient. *Acta Psychiatr Scand 67,* 353–357, 1983.

2

Psychiatric Liability for Patient Violence

STEPHEN RACHLIN

How do we understand the fact that we, as clinicians, can be held legally liable in malpractice suits for the behavior of psychiatric patients? First and foremost, it must be recognized that this is a matter with significant social consequences. Thus, it becomes a public policy issue. In this context, it is the legal, and not the clinical, system which becomes the decision maker. And since the law is not an empirical science (Gutheil, Rachlin, and Mills, 1985), it can impose accountability even absent evidence of our ability to predict or to control what others may do.

BASIC MEDICOLEGAL PRINCIPLES

The standard mnemonic for remembering the elements of professional malpractice is the "four Ds": *d*ereliction of *d*uty *d*irectly causing *d*amages. For the moment, I will skip over the question of damages, as it would be a given in the situation where a patient commits a violent act on the person of another.

From the legal perspective, the analysis begins with duty, something clearly stated to be a matter of law (e.g., *Sukljian v. Ross,* 1986). We all know what our responsibilities are in the traditional therapist-patient relationship, but having an obligation to a third party seems strangely out of place. The law, however, creates a condition wherein a so-called "special relationship," or perhaps even one perceived by the general public as being such, may result in a particular responsibility. This is the mechanism for imposing culpability when a patient injures or kills someone.

It should be recognized that not all situations will result in a legal duty being found or created. For example, in one recent case (*Purdy v. Westchester County,* 1987), a car driven by a nursing home resident smashed into a gas station, causing personal injury. The facility and its medical director were sued for failing to prohibit the person from driving, based on her medical condition. Although the jury found both the home and the physician liable, the judge set aside the verdict. The appeals court agreed with the judge's decision, stating that, as a matter of public policy, there was an insufficient basis for postulating a special relationship, and therefore a duty to restrain the freedom of this individual to operate her car. To impose a duty in this situation, the court continued, would be to create an unreasonable burden. In a different set of circumstances (*Gill v. New York City,* 1987), also reversing a jury verdict, another court determined that it would be unfair and contrary to law to hold a landlord responsible for the injuries inflicted by a mentally ill tenant on a cotenant.

Direct causation, known in law as proximate cause, is a technical term which does not have the apparent meaning one might ordinarily ascribe to it. In order to establish proximate cause, all that must be shown is that the event in question was a substantial factor in bringing about the ultimate result (Goldstein, 1987). In other words, legally sufficient cause, decided by the jury, need meet only a more-likely-than-not test in order to establish liability. This is true even if the event did not have the sole, or even the major, role. Mere passage of time does not dilute "proximate."

Opposing expert testimony is necessary to delineate the relevant professional standards, and deviation therefrom, which constitute the fourth and final element: dereliction. Two experienced defense attorneys put it most succinctly: "As any veteran of the courtroom is acutely aware, the physician can count on his colleagues to supply the needed testimony as to departure" [from acceptable standards of practice] (Ledy-Gurren and Greenman, 1986). Add to this commentary the facts that juries have considerable leeway to decide retrospectively that some other measure could have been taken, to accept idiosyncratic standards proposed by the expert for the plaintiff, and also to express sympathy for the victim (Appelbaum, 1987), it should not be difficult to understand otherwise scientifically incomprehensible verdicts.

The fulcrum of malpractice litigation is often the issue of foreseeability. Expressed in standard negligence law terms, the defendant has to be shown to know, or reasonably expected to know, of the possibility of an unfortunate outcome. At least a modicum of prescience is perhaps useful here. Hindsight is used to judge foreseeability, and this is not the oxymoron it may seem to be. Because damage must occur before this type of lawsuit would be filed, there is no alternative to looking backwards at the particular facts and circumstances. Two cases, with unfavorable conclusions, will serve to illustrate how these medicolegal principles operate.

A patient with a 10-year history of paranoid schizophrenia killed his mother and brother three months after his last treatment contact. There were no specific warning signs of violence, and his wife had stated that she did not think he was a danger. The court focused on what the treating staff should have known, without giving any idea how this could be accomplished (*Bardoni v. Kim,* 1986). They simply stated that the assessment does not turn on information that is known, but on that which is extrinsic. An expert witness for the survivors testified that the clinician improperly relied on the wife's statements, and that the patient's refusal of treatment could make him violent. In a curious footnote, the court stated that it was limiting its decision to psychiatrists, and would not comment as to whether the same duties would fall upon psychologists.

In a different jurisdiction, a patient with an extensive history of psychiatric care was discharged from a voluntary hospitalization when he was no longer hallucinating, delusional, or considered a danger to himself or others. Almost half a year later, the car he was driving crossed the center line and killed someone heading in the opposite direction. The court found the physicians "grossly" negligent, and that this negligence was the proximate cause of death (*Laird v. Buckley*, 1987). The plaintiff's expert testified that more attention should have been paid to his history, he should not have been discharged on high-dose medications, continuing treatment should have been mandated, involuntary commitment pursued, and, finally, that his dangerousness was foreseeable with reasonable medical certainty.

THE DOCTRINE CHANGES

For many years, inpatient facilities and doctors working therein have been held legally liable in situations where it could be shown that they either negligently discharged a patient or negligently allowed him or her to escape, and the patient subsequently inflicted harm on an innocent third person. This is not new law but, rather, standard. It was, and still is, based on the principle that the hospital had actual control over the patient—since he or she was in the physical custody of the hospital, a special relationship arose and created a clear duty to control foreseeable behavior.

The first case in which a court applied similar standards in a noncustodial, i.e., outpatient, setting was that of *Tarasoff v. Regents of University of California* (1974). This is perhaps the one decision in the annals of mental health law best known to psychiatric clinicians. An ex-suitor killed the young woman whose affections he desired, after confiding to his therapist that he harbored such intentions. An abortive attempt to hospitalize him had been made, but no further action was taken. In its first decision on the matter, the California Supreme Court created a new duty, the so-called duty to warn an endangered third party. However, less well known to practitioners is the fact that the court changed its stance two years later.

In what is, in fact, the precedent-setting ruling, the California Supreme Court stated that, "When a therapist determines, or pursuant to the standards of his profession should determine, that his patient presents a serious danger of violence to another, he incurs an obligation to *use reasonable care to protect* [emphasis added] the intended victim against such danger (*Tarasoff v. Regents of University of California,* 1976)." As to professional concerns relative to confidentiality, the court said simply, "The protective privilege ends where the public peril begins."

The good news in the court's change of heart was that warning was modified to allow other, perhaps more appropriate, clinical interventions. One could, for example, arrange either voluntary or involuntary hospitalization. Depending on the patient and his or her relationship with the therapist, one might increase the dose of medication, see the patient more frequently, or use a technique of "contracting" with the patient to control behavior by such means as calling the therapist at any time a destructive impulse arises. The phrase "determine or should determine" is boilerplate negligence law. But the bad news was that the "pursuant to the standards of his profession" terminology remained, despite the fact that there were not then, and are still not today, any such well-developed standards.

Tarasoff spawned a good number of progeny as, increasingly, state courts adopted the doctrine that a therapist has a duty to protect a third party from danger his or her patient may be creating. These are reviewed in a variety of other publications (e.g., Beck, 1985), and to do so here would exceed the purpose of this chapter. However, it is instructive to mention briefly four cases, all decided in 1983, which significantly enlarged the scope of this new obligation imposed on mental health professionals.

A California court extended the duty to protect to a small child whose mother was injured, reasoning that such youngsters are generally in the company of a parent (*Hedlund v. Orange County,* 1983). Another tribunal held evaluating physicians liable in a situation in which no specific threats were made, and the victim was just as aware of her killer's past history of violent behaviors as were the doctors (*Jablonski v. U.S.,* 1983). In Washington, a case which could simply have been handled as a matter of negligent release was instead decided so as to broaden the duty to protect to any member of the public who might be harmed by the patient (*Petersen v. State,* 1983). Finally, a crime committed in a distant location some time after the patient left the hospital was deemed the fault of state psychiatrists, based on a two-year old emergency room note written prior to an earlier admission (*Davis v. Lhim,* 1983).

In Vermont, another novel extension of professional responsibility was created by the courts. Going beyond assaults upon persons, a duty to prevent damage to property was enunciated (*Peck v. Addison County,* 1985). Other jurisdictions have not yet followed suit.

One commentator (Felthous, 1987) has noted that we are now at the point where failure to properly diagnose includes failure to foresee violent acts, and failure to treat includes failure to restrain violent acts. But these are not truly medical problems! Appropriate steps for clinicians to take in potentially explosive circumstances have been enumerated by Appelbaum (1985). First, the degree of danger must be assessed, after all relevant data have been gathered. Of course, an attempt must be made to identify any possible victims. Next, the clinician must select a course of action, taking whatever steps are deemed reasonable. In other words, more than thought is required. Implementation involves not only carrying out a plan of treatment, but also continuing to monitor its effectiveness.

In a decision with which most of us would agree, New York's highest court recently differentiated between those patients treated on an ambulatory basis and those over whom we have greater custody by virtue of their being inpatients: the State's control over, and consequent duty to prevent harm by, a voluntary outpatient, is more limited than its control over a hospitalized patient (*Schrempf v. State of New York,* 1985). Note, of course what was not said—some duty still remains.

Finally, one additional instructive case should be mentioned, for it mixed the two legal claims of negligent release and failure to warn/protect. A schizophrenic patient, in and out of hospitals, killed his mother and injured his father several months after his release from inpatient care. During that stay, he voiced no threats, but did express anger at his parents for having him committed. The doctors were aware of this, considered it reality based, and were of the belief that he was handling his feelings by talking about them. On direct questioning, the parents denied that he had ever given them a reason to be afraid of him. While one expert described the patient as something of a walking time bomb, for whom the only acceptable treatment would be long-term institutionalization, and whose improvement did not warrant release, he also expressed his disagreement with the law on the matter. The other psychiatrists who testified stated that it is impossible to predict violence in the absence of any past or current assaultiveness and, even if it were possible, our abilities in this regard could extend for no more than a few days to a couple of weeks at most. Concluding that sometimes doctors are wrong, the court decided that the physicians in this case should not have known what the patient would do subsequent to discharge (*Soutear v. U.S.*, 1986).

WHAT IS DANGER? SHOULD WE WARN OF IT?

While I have clearly been an advocate for broadening the criteria of dangerousness for the purpose of civil commitment (Rachlin, 1987), it somehow seems that a more narrow definition is in order when discussing potential liability for harm to third parties. Can there possibly be this best of both worlds? Several decisions by the United States Supreme Court have led me to believe that such a utopian stance may not be totally unfounded.

In *Addington v. Texas* (1979), a leading civil commitment case, the Court stated that proof beyond a reasonable doubt was not constitutionally required in order to involuntarily hospitalize someone, whatever (including dangerousness) the basis for admission. The Justices recognized that the profession could not be held to this level of accuracy if sick people were to be helped appropriately. With reference to the sentencing phase of a death penalty case, however, our claimed difficulty predicting danger was rejected (*Barefoot v. Estelle*, 1983). The Court was not persuaded as to our scientific unreliability, indicating that doctors are not always wrong (just most of the time). Finally, where the situation was that of an insanity acquittee seeking release from the hospital, the Justices indicated that violence is not necessary for there to be a finding of dangerousness (*Jones v. U.S.*, 1983). The commission of a crime, here petty larceny, is sufficient to indicate danger. While these three cases may appear to have disparate results, one can at least say that the Supreme Court is willing to vary the definitions and criteria depending on the circumstances.

Generally speaking, clinical knowledge has not yet made significant inroads into court decisions in the sphere of liability for violence. However, context is known to be an important clinical variable in the assessment of danger and the occurrence of violent acts (Stokman, 1984). It is absolutely important for us to understand the interaction between the person and his environment as a factor in attempting any prediction. Simply put, what will the patient meet in the community?

Wettstein (1984) urges a multifactorial equation when a mental health professional is attempting to grasp, or divine, what behavior might be expected from a patient. Not only must the nature, severity and likelihood of any violence be considered, but, which is often overlooked, its imminence as well. He goes on to tell us that the evidence reviewed suggests that, even if the patient is threatening harm, more likely than not he will not act. This point should be widely known to judges and legislators; unfortunately, it is not. How long, it is legitimate to ask, can a damaged person (patient) remain fixed (nonviolent)? How long can his treators be held accountable for his behavior?

In what he calls the first generation of violence prediction studies, Monahan (1984) concludes that we have been wrong twice as often as we have been right. Not overly glum about this fact, he goes on to say that as we improve our research techniques and get better at narrowing the circumstances of our predictions, our abilities may increase. Even so, based on his extensive work in the area, he believes that the real ceiling of our predictive skill may ultimately top out at 50%. While this may not be any better than chance, it could nonetheless be valuable with and for individual patients. Time will tell, but courts are not likely to wait.

Beck (1987), among the most serious students of what *Tarasoff* has wrought, has recently categorized all known decisions on the duty to protect. He reports that, where a patient's violence to a victim was clearly foreseeable—which he defined as two-thirds of the triad of a history of violence, a threat to a specific third party, and an apparent motive—virtually all courts have imposed a duty (and possibly liability as well) upon mental health professionals. In those situations he deemed questionably foreseeable (one of the three conditions), courts usually looked to whether or not professional judgment was exercised, and where the danger was unforeseeable (none of the three), most cases have gone in favor of the doctor and /or treatment teams. I am not nearly as sanguine (Rachlin and Schwartz, 1986), but it must be acknowledged that the sample sizes reviewed are so small as to make valid statistical comparisons impossible. To venture again into terminology of another field of learning, the jury is still out on this one.

Warning a potential victim appears to have found favor within the law. It is a specific, concrete action on the part of the therapist, susceptible to a did-it-or-did-it-not-take-place measure. Its value tends to be assumed, but this is not necessarily the case. In the absence of any evidence that it decreases the incidence of violence, it is inappropriate to presume that warning is a good thing.

Mills (1985) points out that there are risks to such a course of action. The person contacted may become not only frightened, but also wary of the patient, perhaps for a considerable period of time and, perhaps also, unnecessarily (given the inaccuracies in predictive abilities). Will the party warned pay serious attention to the therapist's concern and, if so, what reasonable steps can he or she take of a protective nature? Few can afford to hire private bodyguards, and the police are unlikely to supply officers for this purpose. So, warning may in fact be no more than an empty remedy.

On the other hand, a clinical perspective casts a somewhat different light. I am unaware of any patient who has been helped to grow psychologically by killing or maiming another person. No matter what the psychodynamics, such action would never be of benefit, for infinitely more reasons than the likelihood of apprehension and prosecution. Thus, the competent therapist will, when faced with the possibility of a patient inflicting serious physical harm, take steps to prevent what might loosely be called acting-out. This would be part of the responsibility to the subject of our treatment, just as it would be if the patient were deemed to be in danger of suiciding.

There is some data to indicate that, if the patient is part of the decision to warn and its implementation, the results can be positive (Carlson, Friedman, and Riggert, 1987). Although nobody has documented a large series of cases where this was done, the warning itself can possibly be sufficient as an externally imposed control to assist the patient with his or her behavior. It is a form of limit setting, a rather classical therapeutic technique, and it gives due recognition to the equally obvious fact that the patient may have significant ambivalence over his planned acts. The conventional wisdom, to the extent it exists, is not to warn without telling the patient, and to do so only after other clinical interventions have been ruled out or have failed (e.g., hospitalization, increasing medication dosage, seeing the patient more frequently, etc.).

LEGAL AND CLINICAL RESPONSES

Difficult social problems commonly are the subject of litigation, ultimately to be followed by the somewhat slower legislative process. And this is precisely what has happened with regard to the duty to protect. We have already seen some of what the courts have done; most, but not all, jurisdictions have adopted the *Tarasoff* doctrine, or some variation thereof, when given the opportunity to do so. It is prudent to act as though such a responsibility exists, no matter the location of one's practice.

The American Psychiatric Association has issued a "resource document" on the duty to protect, while the American Psychological Association has put forth a somewhat more official sounding "white paper." Both recognize, and also circumscribe, the duty. Some legislative action has taken place, though not necessarily in response to these pronouncements by professional organizations.

As of this writing, I am aware of laws both establishing and, at the same time, restricting the duty to protect in a number of states. It is of interest to note that among these are California, where this all got started, and Washington, where it reached its most expansive expression. (Other states include Colorado, Indiana, Kentucky, Louisiana, Minnesota, and Montana. Additional jurisdictions are considering such legislation, and some will undoubtedly have enacted it by the time this chapter is read.)

Depending on the exact wording of the particular state law, the professions covered are typically enumerated. A duty to protect is established, under specific circumstances. Usually, these include an overt threat and an identifiable victim, but there may be variations. Finally, the actions expected of the clinician are detailed. Responses sufficient to satisfy the legal obligation include issuing a warning and/or notifying the police, or arranging for hospitalization of the patient. Whether such laws will really affect the incidence and prevalence of violence remains an open question but I, for one, am dubious. These bills restrict clinical judgment and options.

Should we attempt, in addition, to get courts to make some modifications in existing legal standards? Perhaps, but with recognition that the process will be painfully slow. First on any such agenda would be convincing judges that it is not acceptable for them to assume that violent behavior can be clinically diagnosed and treated. The existing technology is immature and, as a result of this fact, Mills (1984) suggests that the criterion for imposing liability be a "substantial departure" from accepted professional standards [rather than "reasonably should have known"]. Does the answer lie in a "no fault" system, as with automobile insurance? Would society accept a worker's compensation-like arrangement? Either is, at the very least, worthy of consideration.

Certainly, one option which might be comparatively simple to institute would be to insist that the experience of expert witnesses match, to some degree, the questions being posed by the litigation (Rachlin and Schwartz, 1986). For example, a psychiatrist who for the past 20 years has concentrated exclusively on outpatient treatment of children should not be considered qualified to make a statement on the criteria for discharge from inpatient care of the young adult chronic patient. Misguided experts can and do confuse their wishes with reality, and do not always express recognition of the limits of resources, particularly vis-à-vis public sector psychiatry. In terms of when to hold a therapist liable for the behavior of an outpatient, we have further suggested that it first be demonstrated that evidence of committability has been ignored.

An interesting approach to the decision to discharge an inpatient who may be at risk for engaging in violent acts has been described by Travin and Bluestone (1987). They have constituted an interdisciplinary disposition committee to engage in systematic deliberations prior to a final determination being made. It is a sad, but valid, commentary that these two psychiatrists have labelled what many of us would call a clinical case conference as a "hearing."

In any assessment of potentially dangerous patients, it is wise to reiterate the steps recommended by Appelbaum (1985): gather information, use the data to make a determination as to an appropriate course of action, then implement and monitor it. One should also recall the suggestion of Wettstein (1984) to look at severity, nature, imminence, and likelihood of violence. To these ideas we (Rachlin and Schwartz, 1986) have added the need to pay particular attention to previous medical records, any past history of violent behavior, and the statements of relatives or friends as being among the prudent steps one can take. Communication within the treatment team (if the situation includes other professionals and paraprofessionals) is crucial, and it is impossible to overstress the importance of careful written documentation of precisely what has been done, the opinions of any supervisors or consultants who may have been involved, and the reasoning behind the decision.

CONCLUSION

We have yet to demonstrate conclusively that any of the thoughts and behaviors outlined in the previous section will prevent or even reduce violence. Be that as it may, all are consistent with high quality patient care, a laudable goal for any clinician. Thus, despite the fact that the question of liability for the behavior of others will not leave the legal arena in the foreseeable future (not only with respect to mental health professionals, but to society in general), the reasons why we intervene relate, or should relate, to the principles and traditions of our several professions.

Lest the reader be misled by some of what I have reported, particularly the cases with outcomes that appear to make little sense, the number of findings of liability for patients' violent acts is still relatively small. Despite the anecdotes, the problem is not out of bounds. Providing high quality professionally acceptable treatment remains not only an ethical percept, but also the best defense against a lawsuit. After all, we do prevail in most cases instituted against us, and the real winner needs always to be the patient. The law should not have to be telling us what constitutes good standards of care.

REFERENCES

Appelbaum, P. S. (1985). Tarasoff and the clinician: Problems in fulfilling the duty to protect. *American Journal of Psychiatry, 142,* 425–429.

Appelbaum, P. S. (1987). Legal aspects of violence by psychiatric patients. In R. E. Hales & A. J. Frances (Eds.), *American Psychiatric Association Annual Review, Vol. 6.* Washington, D.C., American Psychiatric Press.

Beck, J. C. (1985). The psychotherapist and the violent patient: Recent case law. In J. C. Beck (Ed.), *The Potentially Violent Patient and the Tarasoff Decision in Psychiatric Practice.* Washington, D.C., American Psychiatric Press.

Beck, J. C. (1987). The psychotherapist's duty to protect third parties from harm. *Mental and Physical Disability Law Reporter, 11,* 141–148.

Carlson, R. J., Friedman, L. C., & Riggert, S. C. (1987). The duty to warn/protect: Issues in clinical practice. *Bulletin of the American Academy of Psychiatry and the Law,* 15, 179–186.

Felthous, A. R. (1987). Liability of treaters for injuries to others: Erosion of three doctrines. *Bulletin of the American Academy of Psychiatry and the Law, 15,* 115–125.

Goldstein, R. L. (1987). The twilight zone between scientific certainty and legal sufficiency: Should a jury determine the causation of schizophrenia? *Bulletin of the American Academy of Psychiatry and the Law, 15,* 95–104.

Gutheil, T. G., Rachlin, S., & Mills, M. J. (1985). Differing conceptual models in psychiatry and law. In S. Rachlin (Ed.), Legal Encroachment on Psychiatric Practice. *New Directions for Mental Health Services,* No. 25, San Francisco, Jossey-Bass.

Ledy-Gurren, N., & Greenman, L. C. (1986). The psychiatrist's unique dilemma: Liability for the violent acts of patients. *Bower and Gardner Update, 1* (3), 2–7.

Mills, M. J. (1984). The so-called duty to warn: The psychotherapeutic duty to protect third parties from patients' violent acts. *Behavioral Sciences and the Law, 2,* 237–257.

Mills, M. J. (1985). Expanding the duties to protect third parties from violent acts. In S. Rachlin (Ed.), Legal Encroachment on Psychiatric Practice. *New Directions for Mental Health Services*, No. 25, San Francisco: Jossey-Bass.

Monahan, J. (1984). The prediction of violent behavior: Toward a second generation of theory and policy. *American Journal of Psychiatry, 141*, 10–15.

Rachlin, S. (1987). Redefining dangerousness for civil commitment. *Hospital and Community Psychiatry, 38*, 884–886.

Rachlin, S., & Schwartz, H. I. (1986). Unforeseeable liability for patients' violent acts. *Hospital and Community Psychiatry, 37*, 725–731.

Stokman, C. L. J. (1984). Dangerousness and violence in hospitalized mentally ill offenders. *Psychiatric Quarterly, 56*, 138–143.

Travin, S., & Bluestone, H. (1987). Discharging the violent psychiatric inpatient. *Journal of Forensic Sciences, 32*, 999–1008.

Wettstein, R. M. (1984). The prediction of violent behavior and the duty to protect third parties. *Behavioral Sciences and the Law, 2*, 291–317.

CASES CITED

Addington v. Texas, 441 U.S. 418, 99 S.Ct. 1804, 60 L.Ed.2d 323 (1979).

Bardoni v. Kim, 390 N.W.2d 218 (Mich. App. 1986).

Barefoot v. Estelle, 463 U.S. 880, 103 S.Ct. 3383, 77 L.Ed.2d 1090 (1983).

Davis v. Lhim, 335 N.W.2d 481 (Mich. App. 1983).

Gill v. New York City Housing Authority, 130 A.D.2d 256, 519 N.Y.S.2d 364 (1987).

Hedlund v. Superior Court of Orange County, 34 Cal.3d 695, 194 Cal. Rptr. 805, 669 P.2d 41 (1983).

Jablonski by Pahls v. United States, 712 F.2d 391 (9th Cir. 1983).

Jones v. United States, 463 U.S. 354, 103 S.Ct. 3043, 77 L.Ed.2d 694 (1983).

Laird v. Buckley, Del.Super., C.A. No. 79C–JA–97, Taylor, J. (March 2, 1987). (on Westlaw) *aff'd sub nom Naidu v. Laird* 539 A.2d 1064 (Del. Supr., 1988).

Peck v. Counseling Service of Addison County, 499 A.2d 422 (Vt. 1985).

Petersen v. State, 671 P.2d 230 (Wash. 1983).

Purdy v. Public Administrator of Westchester County, 127 A.D.2d 285, 514 N.Y.S.2d 407 (1987) *aff'd* 72 N.Y.2d 1, 530 N.Y.S.2d 513, 526 N.E.2d 4 (1988).

Schrempf v. State of New York, 66 N.Y.2d 289, 496 N.Y.S.2d 973, 487 N.E.2d 883 (1985).

Soutear v. United States, 646 F.Supp. 524 (E.D.Mich. 1986).

Sukljian v. Ross & Son Company, 69 N.Y.2d 89, 511 N.Y.S.2d 821, 503 N.E.2d 1358 (1986).

Tarasoff v. Regents of the University of California, 13 Cal.3d 177, 118 Cal. Rptr. 129, 529 P.2d 553 (1974).

Tarasoff v. Regents of the University of California, 17 Cal.3d 425, 131 Cal. Rptr. 14, 551 P.2d 334 (1976).

PART II

Ethological Issues

3

Psychosocial Correlates of Suicide and Violence Risk

ROBERT PLUTCHIK
HERMAN M. VAN PRAAG

Clinicians have long recognized a relation between aggression and suicide. For example, psychoanalysts have often stated that suicide is an expression of anger turned inward. A number of studies have reported that about 30 percent of violent individuals have a history of self-destructive behavior, while about 10–20 percent of suicidal persons have a history of violent behavior (Bach-Y-Rita and Veno, 1974; Tardiff and Sweillam, 1982; Skodal and Karasu, 1978).

However, relatively little is known about why some people show violence only, some are suicidal, and some are both. If psychiatry is to be of practical help in recognizing and treating individuals, it should identify those variables or factors that predispose an individual to act violently so that suitable interventions can be made.

The purpose of the present paper is to provide an overview of what have been learned in recent years about the factors that contribute to violent behavior. It will have three parts. In Part I we will review studies on variables that contribute to the risk of suicide. In Part II we will describe variables that contribute to the risk of violence. And in Part III we will discuss the interrelations between suicide and violence and will present some of our own recent findings. Finally, we will describe a general model or theory that we believe to be helpful in integrating the observations that have been made.

PART I: SUICIDE

Table 1 illustrates some data that are well known about suicide. The overall suicide rate in the United States is approximately 12 per 100,000 people per year (Pokorny, 1983). However, rates among adolescents and young people have risen in the past decade so that it is now 20/100,000/yr (Hendin, 1986). People over 50 also have a relatively high rate of suicide. Although they make up about one-quarter of the U.S. population, they commit about 40 percent of the suicides (Hendin, 1986). We also know that Whites commit suicide almost 3 times more frequently than Blacks (Pokorny, 1983) and that women make more attempts than males, but men are more likely to complete the suicide. Single veterans commit suicide about 4 times more frequently than married ones (Pokorny, 1983). It is also well known that suicide (as well as homicide) rates vary from one social class to another, from state to state and from country to country. At one time it had been believed that there was a simple inverse relation between suicide and violence so that countries high in suicide were likely to be low in homicide. This is not true and there are countries like Ireland and Norway where both the suicide and homicide rates are low, and countries like the United States where both the suicide and homicide rates are quite high.

TABLE 1
Death Rates by Suicide in the United States in 1982

	Rates per 100,000/yr
White Males	19.4
Black Males	10.8
White Females	5.8
Black Females	2.2
Nevada (Highest State)	29.0
Connecticut (Lowest State)	7.7
Age 20–24 Years	16.0
Age 40–44 Years	17.5
Age 60–64 Years	25.5

In addition to these rather broad sociological variables like race, age, and social class, there are also more individual or personal variables that have been identified. It is pretty well accepted that depression is a risk factor for suicide, as are various other psychiatric diagnoses. Table 2 shows the suicide rates for a large group of 4800 male veterans followed prospectively for five years. Patients with affective disorders have 32 times the likelihood of committing suicide compared to veterans in general. Patients diagnosed as schizophrenic have 20 times the likelihood of suicide of veterans in general. In fact, patients with any psychiatric diagnosis at all have from three to 32 times greater probability of suicide than veterans as a whole. It is thus evident from this prospective study following large numbers of patients that any psychiatric diagnosis indicates an increased risk for suicide.

Another important issue concerns the degree of similarity between suicide attempters and suicide completers. The fundamental question is: Can we study suicide attempters and draw any conclusions about suicide completers? Although there are some differences, there appear to be more similarities. For example, the distribution of diagnoses between those who attempt suicide and those who actually suicide is quite similar (Hendin, 1986). Pokorny (1983) also showed that there appears to be an increas-

TABLE 2
Incidence of Suicide by Diagnostic Category*

Diagnosis	*Suicide Rate per 100,000/yr.*
Affective Disorder	695
Schizophrenia	456
Drug Abuse	194
Alcoholism	187
Personality Disorder	187
Neurosis	150
Organic Brain Syndrome	71
All Veterans	23
U.S. as a Whole	12

*Based on a 5-year follow-up of 4800 veterans (Pokorny, 1983)

ing risk continuum from those who have suicidal ideas to those who make attempts. This is shown in Table 3. Pokorny concludes that "in most respects suicide attempters and suicide completers are similar, that is, they were mostly related to the same predictors, and generally in the same direction" (p. 253).

Sletten, Evenson, and Brown (1973) also reported that actual suicides generally resembled suicide attempters on a variety of diagnostic, demographic and family variables more than they resembled patients who were nonattempters. They concluded that committed suicides are typically drawn from a population of suicide attempters. In addition, the great majority of patients who eventually suicide have thought, planned or attempted suicide in the past (Harkavy-Friedman, Asnis & DiFiore, 1987).

Examining this same point a bit further, Buglass and McCulloch (1970) in England followed a large group of patients who came to a Poison Treatment Center. Those who actually killed themselves in the next three years had risk scores on a series of rating scales similar to those who made attempts.

One other study also confirmed the idea of a continuum between suicide attempts and suicide. Lester, Beck, and Mitchell (1979) looked at depression and hopelessness scale scores in a group of 453 attempted suicides. Fourteen of the patients killed themselves during the next five years. It was found that their depression and hopelessness scores were similar to the group of attempted suicides with the greatest intent to die. This finding was interpreted to mean that it is possible to extrapolate from research findings on attempted suicides the psychological characteristics of completed suicides. The half-dozen studies we have

TABLE 3
Incidence of Suicide in 4800 Veterans as a Function of the Suicidal Spectrum*

Suicidal Spectrum	*Suicide Rate per 100,000/yr.*
Ideas	704
Threats	710
Attempts	805

*Pokorny (1983).

cited on this point all concur in concluding that completed suicides are quite similar to attempted suicides in most respects and that a continuous spectrum exists ranging from suicidal ideas, to gestures, to mild attempts, serious attempts, and finally suicide. What is not yet known are all the important variables that influence an individual's progression along this spectrum of suicidality.

To give some idea of what variables might determine the probability of suicide, we will cite two recent studies. Motto, Heilbron and Juster (1985) evaluated 2753 patients who had been hospitalized for depression and/or suicidal state. In a two-year followup, approximately five percent of the group had committed suicide. Major variables that were correlated with the likelihood of a suicide are shown in Table 4. They include a family history of alcoholism, depression and other psychiatric illnesses, severe impairment in physical health, special stresses, ideas of reference and suicidal impulses, among others.

A recent study evaluated all suicides in San Diego county in California between 1981 and 1983 (Rich, Young and Fowler, 1986). A detailed structured interview was conducted with close family members dealing with demographic, clinical, medical and family history as well as current stressors. The major results are

TABLE 4
Major Risk Factors for Suicide*

1. A Family History of Depression, Alcoholism or Other Emotional Disorders.
2. An Active Bisexual, or an Inactive Homosexual Life-Style.
3. Severe Impairment in Physical Health in the Past Year.
4. Previous Psychiatric Hospital Admissions.
5. Previous Efforts to Obtain Help have been Unsuccessful.
6. Severe Special Stress (Other Than Health or Job).
7. Presence of Suicidal Impulses.
8. Presence of Ideas of Persecution or Reference.
9. Sleeps Too Much.
10. Has Made a Recent Suicide Attempt.

*Based on a 2-year follow-up of 2753 depressed or suicidal patients (Motto, Heilbron and Juster (1985).

summarized in Table 5. The results showed that half the group had had previous psychiatric treatment and that one-fourth of all suicides were in treatment at the time of the suicide. Most of the individuals had talked about committing suicide and almost 40 percent had made a previous suicide attempt.

In terms of the stressors that were identified, physical illness was the most common, especially in the over-age-30 group,

TABLE 5
Variables Related to 283 Suicides in
San Diego County, California, 1981–1983*

	Percent
Below Age 30 Years	47
Above Age 30 Years	53
Prior Psychiatric Treatment	48
In Treatment at Time of Suicide	28
Talked About Own Suicide	67
Made a Previous Suicide Attempt	38
Used Firearms	49
Used Drugs or Poisons for Suicide	20
Stressors	
Death in Family	18
Separation	42
Rejection	42
Illness	45
Financial Trouble	31
Job Problems	12
Unemployed	26
Legal Trouble	8
Major Diagnoses	
Substance-Use Disorder	
Drug	63
Alcohol	77
Affective Disorder	63
Atypical Psychoses	11
Adjustment Disorders	13

*Rich, Young and Fowler (1986).

where 70 percent were reported to have a serious illness. Other important stressors were separation from a spouse, rejection by a lover, and financial problems.

The most common diagnoses were substance-use disorders (77 percent were alcohol abusers), affective disorders (63 percent), atypical psychoses (11 percent), and adjustment disorders (18 percent).

In a review of 15 rating scales for the estimation of suicide risk, Burk, Kurz and Moller (1985) identified nine general categories of variables that have been used as predictors. These are listed in Table 6. They include certain demographic data, evidence of mental illness, social isolation, and recent loss experiences.

Given the extensive research that has been carried out on suicide over the past 30 years or more, why are our tables so general and our conclusions about specific variables so tentative? There are a number of reasons which are summarized in Table 7.

Fundamentally, suicide is a rare event and rare events are inherently difficult to predict. To state this idea another way, prediction of rare events generally produces too many false positives. For example, let us assume that suicide occurs to one person in 10,000 and that we have a predictive test that is 99 percent accurate. If we test 10,000 people, we may still miss the

TABLE 6
Variables Identified as Predictors of Suicide Risk in 15 Different Studies*

1. Evidence of Mental Illness.
2. Previous Suicidal Behavior.
3. Demographic Data (Age, Sex, Race).
4. Evidence of Antisocial Behavior.
5. Presence of Psychopathological Symptoms.
6. Poor Physical Health.
7. Social Isolation.
8. Recent Loss.
9. Severity of Current Suicidal Attempts.

*Burk, Kurz and Moller (1985).

TABLE 7
Difficulties in Research on Suicide

1. Suicide is a Rare Event, So There Are Relatively Few Cases to Study.
2. Subjects Are Not Available For Direct Study After Committing Suicide.
3. Retrospective Data Are Not Often Reliable.
4. Most Suicidal Patients Are Not Given Extensive Batteries of Tests or Ratings to Use in Predictive Studies.
5. Identification of a Suicidal Patient Initiates Efforts to Prevent the Suicide. If Successful, This Weakens the Relation of Predictor to Outcome.

one person who is going to commit suicide, but we will identify approximately 100 people falsely as suicide risks who are in fact not likely to commit suicide.

Second, once a person has suicided it is very difficult to collect accurate data about the individual from family members and others for reasons of shame, guilt, defensiveness, faulty memory, and lack of knowledge. Another important reason for our difficulty in making predictions is that the identification of suicidal patients generally leads to efforts to prevent the suicide. To the extent that this is successful, it attenuates the presumed relation between a predictor variable and an overt suicide.

For all these reasons plus the fact that suicide attempters are apparently fairly similar to suicide completers, it is much easier to study suicide attempters and to then extrapolate our conclusions. Generally speaking, past behavior is the best guide to future behavior.

There are two other important ideas that we should like to present before turning our attention to issues of violence.

First of all, although the statistics of suicide are interesting, we should keep in mind that most of it is sociological and not psychological. The fact that White people commit suicide more frequently than Black people do, or that single people suicide more than married people, gives us no insight into the reasons that any one individual attempts suicide. Such sociological or demographic variables must somehow act through the final common pathway—that is, the individual. We need to identify personal variables that influence attitudes and expectations and behavior if we are to understand why, contrary to our sociological expectations, this *particular* Black, married man, from the middle class has made a suicide attempt. The fact is that the vast majority of people in any given risk category do *not* make suicide attempts.

At best, our efforts will be like playing dice. On any given throw we cannot predict which faces will come up. However, if we make a thousand tosses we can predict very well what the exact distribution of outcomes will be. Thus, in a group of male war veterans in Texas we know that approximately two will kill themselves out of 10,000 in any given year, but we cannot predict which two they will be (Porkorny, 1983). Hopefully, we can improve the odds through research. Thus, in a study reported by Pallis et al. (1982), 1263 suicide attempters were followed for two years. Twelve suicided in the first year. It was learned that 10 of the 12 were in the top quarter of a suicide risk scale. Thus, if someone gets a very high score on this suicide risk scale, and has already made a suicide attempt, then we can say that he (or she) has approximately an 80 percent chance of suiciding in the next year. All of our statements have to be made in probabilistic terms. This argument applies equally well to the prediction of violence.

The second general point concerns the unstable nature of the forces that impel a given individual toward suicide. This may be illustrated by a recent British study of 50 adolescents admitted to a hospital after taking overdoses of drugs (Hawton et al., 1982). The adolescents reported such problems as difficulties with parents or boyfriends, school difficulties, and ill health. In the majority of cases the problems appeared to be transient and most reported considerable improvement within a few weeks. However seven of the patients (14 percent) made another self-poisoning attempt within a year.

These results suggest a kind of cathartic effect of a suicide attempt, an observation that has occasionally been reported in the literature (Platman, Plutchik & Weinstein, 1971). This idea is supported by a recent study reported by us (van Praag & Plutchik, 1986). We compared a group of depressed patients who had been admitted to a hospital subsequent to a suicide attempt, with a group of depressed patients admitted to the same hospital, but who had not made a suicide attempt. The average depression levels of both groups prior to hospitalization were not significantly different. However, the suicidal group showed a significant decrease on all measures of depression within one to two weeks after hospitalization. We interpret this rapid change as evidence for the cathartic effect of a suicide attempt in many people.

The point these illustrations make is that the factors that coexist at any given point in time to precipitate a suicide attempt in a particular individual are unique (and therefore unstable). A specific suicidal act requires exactly the right combination of internal inhibitions, external prohibitions, motivational drive, impulse strength, and situational opportunities. Variations in any of these classes of events can abruptly change the probability of a suicidal act.

PART II: VIOLENCE

Let us turn our attention now to the other side of the coin, to the issue of violence.

Table 8 gives some idea of crime rates for the United States as a whole in 1984. The rate of murder is 7.9 per 100,000 people per year. Forcible rape is 35.7/100,000/yr, while aggravated assault is 290/100,000/yr. These figures for violence are considerably higher than those for suicide.

If we consider the changes in suicide rates over time, we also find no simple relation between the two. For Whites, the suicide rate went from 17.6 to 20.7 over a 22-year period, an 18 percent

TABLE 8
Violent Crime Rates in the United States (1980–1984)

	Rates per 100,000/yr
Murder	7.9
Forcible Rape	35.7
Robbery	205.0
Aggravated Assault	290.0

increase. During the same period, homicide rates increased approximately 300 percent. For Blacks, during the same period, both the suicide and homicide rates increased by about 60 percent. These figures suggest that quite different factors influence suicidality and homicide in Blacks and Whites in America.

In the following discussion, the term "violence" is used to refer to a spectrum of behavior which can and does range from thoughts of harm to others and verbal threats to actual assaultive behavior shown by one person to another which has the effect of producing physical harm or injury. This definition has two immediate implications: (1) that violence implies a dimension of behaviors and not a single act; and (2) that the concept of violence is an inference from various classes of evidence. This latter point is not a new one since the common law clearly distinguishes among various crimes that may have the same outcome (e.g. the death of a person) on the basis of evidence of accident, design or premeditation. The presence of violence is thus a social judgment made about the behavior of others and is, like all judgments, fallible.

An early study of violence (Climent et al., 1973) examined medical and psychiatric correlates of violent behaviors in 95 women prisoners in a Massachusetts prison. A number of different ways of measuring violence in these women was used. These included a self-rating of how frequently the individual showed certain types of violent behaviors. It also included a rating made by a correctional officer based on observed behavior in the prison, and an estimate of the degree of violence involved in the crimes for which the women were incarcerated. Based on these indices, some prisoners were defined as "violent" and others as "not-violent."

When the violent and not-violent women prisoners were compared on all variables, we discovered 12 that significantly discriminated the two groups. These are shown in Table 9. The overall picture that emerges is that the violent inmates were higher on loss of parents at an early age, on medical and neurological problems in their immediate families, on the severity of punishment received within their families, and on easy access to weapons. They also had a tendency to have made more suicide attempts in the past, and to have more menstrual problems (Climent et al., 1974).

We also looked at the relation between violence and homosexuality by comparing self-identified homosexual women with those who were not. We found that the homosexual women were more likely to have engaged in violent crimes (homicide, assault, robbery) and to have had more suicidal thoughts and attempts than the other women. We thus had identified a possible connection between suicidal impulses and violent impulses within the *same* individual (in contrast to the demographic studies that correlate suicide rates vs violence rates in *different* individuals).

The Temporal Lobe Epilepsy Studies

By 1970 enough evidence had accumulated to suggest that neurological dysfunctions could sometimes influence the frequency of violent outbursts in humans (Mark and Ervin, 1970; Monroe, 1970; Roberts and Kiess, 1964). With this belief as the back-

TABLE 9
Variables Significantly Correlated with Violence

Violent Prisoners are Higher On:
1. Mean Number of Neurological Disorders in the Family.
2. Mean Number of Medical Disorders in the Family.
3. Number of Episodic Dyscontrol Symptoms.
4. Self-Reported Homosexuality.
5. Percent Who Suffered Loss* of Mother Before the Age of Ten.
6. Percent Who Reported Severe Punishment From Their Parents.
7. Percent Who Reported Easy Access to Weapons.
8. Percent Who Reported a Suicide Attempt in the Past.
9. Percent Who Reported Menstrual Problems.
Violent Prisoners Are Lower On:
1. Mean Age at Loss* of Father (Approximately 10 vs. 16 Years).
2. Mean Age at Loss* of Mother (Approximately 9 vs. 20 Years).
3. Mean Number of Miscarriages.
4. Number of Symptoms of Neurotic Depression.
5. Percent who Reported Having Had Outpatient Psychiatric Care.

*Loss defined as any permanent separation of child from parent due to death, desertion or separation.

ground, a new investigation was launched by Ervin with the aim of identifying violent individuals in the community and of studying them intensively using medical, neurological and psychometric indices (Plutchik, Climent and Ervin, 1976). The investigation hoped to collect data on a group of self-referred persons who suffered from episodic outbursts of violence and to compare them to other groups. It was hypothesized that the greater the frequency and intensity of violent behaviors shown by a group of individuals, the greater the probability of various other classes of abnormalities, such as medical problems, soft and hard neurological signs, and a history of psychiatric difficulties.

We administered a battery of tests to 11 different groups (a total of 309 individuals) which included self-referred violent persons, male and female prisoners, psychiatric outpatients, college students, neurology patients, and epileptics. Figure 1 shows the mean scores of each of the groups on one of our measures, the FAV, which is a self-report index of violent impulses and behav-

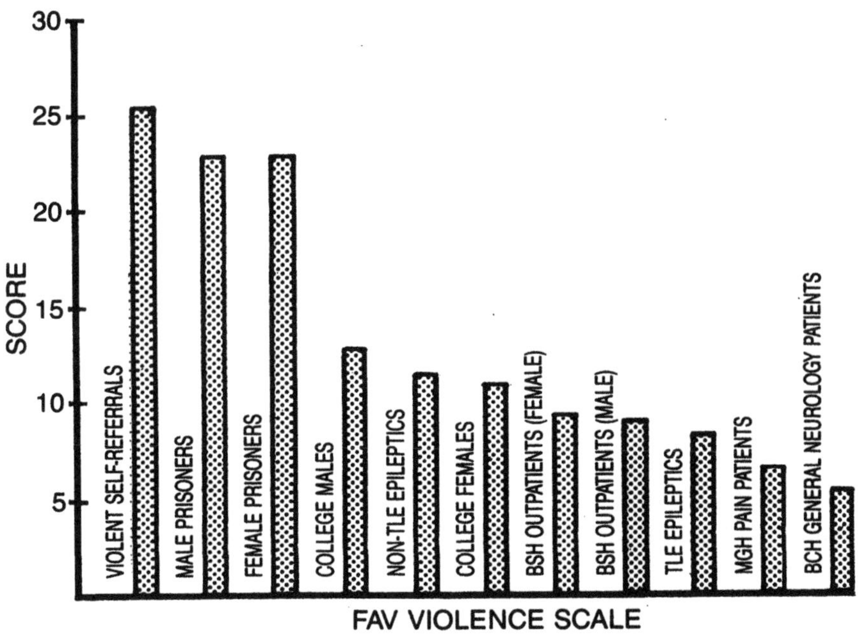

Figure 1. Mean scores obtained by eleven different groups on FAV self-reported violence scores.

iors in which the individual has engaged. The self-referred violent patients scored highest on this scale, thus contributing to the construct validity of the scale. They are significantly higher than all the other groups except the prisoners. The male and female prisoners also score quite high on the FAV Scale. College students fall near the middle of the distribution of groups, and the temporal lobe epileptics fall toward the low end of the scale.

A second analysis of the data was based on the computation of intercorrelation matrixes for all variables. This was done separately for each of seven groups: the male and female prisoners, the male and female college students, the male and female psychiatric outpatients, and the violent self-referred patients. Table 10 presents those variables found to be significantly correlated with FAV violence scores in two or more groups (correlations which are highly significant and are essentially independent replications of a relationship).

TABLE 10
Variables Significantly Correlated with the FAV Violence Scale in Two or More of Seven Groups

Variable	*Number of Groups*	*Mean Correlation*
History of Family Violence	7	.42
Monroe Scale (Epileptiform Dyscontrol States)	7	.61
Total Number of Problems (Health, Job, Social, etc.)	5	.39
Number of Behavior Problems (Truancy, Drugs, etc.)	5	.61
Schizophrenia Scale (Subset of MMPI Items)	4	.50
FAS Sex Drive Scale	3	.50
Number of Emotional Problems	3	.44
EPI Aggression Score	2	.55
EPI Timidity Score	2	-.39
Number of Behavior Problems in Family Members	2	.53
Psychopathic Deviate Scale (Subset of MMPI Items)	2	.75

The results show high correlations between a history of family violence (frequent spankings, fights, and observation of parental quarrels and fights) and the extent of violence in the subjects. This is found in every group. Similarly, scores on signs of episodic discontrol are correlated with scores on the violence scale in all seven groups. Other highly significant correlations with violence are the total number of life problems, signs of schizoid thinking, and intense sex drive.

Another study was carried out at a prison for men. This prison had a psychiatric unit which routinely evaluated prisoners referred by the courts for competency (to stand trial) and for responsibility (for one's acts). This latter judgment, in essence, is an estimate of the "craziness" of the prisoner.

Fifty prisoners completed a battery of tests. We then compared the 37 prisoners who had committed violent crimes such as armed robbery, assault and rape with the 13 prisoners who had committed nonviolent crimes such as burglary or forgery. We found that the violent prisoners had fewer social contacts and had higher scores on drug and alcohol use, and on an index of distrust. We then correlated the FAV self-report measure of violent tendencies with each of the tests of the battery and found 13 significant correlations as shown in Table 11.

The data indicate that people who describe themselves as high on a self-report violence scale have had troubled early school experiences, have seen violence in their own families, have a sociopathic social history (e.g., previous trouble with the law), have signs of poor impulse control, have a high sex drive, have a high tendency toward suicidal actions, have many soft neurological signs and symptoms, have a tendency to lie about themselves, and have engaged in numerous sadistic acts such as setting fires, killing animals, or beating people up. It was also found that prisoners who had a history of hospitalization for a psychiatric problem were more likely to report higher violence scores than those prisoners without such a history.

Discussion and Synthesis

We have described a number of investigations that have dealt with the problem of violence in humans. While not every study had produced identical results, there are enough consistencies to enable some tentative conclusions to be drawn.

TABLE 11
Correlations between the FAV Self-Report Violence Scale and other Variables*

Troubled Early School Experiences	+.74
Monroe Dyscontrol Scale	+.73
Poor Impulse Control Scale	+.67
Sex Drive Scale	+.67
Family Violence Scale	+.62
Suicide Potential Scale	+.61
Neurological Syndrome Checklist	+.52
Lie Scale of the MMPI	+.49
Sadism Scale	+.45
EPI Aggressiveness Scale	+.44
Sociopathic Social History	+.44
EPI Timidity Scale	−.42
EPI Trust Scale	−.41

*Based on 50 prisoners referred for evaluation for competency and for responsibility.

1. The presence of violence as well as its degree is always an inference from various kinds of evidence. We should distinguish between accidents that result in assaults and assaults that are premeditated.
2. On a comparative scale, violent acts are relatively rare events, and are therefore difficult to predict. Any given act of violence requires the simultaneous occurrence of a large variety of background variables plus a triggering stimulus in the environment.
3. By their very nature, violent acts are the vectorial resultant of a variety of forces that are acting simultaneously. The emotion of anger and the impulse to destroy conflict with various control and inhibitory mechanisms that each human being possesses. The violent outcome occurs when the control mechanisms are inadequate to the task.
4. There are six classes of variables that interact to influence the occurrence of a given act of violence. These are:
   1) Past history variables
   2) Family variables
   3) Constitutional and medical variables
   4) Personality variables

5) Environmental variables
6) Chance events

5. Of considerable importance is the fact that there are a number of variables that have been found to be negatively correlated with the occurrence of violence. These are:
   1) A high number of symptoms of depression
   2) A high number of symptoms of anxiety
   3) Previous outpatient psychiatric care
   4) A history of drug addiction (in contrast to alcohol addiction)
   5) High scores on the Timidity and Trust scales of the Emotions Profile Index (Plutchik and Kellerman, 1974)

The implication of these ideas is that there are certain factors that increase the likelihood of violence and others that decrease it. The exact values of these variables at any given moment determine the probability of an act of violence.

PART III: THE INTERACTION OF SUICIDE AND VIOLENCE

We have examined a number of studies that have identified factors related to suicide and other studies that have identified factors related to violence. Some of these factors appear to be identical: for example, early loss of parents, experience of violence in the home, and possibly use of alcohol. There is thus reason to believe that some kind of relation exists between violent and suicidal acts. This part of our presentation will deal with this issue.

Newspapers periodically remind us of the close connection between violence and suicide. Headlines frequently tell us of people who murder and then commit suicide. The Guyana incident with Reverend Jones is one well known example, and a more recent one is the Oklahoma killings in which a postman shot 14 coworkers and then killed himself.

A few reports have looked at the statistics of homicide followed by suicide. The classic study by West (1966) examined data in England and Wales for the period from 1954–1961. He reported that the murder-suicide rate was 33 percent. In contrast, it was 42 percent in Denmark, 22 percent in Australia, 4 percent in Philadelphia, 2 percent in Los Angeles (Allen, 1983), and 1–2 percent in North Carolina (Dalmer and Humphrey, 1980). In the Los Angeles study, it was found that in the majority of the homicide-suicide cases, the reason for the murder seemed to be an unbalanced, quarrelsome love relationship between husband and wife, or lovers. A smaller group consisted of elderly individuals struggling with illness and financial problems. In 50 percent of the incidents, alcohol was found in the blood of victims and offenders alike. In the North Carolina study, the offenders were more similar to suicide-only individuals on demographic characteristics and dissimilar to homicide-only offenders. It was suggested that the killing of a family member is a part of the evolving steps toward suicide.

Other evidence of a connection between violence and suicide comes from the literature on the effects of crowding in prisons (Cox, Paulus and McCain, 1984). A major review indicates that population increases in prisons are associated with increased rates of suicide, disciplinary infractions (violence), psychiatric commitment, and death. Decreases in prison populations are associated with decreases in assaults, suicide attempts, and death rates. The authors of this review suggest that the underlying reasons for these effects of crowding are the increases in uncertainty, goal interference, and cognitive load.

In the past few years a number of empirical studies have shown connections between suicidal impulses and violent impulses. For example, Shafii and his colleagues (1985) performed a psychological autopsy on 20 adolescents who had completed suicide and contrasted their behavior and personality with those of a group of matched-pair controls (friends) (Table 12). They found that the majority of suicides had expressed suicidal thoughts or attempts in the past, had a friend who had attempted suicide, had abusive parents, felt isolated and lonely, and had engaged in antisocial behavior. Antisocial behavior was defined as physical fights, firesetting, shoplifting, selling drugs, or prostitution. The authors conclude that a large number of the suicide victims had also been destructive toward others.

A similar connection was reported by Bach-Y-Rita and Veno (1974). In California, 62 habitually violent inmates sent to a special facility were interviewed. Most had used weapons on other persons and many had assaulted members of their own family. It was found that half of the patients admitted seriously attempting to harm themselves, and 42 percent had mutilated their bodies in such a way as to produce scars. The rate of self-injuries was six times that of a typical prison population. The self-destructive prisoners were more likely to have used a weapon on someone else. More than half of these violent prisoners had observed their parents engaged in physical fights. It was also found that the most self-destructive prisoners were also judged to have an impulsive character disorder.

In a related series of studies, Tardiff and his colleagues examined the records of large numbers of psychiatric outpatients and inpatients. Of 2916 outpatients at two private hospitals, 2–3 percent were physically assaultive toward others a few days before evaluation (Tardiff and Koenigsberg, 1985). In contrast, 10 percent of patients admitted to the inpatient service at the same private hospitals were assaultive (Tardiff, 1984), while 7 percent of chronic state hospital patients were found to be assaultive in the 3 months preceding the survey (Tardiff and Sweillam, 1982).

TABLE 12
Variables that Discriminated between Adolescents who Committed Suicide and Matched-Pair Control Subjects*

Variables
1. Had Expressed Suicidal Ideas, Threats, or Had Made a Previous Attempt.
2. Antisocial Behavior (e.g. Shoplifting, Firesetting, Physical Fights, School Problems, Selling Drugs, Prostitution).
3. Sibling or Friend Had Attempted Suicide.
4. Frequent Use of Non-Prescribed Drugs or Alcohol.
5. Physical or Emotional Abusiveness by Parents.
6. Previous Psychiatric Treatment.
7. Parent or Adult Relative Had Made Suicidal Threats, Attempts or an Actual Suicide.
8. Isolation (e.g. Lack of Close Friends, Loneliness, Extreme Sensitivity).

*Shafii et al., 1985.

When the occurrence of suicidal problems is measured over a long period of time, there is a positive correlation between suicidal behavior and assault. Assaultive patients were more likely to have delusions, hallucinations, inappropriate affect, and feelings of depression than nonassaultive patients. Both male and female assaultive patients were 3–4 times more likely to have attempted suicide than nonassaultive patients.

In an earlier study, Tardiff and Sweillam (1980) examined the association between assaultiveness and suicidality in 9,365 patients admitted to public hospitals in a one-year period (1975). They found that men who were assaultive were twice as likely to have made suicide attempts than were men who were not assaultive. They also found that patients who were both assaultive and suicidal were most likely to have abused drugs. In a separate study of suicidal inpatients, they found that 14 percent of male inpatients and 7 percent of female patients were assaultive at the time of or just prior to admission. For both sexes, assaultive suicidal patients were more likely to have delusions, hallucinations, agitation and feelings of suspicion than the nonassaultive suicidal patients.

In a similar study in a rural English community (Barraclough et al., 1974), a group of 100 suicides who had previously been seen by a psychiatrist were compared to 100 matched control patients. About 18 percent of the suicides had shown evidence of violent behaviors (in nurses and social workers notes) while only 6 percent of the controls had shown violent behavior.

In a related study, Skodal and Karasu (1978) found that 17 percent of patients appearing at a psychiatric emergency room were considered to be violent and that another 17 percent were judged to be suicidal. About 30 percent of the violent patients were also suicidal. Of the 62 patients in the violent sample, 65 percent were believed to have a major disturbance in perception, cognition, and reality testing resulting from psychosis, organicity, or intoxicants.

Following this same train of thought, Weissman, Fox and Klerman (1973) compared 29 depressed (but not suicidal) women with 29 matched suicide attempters. There were no differences between the two groups in degree of depression, but the suicide attempters were more hostile during the psychiatric interview, had used drugs more often, had more criminal convictions, and had more arguments with family and friends as a general lifestyle.

Five other studies have also reported a connection between suicidal behavior and violent behavior. Inamdar, Lewis and their colleagues (1982) examined the records of 51 hospitalized, psychotic adolescents. Of these patients, two-thirds had been violent, almost half had been suicidal, and 28 percent had been both violent *and* suicidal. These general findings were more pronounced in boys than in girls. These authors conclude that violent behavior in adolescents is used to diagnosis the patients as sociopaths or conduct disorders and to dismiss suicidal behaviors as conscious manipulations. In contrast, they believe that these behaviors reflect the possibility of psychotic processes and real risks.

A similar connection between violence and suicidality was reported by Alessi et al. (1984). They used a structured interview (SADS) with 71 juvenile delinquents who had been arrested for violent felonies and assaultive behavior in the program. They found that six out of 10 delinquents had made suicide attempts in the past. They also found no difference in the distribution of suicide attempts for those with major affective disorders, thought disorders or other psychiatric disorders.

The studies that have been described are consistent in showing a strong connection between suicidality and aggressiveness.

In addition several careful medical evaluations of violent individuals have revealed a surprisingly high level of neurological and EEG abnormalities, soft neurological signs, head injuries in children, and occasional blackouts (Elliot, 1987; Mark and Ervin, 1970; Merikangas, 1981). Violent individuals have also been found in many cases to have ingested various chemicals. Both alcohol and amphetamines have been reported to induce violent behaviors and the two in combination are even more potent (Mello and Mendelsohn, 1972). In the early part of this century "epidemics of insanity" were reported among rubber and rayon workers accidentally poisoned by carbon disulfide. These workers showed symptoms of depression, extreme irritability, uncontrolled anger and acute mania, and there were many cases of attempted suicide as well as homicide. These points are made to simply suggest that there may be biological aspects to the presence of severe and chronic violent behaviors.

A Theoretical Model of Suicidality and Violence

We have reviewed a large number of empirical findings about the nature of suicide and violence and have seen that there is unequivocal evidence of a relation between them. The relation is not a simple one. The old psychoanalytic idea that suicide is violence turned inward has some validity but it does not help us understand why some violent people are suicidal and why others are not. In order to answer such questions, we need to identify the variables that influence both violence and suicide risk in individuals. And we need to examine these questions from the broadest perspective we can find.

The conception that we have found most helpful is a broad ethological-evolutionary one that looks for general principles and common elements across species. One such general principle is the universality of aggression (which refers to complex patterns of behavior connected with fight and defense in all species). The ethologists have pointed out that aggressive behavior serves to increase the probability of access to resources, helps deal with conflicts among individuals, and increases the chances of successful courtship and mating. The overall function of aggression is that it increases the chance of individual survival as well as inclusive fitness, i.e., the likelihood of gene representation in future generations.

In addition, neurophysiological research over many decades has established the existence of brain structures that organize patterns of aggressive behavior (e.g. lateral hypothalamus, ventral tegmental areas, midbrain central gray area, and the central and anterior portions of the septum). Recent research has also shown that various neurotransmitter systems are involved in the expression of aggression. For example, animals fed a tryptophan-free diet became increasingly aggressive, implying that low serotonin levels are associated with a risk of violent behavior (Gibbons, Barr et al., 1979).

Finally, the recent literature on behavioral genetics has revealed that many, if not most, emotional characteristics are heritable. Aggressivity has been shown to be heritable in mice and dogs

(Fuller, 1986), and human studies of personality and temperament have also indicated significant genetic components in assertiveness, extraversion and dominance (Loehlin, Horn and Willerman, 1981; Loehlin and Nichols, 1976; Wimer and Wimer, 1985).

A recent review of the literature on predation within species (i.e. cannibalism) has demonstrated that the killing and eating of an individual of one's own species is very widespread. It has been observed in about 1300 species, including humans (Polis, 1981). It appears to have a strong genetic component, although its frequency can be affected by the availability of food supplies. In some species, cannibalism has a major influence on population size. It has been observed in at least 14 species of carnivorous mammals: lion, tiger, leopard, cougar, lynx, spotted hyena, golden jackel, wolf, cayote, dingo, red fox, artic fox, brown bear, and grasshopper mice. In most such cases, adults preyed on immature animals and cubs. Cannibalism has also been reported in 60 human cultures (Schankman, 1969).

This brief overview suggests that aggressive behavior has fundamental importance for survival and for regulation of populations in humans and lower animals. The evidence clearly indicates that there are neurological structures and biochemical processes that are intimately connected with aggressive behavior, and that there are genetic contributions to the individual differences seen in aggressive traits.

Ethological research has further indicated what classes of events tend to trigger aggressive impulses. Generally speaking, threats, challenges, changes in hierarchical status, and various losses tend to increase aggressive impulses (Blanchard and Blanchard, 1984). However, we need to distinguish between aggressive impulses and aggressive behavior (or violence). Whether or not the aggressive impulse is expressed in the form of overt action, i.e., violent behavior, depends on the presence of a large number of forces, some of which act as amplifiers of the aggressive impulse and some act to attenuate the impulse. Examples of amplifiers are: extensive school problems in the history of the individual, a history of assaultive acts, pervasive feelings of distrust, easy access to weapons, and a tolerant attitude toward the expression of violence. Examples of attenuators are: a timid personality style, close family ties, and appeasement from others. These variables interact in complex ways and determine the probability that the aggressive impulse will be expressed in overt violent behavior. We call these factors Stage I countervailing forces.

Overt action, however, requires a goal object toward which it is directed. The model assumes that a separate set of variables determines whether the goal of aggressive actions will be other people or oneself. A major study we carried out recently provides some insight into the variables that determine the goal object.

In this study we interviewed 100 psychiatric inpatients and obtained data on 30 variables for each patient. The major scales used are listed in Table 13. We considered these variables possible predictor variables that would be used to predict two outcome measures: a self-report measure of suicide risk and a self-report measure of violence risk. These measures had been

TABLE 13
Major Scales Used in the Study of Suicide and Violence Risk*

Depression
Hopelessness
Marital Problems
Impulsivity
Dyscontrol
Physical Symptoms
Attitudes Toward Suicide
MMPI Scales
Life Problems Checklist
Violence Risk
Suicide Risk
Recent Psychiatric Symptoms
Family Violence
Social Network
Menstrual Problems
Early School Problems
Coping Styles

*Plutchik, van Praag, and Conte (1985).

independently determined to be related to a history of suicide attempts or to a history of acting-out behavior.

The results of this study revealed that certain variables correlate with suicide risk but not violence, and that other variables correlate with violence risk but not suicide. The correlates of suicide risk alone are: depression, a large number of life problems (including work, medical and family problems), feelings of hopelessness, and recent psychiatric symptoms. In contrast, the correlates of violence risk alone are: impulsivity, problems with the law, menstrual problems in women, and recent life stresses. These two sets of variables that determine the goal of the aggressive impulse, we refer to as Stage II countervailing forces. The presence and interaction of these various countervailing forces determine both the strength of aggressive behavior and the goal of the aggressive behavior. The complete model is shown in Figure 2.

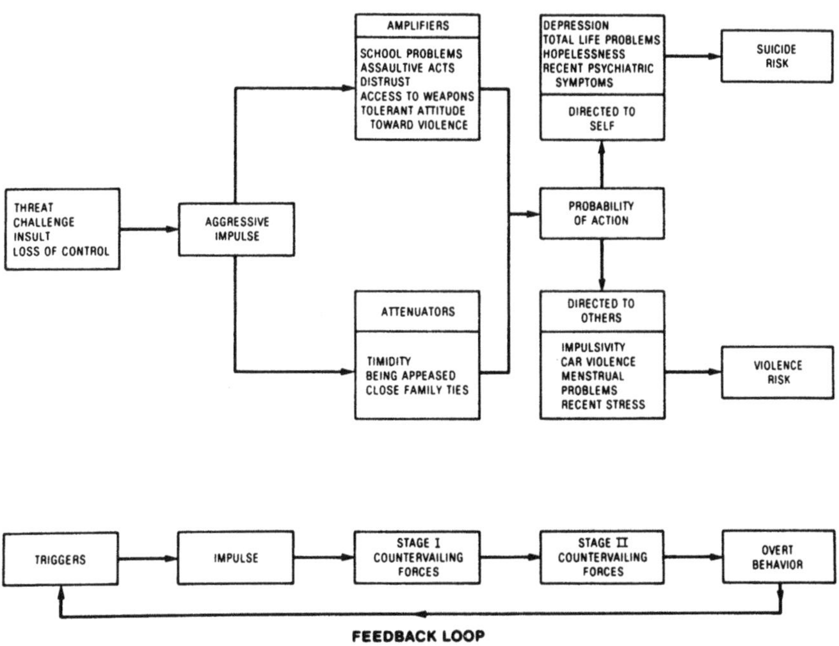

Figure 2. Two-stage model of suicide and violence.

We believe this model is useful in several ways. First, it sensitizes clinicians about the key variables to consider when evaluating a patient for risk of suicide or violence. In current research we have already found the scores on the various tests we use to be quite helpful to clinicians who are faced with the difficult task of evaluating a particular patient's risk of suicide or violence. Second, the model identifies the special variables that relate to suicide risk in contrast to the special variables that relate to violence risk. And third, it directs our attention to the search for additional variables that may act to attenuate or inhibit violent or suicidal impulses in accord with the idea of countervailing (or counterbalancing) variables. And last but not least, it places the study of human suicide and violence into a broad evolutionary framework so that it can be seen as an aspect of several interrelated sciences.

REFERENCES

Alessi, N. E., McManus, M., Brickman, A., & Grapentine, L. (1984). Suicide behavior among serious juvenile offenders. *American Journal of Psychiatry, 141,* 286–287.

Allen, N. H. (1983). Homicide followed by suicide: Los Angeles, 1970–1979. *Suicide and Life Threatening Behavior, 13,* 155–165.

Bach-Y-Rita, G., & Veno, A. (1974). Habitual violence: A profile of 82 men. *American Journal of Psychiatry, 131,* 1015–1017.

Barraclough, B. M., Bunch, J., Nelson, B., & Sainsbury, P. (1974). A hundred cases of suicide: Clinical aspects. *British Journal of Psychiatry, 125,* 355–372.

Blanchard, D. C., & Blanchard, R. J. (1984). Affect and aggression: An animal model applied to human behavior. In R. J. Blanchard & D. C. Blanchard (Eds.), *Advances in the Study of Aggression,* Vol. I. New York: Academic Press.

Buglass, D., & McCulloch, J. W. (1970). Further suicidal behavior: The development and validation of predictive scales. *British Journal of Psychiatry, 116,* 483–491.

Burk, F., Kurz, A., & Moller, H. J. (1985). Suicide risk scales: Do they help to predict suicidal behavior? *European Archives of Psychiatry and Neurological Sciences, 235,* 153–157.

Climent, C. E., Raynes, A. Rollins, A., & Plutchik, R. (1974). Epidemiological studies of female prisoners II. Biological, psychological and social correlates of drug addiction. *International Journal of the Addictions, 9,* 345–350.

Climent, C. E., Rollins, A., Ervin, F. R., & Plutchik, R. (1973). Epidemiological studies of women prisoners, I: Medical and psychiatric variables related to violent behavior. *American Journal of Psychiatry, 130,* 985–990.

Cox, V. C., Paulus, & McCain, G. (1984). Prison crowding research: The relevance for prison housing standards and a general approach regarding crowding phenomena. *American Psychologist, 39,* 1148–1160.

Dalmer, S., & Humphrey, J. A. (1980). Offender-victim relationships in criminal homicide followed by offenders suicide, North Carolina 1972–1977. *Suicide and Life-Threatening Behavior, 10,* 106–118.

Elliot, F., (1987). Neuroanatomy and neurology of aggression. *Psychiatric Annals, 17,* 385–388.

Fuller, J. L. (1986). Genetics and emotions. In R. Plutchik & H. Kellerman (Eds.), *The Biological Foundations of Emotions.* New York: Academic Press.

Gibbons, J. L., Barr, G. A., Bridger, W. H., & Leibowitz, S. F. (1979). Manipulation of dietary tryptophan: Effects on mouse killing and brain serotonin in the rat. *Brain Research, 169,* 139–153.

Harkavy-Friedman, J. M., Asnis, G. M., & DiFiore, J. (1987). The prevalence of specific suicidal behaviors in a high school sample. *American Journal of Psychiatry, 144,* 1203–1206.

Hawton, K., Cole, D., O'Grady, J., & Osborn, M. (1982). Motivational aspects of deliberate self-poisoning in adolescents. *British Journal of Psychiatry, 141,* 286–291.

Hendin, M. H. (1986). Suicide: A review of new directions in research. *Hospital & Community Psychiatry, 37,* 148–154.

Inamdar, S. C., Lewis, D. O., Siomopoulous, G., Shanok, S. S., & Lamela, M. (1982). Violent and suicidal behavior in psychotic adolescents. *American Journal of Psychiatry, 139,* 932–935.

Lester, D., Beck, A. T., & Mitchell, B. (1979). Extrapolation from attempted suicides to completed suicides: A test. *Journal of Abnormal Psychology, 88,* 78–80.

Loehlin, J. C., Horn, J. M., & Willerman, L. (1981). Personality resemblance in adoptive families. *Behavior Genetics, 11,* 309–330.

Loehlin, J. C., & Nichols, B. C. (1976). *Heredity, Environment and Personality: A Study of 850 Twins.* Austin: University of Austin Press.

Mark, V. H., & Ervin, F. R. (1970). *Violence and the Brain*. New York: Harper & Row.

Mello, N. K., & Mendelsohn, J. (1972). Drinking patterns during work contingent and non-contingent alcohol acquisition. *Psychosomatic Medicine, 34,* 139–164.

Merikangas, J. R., (1981). The neurology of violence. In J. R. Merikangas (Ed.), *Brain-Behavior Relationships*. Lexington, Mass.: Lexington Books.

Monroe, R. R. (1970). *Episodic Behavioral Disorders*. Cambridge, Mass.: Harvard University Press.

Motto, J. A., Heilbron, D. C., & Juster, R. P. (1985). Development of a clinical instrument to estimate suicide risk. *American Journal of Psychiatry, 142,* 1061–1064.

Pallis, D. J., Barraclough, D. M., Levey, A. B., Jenkins, J. S., & Sainsbury, P., (1982). Estimating suicide risk among attempted suicides: I. The development of new clinical scales. *British Journal of Psychiatry, 141,* 37–44.

Platman, S. R., Plutchik, R., & Weinstein, B. (1971). Psychiatric, physiological, behavioral and self-report measures in relation to a suicide attempt. *Journal of Psychiatric Research, 8,* 127–137.

Plutchik, R., Climent, C., & Ervin, F. (1976). Research strategies for the study of human violence. In W. L. Smith & A. Kling (Eds.), *Issues in Brain/Behavior Control*. New York: Spectrum.

Plutchik, R., & Kellerman, H. (1974). *Manual of the Emotions Profile Index*. Los Angeles, California: Western Psychological Services.

Pokorny, A. D. (1983). Prediction of suicide in psychiatric patients. *Archives of General Psychiatry, 40,* 249–257.

Polis, G. A. (1981). The evolution and dynamics of intraspecific predation. *The Review of Ecology and Systematics, 12,* 225–252.

Rich, C. L., Young, D., & Fowler, R. C. (1986). San Diego suicide study: I. Young vs. old subjects. *Archives of General Psychiatry, 43,* 577–582.

Roberts, W. W., & Kiess, H. O. (1964). Motivational properties of hypothalamic aggression in cats. *Journal of Comparative* and *Physiological Psychology, 58,* 187–193.

Schankman, P. (1969). Le roti et le bouilli: Levi-Strauss' theory of canabalism. *American Anthropologist, 71,* 54–69.

Shafii, M., Carrigan, S., Whillinghil, L., & Derrick, A. (1985). Psychological autopsy of completed suicide in children and adolescents. *American Journal of Psychiatry, 142,* 1061–1064.

Skodal, A. E., & Karasu, T. B. (1978). Emergency psychiatry and the assaultive patient. *American Journal of Psychiatry, 135,* 202–205.

Sletten, I. W., Evenson, R. C., & Brown, M. L., (1973). Some results from an automated statewide comparison among attempted, committed, and non-suicidal patients. *Life-Threatening Behavior, 3,* 191, 197.

Tardiff, K. (1984). Characteristics of assaultive patients in private hospitals. *American Journal of Psychiatry, 141,* 1231–1234.

Tardiff, K., & Koenigsberg, H. W. (1985). Assaultive behavior among psychiatric outpatients. *American Journal of Psychiatry, 142,* 960–963.

Tardiff, K., & Sweillam, A. (1980). Assault, suicide and mental illness. *Archives of General Psychiatry, 37,* 164–169.

Tardiff, K., & Sweillam, A. (1982). Assaultive behavior among chronic inpatients. *American Journal of Psychiatry, 159,* 212–215.

van Praag, H. M., & Plutchik, R. (1986). An empirical study on the "cathartic effect" of attempted suicide. *Psychiatry Research, 16,* 123–130.

Weissman, M., Fox, K., & Klerman, G. (1973). Hostility and depression associated with suicide attempts. *American Journal of Psychiatry, 130,* 450–455.

West, D. J. (1966). *Murder Followed by Suicide.* London: Heinemann.

Wimer, R. E., & Wimer, C. C. (1985). Animal behavior genetics: A search for the biological foundation of behavior. *Annual Review of Psychology, 36,* 171–218.

4

Aggression: Integrating Ethology and the Social Sciences

ROBERT A. HINDE

The understanding of aggressive behavior demands an eclectic approach. This chapter presents an overview that goes some way towards indicating how biological/ethological data can be integrated, or I would prefer to say *must* be integrated, with those of the social scientist. This integration is sought through an emphasis on the necessity for the scientist and/or clinician to cross and recross between different levels of social complexity.

To understand the behavior of an individual it is necessary to come to terms with the causal interrelations between successive levels of physiological complexity: subcellular, cellular, organ, system, and individual levels. Beyond that, to understand social behavior it is necessary to come to terms with successive levels of social complexity: short-term interactions, dyadic and more complex relationships involving sequences of interactions each affected by the preceding ones, and social groups involving networks of relationships. Each of these levels has properties that are not relevant to lower ones; for instance, the relationships within a group may be arranged centrifocally, hierarchically, linearly, etc.—properties not relevant to the individual relationships.

Furthermore, each of these levels affects and is affected by those on either side (Figure 1). For instance, the course of an interaction is affected by characteristics of the participating individuals and by the nature of the relationship in which it is embedded, but the characteristics individuals display are affected by

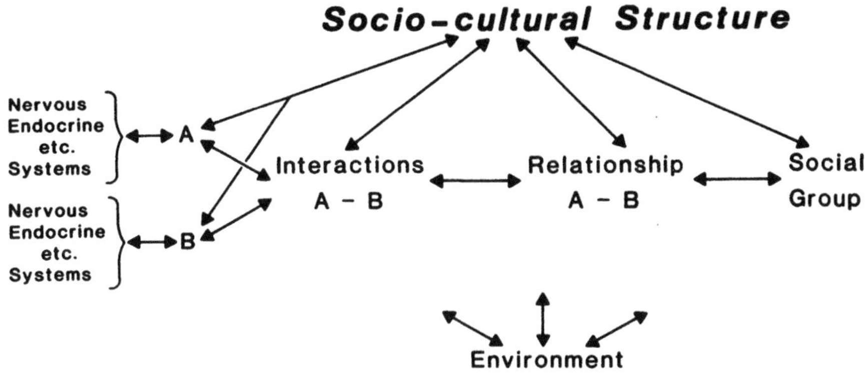

Figure 1. Dialectical relations between successive levels of social complexity.

the interaction in which they are involved, and in the longer term the characteristics that they can display are affected by the interactions and relationships that they have experienced in the past. Again the nature of a relationship depends on the nature of its constituent interactions and on the group in which it is embedded, while the nature of that group depends on that of its constituent relationships. In addition, each of these levels affects, and is affected by, the values, norms and beliefs of the society in which they are set, and by the institutions with their constituent roles in that society. These are referred to here as the sociocultural structure of that society (Hinde, 1987).

To exemplify this, consider the genesis of snake phobias. Children who have never previously seen a snake start to show fear of snakes in their early years (Prechtl, 1950). The extent of their fear depends in part on the response of their caregiver. The social referencing involved in such situations has been studied in some detail (e.g., Emde, 1984), and can be seen as an aspect of attachment (Bretherton, 1985); it is known also in monkeys (Seyfarth & Cheney, 1986). Thus, both initial predispositions and learning play a part in the development of a fear of snakes (Delprato, 1980). Some children subsequently develop snake phobias (Marks, 1987). Now snakes have played a very important part in the mythology of many cultures—a part beautifully illustrated in von Cranach the Elder's *Adam and Eve* or the startling Rubens

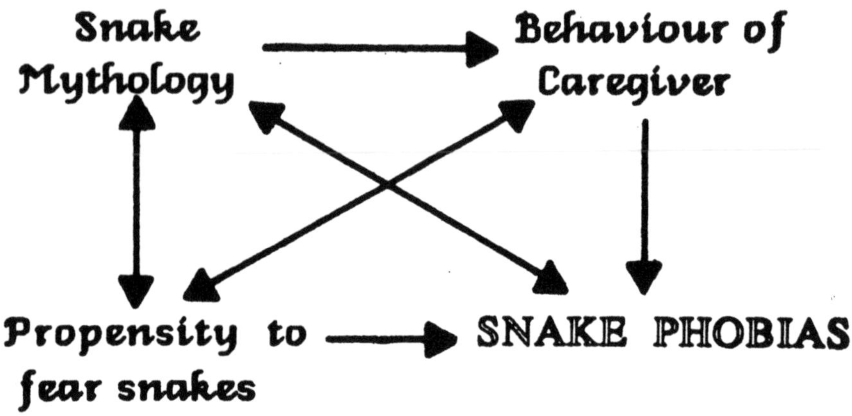

Figure 2. The genesis of snake phobias—crossing the levels of social complexity.

paintings of the lost souls being cast down into hell with snakes gnawing at their genitals. Thus, the suggestion here is that the genesis of snake phobias depends in part on the mythology, the mythology depends in part on the human predisposition to fear snakes, and the two are related through personal relationships with the caregiver and others (Figure 2). Full understanding requires us to come to terms with the dialectical relations between successive levels of social complexity.

We may turn now to the more specific issue of aggressive behavior. Aggressive behavior is defined here as behavior directed towards causing harm to others. Although the two are often associated, aggressiveness is to be distinguished from assertiveness, which need involve no tendency to cause harm. Unfortunately phrases used in common speech, such as "the aggressive salesman," often neglect this distinction.

Behavior directed towards causing harm to others often involves risk of injury to the aggressor. For that reason, aggressive behavior is often associated with elements of fear, withdrawal or submission. The complex of aggressive behavior, threat, fleeing and submission is often referred to as "agonistic behavior" by ethologists (Scott and Fredericson, 1951).

There have been three views about the nature of threat. Darwin (1872) regarded it as an "expression of the emotions." Ethologists, fascinated by the complexity of the threat behavior shown by many species, pointed out that much of that complexity could be understood on the view that threat behavior depends on conflicting behavioral tendencies—to attack, to flee, and to pursue the activity interrupted by the rival. The evidence for this view came from a number of sources (Tinbergen, 1948, 1959; Hinde, 1970), the following being amongst the most important:

(a) The situation in which the threatening behavior occurs. For instance a territorial bird attacks intruders on its own territory, flees from rivals if on a neighboring territory, and threatens only on the boundaries, where tendencies to attack and to flee are in balance.

(b) Behavior accompanying the threat. Thus a threatening individual may edge towards or away from the rival or adopt a compromise by circling around him/her.

(c) The nature of the threat posture. These often contain elements of attack or flight, though such elements have often been "ritualized" to increase the signal value of the threat.

(d) The behavior that precedes or follows the threat. Thus threat postures are often followed by an attack on or escape from the rival.

More recently, ethologists have argued that threat behavior can also be seen as a process of negotiation, signaling not just the emotional state of the threatening individual but a message of the type, "If you approach, I may attack" (Hinde, 1985). The data, in fact, show that whether or not a threat posture is followed by attack depends in part on the behavior of the threatened individual (Bossema and Burgler, 1980).

Ambivalence in the threat posture of birds may seem far removed from the problems of human aggression, but it raises two issues important in the present context. First, the three approaches to the study of threat behavior outlined above involve a progression from a purely affective or emotion model to one more in terms of cognitive processes. Whilst physiological studies of aggressive behavior tend to lay emphasis on subcorticalprocesses, it is essential to remember that, in much human aggression, cognitive processes are crucial.

Second, the emphasis on ambivalence facilitates understanding of the heterogeneity of aggressive behavior. Whilst this heterogeneity is widely recognized, some investigators still seek for unitary explanations of human aggression, and there is no general agreement as to how aggressive behavior should be categorized. For example, Tinklenberg and Ochberg (1981), discussing the bases of violence in adolescents, distinguished between Instrumental (the planned use of aggression to achieve a particular end), Emotional (performed in anger or fear), Felonious (occurring in the course of another crime), Bizarre (psychopathic), and Dyssocial (having the approval of the reference group) violence and aggression. Ervin (this volume) has distinguished between different types of aggressive behavior according to their social acceptability—a continuum which incidentally runs from cases in which cognitive factors play at most a primarily inhibitory role, as in the aggressive behavior associated with rabies, to those in which the aggression is primarily cognitive in origin, as in the aggression shown by police and soldiers in the course of their duty. Even the aggressive behavior of preschool children is heterogeneous. It has been divided into Instrumental or Specific Aggression, concerned with possession of an object or access to space; Hostile or Teasing Aggression, without any such apparent objective; Games Aggression, escalating out of rough-and-tumble play; and Defensive Aggression, given in response to an attack (e.g., Feshbach, 1970; Manning, Heron and Marshall, 1978).

The ethological view that aggressive behavior may involve more than one type of motivation helps to bring order to some of this diversity. For instance specific aggression can be seen as involving both aggressiveness and specific acquisitiveness (the motivation to acquire the object in question), whilst in other cases aggressiveness and assertiveness (motivation to enhance one's status) may be involved. If one makes the gross simplifying assumption that only these three motivations are involved, the situation might be approximated by the diagram in Figure 3, with aggression occurring when the three motivations were represented by a point above the striped surface.

Recognition of the diversity and motivational heterogeneity of aggressive behavior is important for studies of its physiological bases. As Olivier et al. (this volume) have shown, demonstration of the specificity of pharmacological agents for aggressive

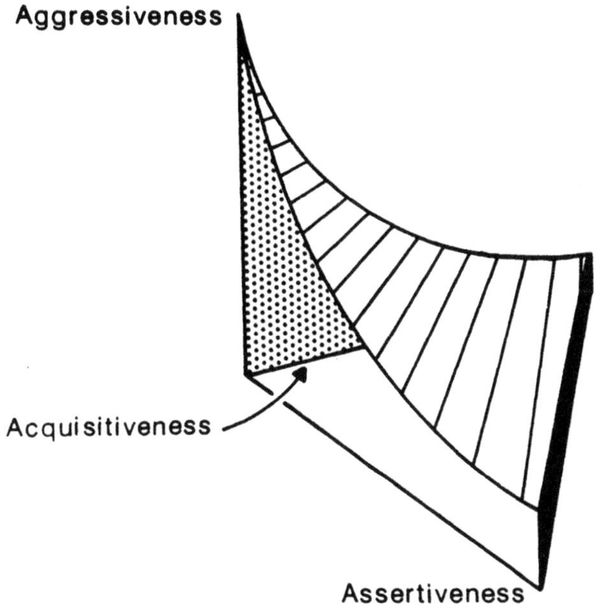

Figure 3. Diagrammatic representation of the occurrence of aggression based on aggressiveness, acquisitiveness and assertiveness. Aggression will occur above the striped area.

behavior requires both that they be shown not to affect other types of behavior and that they affect aggression in diverse contexts.

The issue of motivational complexity raises also the issue of cross-situational consistency, for an individual's motivational (and emotional) state varies with the situation. When the focus is on pathological aggression, it is necessary to categorize individuals according to their propensity for aggression in general, though in practice the nature of the situations most likely to precipitate aggressive behavior may be a matter of considerable concern. In our own studies of preschool age children at home and in school, situational factors appeared to be crucial: rank order correlations between aggression (and other types of behavior) at home and at school were low and mostly nonsignificant. This of course is entirely compatible with a relationships approach (Figure 1), which emphasizes that the social situation as well as individual characteristics determines the behavior shown. Whether the behavior of four-year-olds is more labile across situations than that of adults is at present an open issue.

Although there were few significant correlations between the behavior of these four-year-olds at home and at school, there were meaningful relations between the two. For instance, children who spent much time in joint activities with their mothers and had frequent positive interactions with them at home tended to have infrequent interactions with peers in school, but these interactions were of a generally positive nature. Maternal warmth coupled with moderate control at home was associated with least aggression in school (Baumrind, 1971; Hinde and Tamplin, 1983). These findings can be partially understood in terms of combinations of child characteristics. Children high on the temperamental characteristics Active and Moody tended to have few positive interactions with their mothers at home, but Moody children tended to interact frequently with peers in school, and Active children tended to have a high proportion of interactions involving hostility. It is a reasonable supposition that the lack of positive interactions at home was a consequence of a tensionful mother-child relationship induced in part by the child's characteristics, and that those characteristics were expressed in a different way in school (Hinde, 1985).

One issue, somewhat mundane but of considerable importance for understanding the cross-situational consistency/inconsistency of aggressive behavior, concerns the misleading nature of correlation coefficients in this context. When the home correlates of aggressive behavior were investigated by different statistical techniques (linear correlation, multiple regression, continuous discriminant analysis, and categorical discriminant analysis), these techniques (each often referred to as providing the "truth") laid emphasis on different home variables. This was partly due to the fact that aggression in school was related to a variety of different indicators of tension at home (e.g., disobedience or disconfirmation of the mother), and in part to the fact that the mothers of the few most aggressive and of the least aggressive children tended to be permissive, whilst those of the moderately aggressive children were controlling (Hinde and Dennis, 1986).

One issue crucial for understanding the aggressive behavior of preschool children, and its cross-situational consistency/inconsistency, concerns the value systems of the child's interactants at home and school. This first came to our attention in the context of shyness. Although boys and girls did not differ on shyness as assessed from a temperamental characteristics interview of the mother (Garside et al., 1975), shy girls tended to have better relationships with their mothers and other family members than non-shy girls, whilst shy boys tended to have worse relationships than non-shy boys. Comparable findings have been obtained by Radke-Yarrow (1988). A variety of lines of evidence indicate that the difference stems from the parental value systems—parents like little girls to be shy, but do not like little boys to be shy.

The differences carry over into preschool behavior. Again, girls and boys did not differ in Assertiveness as assessed from the maternal interview, but this characteristic had very different correlates in preschool. Assertive girls tended to have more tensionful relationships with teachers than nonassertive girls, whilst assertive boys tended not to interact with the teachers but to control their peers. Such examples indicate the importance of parental value systems in the personality development of young children.

The sociocultural structure is even more important in the most dramatic form of aggression of which man is capable—modern international war. Whilst the aggressive behavior of preschool children can be understood reasonably well in terms of propensities such as aggressiveness, acquisitiveness and assertiveness, modern war is an institution, with a wide variety of constituent roles—generals, soldiers, politicians, scientists, munition workers, nurses, and so on. Just as the role of husband or wife within the institution of marriage each has its own inherent rights and duties, and these rights and duties are major determinants of their behavior, so also are the various roles in the institution of war crucial determinants of the behavior of their incumbents (Figure 4). The behavior of the soldier in battle in-

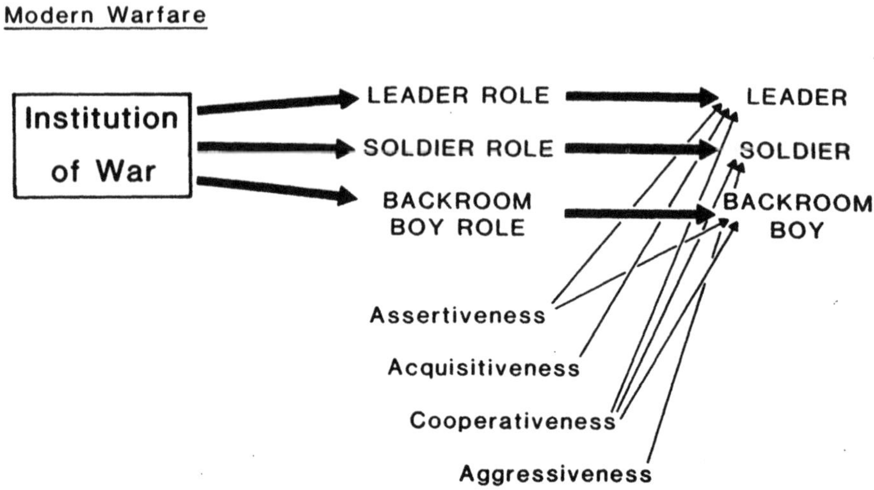

Figure 4. The institution of war and its constituent roles.

volves aggressiveness only to a very limited extent and in special situations. Propensities to obey, to cooperate with friends, and perhaps assertiveness, may play a role. But the major determinants of his behavior are beliefs concerned with the duties inherent in his role. Here cognitive factors play a crucial part in aggressive behavior.

To understand the bases of modern war, then, we must try to understand the genesis of the institution of war (Figure 5). The sources of the institution of war are to be sought in historical, religious and economic factors that it is beyond my competence to discuss. However it is important to remember that the maintenance of the institution of war and, indeed, the operation of those historical, religious and economic factors, are made possible because humans are what they are. And what humans are depends on a complex interplay between social and biological factors. For instance, the maintenance of the institution of war depends in large measure on propaganda, and the propaganda uses aggressive images and plays on aggressive motivation. In war we are exhorted to "Defend little Belgium from the aggressor" or to "Fight on the beaches" to defend our homeland. Again, the propaganda creates an image of the enemy as subhuman, evil and dangerous (Wahlström, 1987). This again involves

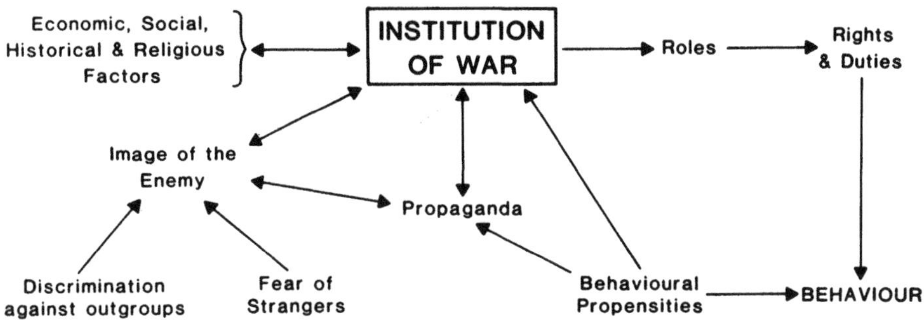

Figure 5. The institution of war.

a play on basic human propensities—the fear of strangers which first appears at about nine months but remains with us in some degree throughout our lives, and the tendencies to differentiate our own group from outgroups and to see transition between ingroup and outgroup as more difficult than is actually the case (Tajfel, 1978). Even in peacetime, politicians and the media play on these propensities. An important step towards undermining the institution of war involves increasing public awareness of human susceptibilities in this direction.

This essay attempts to point the way towards an integration of the approaches of the biologist and the social scientist in the study of aggression. The term biology, so often interpreted in American science to mean only physiology, embraces also the theory of evolution. Can the theory of evolution help us to understand human aggression? This issue can be discussed only briefly here, but an answer is implicit in much of what has been said. On the one hand, man is endowed with the potential for aggressive behavior, and it is reasonable to suppose that aggressive propensities have been shaped by natural selection. This does not mean that humans are inevitably aggressive, for natural selection operates to produce propensities which can lead to action as appropriate, and has given us the ability to cooperate as well as to compete and to behave aggressively. Whilst there can be no proof of the role of natural selection in shaping the details of human aggression, an evolutionary approach does help to integrate what otherwise appear as isolated facts. For instance our greater propensity to behave aggressively towards strangers than towards known individuals, and toward non-kin as opposed to kin, might well have been adaptive in our environment of evolutionary adaptedness.

An evolutionary perspective is even suggestive over questions concerning the ontogeny of aggression. Why should it be that having parents who are cold and harshly controlling in childhood should predispose individuals to aggression and to behavior problems in adolescence? Is it because natural selection has operated so that individuals adopt a developmental trajectory that will fit them for (biological) success in the environment they will encounter in adulthood, and the best predictor of that environment is the childhood one? Are children brought up in loving, authoritative families less likely to be aggressive because cooperation is likely to be a better subsequent strategy? Such an approach would also suggest that natural selection would have produced some flexibility consequent upon post-infancy pre-adulthood experience, a suggestion compatible with the data. Whilst the role of natural selection here can be no more than a matter of speculation, critically applied it can integrate a surprising wealth of facts about human behavior and human relationships (Hinde, 1987).

On the other hand, this approach must not be taken too far. The values, beliefs and institutions of the sociocultural structure are, as we have seen in the case of the institution of war, the product of diverse human propensities that, in interaction with each other within and between individuals, produce historical, religious and economic forces only distantly related to the basic human propensities which were structured by natural selection in our environment of evolutionary adaptedness. Much behavior determined by the current values of western society cannot be seen as a direct product of natural selection. Indeed, the circumstances in which adherence to the cultural dictum, "Dulce et decorum est, pro patria mori," is conducive to the actors' reproductive success must be very rare.

The goal of the scientist must be to produce simplifying generalizations. However that must not lead him to yield to the temptation of neglecting the complexity of the phenomena he studies. Nowhere is this more true than in the study of aggression. Physiological analysis may tell us all we need to know about some cases of pathological aggressiveness. Social forces may be crucial in determining much of the aggression in our society. But full understanding requires us to come to terms with how those social forces shape our behavioral propensities and how our physiological and more broadly biological nature shapes those social forces. We must cross and recross between the levels of social complexity and understand the dialectical relations between them (Groebel & Hinde, 1988).

REFERENCES

Baumrind, D. (1967). Child care practices anteceding three patterns of preschool behaviour. *Genetic Psychology Monographs, 75,* 43–88.

Baumrind, D. (1971). Current patterns of parental authority. *Devel. Psychol. Mono., 4,* (1, Pt. 2).

Bossema, I., & Burgler, R. R. (1980). Communication during monocular and binocular looking in European jays. *Behaviour, 74,* 274–83.

Bretherton, I. (1985). Attachment theory: Retrospect and prospect. In I. Bretherton & E. Waters (Eds.), *Growing Points of Attachment Theory and Research.* Monographs of the Society for Research in Child Development, Vol. 50. Nos. 1–2, 3–38.

Darwin, C. (1872). *The Expression of the Emotions in Man and Animals.* John Murray: London.

Delprato, D. (1980). Hereditary determinants of fears and phobias, a critical review. *Behaviour Therapy, 11,* 79–103.

Emde, R. (1984). The affective self. In J. D. Call, E. Galenson, & R. L. Tyson (Eds.), *Frontiers of Infant Psychiatry.* New York: Basic Books.

Feshbach, S. (1970). Aggression. In P. H. Mussen (Ed.), *Carmichael's Manual of Child Psychology, II,* New York: Wiley.

Garside, R. F., Birch, H., & Scott, DMcI. et al., (1975). Dimensions of temperament in infant school children. *J. Child Psychol. Psychiatry Allied Discip., 16,* 219–231.

Groebel, J., & Hinde, R. A. (Eds.) (1988). *Aggression and War: Their Biological and Social Bases.* Cambridge: Cambridge University Press.

Hinde, R. A. (1970). *Animal Behaviour.* New York: McGraw-Hill.

Hinde, R. A. (1985). Home correlates of aggressive behavior in preschool. In J. M. Ramirez & P. F. Brain (Eds.), *Aggression: Functions and Causes.* Spain: C.I.C.A. & P.W.P.A.

Hinde, R. A. (1986). Some implications of evolutionary theory and comparative data for the study of human prosocial and aggressive behaviour. In D. Olweus, M. Radke-Yarrow, & J. Block (Eds.), *The*

Development of Antisocial and Prosocial Behavior. London: Academic Press.

Hinde, R. A. (1987). *Individuals, Relationships and Culture*. Cambridge: Cambridge University Press.

Hinde, R. A., & Dennis, A. (1986). Categorizing individuals: An alternative to linear analysis. *International Journal of Behavioral Development, 9,* 105–119.

Hinde, R. A., & Tamplin, A. (1983). Relations between mother-child interaction and behaviour in preschool. *British Journal of Developmental Psychology, 1,* 231–257.

Manning, M., Heron, J. & Marshall, T. (1978). Styles of hostility and social interactions at nursery, at school and at home. An extended study of children. In L. A. Hersov, M. Berger, & D. Shaffer (Eds.), *Aggression and Anti-Social Behaviour in Childhood and Adolescence*. Oxford: Pergamon Press.

Marks, I. M. (1987). *Fears and Phobias*. New York: Academic Press.

Prechtl, H.F.R. (1950). Das Verhalten von Kleinkindern gegenuber Schlangen. *Weiner Zeitsf. Philosophie, Psychologie und Paedagogie, 2,* 68–70.

Radke-Yarrow, M. (1988). Child development in a network of relationships. In R. A. Hinde & J. Stevenson-Hinde (Eds.), *Relationships within Families*. Oxford: Oxford University Press.

Scott, J. P., & Fredericson, E. (1951). The causes of fighting in mice and rats. *Physiol.Zool., 24,* 273–309.

Seyfarth, R. M., & Cheney, D. L. (1986). Vocal development in vervet monkeys. *Animal Behaviour, 34,* 1640–58.

Tajfel, H. (Ed.) (1978). *Differentiation between Social Groups*. London: Academic Press.

Tinbergen, N. (1948). Social releasers and the experimental method required for their study. *Wilson Bull., 60,* 6–51.

Tinbergen, N. (1959). Comparative studies of the behaviour of gulls (Laridae): A progress report. *Behaviour, 15,* 1–70.

Tinklenberg, J. R., & Ochberg, F. M. (1981). Patterns of adolescent violence: A California sample. In D. A. Hamburg & M. B. Trudeau (Eds.), ***Biobehavioral Aspects of Aggression.*** New York: Alan R. Liss, Inc.

Wahlström, R. (1987). The image of enemy as a psychological antecedent of warfare. In J. M. Ramirez, R. A. Hinde, & J. Groebel (Eds.), ***Essays on Violence.*** Seville: Publicaciones de la Universidad de Sevilla.

5

Serotonergic Involvement in Aggressive Behavior in Animals

BEREND OLIVIER
JAN MOS
MARTIN TULP
JACQUES SCHIPPER
SJAAK DEN DAAS
GEERT VAN OORTMERSSEN

For quite a while serotonin (5-HT) has been implicated in the control of aggressive behavior in animals (Valzelli, 1981) and man (Mühlbauer, 1985). This does not imply, however, that serotonin is "the" neurotransmitter of aggression, because a number of other neurotransmitters have been suggested to be involved in the modulation of aggressive behavior—e.g. catecholamines (Eichelman and Thoa, 1973) and acetylcholine (Smith et al., 1970). Although multiple-transmitter modulation is more likely for complex sets of behaviors like aggression, many aspects of the important modulatory role of serotonin in several types of agonistic (aggression, defense, and flight) behavior in animals and man remain to be elucidated (Miczek, 1987; Miczek and Barry, 1976; Valzelli, 1984).

Early work on 5-HT and aggression indicated that a general 5-HT activation decreased aggression whereas an overall inactivation of 5-HT (achieved by various manipulations) led to en hanced aggression (e.g. Valzelli, 1981). However, the increased

We thank Mrs. M. Mulder for typing the report and Ruud van Oorschot for technical support.

knowledge about the neuroanatomy, neurochemistry and neuropharmacology of the 5-HT CNS systems on the one hand and about the existing different types of aggressive behaviors on the other hand, suggests a much more complicated pattern of the involvement of 5-HT in agonistic behavior. The neuroanatomical distribution of 5-HT receptors and localization of cell groups of 5-HT in the CNS and their differential projections (cf. Pazos and Palacios, 1985; Pazos et al., 1985; Steinbusch, 1981) indicate that it is no longer justifiable to speak about an unidimensional role of 5-HT in any aggression paradigm. Moreover, the recent differentiations in 5-HT receptor (sub)types or binding sites (Arvidsson et al., 1986; Hoyer et al., 1985; Peroutka, 1986; Richardson and Engel, 1986) and their distinct functional roles delineate the possibilities of a functional discrimination in the 5-HT systems in the CNS with regard to different kinds of agonistic behavior.

The present contribution first demonstrates the problems in the interpretation of 5-HT turnover and aggressive behavior in two rat strains and in two lines of wild house mice selected for high or low spontaneous aggression. Following this, a short neurochemical profile of the serotonergic drugs used will be given. The remaining section will then give a description of the behavioral effects of several drugs with a differential 5-HT mechanism of action using a variety of animal agonistic behavior models. In the latter part, emphasis will be placed on the behavioral effects of specific anti-aggressive drugs, serenics.

5-HT TURNOVER AND SPONTANEOUS AGONISTIC BEHAVIOR IN RODENTS

Support for the relationship between neural 5-HT activity and aggressive behavior in animals is not unequivocal. This is largely due to the lack of direct correlations between the spontaneous neurophysiological activity of (subsets of) 5-HT neurones in the CNS and measures of ongoing aggressive behavior. One part of the available evidence is the correlation between levels of 5-HT and 5-HIAA (or 5-HT turnover) in certain specific brain areas with some forms of aggressive behavior (c.f. Daruna, 1978). More evidence stems from different pharmacological manipulations of the 5-HT system and the effects on some parameters of aggression (for a review see Miczek, 1987). Thus it was observed that depleting 5-HT in the brain, facilitated or elicited various kinds of aggressive behavior in the rat, e.g. predation (Applegate, 1980; Valzelli et al., 1981; Vergnes & Kempf, 1981, 1982) and shock-induced fighting (defense) (Kantak et al., 1981; Knutson et al., 1979; Sheard & Davis, 1976). In a resident-intruder paradigm in rats, Vergnes et al. (1986) showed that depletion of 5-HT by PCPA administration enhanced offense when the resident was treated but had no effect on defensive behavior of the intruder when the latter was treated. This suggests that 5-HT plays a role in modulating offense, but not defense or submissive behavior.

Attempts were made in our laboratory to assess the relationship between spontaneous 5-HT turnover in the CNS and different forms of aggressive behavior. The purpose of the experiments was to determine whether rat strains with different propensities to both kill mice *and* engage in more intensive agonistic interactions with conspecifics varied in terms of their 5-HT activity. Moreover, we studied 5-HT turnover in the brain of two genetically selected lines of wild house mice—one selected for a high level of aggression, the other for a low level (Van Oortmerssen and Bakker, 1981; Van Oortmerssen et al., 1985).

As a measure of 5-HT activity in rats, the ratio between 5-HIAA/5-HT was measured, which gives an indication of the 5-HT turnover (Shannon et al., 1986). Two rat strains were used, the TMD-S3 and the Wistar. Animals were housed singly for 4 weeks and tested once weekly for mouse killing and aggression towards a naive male intruder. Both strains were compared with regard to 5-HT turnover in striatum and cortex and aggressive behavior (mouse-killing behavior and resident-intruder aggression). Moreover, intra-strain correlations were computed for 5-HT turnover and aggression.

Figure 1 shows the lack of correlation in individual rats between the level of 5-HT turnover (in the striatum) and two measures of aggressive behavior, namely the total time spent on

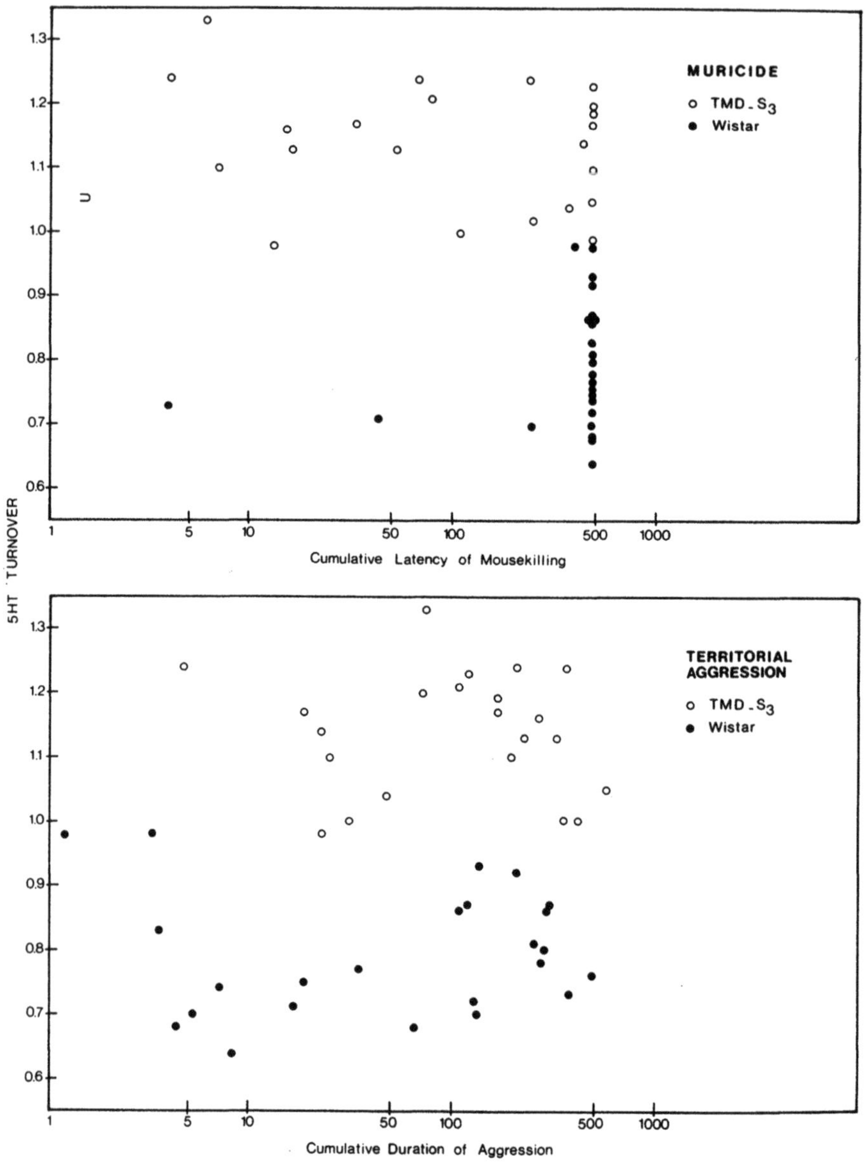

Figure 1. In the upper panel, the 5-HT turnover (5-HIAA/5-HT ratio) in the striatum is plotted versus the cumulative killing latency in 4 consecutive tests for the two strains of rats. Wistar rats show virtually no spontaneous mouse-killing behavior, therefore no correlation with 5-HT turnover could be computed. S3 rats spontaneously kill mice, but this index is not correlated with 5-HT turnover. In the lower panel,

the correlation between 5-HT turnover in the striatum and the % of total time spent on aggression during 4 consecutive intruder tests is plotted for the rat strains. No significant correlation was found between 5-HT turnover and aggression. 5-HT turnover in S3 rats is higher than in Wistars, but the total time spent on aggression did not differ significantly.

fighting in a resident-intruder paradigm and the killing latency in the muricide data. S3 rats show a significantly higher incidence of mouse killing than Wistar rats (63% vs 13%) but also a higher 5-HT turnover. This contradicts the general inhibitory role of 5-HT in (predatory) aggression as proposed by Valzelli (1981) and actually suggests a facilitative role of the neurotransmitter. However, the intra-strain analysis shows that there is no such correlation within the S3 strain between muricidal behavior and 5-HT turnover in the striatum. Similar effects were found for 5-HT turnover in the cortex (data not shown). Thus neither the inter-strains comparison nor the intra-strain analysis reveals a definite relationship between this measure of 5-HT turnover and muricidal responses.

In the Resident-Intruder paradigm, no clearcut difference was noted in the time spent on aggression by S3 and Wistar rats against intruders. There was also no correlation between individual 5-HT turnover in the striatum and cortex and aggression levels in either strain. Although S3 rats did not spend more time on aggression, they were more vigorous fighters as they caused more wounds on the opponents. These data do not indicate a direct relationship between this measure of 5-HT activity and aggression, although in other areas in the CNS such correlations may exist. Other measures of 5-HT turnover, e.g. 5-HTP accumulation after NSD-1015 treatment may reveal correlations not revealed with the present techniques. Although currently technically complicated, it would be more relevant to measure the actual 5-HT turnover during aggressive interactions.

In a second experiment, two genetically selected lines of wild house mice (Van Oortmerssen and Bakker, 1981) were used, which had either short attack latencies (SAL-line) or long attack latencies (LAL-line). After determination of their aggressive behavior, male mice of each line were rapidly decapitated and their whole brains were used to measure levels of monoamines and their metabolites. The results are shown in Table 1.

Turnover indications of DA, as measured by the ratios 3, 4 dihydroxy-phenylacetic acid/dopamine (DC/DA) and homovanillic acid/dopamine (HVA/DA), did not show significant differences between the SAL- and LAL-lines. The only difference in levels measured is that of serotonin, which is lower in the SAL-mice. Although the ratio 5-HIAA/5-HT was higher in the SAL-mice, this was not statistically significant. However, the number of animals used is low and whole brain measurements are not highly refined. The available evidence suggests that a high-aggressive strain of mice (SAL) may have a higher 5-HT turnover than a low-aggressive strain, thereby confirming the rat data presented before.

Another, and perhaps more fruitful, way to investigate the role of 5-HT in aggression may be the manipulation of central 5-HT activity with different pharmacological tools. This approach will be elaborated in the remainder of this chapter. Essentially, serotonergic drugs with different mechanisms of action were used and their effects on aggression established using several behavioral paradigms. In these experiments we will assume that the drugs with different receptor affinities are acting equally on the different neuroanatomical subsystems of the 5-HT system.

TABLE 1
HPLC-Measurements of the Levels of Noradrenaline (NA), 3,4 Dihydroxyphenylacetic Acid (DC), Dopamine (DA), Homovanillic Acid (HVA), 5-Hydroxyindoleacetic Acid (5-HIAA), and Serotonin (5-HT) in Whole Brain of Wild Mice Either Belonging to the Short-Attack-Latency (SAL) Line (N=5) or the Long-Attack-Latency (LAL)-Line (N=5)

	Mean Concentration (± SEM) in ng/g Total Brain					
	NA	*DC*	*DA*	*5-HIAA*	*HVA*	*5-HT*
LAL	811 ± 37	113 ± 9	635 ± 38	343 ± 21	249 ± 27	722±10
SAL	782 ± 15	133 ± 9	629 ± 10	332 ± 22	274 ± 24	617±15*

*$p<0.05$ Student-t-test: different from the LAL-line.

NEUROCHEMICAL PROFILE OF 5-HT DRUGS USED

The following section first provides a short description of the neurochemical profiles of some of the serotonergic drugs used. Two functional parameters are given, namely 5-HT agonistic activity *in vitro* on the presynaptic autoreceptor and modulation of 5-HT turnover *in vivo*. First we will give the data on the receptor affinities.

Receptor Binding (Table 2)

Of the drugs tested in behavioral studies of aggression, several compounds have a high affinity for 5-HT_{1A} binding sites relative to 5-HT_{1B} or 5-HT_2 [5-methoxy-N,N-dimethyltryptamine, 8-OH-DPAT (8-hydroxy-2-di-N-propylamino) tetralin], buspirone and ipsapirone (TVX-Q 7821)]. Others have about equal affinity for 5-HT_{1A} and $_{1B}$ sites; RU 24969 [5-methoxy-3-(1,2,3,6-tetrahydro-4-pyrimidyl) indole succinate], DU 28853 (eltopramine), whereas TFMPP (trifluoromethyl phenylpiperazine) and quipazine exert some preference for 5-HT_{1B} sites. In general, affinity of these compounds for 5-HT_2 receptors is relatively low. Of course, several compounds also have affinity for other receptors and in some cases (e.g. buspirone-D_2) it is possible that those affinities cause interfering biological activity.

Autoreceptor Modulation of 5-HT Release (Table 3)

5-HT release from nerve terminals is subjected to negative feedback via presynaptic 5-HT receptors. It has been proposed by various authors (Engel et al., 1986; Middlemiss, 1984) that these 5-HT autoreceptors are of the 5-HT_{1B} type as defined by radioligand-binding studies. Several 5-HT agonists inhibit the 5-HT release *in vitro* as measured by the potassium or electrically-stimulated release of pre-stored (^{3}H) 5-HT from brain slices (Göthert, 1980). As indicated by the pD_2 values in table 3, 5-HT, RU24969, 5-Me-O-DMT, TFMPP and DU 28853 act as agonists at the presynaptic autoreceptors. Compounds with a high affinity for the 5-HT_{1A} binding site, such as 8-OH-DPAT, bus-

TABLE 2

Affinity of Serotonin and Several Other Serotonergic Compounds for 18 Receptor (Sub)Types Expressed as pK_i's ($-\log K_i$). All Data Are Based on At Least Three Measurements.

Receptor (Sub)type	*Serotonin*	*RU24969*	*5-Me-O-DMT*	*TFMPP*	*Flupazine*	*DU28853*	*8-OH-DPAT*	*Quipazine*	*Buspirone*	*Ipsapirone*	*MDL72222*	*Ritanserine*	*Fluvoxamine*	*Methysergide*	Brain Area	[³H]-ligand	Reference
5-HT_{1A}	8.4	8.1	8.2	6.7	6.4	7.4	8.6	5.6	7.8	8.3	<5.2	6.1	<5.2	7.7	fc	8-OH-DPAT	Gozlan et al. (1983)
5-HT_{1B}	8.4	8.1	7.3	7.5	5.7	7.2	5.8	6.6	5.2	5.6	<4.5	6.2	<5.2	7.3	fc	Serotonin (*)	Sills et al. (1984)
5-HT_2	5.9	5.8	5.6	6.1	5.8	5.8	<5.2	6.0	6.0	5.6	<5.3	8.5	5.2	7.8	fc	Spiperone	Creese and Snyder, (1974)
$alpha_1$	4.4	5.9	—	5.9	5.8	6.1	5.6	5.4	6.0	6.6	<5.4	7.1	5.6	<5.4	tb—cb	Prazozine	Timmermans et al. (1981)
$alpha_2$	4.8	5.6	—	5.8	4.1	5.5	6.5	5.9	<5.3	5.6	<5.3	6.5	4.8	5.5	tb—cb	Clonidine	U'Pritchard et al. (1977)
$beta_{1/2}$	4.4	6.4	—	6.4	<4.3	6.7	<5.2	5.9	<5.2	<5.2	<5.3	<5.3	5.0	<5.2	cc	Dihydroalprenolol	Nahorski (1978)
DA_1	5.4	<5.1	—	<5.1	4.7	<5.1	<5.1	<5.1	<5.1	5.2	<5.1	—	<5.1	—	tb	Mepyramine	Tran et al. (1978)
DA_2	4.8	5.9	—	6.1	5.6	6.0	5.7	<5.4	7.4	6.4	5.5	7.9	5.9	6.8	tb—cb	QNB	Yamamura and Snyder (1974)
his-H_1	—	<5.3	—	5.6	5.6	5.4	<5.3	5.9	6.0	5.9	6.0	7.9	<5.3	—	Caudate	Dopamine	Burt et al. (1976)
muscarinic	—	<5.6	—	<5.6	4.5	<5.6	5.7	<5.4	<5.4	<5.3	5.8	—	4.4	6.8	Striatum	Spiperone	Creese et al. (1977)

mu-opiate	—	5.2	—	<5.2	5.1	<5.2	<5.2	<5.1	5.1	<5.3	<5.3	—	<5.2	—	tb—cb	Naloxone	Pert and Snyder (1974)
kappa-opiate	—	<5.2	—	<5.2	<5.2	<5.2	<5.2	<5.2	5.6	5.1	<5.2	—	<5.2	<5.2	tb—cb	EKC	Hiller and Simon (1980)
delta-opiate	—	4.8	—	<5.1	<5.1	<5.1	<5.0	<5.1	<5.1	<5.1	<5.1	—	<5.1	<5.1	tb-cb	DADLE	Leslie et al. (1980)
BDZ	<4.1	<5.1	—	<4.1	<5.1	<5.2	<5.1	<5.1	<5.1	<5.1	<5.1	—	<5.1	—	tb	Diazepam	Braestrup and Squires (1978)
gaba	—	<5.2	—	<5.2	<5.2	<5.2	<5.2	5.1	<5.2	<5.2	5.5	—	<5.1	<5.2	cb	Muscimol	Herschel and Baldessarini (1978)
glycine	<4.2	<5.2	—	<5.2	<5.2	<5.0	<5.2	5.3	<5.2	<5.2	<5.6	—	<5.2	<5.2	m + p	Strychnine	Muller and Snyder (1978)
TRH	<4.1	<5.0	—	<5.0	<5.0	<5.0	<5.0	<5.0	<5.0	<5.1	<5.0	—	<4.1	<5.0	tb-cb	MeTRH	Taylor and Burt (1981)
CCK	<5.1	<5.1	—	<5.1	<5.1	<5.1	<5.1	<5.1	<5.1	<5.1	<5.1	<5.1	<5.1	—	cc	CCK-8	Van Dijk et al. (1984)

K_1 (nM) is calculated from IC_{50}-values via the Cheng-Prusoff equation.
(*)In this essay 3.10^{-8}M unlabelled 8-OH-DPAT is added to the incubation in order to block 5-HT_{1A}-receptors.
tb = total brain; fc = frontal cortex; cb = cerebellum; cc = cerebral cortex; m = medulla; p = pons

pirone and ipsapirone, do not affect 5-HT release, indicating a lack of agonistic activity on the 5-HT autoreceptor. The phenylpiperazines, TFMPP and DU 28853, show activity comparable to 5-HT but their intrinsic activities classify them as partial agonists.

5-HT Turnover In Vivo (Table 3)

After inhibition of the aromatic-L-amino-acid decarboxylase by NSD 1015, 5-hydroxytryptophan (5-HTP) accumulates in brain

TABLE 3
In vitro 5-HT release and ED_{50} for the 5-HTP Accumulation of 5-HT Agonists

	5-HT Release In Cortex[1]		*5-HTP Formation*[2]
	pD_2	α	ED_{50} *mg/kg*
5-HT	7.7	1.0	—
RU24969	8.0	0.8	1.0
5-Me-O-DMT	5.5	0.9	<10
TFMPP	7.7	0.7	1.9
DU 28853	7.6	0.4	0.3
Fluprazine	<5.5	0	—
8-OH-DPAT	<5.0	0	0.2
Quipazine	<5.0	0	>10
Buspirone	<6.0	0	<10
Ipsapirone	<6.0	0	<10

— = not tested

[1]The effects of putative 5-HT agonists on K^+ (20 mM)-evoked ^3H-5-HT release from rat cortex slices. Neuronal 5-HT uptake was blocked during superfusion by fluvoxamine (10 μmol/l). Agonists were added to the superfusion medium 15 min before stimulation. pD_2 values and intrinsic activity (α) are calculated from the concentration-response curves.

[2]Effects of 5-HT agonists on 5-HTP formation in striatum of rats. Agonists were given 60 min and NSD 1015 (100 mg/kg IP) 30 min before decapitation. 5-HTP levels were determined by use of HPLC with electrochemical detection. Doses necessary to induce half-maximal inhibition of 5-HTP levels were determined from the dose-response curves. All compounds were given orally except 5-Me-O-DMT and 8-OH-DPAT which were given intraperitoneally.

regions containing 5-HT terminals. The rate of accumulation of 5-HTP has been used as an index of 5-HT neuronal activity (Carlsson et al., 1972). 5-HT agonists inhibit 5-HTP accumulation and it has been suggested that this is due to a negative feedback mechanism (Arvidsson et al., 1986). The 5-HT agonists that inhibited 5-HT release *in vitro* also reduced 5-HTP accumulation *in vivo*. Interestingly, 8-OH-DPAT also reduces 5-HTP accumulation. The *in vitro* data suggest that it is unlikely that the 5-HT_{1A} compounds reduce 5-HT neuronal activity via presynaptic receptors mediating 5-HT release. It is possible that another presynaptic feedback mechanism, which modulates synthesis rather than the release mechanism, exists via 5-HT_{1A} receptors. On the other hand, one cannot exclude the possibility that a postsynaptic 5-HT_{1A} receptor is involved, resulting in a "long-loop" feedback mechanism as known for e.g. dopaminergic neurones. Definitely, further research will be necessary to unravel the mechanisms involved in the modulation of 5-HT neuronal activity via 5-HT receptor subtypes *in vivo*.

EXPERIMENTAL MODELS TO STUDY AGONISTIC BEHAVIOR IN RODENTS

Aggressive behavior, as observed in a variety of aggression models, consists of an extensive number of components that have complex functions and that have been organized in certain patterns and sequences resulting in species-specific behavior. Depending on the animal model used (i.e., the environmental situation), each model delivers its own set of species-specific behaviors. The distinction between the different types of aggression occurring in different models is mainly based on the frequency distribution of the possible behavioral repertoire of the species involved. A defending and offending rat make use of the same set of behavior elements, but because of a different frequential and sequential distribution of the elements, the behavior can be classified into offensive or defensive. It is current terminology to refer to aggressive interactions between animals by the term "agonistic behavior," derived from the ethological vocabulary. Agonistic behavior refers to all elements of behavior present in situations of conflict, and includes attack, defense and flight behaviors. Agonistic behavior is limited to intraspecific interactions, and does not hold for interspecific interactions like predatory behavior. Agonistic behavior represents interactions between two (or more) combating animals.

The nature of such interactions is usually highly specific, often ritualized and determined by environmental conditions. The initial, appetitive phase of agonistic behavior, consists of approach of one (or both) combatants and start of introductory social behavior (investigation). Most often, a clear distinction then appears between offensive and defensive behavior. One animal shows the elements (acts, postures and signals) belonging to the offensive repertoire, the other one engages in activities belonging to defense, submission and flight. Such a division in agonistic behavior is observed in a very wide range of animals, from low to very high ranking on the evolutionary scale. However, an animal which behaves defensively in a certain situation (e.g. the territory of a stranger) may behave very offensively in its own territory. This underlines the hypothesis that offense, defense, submission and flight belong to one continuum of agonistic behavior, with on one side pure offense (attack), on the other side pure defense (flight). The situation in which the animal finds itself determines the behavioral strategy for the most part. Of course, internal stimuli (e.g. hormones, previous experience) also partly determine the strategy chosen by an animal.

Animal Models

The aforenamed dichotomy in aggressive behavior, the offense-defense continuum, is present in a number of different animal models presently in use for the testing of agonistic behavior in animals, specifically in rodents (cf. Miczek and Krsiak, 1979). In the following section, a description will be given of the most frequently used animal aggression models and an attempt to indicate the value of the model for testing of anti-aggressive drugs will be delineated.

Offensive Aggression Models

The most frequently used manipulation to induce aggression is isolation of animals for some period of time. Male laboratory mice show attack behavior after several weeks of isolation (Valzelli, 1969). This *isolation-induced aggression* model is one of the most frequently used aggression models in behavioral pharmacology (Malick, 1979). Because isolated male mice show a full repertoire of agonistic behaviors (Krsiak, 1974; Miczek and Krsiak, 1979), this isolation-induced aggression model can also be used in an ethological way, giving the possibility of detecting very specific drug effects (cf. Olivier and Van Dalen, 1982). The model mainly represents offensive aspects of agonistic behavior, but in some animals defensive aspects prevail so that this behavioral model can be elegantly used to differentiate between several drugs that influence agonistic behavior (Janssen et al., 1960; Krsiak, 1975, 1979; Malick, 1979; Miczek, 1987).

A comparable model is the *intermale aggression* model in rats and mice. In this model, a relatively short isolation period is used to increase the probability of aggression against a conspecific male in a short test (Olivier, 1981; Olivier and Van Dalen, 1982). In this test, a very diverse pattern of activities is present because such a situation elicits a mixture of offensive-defensive behavior.

This model can differentiate more specifically between different putative anti-aggressive drugs and is more interesting in this respect because it shows properties of compounds which are revealed only partially, or not at all, by common pharmacological test models, e.g. isolation-induced aggression (cf. Miczek and Barry, 1976; Miczek and Krsiak, 1979; Olivier, 1981).

Another animal model with increasing use in pharmacology is the *resident-intruder paradigm* or *territorial aggression* model (Adams, 1976). In such a situation, a male rat (or mouse) is housed with a female, a situation which more closely resembles the natural situation (Barnett, 1975; Lore and Flannelly, 1977). When such territorial males meet a strange male intruder in their territory, heavy fighting may occur. This aggression is considered as offensive and resembles aggression occurring in nature (Blanchard and Blanchard, 1977; Miczek, 1979). This resident-intruder paradigm differs from both isolation-induced aggression in mice and intermale aggression in rats, because no (prolonged) isolation occurs, which may lead to behavioral and neurochemical anomalies (Valzelli, 1973). Moreover, resident-intruder paradigms have a very wide species generality (Van Hooff, 1977; Wilson, 1975), probably including man, whereas isolation-induced aggression is much more restricted to certain species (Miczek and Krsiak, 1979). The offensive aggression seen in the territorial situation resembles to a great extent that seen in intermale aggression (although the latter has more defensive components), and both models are very potent in the investigation of specificity and the behavioral mode of action of several drugs with anti-aggressive qualities (cf. Olivier, 1981; Olivier et al., 1984a; Van der Poel et al., 1984).

Aggression similar to that of offensive territorial males can be induced by electrical stimulation in the *hypothalamus* of male and female rats (Kruk et al., 1979; Kruk and van der Poel, 1980; Mos et al., 1987). Overt attack behavior is used as the behavioral characteristic; the current threshold is used to judge the anti-aggressive potency of the compound. Since stimulation of the same electrode can be used to measure drug effects on aversive qualities of the current and to measure sedation or stimulation (via locomotion), the model makes it possible to estimate the specificity of the anti-aggressive effect of the drug.

Although males behave, in many different situations, more aggressively than females (Moyer, 1976), females certainly can be aggressive. One of these situations is *maternal aggression* where a lactating animal with young will behave aggressively towards a large variety of intruders. The stimulus situation which elicits this type of aggressive behavior involves the proximity of some threatening objects to the female's young. In rats, maternal aggression is most pronounced during the first part of the lactating period (Erskine et al., 1978a,b; Olivier and Mos, 1986a). Such aggression performed by a lactating female can be considered as offensive (Van der Poel et al., 1984) although some authors describe it as partly defensive (Moyer, 1976).

In summary, in all these models the offensive aspects of aggression are emphasized. Offensive aggression is always characterized by the taking of initiative and inflicting of wounds (injury) upon the opponent (Blanchard et al., 1977b; Miczek and Krsiak, 1979; Olivier, 1981).

Defensive Aggression Models

In the foregoing models the offensive aspects of aggression were emphasized. In contrast, defensive aggression lacks active approach and no wounds (or incidental wounds on the snout) are made on the attacker. A much used aggression-model in pharmacology is *foot-shock* or *pain-induced* aggression, which is presently conceived of as a defensive aggression model (Blanchard et al., 1977a). Electrical shock to the hindpaws of a pair of rats or mice can evoke defensive behavior (Ulrich and Azrin, 1962), consisting of mutual defensive postures and squealing. These reactions are well integrated, but no complete sequences of fighting and no signs of offensive (threat) displays are present, at least in rats. An interfering factor in such a model is that the behavior-releasing stimulus (pain) can be masked by analgesic properties of psychoactive drugs. The latter fact and the very restricted behavioral repertoire in this paradigm limit the use of this defensive model to test anti-aggressive properties of drugs, although it has been (Valzelli, 1978) used extensively to assess such qualities and still is used.

Another, more natural model of defense is that in which a rat defends itself against an attacking conspecific, e.g. an intruder in the rat resident-intruder paradigm or in maternal aggression (Olivier and Mos, 1986b). This *defensive behavior* model reveals that defending rats have special tactics to defend the more vulnerable parts of their body. In naturally occurring situations, such animals mostly flee from the territory of the residential male or lactating female (Barnett, 1975), but when this is impossible, as is often the case in the semi-natural laboratory settings, they defend themselves by defensive upright postures, fleeing, crouching, emission of ultrasonic sounds, and submissive postures. Mostly these behaviors are aimed at protecting the back, the area where most wounds are inflicted by attacking rats (Mos et al., 1984). Although this model involves at least two rats, an offensive and a defensive one, it gives the opportunity to measure the capacities of the defending animal when it is treated with a psychoactive drug. When the behavior of the defender is assessed by ethological methods, this may provide a very subtle way of describing the effects of drugs. This defensive model has found limited use in psychopharmacological research on aggression, despite its obvious advantages (cf. Olivier and Mos, 1986b).

Predatory Aggression

A much used aggression model is mouse-killing by rats (muricide). This *predatory* or *interspecific aggression* model can be conceived as predatory attack on a prey, whereas the behavior of the mouse can be considered as defense against the predator. The *muricide model* has been used extensively to assess anti-aggressive qualities of drugs, but is of limited value because there is a lot of dispute whether its main motivational background stems from aggressive or feeding behavior (Baenninger, 1978), or from both. Moreover, muricide differs also from intraspecific aggression with regard to the neuroanatomical, physiological and hormonal mechanisms (Moyer, 1976). The typical behavior elements of this predatory behavior involve chasing, seizing and biting the mouse at the cervical spine level.

No concomitant agonistic displays such as sounds, threatening or pilo-erection occur, indicating that this behavior differs markedly from agonistic (intraspecific) behavior. Nevertheless, the model gives some clues to activities of drugs and can be used for comparative reasons along with the agonistic models (cf. Valzelli, 1978).

SEROTONERGIC DRUGS AND OFFENSIVE AGGRESSION

Isolation-Induced Aggression in Mice

When a male mouse is isolated for some time and subsequently confronted with a male group-housed intruder mouse, intense agonistic interactions may occur, including threat, chasing and biting (see Miczek, 1987 for a review of the important variables determining this kind of aggression). Although this paradigm has been suggested to model a psychopathology (Garattini and Valzelli, 1981; Valzelli, 1973), more recent studies, assessing ethological, pharmacological and endocrinological features, strongly suggest that such isolated males are highly similar to adult male mice in nature defending their territory (Blanchard et al., 1979; Brain, 1975; Crawley et al., 1975; Miczek and O'Donnell, 1978).

The effects of serotonergic drugs were studied in two set-ups. First, in a relatively simple screening test, the ED_{50} for inhibition of aggression was determined (according to the methods of Tedeschi et al., 1959). Although the results given in Table 4 show that a substantial number of drugs inhibit aggression, it is unclear from these values which behavioral inhibitory mechanisms are involved. Therefore, more detailed ethological studies were performed, which, by taking into account a broader reper-

TABLE 4
ED_{50}-Values for Isolation-Induced Aggression in Male Mice

Drug	*ED_{50} (mg/kg PO)*
RU24969	0.7
5-Me-O-DMT	4.2
TFMPP	0.2
DU 28853	0.4
Fluprazine	1.2
8-OH-DPAT	0.3(IP)
Quipazine	>38
Buspirone	>20
Ipsapirone	>20
Fluvoxamine	70
Fenfluramine	10
Methysergide	>10
Ritanserine	>10 (IP)
MDL72222	>10

Drugs were given orally 60 min. before testing suspended in 1% tragacanth.

toire of behaviors, may indicate more specifically *how* aggression was reduced.

The methodology used has been described in detail in Olivier and Van Dalen (1982) and Olivier et al. (1986d). Briefly, the behavior of the isolate was recorded in a neutral cage using 16 categories to describe the ongoing behavior (during 5 min confrontations between a 4–8 week isolated male mouse and a group-housed male conspecific). This approach permits a direct, simultaneous measurement of drug effects on aggressive and non-aggressive behaviors, revealing the specificity of drug action (cf. Miczek, 1987; Miczek and Krsiak, 1979). Figure 2 summarizes how seven 5-HT drugs affect such behavior.

DU 28853 exhibited a nice dose-dependent decrease in aggression with a concomitant increase in social interest, whereas non-social activities (mainly exploration) were also somewhat enhanced. It is especially noteworthy that no sedation was evident even at the dose of 20 mg/kg, which is 40 times the ED_{50} of isolation-induced aggression. Although defense seems to be dramatically enhanced, it has to be remembered that under control conditions, defense hardly occurs, whereas at doses where aggression no longer is present (1 mg/kg and higher) animals defend themselves against obtrusive intruders. A similar reasoning may hold for avoidance.

A more detailed pattern for DU 28853's behavioral effects is given in Table 5. A rather similar pattern emerges for fluprazine and TFMPP (for full descriptions see Olivier et al., 1987). Fluvoxamine, a specific 5-HT reuptake blocker (Claassen et al., 1979), also decreases aggression, but in a less specific way because it is accompanied by decreases in social interest and avoidance. 8-OH-DPAT, a specific 5-HT_{1A}-agonist (Middlemiss and Fozard, 1983) reduced aggression but also decreased non-social activities somewhat, and reduced defense (at 1 mg/kg) and avoidance. RU 24969, a mixed $5\text{-HT}_{1A/1B}$-agonist (Tricklebank, 1985) reduces aggression at the highest dose tested, concomitantly increasing avoidance.

To further illustrate the anti-aggressive activity of *the serenics,* fluprazine (Olivier and Van Dalen, 1982; Van der Poel et al., 1982) was tested in wild house mice. The latter were selected for a high level of aggression, which was measured by the attack

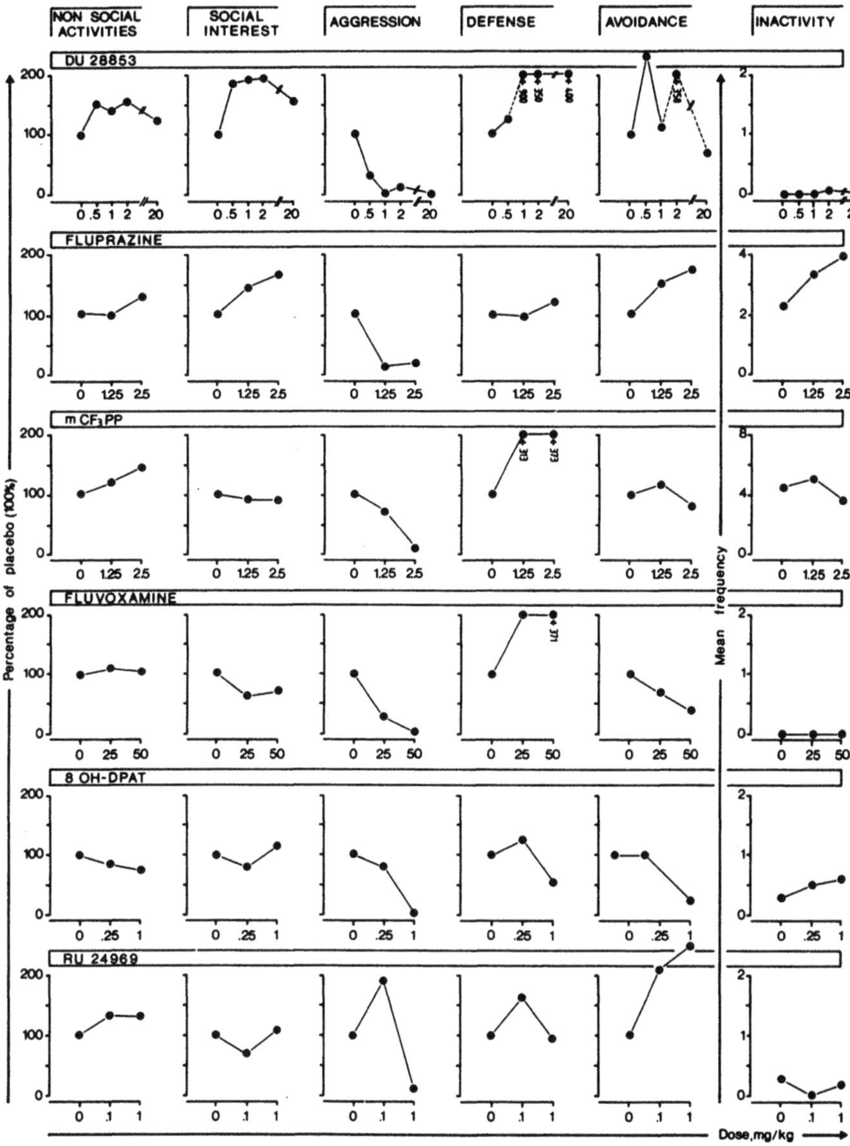

Figure 2. Effects of DU 28853, fluprazine, metaCF$_3$phenylpiperazine (mCF$_3$PP or TFMPP), fluvoxamine, 8-OH-DPAT and RU 24969 on six behavioral categories in intermale aggression in mice.

latency when confronted with a male opponent (Van Oortmerssen et al., 1985). In a first experiment, 16 wild male mice were used which were selected for Short Attack Latencies (<100 sec). In 3 trials of 10 mins each, all mice gained a stable and short

TABLE 5
Acute Oral Effects of DU 28853 on
Intermale Aggression in Mice

	Mean Frequency (N/5 min)				
Behavior elements	*DU 28853 (mg/kg p.o.)*				
Dose:	0	0.5	1	2	20
Nonsocial activities:					
Exploration	18.1	28.6	28.1	28.4	23.9
Rearing	1.1	3.8	1.2	4.9*	1.2
Attention	4.6	4.3	5.5	5.2	5.6
Body care	0.9	1.2	0.5	0.3	0.4
Social activities:					
Introductory social	18.1	41.8*	43.5**	44.6**	34.9
Social investigation	34.3	56.6**	57.9**	53.8**	48.5**
Crawling under	7.3	11.0	12.6	16.9*	10.5
Aggressive activities:					
Introductory aggressive	29.8	10.2*	0.7**	3.9**	—**
Aggression	8.5	2.0	0.1**	1.1**	—**
Tail rattling	23.1	5.9**	—**	3.1**	0.1**
Defensive activities:					
Defensive posture	0.3	0.3	3.1	0.9	1.1
Flight	0.1	0.2	0.5	0.5	0.5
Inactivity:					
Immobile	—	—	—	0.1	—
Immobile alert	—	—	—	—	—
Avoidance	1.2	5.1	2.4*	4.3**	1.5
Sexual behavior	1.2	0.5	0.2	—	0.1

DU 28853 was given 60 min. before testing lasting 5 min.
* significant difference ($p<0.05$, t.t.) between 0 and other doses.
**significant difference ($p<0.01$, t.t.) between 0 and other doses.

attack latency (fig. 3A-pre value). In the fourth trial 8 mice were injected intraperitoneally with saline and 8 mice with 20 mg/kg i.p. fluprazine (30' before testing). Fig. 3A clearly shows the antiaggressive activity of fluprazine after acute administration. Also after minipump administration (fig. 3B) for 7 days, fluprazine (400 mg/kg/day) exerted considerable antiaggressive activity.

The behavioral patterns observed after fluprazine in these wild mice confirm the specific anti-aggressive profile of this class of drugs in domestic and wild animals and point to the universality of the drug's effects: specific inhibition of aggression in every species tested so far.

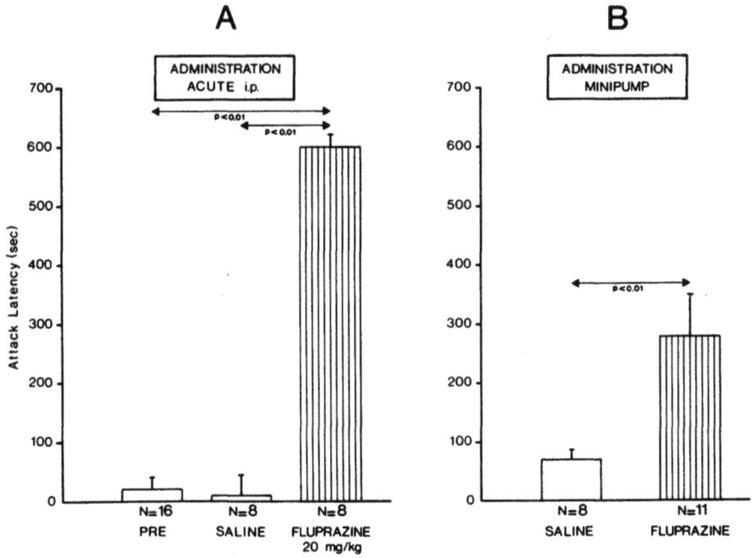

Figure 3. The effects of fluprazine, given acutely (A) (i.p. and 30 mins before testing in a volume of 0.2 ml/kg body weight) or via Alzet ® osmotic minipumps (B) filled either with saline or 400 mg/kg day fluprazine, on the attack latencies (in sec) of wild house mice of the SAL-line.

Resident-Intruder Aggression in Rats

Rats may be considered as socially living animals (Barnett, 1975; Timmermans, 1978) and male rats defend territories (Barnett, 1975) against unfamiliar intruders. This territorial behavior can be easily demonstrated under semi-natural laboratory conditions using domesticated and inbred strains of rats (Blanchard and Blanchard, 1984; Lehman and Adams, 1977; Olivier, 1977). Introduction of a strange male in such territories evokes a complete agonistic repertoire, similar to that occurring under natural circumstances (Barnett, 1975; Timmermans, 1978). Details of the methods are provided in Olivier (1981) and Olivier et al. (1984a). Briefly, male rats (residents) living together with a female in a large territory cage were confronted during 10 min with a strange male intruder. Behavior was recorded using ethograms as described previously (Olivier, 1981). Drugs were given 30 min (IP) or 60 min (PO) before testing. Animals were tested once a week and treatments (vehicle and 3 doses of a drug) were randomized according to a Latin square design.

The results for DU 28853, TFMPP, 5-Me-O-DMT, fluvoxamine and buspirone are shown in Figure 4. The behavioral effects are shown on four main behavioral categories: aggression, social interest, exploration and inactivity. Each category comprises several behavioral elements (cf. Olivier et al., 1984a, 1987) and adequately reflects the general effects of drugs on (social) behavior. DU 28853 dose-dependently reduced aggression without a concomitant decrease in social interest. The individual behavioral elements belonging to aggression and social interest are depicted in Figures 5 and 6 respectively. Exploration is not changed or even somewhat enhanced. Although inactivity is not significantly enhanced, at the highest dose, there is a tendency for this aspect to increase, presumably indicating that it replaces the time normally spent on aggression. A similar pattern occurs after TFMPP and (not shown) fluprazine. 5-Me-O-DMT reduces aggression in a nonspecific way, indicated by a simultaneous decrease in social interest and an increase in inactivity. Fluvoxamine has no dramatic effects at the doses used, but the general pattern indicates a nonspecific inhibitory effect on ag-

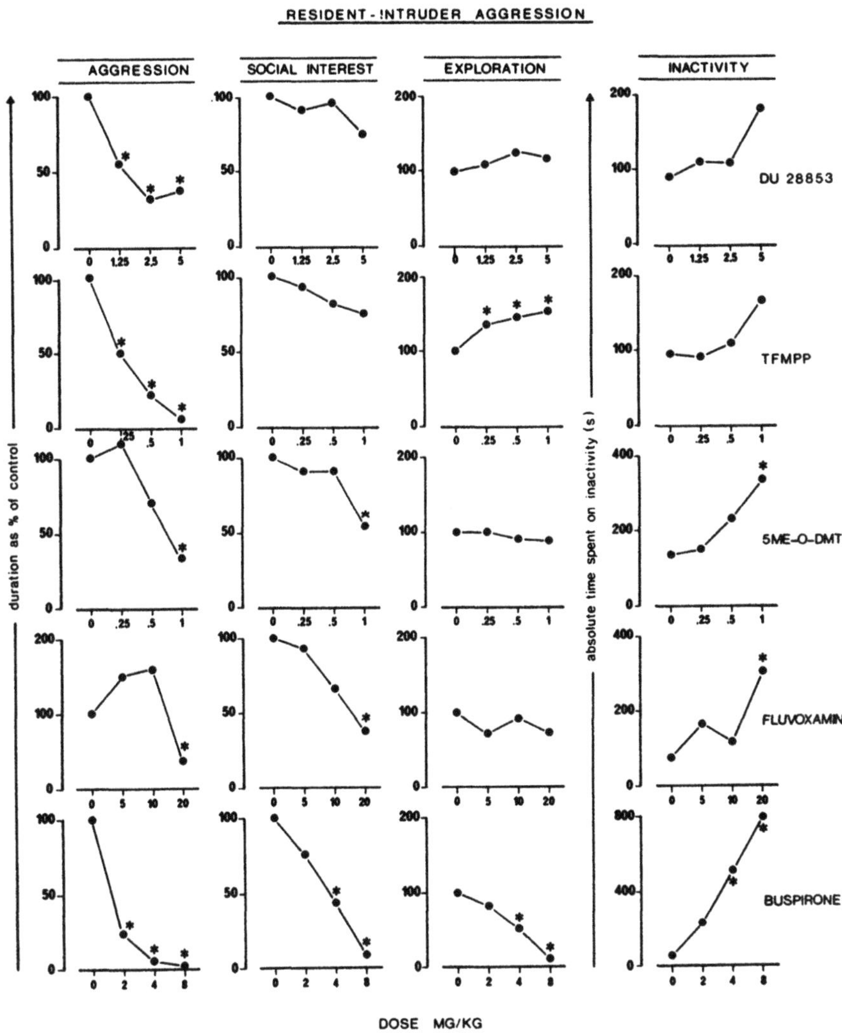

Figure 4. The effects of DU 28853, TFMPP, 5-Me-O-DMT, fluvoxamine and buspirone on four behavioral categories in resident-intruder aggression in rats.

gression. Buspirone nonspecifically reduces aggression as the compound is quite sedative at doses suppressing attacks (cf. Olivier et al., 1984a) in such tests.

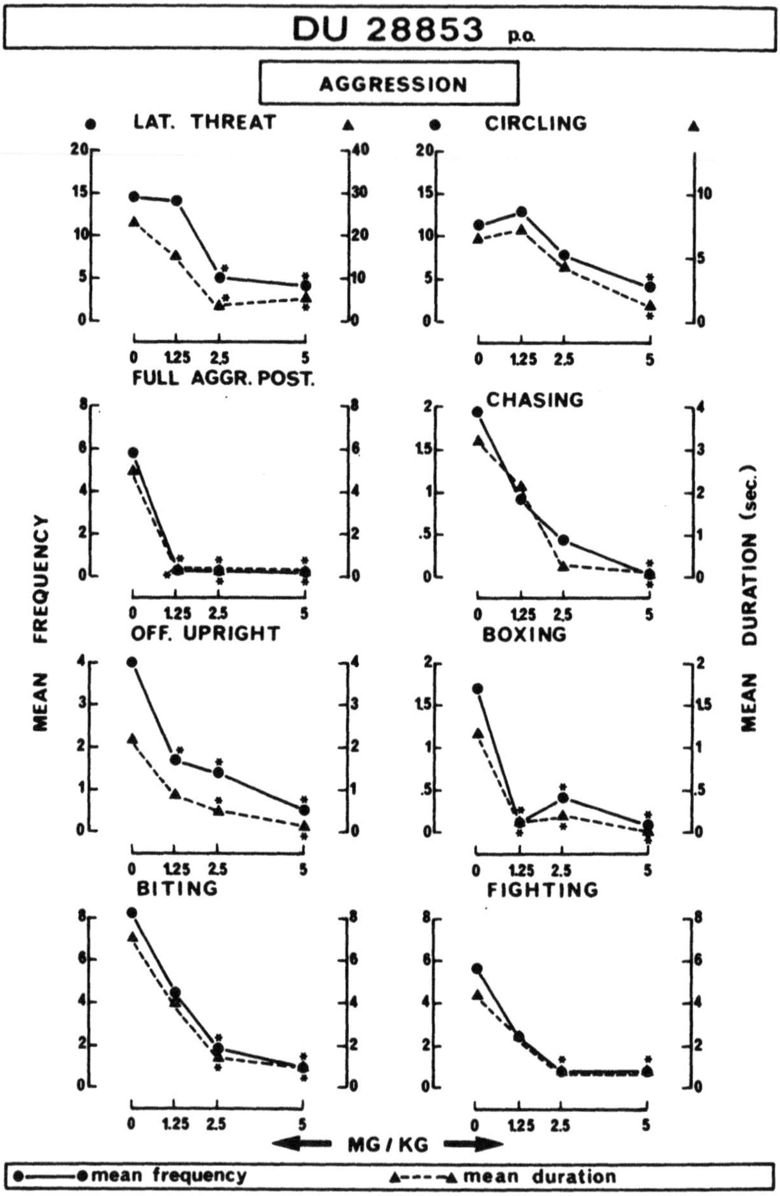

Figure 5. Effect of DU 28853 on Aggressive behavior in resident-intruder (territorial) aggression towards intruders in male rats.

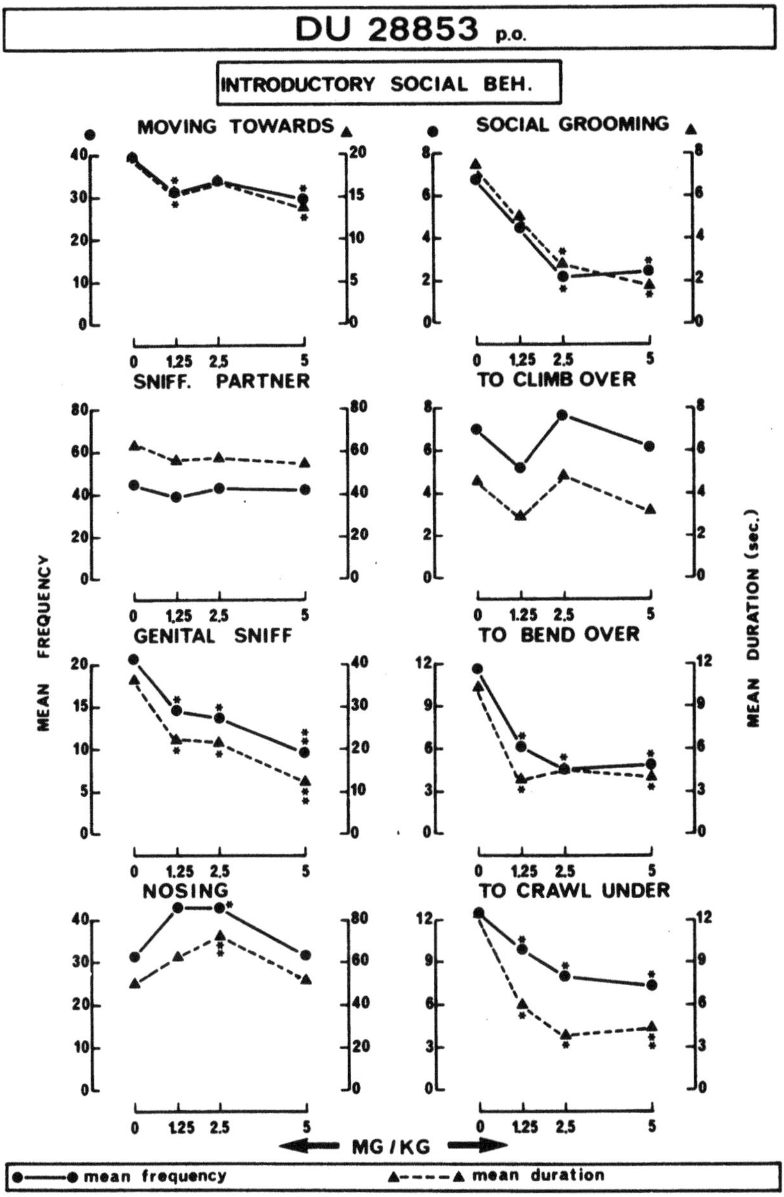

Figure 6. Effect of DU 28853 on Introductory Social Behavior (ISB) in resident-intruder aggression (territorial aggression) in male rats.

Colony-Aggression

Rats living in groups of male and female rats show a hierarchically organized group structure (Barnett, 1975; Lore and Flannelly, 1977; Timmermans, 1978). Typically, a dominant or α-male emerges, which stays for long periods in such a role (Blanchard et al., 1977b). The remaining males are subordinates (Dijkstra et al., 1984; Mos et al., 1984) which—like females—normally do not take part in attacks on strange male intruders (Blanchard et al., 1977b; Blanchard and Blanchard, 1981, 1984). The attractiveness of a colony situation for studying drug effects is that one can treat all males, only the α-male or the subordinates, and that one can remove several members, as e.g. the α-male and see what happens when a strange intruder is placed into the colony. In the present experiment, a limited colony has been used consisting of two males and one female. During colony formation the emergence of dominance/subordinance was tested by using weekly intruder tests. Typically, after a couple of weeks one male, the α-male, performs most of the attacks on the intruder. After reaching such a stable hierarchy-situation, drug experiments were performed. In this experimental set-up no extensive experiments with serotonergic drugs have been performed till now, and instead the effects of alcohol and chlordiazepoxide will be shown.

Figure 7 shows the results of acute treatment with respectively DU 28853 and, as reference compounds, chlordiazepoxide and ethylalcohol on the duration of aggression (all summed aggression elements) during a 15-min encounter with an intruder. Four kinds of interactions are possible: between the α-male and the intruder, between the subordinate and the intruder, between the α-male and the subordinate jointly against the intruder, and between the α-male and the subordinate. DU 28853 clearly reduced aggression in all interactions in a dose-dependent way. Fluprazine was only tested in one dose (16 mg/kg i.p.) which also clearly reduced all types of interaction (figure not shown).

Chlordiazepoxide (CDP) had a biphasic effect on aggression (Figure 8), increasing it at 5 and 10 mg/kg (except in the dominant vs. subordinate interaction). Moreover, chlordiazepoxide differentially affected the dominant and subordinate males. The

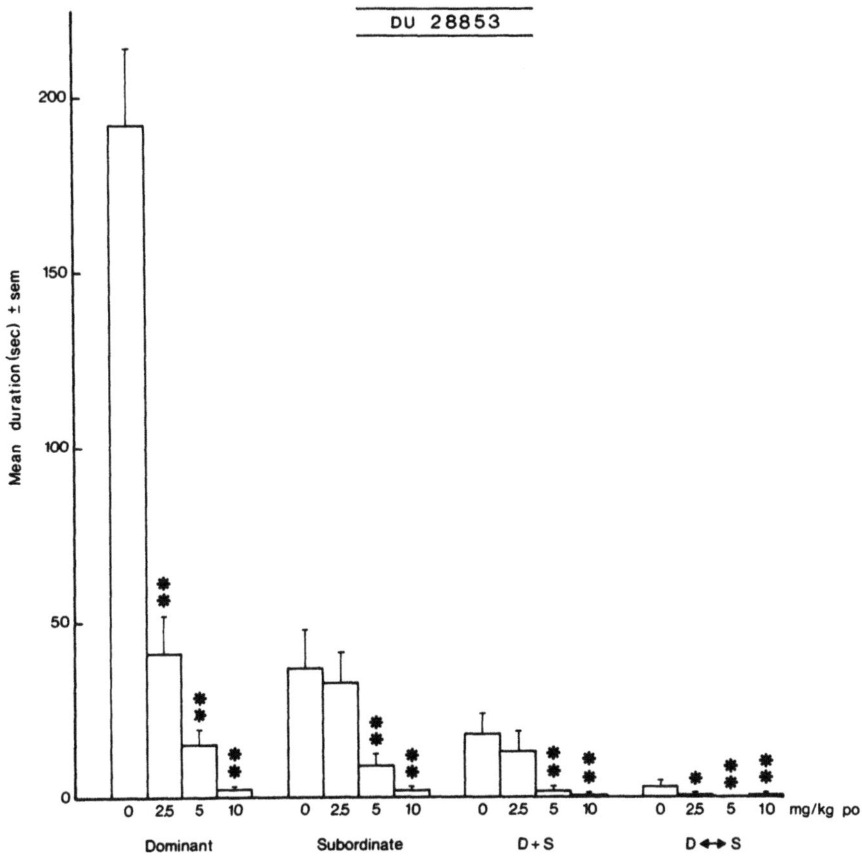

Figure 7. Effects of DU 28853 on the aggressive behavior of the dominant male and the subordinate male in a colony situation. The aggressive behavior towards the intruder or towards the members of the colony is depicted.

pro-aggressive action of CDP was more marked in the subordinate than in the dominant male (around 300% in the subordinate and approximately 150% in the dominant male). This pro-aggressive action of CDP has been described before (Olivier et al., 1985, 1986; Olivier and Mos, 1986 a, b) in several aggression paradigms (for a review see Mos and Olivier, 1987).

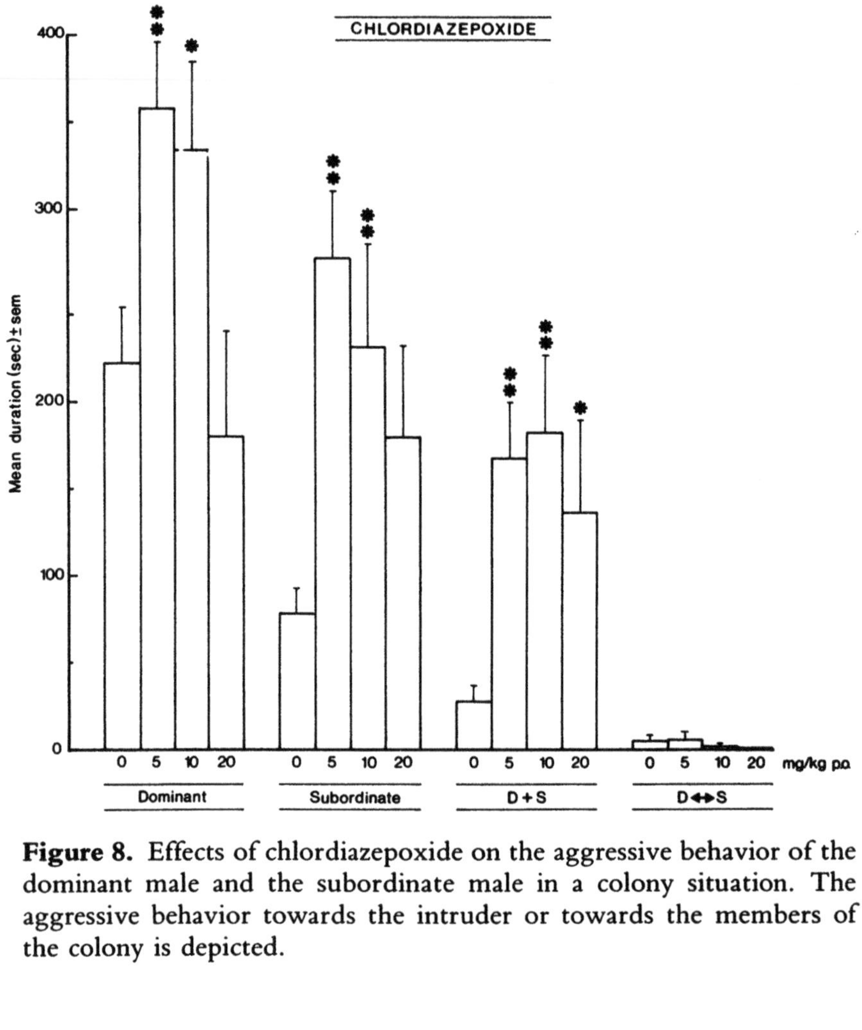

Figure 8. Effects of chlordiazepoxide on the aggressive behavior of the dominant male and the subordinate male in a colony situation. The aggressive behavior towards the intruder or towards the members of the colony is depicted.

Ethylalcohol had no clear effects on aggression in any type of interaction, except in the dominant vs. intruder at the highest dose, where aggression was reduced (Figure 9). The absence of effects on aggression in low to moderate alcohol doses (2 g/kg) in this colony-paradigm confirms earlier data obtained in resident-intruder aggression, maternal aggression (Olivier and Mos, 1986a) and hypothalamically-induced aggression (Kruk et al., 1987). For a review of alcohol effects see Winslow et al.

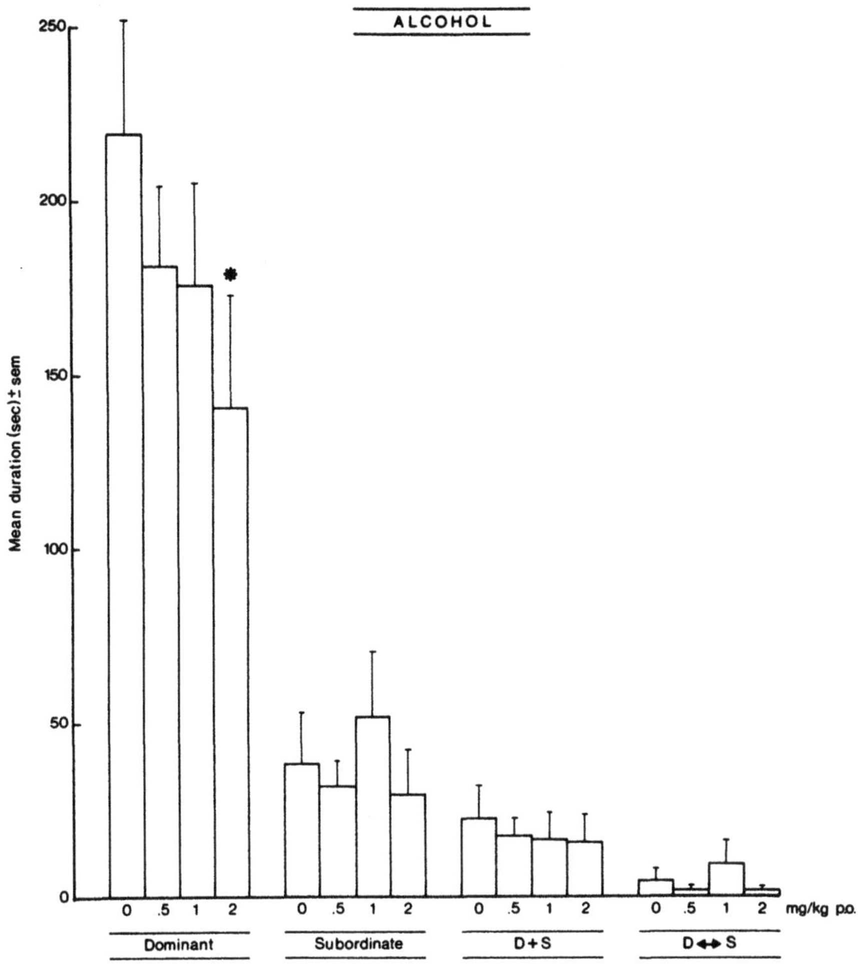

Figure 9. Effects of ethylalcohol on the aggressive behavior of the dominant male and the subordinate male in a colony situation. The aggressive behavior towards the intruder or towards the members of the colony is depicted.

(1987), Blanchard et al. (1987) and Olivier and Mos (1986a). Under specific conditions alcohol may lead to pro-aggressive actions (Winslow et al., 1987), but neither we (Olivier and Mos,

1986a), nor others (Brain, 1986; Blanchard and Blanchard, 1987) were able to detect such actions.

Hypothalamically-Induced Behavior in Rats

Electrical stimulation of specific sites in the hypothalamus of rats (Koolhaas, 1978; Kruk et al., 1979) in the presence of an appropriate goal object (i.e. a conspecific) may induce aggressive behavior, resembling normal offensive aggression (Kruk et al., 1979; Kruk and Van der Poel, 1980; Olivier et al., 1983). Hypothalamic aggression in male rats is sensitive to manipulation of androgen levels (Bermond et al., 1982). Moreover, it can be induced in an area (Kruk et al., 1983) roughly coinciding with the areas where levels of circulating sex hormones are regulated. In this same area, in female rats also aggression can be elicited (Kruk et al., 1984; Mos et al., 1987). Such aggressive behavior can be easily reproduced under constant circumstances, thereby meeting an important requirement for a model to study aggression. In this model the effects of DU 28853 were assessed and compared to a number of reference compounds. Previous studies have shown that serenics (Van der Poel et al., 1982; Olivier et al., 1986a, b) exert a specific profile in this hypothalamic-induced aggression paradigm both in males and females. Electrical stimulation in the hypothalamus of male and female rats (Kruk et al., 1979; Kruk et al., 1984) may, apart from aggressive behavior, also induce locomotion and teeth-chattering. The effects of drugs are measured in changes in the current thresholds needed to evoke the respective behaviors (Van der Poel et al., 1982). Comparison of the effects on the different thresholds gives information about the specificity of the drug effect. A specific anti-aggressive effect is present when only the thresholds for aggression and teeth-chattering are enhanced and locomotion is either unaffected or decreased. Table 6 shows the changes in thresholds for aggression, teeth-chattering and locomotion after treatment with DU 28853, fluprazine, and for comparative reasons chlordiazepoxide and haloperidol.

DU 28853 markedly enhanced the threshold currents for aggression and to a lesser extent for teeth-chattering, whereas the threshold for locomotion was decreased, indicating the specific

TABLE 6

Mean Thresholds (μAmp) ± SEM for Aggression, Teeth-Chattering and Locomotion in Hypothalamically-Induced Behavior in Rats

Drug	*Behaviors*	*Dose 0*	*2*	*4*	*8 mg/kg p.o.*
DU 28853	Aggression (N=6)	42.9 ± 3.8	90.9 ± 13.9	85.3 ± 15.7	100.5 ± 16.6
	Teeth-chatter (N=10)	32.3 ± 3.8	37.0 ± 4.3	37.5 ± 4.2	36.8 ± 4.1
	Locomotion (N=5)	60.3 ± 9.7	43.3 ± 4.6	37.0 ± 9.3	40.2 ± 11.1
		Dose 0	*5*	*10*	*20*
Fluprazine	Aggression (N=4)	35.4 ± 6.6	54.6 ± 9.0	49.2 ± 3.9	69.2 ± 16.9
	Teeth-chatter (N=10)	28.1 ± 3.7	35.6 ± 4.4	36.6 ± 4.4	44.9 ± 5.8
	Locomotion*	n.d.	n.d.	n.d.	n.d.
		Dose 0	*5*	*10*	*20*
Chlordia zepoxide	Aggression (N=7)	45.0 ± 4.2	43.8 ± 9.0	38.8 ± 4.6	70.8 ± 30.0
	Teeth-chatter (N=11)	37.0 ± 4.1	38.3 ± 3.9	38.8 ± 3.2	42.3 ± 3.9
	Locomotion (N=6)	84.5 ± 13.6	116.5 ± 33.5	126.1 ± 25.6	140.3 ± 24.7
		Dose 0	*05*	*1*	*2*
Halo peridol	Aggression (N=4)	31.5 ± 9.1	>200	>200	>200
	Teeth-chatter (N=9)	28.0 ± 4.9	31.3 ± 4.9	33.0 ± 6.4	40.9 ± 11.8
	Locomotion+	n.d.	n.d.	n.d.	n.d.

n.d. = not determined; n = number of animals

* in i.p. experiments (Van der Poel et al., 1982) the locomotion thresholds were not enhanced.

+ because of the long duration of action of haloperidol, thresholds were not reproducible, but clearly enhanced.

ity of action on aggression (Figure 10). Fluprazine had a comparable effect on aggression but did not influence locomotion (see Van der Poel et al., 1982), whereas haloperidol enhanced aggression, teeth-chattering (slightly) and locomotion thresholds at the same time, indicating its nonspecific effects. Chlordiazepoxide had no effect on aggression and teeth-chattering thresholds at lower dosages and enhanced the thresholds for both aggression and locomotion only at the highest dose, presumably indicating the muscle relaxant properties at that dose.

Recent evidence (Kruk et al., 1987) showed that this EBS-induced behavior paradigm in rats shows a quite specific profile for serenics; enhancement of thresholds for aggression and teeth-chattering, no effect or even a decrease on locomotion thresholds, and no effect on switch-off behavior, a measure for the interference of a drug with the aversive qualities also resulting from electrical brain stimulation.

Several reference drugs from different classes were tested in our laboratory or in the Pharmacological Laboratory of the University of Leiden (Kruk et al., 1987). d-Amphetamine (0.5 till 2 mg/kg i.p.) had no effect on aggression, teeth-chattering and switch-off behavior, but decreased the locomotion threshold, illustrating its stimulatory action. Scopolamine, a (muscarinic) anticholinergic drug, had (at 0.25 to 1.0 mg/kg i.p.) no effect on aggression and teeth-chattering, but decreased locomotory thresholds also and decreased switch-off thresholds. Alcohol, up to a dose of 2 g/kg orally, had no effect on any parameter, which was also observed after naloxone (0.1–10 mg/kg, i.p.), an opiate antagonist. Quipazine, a nonspecific 5-HT-agonist, had a quite nonspecific action in EBS-behaviors: increases in all thresholds, indicating its behavioral nonspecificity. 8-OH-DPAT, a specific 5-HT_{1A}-agonist had, at doses between 0.05 and 0.2 mg/kg i.p., no effects, whereas TFMPP, a more specific 5-HT_{1B}-agonist, and a putative metabolite of fluprazine, exerted a specific effect at 0.5–2 mg/kg (i.p.) on aggression (and teeth-chattering) without interference with locomotion. Interestingly, TFMPP enhanced switch-off thresholds indicating at least that the anti-aggressive action is not caused by fear-induction. dl-Propranolol, a β-adrenergic blocker (at 5–20 mg/kg i.p.) also had a specific anti-aggressive profile: it inhibited aggression and teeth-chattering but had no influence on locomotion and switch-off.

Summarizing, serenics like DU 28853 have a specific profile in this hypothalamic-induced behavioral model; enhancement of

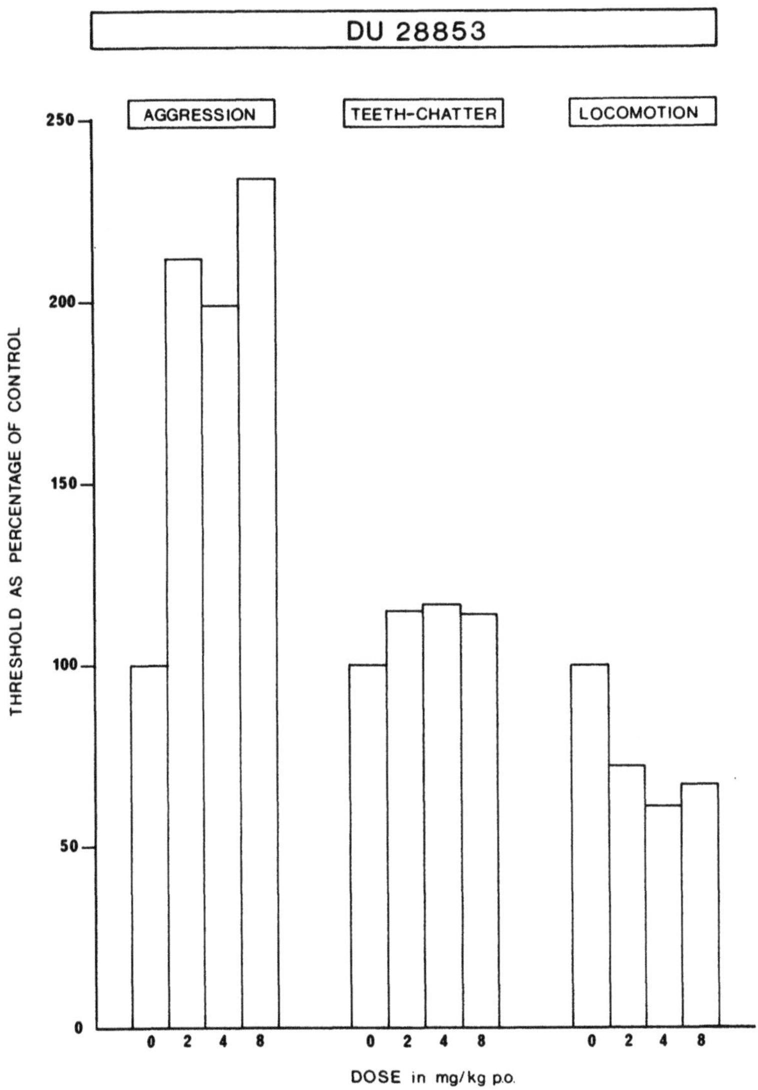

Figure 10. Effects of DU 28853 on the thresholds for aggression, teeth-chatter and locomotion in EBS-induced behavior.

aggression-related behaviors, without such disturbing side effects as sedation or muscle relaxation, or fear-enhancing effects as revealed by enhancement of threshold currents for stimulation-escape (switch-off behavior).

Maternal Aggression in Rats

The majority of studies on animal aggression deal with interactions of studies between males (Moyer, 1976). However females can be quite aggressive under certain conditions, as for instance in hypothalamically-induced aggression in rats (Kruk et al., 1984; Mos et al., 1987), aggression in non-oestrus hamsters (Floody and Pfaff, 1977; Payne and Swanson, 1970) and maternal aggression in several rodent species (mice, voles, rats, hamsters; cf. Floody, 1983; Svare and Mann 1983). In the female analogue of the resident-intruder paradigm, female rats display appreciable levels of aggression against female intruders, but to a lesser extent against male intruders. In general, however, attack frequencies in female aggression are lower than in males (Blanchard and Blanchard, 1981, 1984; De Bold and Miczek, 1984). The use of a female aggression paradigm for psychopharmacological purposes has been very restricted and only recently some developments have started, especially using maternal aggression in female rats (Olivier and Mos, 1986a; Olivier et al., 1985, 1986 b,d) and female mice (Yoshimura, 1987).

Maternal aggression is bound to a restricted postpartum period (Erskine et al., 1978a,b, 1980; Svare and Gandelman, 1973; Olivier and Mos, 1986a) in which the lactating female is highly aggressive against strange intruders, in particular males (Wise, 1974; Svare, 1977; Takahashi and Lore, 1982). Aggression is, at least in mice, dependent upon stimuli from the litter, especially suckling (Svare et al., 1980). Although suckling and growth of the nipples are necessary conditions for the display of maternal aggression, changes in suckling-induced prolactin levels are not necessary (Svare, 1981). Maternal aggression seems very purposeful, viz, protection of the offspring and occurs universally over the animal kingdom including humans.

The effects of DU 28853 and a number of serotonergic compounds were studied in a maternal aggression paradigm, specifically developed in our laboratory to test psychoactive drugs (Olivier and Mos, 1986a,b; Olivier et al., 1985, 1986a,b,c,d). The lactation period 3–12 days after birth appears a relatively stable time to perform aggression tests using the females as their own controls (Olivier et al., 1985, 1986b; Olivier and Mos, 1986a; Mos and Olivier, 1986). Furthermore, a test duration of five minutes suffices, because after that period aggression stabilizes at a low level (Olivier et al., 1987). The behavioral structure of maternal aggressive behavior did not change over time during day 3 to 12. This structure illustrates the purely offensive motivation of the female (Olivier et al., 1987). All her behavior is oriented towards the intruder and her behavior does not strongly depend on the qualities (male, female or castrated) of the strange intruder or its behavior (Mos and Olivier, 1987). This suggests, contrary to earlier suggestions (Svare and Mann, 1983), that maternal aggression is one of the purest forms of offensive behavior (cf. Van der Poel et al., 1984) although its primary function may be conceived as defense of the young.

Several drugs were tested using this paradigm, during test periods of 5 minutes. Each female was repeatedly tested on alternate days between post-partum days 3 to 12. Testing occurred every other day with vehicle or drug (several doses) alternated with "wash-out" days. For the sake of comparison the mean number of bite attacks/minute is presented, a measure which is corrected for the latency to the first attack (Figure 11).

This representation of the data shows that most serotonin-modulating drugs tested thus far inhibit aggression, although there are vast differences between drugs. 8-OH-DPAT, a specific 5-HT_{1A} agonist (Table 2) has a somewhat peculiar profile in that aggression suddenly decreases without a clear dose-response distribution. Behaviorally, this inhibition is also manifest in a sudden drop in interest in the intruder and a high increase in inactivity (see Figure 12). Other 5-HT agonists (of the 1B, mixed 1A/1B and mixed 1/2-types) all have regular dose-dependent, inhibitory effects on aggression (Figure 11). However, more refined behavioral analyses reveal substantial differences between the drugs involved (Figure 12). Quipazine, a nonspecific 5-HT agonist, clearly has a very nonspecific behavioral profile: decreases in aggression and social interest and a strong increase in inactivity (cf. Olivier and Mos, 1986a). The 5-HT_{1B} agonist, TFMPP and both mixed $5\text{-HT}_{1A/1B}$ agonists RU24969 and DU28853 (and also the putative weak $5\text{-HT}_{1A/1B}$ agonist fluprazine (Bradford et al., 1984)), have a similar profile in this female paradigm, namely reducing aggression whilst increasing social interest, exploration, pup care and inactivity.

SEROTONERGIC DRUGS AND DEFENSIVE AGGRESSION

One of the most frequently used models in the psychopharmacology of aggression is foot shock-induced defense in mice or rats. However, several recent studies have shown that this kind of aggression is primarily defensive (Blanchard et al., 1977a, 1978; Rodgers, 1979; Scott, 1966). Although the defensive responses are readily evoked by electric footshock (Ulrich and Azrin, 1962) or drugs (Sbordone et al., 1981), there are a number of constraints in this model. It is difficult to dissociate nonspecific motor effects from specific effects on defense, whereas alterations in pain reactivity may obscure effects on behavior. Therefore one should be very cautious in interpreting drug effects in this "defense" model.

A more natural defensive model is the *resident-intruder* paradigm, in which the intruder is attacked by a resident male or lactating female and has to defend itself (Miczek and Krsiak, 1981; Olivier and Mos, 1986b; Rodgers, 1981). In this situation a defending rat displays all the behavioral elements occurring in natural situations such as defensive upright postures, freeze-crouch postures, full submissive posture, fleeing and vocalizations (sonic and ultrasonic). This model gives the opportunity to record effects of psychotropic agents on the complete defensive behavioral repertoire.

Effect on Foot Shock-Induced Defense in Mice

Antidefense activity was determined according to a modification of the test method described by Tedeschi et al. (1959). Five selected pairs of male albino mice were used for each dose of the

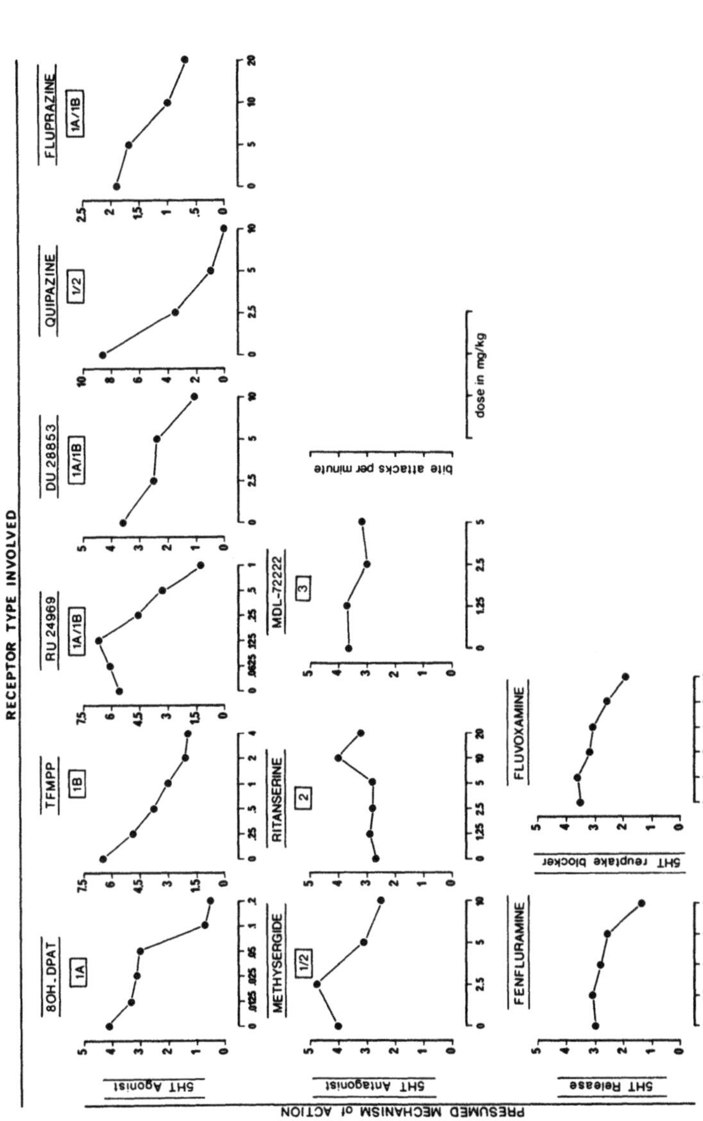

Figure 11. The mean number of bite attacks/minute (± SEM) is shown for a number of serotonergic drugs in the maternal aggression tests in rats. This measure is corrected for the latency to first attack.

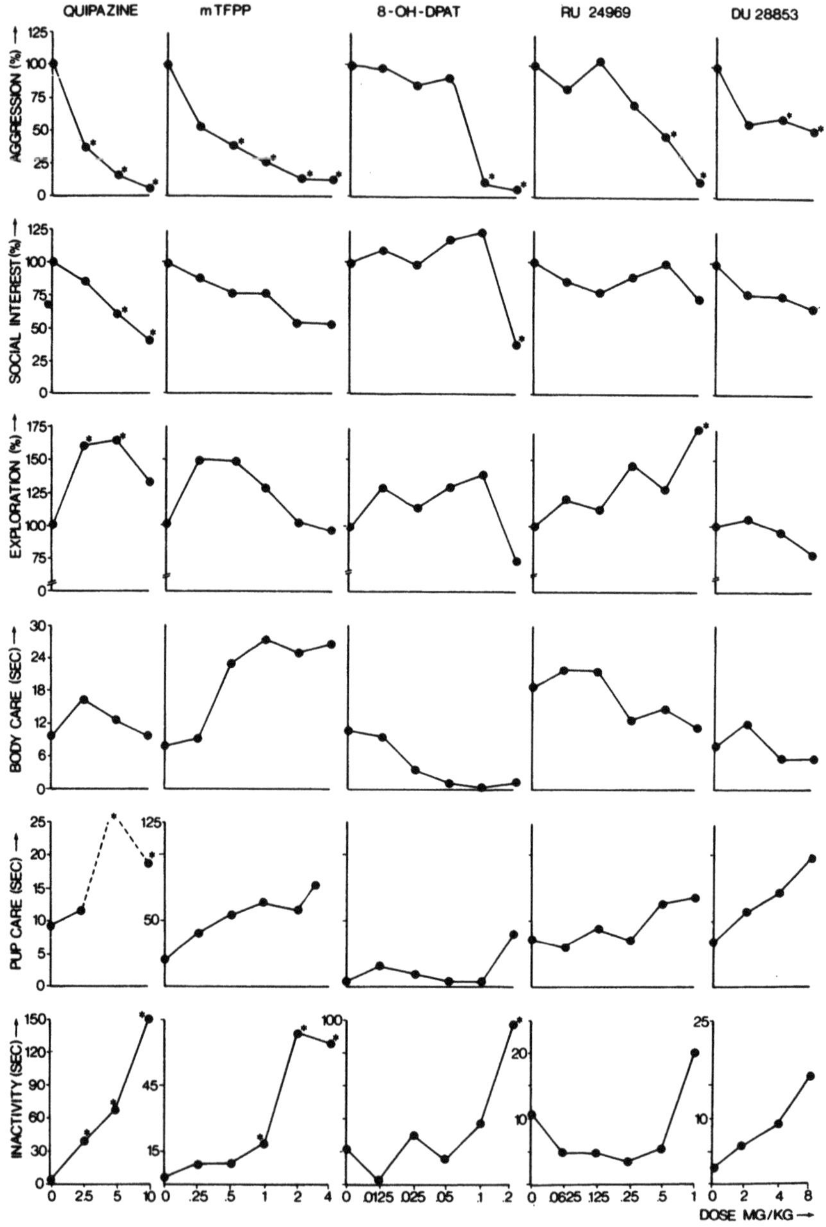

Figure 12. Effects of five serotonergic drugs on the mean duration of six behavioral categories in maternal aggression in rats. Data are expressed either as % of vehicle (0 mg/kg) or as mean duration (sec).

test compound. The test compounds were orally administered to the pairs of mice in a range of doses, and the mice were tested for fighting episodes and paralysis 60 minutes later. Pairs of mice showing three or more fighting episodes within three minutes were considered as not being protected by the test compound. Lack of paralysis was assessed by the ability of mice, hanging by their forelimbs from a thin bar to bring their hind limbs on to the bar within 3 seconds. The ED_{50}-values for antidefensive activity or flaccidity (being the dose preventing fighting episodes in half the pairs of mice, or causing paralysis), were calculated according to the method of Horn (1956). To indicate the specificity of the antidefense effect the ratio flaccidity/defense is given; high values indicate specific antidefense effects, whereas low values suggest strong interfering effects from such factors as muscle relaxation.

As can be seen from Table 7, DU 28853 has no activity in this paradigm, neither on defense nor on muscle tone. Fluprazine shows marked activity against foot shock-induced aggression in doses which do not influence muscle tone. Chlordiazepoxide, a benzodiazepine which has been added as a reference compound, nicely illustrates its well-known muscle relaxing effects. Fluvoxamine has no effect up to doses >215 mg/kg po.

Defensive Behavior of Intruders in Maternal Aggression

Those forms of agonistic behavior in which elements of initiative and approach prevail belong to offensive aggression. This

TABLE 7
Effect on Foot Shock-Induced Defense in Mice

		Oral ED_{50}-Value ± SEM (mg/kg)		
Compound	*n*	*defense*	*flaccidity*	*ratio F/D*
DU 28853	1	>46.4	>46.4	?
Fluprazine	3	2.4±0.6	>40	>20
Chlordiazepoxide	9	15.4±1.6	11.7±1.8	0.76
Fluvoxamine	3	>215	>215	?

Mean ED_{50}-value of repeated experiments
n = number of experiments

offense contrasts with defense, in which fighting is merely a response to being attacked, without initiative and essentially "reactive." Flight and submission are behaviors aimed at escaping or preventing further agonistic interactions (cf. Dixon and Kaesermann, 1987). Some of the drugs known to suppress aggression effectively have highly undesirable effects: for example, neuroleptics decrease activity, including social interest, whereas low doses of benzodiazepines may even increase aggression (Olivier et al., 1985). However, aggression is not always detrimental. Ideally, drugs should inhibit aggression but leave animals competent to deal with situations that require initiative and adequate defense and flight in response to threat and danger. To test the effects of drugs on this aspect of defensive/flight behavior, we tested drug-treated male intruders in an aggression paradigm, where they will be heavily attacked by lactating females and are strongly dependent on their own defensive capabilities.

Figure 13 summarizes the effects of several compounds (DU 28853, fluprazine, and as reference compounds chlordiazepoxide, haloperidol, d-amphetamine and naloxone) both on the behavior of the treated (direct drug effects) and untreated lactating female (indirect drug effects) and on the behavior of the treated intruder (direct drug effects). In the latter case three categories have been used to describe the behavior; *immobility,* reflecting all inactive defense behaviors such as inactive on back, crouching, inactive upright posture, sitting and lying; *defense,* reflecting all active defensive/flight elements including active upright posture, active on back (keep off lying), avoid and flight; *exploration* involving rearing, locomotion, attention and sniffing. Serenics (DU 28853 and fluprazine) clearly reduce the attacks of the lactating female when the female is treated, but have no significant effects on the (untreated) female when the intruders are treated.

Figure 13 shows the effect of acute DU 28853 treatment of the intruders on the attack behavior of the untreated females. No significant effects were noted on the frequency of bite attacks on the attack latency, although at 2 mg/kg there was a tendency of a decreased number of attacks on these intruders. This indicates that the qualities of DU 28853 treated intruders to evoke aggression from the lactating females are not drastically changed.

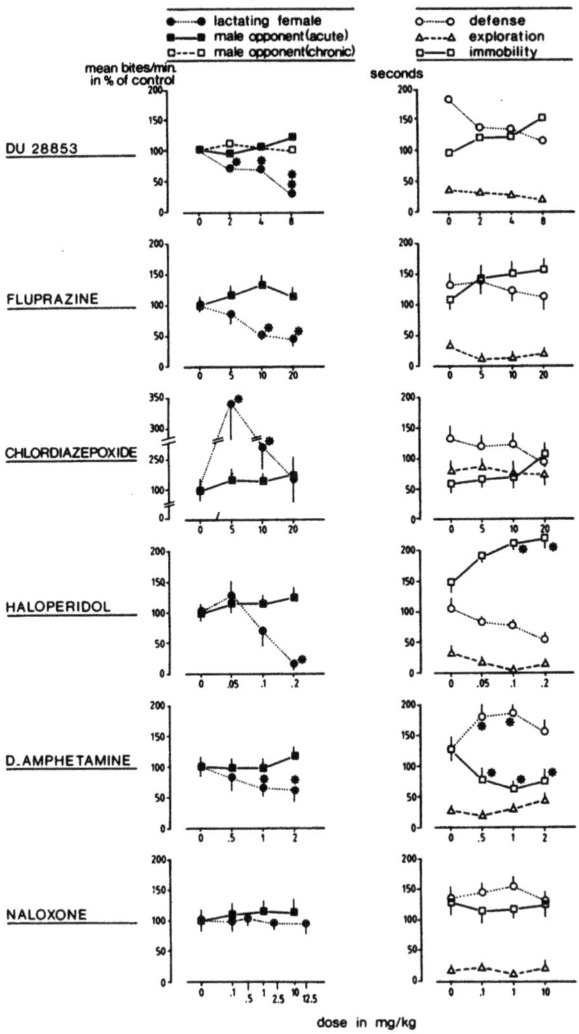

Figure 13. The effects of 6 psychotropic drugs on offensive behavior of lactating females (left-hand panel) or defensive behavior of the male intruder (right-hand panel). In the left-hand panel either the lactating female is treated (direct drug effects) or the male opponent (indirect drug effect), but in both cases the behavior of the female is recorded. In the left-hand panel the mean bites/min (± SEM) as percentage of control (=100%) are used, in the right-hand panel mean duration (± SEM) in sec.

Results of exploration, defensive behavior and immobility of male intruder rats against lactating females are summarized in fig. 13, right-hand panel. The categories (attention, social interest and flight) comprise only a very small proportion of total time. Moreover, no major effects were noted in these categories after drug treatment and they are therefore not shown. The mean duration of the behavioral categories shows some considerable variation, determined both by individual reactions of intruders and the aggression level of the lactating females. Due to this variability, exploration was never significantly changed by drug treatment of the intruder. Although amphetamine treatment increased exploration somewhat, most of the time was spent on defense. Haloperidol tended to decrease exploration, in accordance with the known sedative action of this drug. Fluprazine, CDP and naloxone did not affect exploration. Fluprazine, although effectively reducing offensive aggression, does not decrease the defensive capacities of male intruders. At the highest dose a nonsignificant decrease in defense is seen following CDP treatment of the intruders. Naloxone has no influence on defense, whereas defense is increased by d-amphetamine. Haloperidol dose-dependently reduces the time spent on defense, although this did not quite reach the 5 percent significance level. As expected, immobility increased after haloperidol and decreased after amphetamine. The other drugs, including fluprazine, did not significantly affect immobility.

Summarizing, drugs of various classes differentially influenced offense and defense in maternal aggression. CDP increased aggression at lower doses but left defense intact. Haloperidol decreased both offensive and defensive behavior, d-amphetamine suppressed offense in the lactating females but increased defense of the male opponents. Naloxone, an opiate antagonist, changed neither offense nor defense in this maternal aggression paradigm. The probable antagonism of defeat-induced analgesia (Miczek et al., 1984) apparently does not modify the behavior of the attacked opponent. Fluprazine and DU 28853 markedly suppressed offensive aggression in maternal rats but had no effect on adequate defense and flight.

These findings, although in agreement with expectations derived from the literature (Flannelly et al., 1985), suffer in part from the high levels of aggression displayed by the females in the defense experiments. This high aggressive motivation leaves little opportunity for the male intruders to display social behavior or exploration. The clear-cut dominance of the females suppresses the extent to which social interactions may develop during the test period, and may thus mask some more subtle drug effects, notably the proaggressive effects claimed for amphetamine and CDP when given to the opponent (Miczek, 1974). Nevertheless, the data obtained strengthen the unique profile of the serenics in the field of aggression, defense and social stress. Since aggression usually results in wounding the opponent (Mos et al., 1984) effective control of aggressive behavior may be very beneficial, especially for the victims. The decreased aggression, concomitant with intact integrity of social interest and defense, implies that serenics are good candidates for the effective alteration of abnormal towards adapted social behavior.

SEROTONERGIC DRUGS AND MOUSE KILLING BEHAVIOR IN RATS

When rats are confronted with a mouse, some individuals will attack and kill it, although most strains show a very low (<25%) incidence of such spontaneous behavior (Walsh, 1982). Mouse killing is classified as predatory aggression (Karli, 1956; Rossi, 1975) on the basis of its behavioral topography (seizing in the neck followed by cervical dislocation), its very short latency, and the fact that it is mostly followed by eating the prey (Rossi, 1975). Although this interspecies model certainly reflects aspects other than intraspecific agonistic behavior, it is of value in determining psychoactive properties of drugs. Moreover, by assessing the concomitant behavioral effects (scoring of sedation) a first indication can be obtained about the specificity of a drugs's inhibitory effect.

In this study, rats of the TMD-S3 strain were used, a strain which has a high spontaneous mouse killing frequency (Olivier et al., 1984b; Walsh, 1982). Experienced rats kill a mouse immediately upon confrontation; all killing latencies are reliably less than 1 min. By measuring the killing latency during a 30 min test after giving the drug 30 min. prior to the test (IP), one can estimate the *lowest effective dose* (LED) which significantly inhibits muricide.

Table 8 shows the LED's of several serotonergic compounds. Serenics (fluprazine, TFMPP, DU 28853) inhibit muricidal behavior in a specific way, both in males and females. 8-OH-DPAT does not inhibit muricide. RU 24969 effectively inhibits muricide, although some stimulatory action of the compound may interfere with the killing behavior. Quipazine, fenfluramine and fluvoxamine inhibited muricide, but not in a behaviorally specific way. Methysergide and ritanserine (5-HT antagonists) had no inhibiting effects on mouse-killing whereas 5-Me-O-DMT (a 5-HT_1 agonist) exerted a specific antimuricidal effect. Buspirone nonspecifically inhibited mouse-killing only at higher doses, whereas ipsapirone, another 5-HT_{1A} agonist, had no such effect.

TABLE 8
Effects of Serotonergic Drugs on Muricide in Rats

Drug	*LED (mg/kg IP)*		*Specificity of Inhibiting Effect**
	in Males	*in Females*	
Fluprazine	8	40	+
TFMPP	2	0.5	+
8-OH-DPAT	>5	>5	–
RU24969	1	2	+/–
DU 28853	5	20	+
Quipazine	4	4	–
Fenfluramine	2	4	–
Fluvoxamine	20	10	+/–
Methysergide	>20	>30	0
Ritanserine	>20	>20	0
5-Me-O-DMT	1	5	+
Buspirone	10	15	–
Ipsapirone	>10	>10	0

Data are expressed as LED required to inhibit mouse killing.
* + means behaviorally specific effects; – means nonspecific inhibition by e.g. sedation or motoric disturbances; 0 no inhibition.

DISCUSSION

The present contribution outlines the behavioral effects of several serotonergic drugs with different mechanisms of action on diverse aggression paradigms using mice and rats. This approach has several pitfalls, e.g. it is assumed that the effects of drugs can be solely explained by their actions on receptors in the brain, although 5-HT receptors are also located abundantly in the periphery (see Richardson and Engel, 1986). Moreover, after peripheral administration of drugs, pharmacokinetic processes may lead to unexpected pharmacodynamic results. It is therefore quite conceivable that data obtained with *in vitro* receptor binding do not directly predict actual *in vivo* (behavioral) effects. This should be kept in mind when interpreting behavioral effects although as long as clearly distinct behavioral effects are noted, one is apt to neglect the above-mentioned consideration.

The data obtained in this paper are related to the hypothesis that the behavioral changes induced by the drugs are in some way related to their *in vitro* pharmacological profile (see Tables 2 and 3 for a short summary). Table 9 summarizes, in a very general way, how the different 5-HT drugs tested exert their behavioral effects in several aggression paradigms in mice and rats.

The last column indicates the most likely serotonergic mechanism of action based on our own research and on the available literature on binding studies (e.g. Arvidsson et al., 1986) and several behavioral studies including drug discrimination (e.g. Arvidsson et al., 1986; Glennon, 1986; Glennon et al., 1982, 1984). Although we still lack drugs with certain specific 5-HT properties, e.g. 5-HT_2 agonists and 5-HT_1(A and B) antagonists, the available data summarized in Table 4 suggest that the 5-HT_{1B} binding site plays a specific modulatory role in aggressive behavior. The 5-HT_{1A} site does not seem to play a specific role because 8-OH-DPAT, 5-Me-O-DMT, buspirone and ipsapirone either have no anti-aggressive activity or display a nonspecific effect. Moreover, the 5-HT_2 site also seems not to be directly involved in the modulation of aggressive behavior, although the lack of more specific 5-HT_2 agonists means that this statement cannot be verified. A similar argument may hold for the $5\text{-}HT_3$ site, although it is not even clear whether there is a central location where $5\text{-}HT_3$ ligands may bind.

Of course, almost every compound will eventually cause an inhibition of aggressive behavior, but it is assumed that such an effect must be specific on aggression and should not involve effects on other behavioral systems, like exploration, motor activity, defensive capabilities and social interest. The use of ethological methodologies shows that it is possible to simultaneously measure these several aspects of agonistic behavior occurring between competing conspecifics, whether they are mice or rats (see Olivier et al., 1984b, 1986a). On the basis of this simultaneous measurement of all ongoing behavior, we have developed a new class of psychoactive drugs termed "serenics" (Olivier et al., 1986d; Olivier and Mos, 1986b; Bradford et al., 1984). Serenics, represented here by fluprazine and DU 28853, appear to have their main effects on the 5-HT neuronal systems, especially via the $5\text{-}HT_{1B}$ binding sites, although a contribution from the $5\text{-}HT_{1A}$ site cannot be completely ruled out. Therefore, the general hypothesis that 5-HT activity is inversely correlated with aggression seems no longer tenable. A more refined hypothesis should specify a role for $5\text{-}HT_{1B}$ receptors.

Before this can be done, a considerable amount of work has to be performed and new pharmacological tools (especially specific $5\text{-}HT_{1A}$ and $5\text{-}HT_{1B}$ antagonists and $5\text{-}HT_2$, $5\text{-}HT_3$ agonists) have to be available.

The presence of $5\text{-}HT_{1B}$ receptors in several areas known to be involved in the modulation of agonistic behavior (Albert et al., 1982) lends support to a direct regulation of such behavior by a $5\text{-}HT_{1B}$-related mechanism.

The different 5-HT receptor types have been shown to be differentially localized in the CNS by the use of quantitative autoradiography (Pazos and Palacios, 1985; Pazos et al., 1985). $5\text{-}HT_{1B}$ sites were present in high density in the globus pallidus, dorsal subiculum, substantia nigra and the olivary pretectal nucleus, whereas the highest density of $5\text{-}HT_{1A}$ sites was found in the dentate gyrus of the hippocampus and the lateroseptal nucleus. The neocortex and the hypothalamus also showed high concentration of both types of receptors. In contrast, the density of $5\text{-}HT_1$ receptors in the brainstem and spinal cord was low.

TABLE 9

Effects of Serotonergic Drugs on Several Aggression Paradigms in Mice (m) and Rats (r)

Drug	Isolation Induced Aggression (m)	Intermale Aggression (m)	Footshock induced Defense (m)	Resident-Intruder Aggression (r)	Maternal Aggression (r)	EBS (r)	Muricide (r)	*Putative 5-HT mechanism of action*
Fluprazine	↓	(↓)	(↓)	(↓)	(↓)	(↓)	(↓)	1A,1B and 2 agonist
TFMPP	↓	(↓)	nt	(↓)	(↓)	(↓)	(↓)	1B-agonist (partial)
DU 28853	↓	(↓)	—	(↓)	(↓)	(↓)	(↓)	1A,1B-agonist (partial)
RU24969	↓	(↓)	nt	nt	(↓)	nt	↓	1A,1B-agonist
5-Me-O-DMT	↓	nt	nt	↓	nt	nt	↓	1A-agonist
Quipazine	—	nt	nt	↓	↓	↓	↓	weak 1,2-agonist
8-OH-DPAT	↓	↓	nt	nt	↓	—	—	1A-agonist
Buspirone	—	nt	nt	↓	↓	nt	↓	1A-agonist
Ipsapirone	—	nt	nt	nt	↓	nt	—	1A-agonist
Fluvoxamine	↓	↓	nt	↓	(↓)	↓	↓	reuptake blocker
Methysergide	—	nt	nt	nt	—	—	—	1,2-antagonist
Ritanserine	—	nt	nt	nt	—	nt	—	2-antagonist
Fenfluramine	↓	nt	nt	↓	↓	nt	↓	release
MDL 72222	—	nt	nt	nt	—	nt	nt	3-antagonist

(↓) specific behavioral decrease; ↓ nonspecific behavioral decrease; — no effect; nt not tested. EBS = Electrical brain stimulation-induced aggression.

Moreover, it should not be forgotten that 5-HT is very widely involved in many other kinds of behavioral and motoric systems (see reviews by Green, 1985; Osborne, 1982; Soubrié, 1986). Recent evidence shows that 8-OH-DPAT enhances food intake (Dourish et al., 1985) and sexual behavior (Ahlenius et al., 1981). In contrast, specific 5-HT_{1B} agonists like TFMPP decrease food intake and sexual behavior (Olivier, 1987). This holds also for the mixed 5-$HT_{1A/1B}$ agonists DU 28853 and RU24969 (Olivier, unpublished results).

It is clear that further studies await the development of more specific, 5-HT pharmacological tools and localized brain studies which will facilitate the unravelling of the complex modulation by 5-HT receptor subtypes of agonistic and other behaviors.

REFERENCES

Adams, D.B. (1976). The relation of scent-marking, olfactory investigation, and specific postures in the isolation-induced fighting of rats. *Behaviour,* 56, 286–297.

Ahlenius, S., Larsson, K., Svensson, L., Hjorth A., & Carlsson, A., et al. (1981). Effects of a new type of 5-HT receptor agonist on male rat sexual behavior. *Pharmacol Biochem Behav, 15,* 785–792.

Albert, D. J., & Walsh, M. L. (1982). The inhibitory modulation of agonistic behavior in the rat brain: A review. *Neurosci Biobehav Rev, 6,* 125–143.

Applegate, C. D. (1980). 5,7-Dihydroxytryptamine-induced mouse killing and behavioral reversal with ventricular administration of serotonin in rats. *Behav Neural Biol, 30,* 178–190.

Arvidsson, L. E., Hacksell, U., & Glennon, R. A. (1986). Recent advances in central 5-hydroxytryptamine receptor agonists and antagonists. *Progress in Drug Research,* Vol. *30,* Birkhaüser Verlag, Basel, Boston, Stuttgart, pp. 365–471.

Baenninger, R. (1978). Some aspects of predatory behavior. *Aggr Behav, 4,* 287–311.

Barnett, S. A. (1975). *The Rat. A Study in Behavior.* The University of Chicago Press: Chicago and London.

Bermond, B., Mos, J., Meelis, W., Poel v.d., A. M., & Kruk, M. R. (1982). Aggression induced by stimulation of the hypothalamus: Effects of androgens. *Pharmacol Biochem Behav, 16,* 41–45.

Blanchard, R. J., & Blanchard, D. C. (1977). Aggressive behavior in the rat. *Behav Biol, 21,* 197–224.

Blanchard, R. J., & Blanchard, D. C. (1981). The organisation and modelling of animal aggression. In P. F. Brain & D. Benton (Eds.), *The Biology of Aggression.* Sijthof and Noordhoff, Alphen a.d. Rijn, pp. 529–561.

Blanchard, D. C., & Blanchard, R. J. (1984). Affect and aggression: An animal model applied to human behavior. In R. J. Blanchard & D. C. Blanchard (Eds.), *Advances in the Study of Aggression,* Vol I. Academic Press, Orlando, pp. 1–62.

Blanchard, R. J., & Blanchard, D. C. (1987). Alcohol and aggression in animal models. In B. Olivier, J. Mos, & P. F. Brain (Eds.), *Ethopharmacology of Agonistic Behavior in Animals and Humans.* Martinus Nijhoff, Dordrecht, pp. 145–161.

Blanchard, R. J., Blanchard, D. C., & Takahashi, L. K. (1977a). Reflexive fighting in the albino rat: Aggressive or defensive behavior? *Aggr Behav, 3,* 145–155.

Blanchard, R. J., Blanchard, D. C., Takahashi, L. K., & Kelly, M. J. (1977b). Attack and defensive behaviour in the albino rat. *Anim Behav, 25,* 622–634.

Blanchard, R. J., Blanchard, D. C., & Takahashi, L. K. (1978). Pain and aggression in the rat. *Behav Biol, 23,* 291–305.

Blanchard, R. J., O'Donnell, V., & Blanchard, D. C. (1979). Attack and defensive behaviors in the albino mouse (Mus musculus). *Aggr Behav, 5,* 341–352.

Bradford, L. D., Olivier, B., Van Dalen, D., & Schipper J. (1984) Serenics: The pharmacology of fluprazine and DU 28412. In K. A. Miczek, M. R. Kruk, & B. Olivier (Eds.), *Ethopharmacological Aggression Research.* Alan R. Liss, New York, pp. 191–207.

Braestrup, Squires R. F. (1987). Pharmacological characterisation of benzodiazepine receptors in the brain. *Eur J Pharmacol, 48,* 263–270.

Brain, P. F. (1975). What does individual housing mean to a mouse? *Life Sci, 16,* 187–200.

Brain, P. F. (1986). *Alcohol and Aggression.* Croom Helm, London.

Burt, D. R., Creese, I., & Snyder, S. H. (1976). Properties of (^{3}H) haloperidol and (^{3}H) dopamine binding associated with dopamine receptors in calf brain membranes. *Mol Pharmacol, 12,* 800–812.

Carlsson, A., Davis, J. N., Kehr, W., Lindquist, M., & Atack, C. V. (1972). Simultaneous measurement of tyrosine and tryptophan hydroxylase activities in brain in vivo using an inhibitor of the aromatic amino acid decarboxylase. *Naunyn-Schmiedeberg's Arch Pharmacol, 275,* 153–168.

Claassen, V. C., Davies, J. E., Hertting, G., & Placheta, P. (1979). Fluvoxamine, a specific 5-hydroxytryptamine uptake inhibitor. *Br J Pharmacol, 60,* 505–516.

Crawley, J. N., Schleidt, W. M., & Contrera, J. F. (1975). Does social environment decrease propensity to fight in male mice? *Behav Biol, 15,* 73–83.

Creese, I., Schneider, R., & Snyder, S. H. (1977). (^{3}H) Spiroperidol labels dopamine receptors in rat pituitary and brain. *Eur J Pharmacol, 46,* 377–381.

Creese, I., & Snyder, S. H. (1978). (^{3}H) Spiroperidol labels serotonin receptors in rat cerebral cortex and hippocampus. *Eur J Pharmacol, 49,* 201–202.

Daruna, J. H. (1978). Patterns of brain monoamine activity and aggressive behavior. *Neurosci Biobehav Rev, 2,* 101–113.

DeBold, J. F., & Miczek, K. A. (1984). Aggression persists after ovariectomy in female rats. *Horm Behav, 18,* 177–190.

Dijkstra, H., Olivier, B., & Mos, J. (1984). Dominance maintenance and intruder attack in laboration colonies of rats: Different models for the psychopharmacological control of aggression. *Aggr Behav, 10,* 149.

Dixon, A. K., & Kaesermann, H. P. (1987). Ethopharmacology of flight behavior. In B. Olivier, J. Mos, & P. F. Brain (Eds.), *Ethopharmacology of Agonistic Behaviour* in *Animals and Humans.* Martinus Nijhoff, Dordrecht, pp. 46–79.

Dourish, C. T., Hutson, P. H., & Curzon, G. (1985). Characteristics of feeding induced by the serotonin agonist 8-hydroxy-2-(Di-n-propylamino) tetralin (8-OH-DPAT). *Brain Res Bull, 15,* 377–384.

Eichelman, B. S., & Thoa, N. B. (1973). The aggressive monoamines. *Biol Psychiatry, 6,* 143–164.

Engel, G., Göthert, M., Hoyer, D., Schlicker, E., & Hillenbrand, K. (1986). Identity of inhibitory presynaptic 5-hydroxytryptamine (5-HT) autoreceptors in the rat brain cortex with 5-HT$_{1B}$ binding sites. Naunyn-Schmiedeberg's *Arch Pharmacol, 332,* 1–7.

Erskine, M. S., Barfield, R. J., & Goldman, B. D. (1978a). Intraspecific fighting during late pregnancy and lactation in rats and effects of litter removal. *Behav Biol, 23,* 206–218.

Erskine, M. S., Barfield, R. J., & Goldman, B. D. (1980). Postpartum aggression in rats: II Dependence on maternal sensitivity to young and effects of experience with pregnancy and parturition. *Comp Physiol Zool, 94,* 495–505.

Erskine, M. S., Denenberg, V., H., & Goldman, B. D. (1978b). Aggression in the lactating rat: Effects of intruder age and test arena. *Behav Biol, 23,* 52–66.

Flannelly, K. J., Muraoka, M. Y., & Blanchard, D. C. (1985). Specific antiaggressive effects of fluprazine hydrochloride. *Psychopharmacology, 87,* 86–89.

Floody, O. R. (1983). Hormones and aggression in female animals. In B. B. Svare (Ed.), *Hormones and Aggressive Behaviour.* Plenum Press, New York and London, pp. 39–89.

Floody, O. R., & Pfaff, D. W. (1977). Aggressive behaviour among female hamsters: The hormonal basis for fluctuations in female aggressiveness correlated with estrous state. *J Comp Physiol Psychol, 91,* 443–446.

Garattini S., & Valzelli, L. (1981). Is the isolated animal a possible model for phobia and anxiety? *Progr Neuro-Psychopharmacol, 5,* 159–165.

Glennon, R. A. (1986). Site selective serotonin agonists as discriminative stimuli. *Psychopharmacology, 89* (S1), 135.

Glennon, R. A., McKenney, J. D., & Young, R. (1984). Discrimination stimulus properties of the serotonin agonist 1-(3-trifluoromethylphenyl) piperazine (TFMPP). *Life Sci, 35,* 1475–1480.

Glennon, R. A., Rosecrans, J. A., & Young, R. (1982). The use of the drug discrimination paradigm for studying hallucinogenic agents. In F. C. Colpaert, & J. L. Slangen (Eds.), *Drug Discrimination: Applications in CNS Pharmacology.* Elsevier Biomedical Press, Amsterdam, pp. 69–98.

Göthert, M. (1980). Serotonin receptor mediated modulation of Ca^{2+} dependent 5-hydroxytryptamine release from neurones of the rat brain cortex. Naunyn-Schmiedeberg's *Arch Pharmacol, 314,* 223–230.

Gozlan, H., El Mestikawy, S., Pichat, L., Glowinsky, J., & Hamon, M. (1983). Identification of presynaptic serotonin autoreceptors using a new ligand: ^{3}H-PAT. *Nature, 305,* 140–142.

Green, A. R. (1985). *Neuropharmacology of Serotonin.* Oxford University Press, Oxford, pp. 1–436.

Herschel, M., & Baldessarini, R. J. (1979). Evidence for two types of binding of (^{3}H) GABA and (^{3}H) muscimol in rat cerebral cortex and cerebellum. *Life Sci,* 1849–1854.

Hiller, J. M., & Simon, E. J. (1980). Specific high affinity (^{3}H) ethylketocyclazocine binding in rat central nervous system: Lack of evidence for k-receptors. *J Pharmacol Exp Ther, 214,* 516–519.

Hinde, R. A. (1974). *Biological Bases of Human Social Behaviour.* McGraw-Hill, New York.

Horn, H. J. (1956). Simplified LD_{50} (or ED_{50}) calculations. *Biometrics, 12,* 311–322.

Hoyer, D., Engel, G., & Kalkman, H. O. (1985). Molecular pharmacology of 5-HT_1 and 5-HT_2 recognition sites in rat and pig brain membranes. Radioligand binding studies with [^{3}H] 5-HT, [^{3}H] 8-OH-DPAT, (–) [^{125}I] iodocyanopindolol, [^{3}H] mesulergine, and [^{3}H] ketanserin. *Eur J Pharmacol, 118,* 13–23.

Janssen, P. A. J., Jagenau, A. H. M., & Schellekens, K. H. J. (1960). Chemistry and pharmacology of compounds related to 4-(4-hydroxy-4-phenyl-piperidino)-butyrophenone. Part IV. Influence of haloperidol (R 1625) and of chlorpromazine on the behavior of rats in an unfamiliar "open field" situation. *Psychopharmacologia, 1,* 389–392.

Kantak, K. M., Hegstrand, L. R., & Eichelman, B. (1981). Facilitation of shock-induced fighting following intraventricular 5,7-dihydroxytryptamine and 6-hydroxy dopa. *Psychopharmacology, 74,* 157–160.

Karli, P. (1956). The Norway rat's response to the white mouse: An experimental analysis. *Behaviour, 10,* 81–103.

Knutson, J. F., Kane, N. L., Schlosberg, A. J., Fordyce, D. J., & Simansky, K. J. (1979). Influence of PCPA, shock level, and home cage conditions on shock-induced aggression. *Physiol Behav, 23,* 897–907.

Koolhaas, J. M. (1978). Hypothalamically induced intraspecific aggressive behavior in the rat. *Exp Brain Res, 32,* 365–375.

Krsiak, M. (1974). Behavioral changes and aggressivity evoked by drugs in mice. *Res Comm Chem Pathol Pharmacol, 7,* 253–257.

Krsiak, M. (1975). Timid singly-housed mice: Their value in prediction of psychotropic activity of drugs. *Br J Pharmacol, 55,* 141–150.

Krsiak, M. (1979). Effects of drugs on behaviour of aggressive mice. *Br J Pharmacol, 65,* 525–533.

Kruk, M. R., & Van der Poel, A. M. (1980). Is there evidence for a neural correlate of an aggressive behavioural system in the hypothalamus of the rat? *Prog Brain Res, 53,* 385–390.

Kruk, M. R., Van der Poel, A. M., & De Vos-Frerichs, T. P. (1979). The induction of aggressive behaviour by electrical stimulation in the hypothalamus of male rats. *Behaviour, 70,* 292–322.

Kruk, M. R., Van der Laan, C. E., Mos, J., Van der Poel, A. M., Meelis, W., & Olivier, B. (1984). Comparison of aggressive behaviour induced by electrical stimulation in the hypothalamus of male and female rats. *Progr Brain Res, 61,* 303–314.

Kruk, M. R., Van der Poel, A. M., Lammers, J. H. C. M., Hagg, T., De Hey, A. M. D. M., & Oostvegel, S. (1987). Ethopharmacology of hypothalamic aggression in the rat. In B. Olivier, J. Mos, P. F. Brain (Eds.), *Ethopharmacology of Agonistic Behaviour in Animals and Humans.* Martinus Nijhoff, Dordrecht, pp. 33–45.

Kruk, M. R., Van der Poel, A. M., Meelis, W., Hermans, J., Mostert, P. G., Mos, J., & Lohman, A. H. M. (1983). Discriminant analysis of the localization of aggression-inducing electrode placements in the hypothalamus of male rats. *Brain Res, 260,* 61–79.

Lehman, M. N., & Adams, D. B. (1977). A statistical and motivational analysis of the social behaviors of the male laboratory rat. *Behaviour, 61,* 238–275.

Leslie, F. M., Chavkin, C., & Cox, B. M. (1980). Opioid binding properties of brain and peripheral tissues: Evidence for heterogeneity in opioid ligand binding sites. *J Pharmacol Exp Ther, 214,* 395–402.

Lore, R., & Flannelly, K. (1977). Rat societies. *Sci Am, 236,* 106–116.

Malick, J. B. (1979). The pharmacology of isolation-induced aggressive behavior in mice. In W. B. Essman, & L. Valzelli (Eds.), *Current Developments in Psychopharmacology.* New York, Spectrum Publications Inc., Vol. 5: 1–27.

Miczek, K. A. (1974). Intraspecies aggression in rats: Effects of d-amphetamine and chlordiazepoxide. *Psychopharmacology, 39,* 275–301.

Miczek, K. A. (1979). A new test for aggression in rats without aversive stimulation: Differential effects of d-amphetamine and cocaine. *Psychopharmacology, 60,* 253–259.

Miczek, K. A. (1987). The psychopharmacology of aggression. In L. L. Iversen, S. D. Iversen, & S. H. Snyder (Eds.), *Handbook of Psychopharmacology.* Vol. 19: *Behavioural Pharmacology.* New York: Plenum Press, pp. 183–328.

Miczek, K. A., & Barry, H. (III) (1976). Pharmacology of sex and aggression. In S. D. Glick, & J. Goldfarb (Eds.), *Behavioural Pharmacology.* C. V. Mosby, St. Louis, pp. 176–257.

Miczek, K. A., DeBold, J. F., & Thompson, M. L. (1984). Pharmacological, hormonal and behavioral manipulation in the analysis of aggressive behavior. In K. A. Miczek, M. R. Kruk, & B. Olivier (Eds.), *Ethopharmacological Aggression Research.* Alan R. Liss, New York, pp. 1–16.

Miczek, K. A., & Krsiak, M. (1979). Drug effects on agonistic behaviour. In T. Thompson & P. B. Dews (Eds.), *Advances in Behavioral Pharmacology.* New York, Academic Press, Vol. 2, 87–162.

Miczek, K. A., & Krsiak, M. (1981). Pharmacological analysis of attack and flight. In P. F. Brain & D. Benton (Eds.), *Multidisciplinary Approaches to Aggression Research.* Elsevier/North-Holland Biomedical Press, pp. 341–354.

Miczek, K. A., & O'Donnell, J. M. (1978). Intruder-evoked aggression in isolated and nonisolated mice: Effects of psychomotor stimulants and l-dopa. *Psychopharmacology, 57,* 47–55.

Miczek, K. A., & Winslow, J. T. (1986). Psychopharmacological research on aggressive behaviour. In A. J. Greenshaw & C. T. Dourish (Eds.), *Experimental Psychopharmacology.* Humana Press, Clifton, New Jersey, pp. 27–113.

Middlemiss, D. N. (1984). 8-hydroxy-2-(di-n-propylamino) tetralin is devoid of activity at the 5-hydroxytryptamine autoreceptor in rat brain. *Naunyn-Schmiedeberg's Arch Pharmacol, 327,* 18–22.

Middlemiss, D. N., & Fozard, J. R. (1983). 8-hydroxy-2-(di-n-propylamino) tetralin discriminates between subtypes of the 5-HT_1 recognition sites. *Eur J Pharmacol, 90,* 151–153.

Mos, J., & Olivier, B. (1986). Ro 15-1788 does not influence post-partum aggression in lactating female rats. *Psychopharmacology, 90,* 278–280.

Mos, J., & Olivier, B. (1987). Pro-aggressive actions of benzodiazepines. In B. Olivier, J. Mos, & P. F. Brain (Eds.), *Ethopharmacology of Agonistic Behaviour in Animals and Humans.* Martinus Nijhoff, Dordrecht, pp. 187–206.

Mos, J., Olivier, B., Lammers, J. H. C. M., Van der Poel, A. M., Kruk, M. R., & Zethof, T. (1987). Pregnancy and lactation do not interact with current thresholds for brain stimulation-induced aggression in female rats. *Brain Res, 404,* 263–266.

Mos, J., Olivier, B., Van Oorschot, R., & Dijkstra, H. (1984). Different test situations for measuring offensive aggression in male rats do not result in the same wound patterns. *Physiol Behav, 32,* 453–456.

Moyer, K. E. (1976). *The Phychobiology of Aggression.* Harper & Row, Publishers: New York. Hagerstown, San Francisco, London.

Mühlbauer (1985). Human aggression and the role of central serotonin. *Pharmacopsychiatry, 18,* 218–221.

Muller, W. E., & Snyder, S. H. (1978). Strychnine binding associated with synaptic glycine receptors in rat spinal cord membranes: Ionic influences. *Brain Res, 147,* 107–116.

Nahorski, S. (1978). Heterogeneity of cerebral adrenoceptor binding sites in various vertebrate species. *Eur J Pharmacol, 51,* 199–209.

Olivier, B. (1977). The ventromedial hypothalamus and aggressive behavior in rats. *Aggr Behav, 3,* 47–56.

Olivier, B. (1981). Selective anti-aggressive properties of DU 27725: Ethological analysis of intermale and territorial aggression in the male rat. *Pharmacol Biochem Behav, 14* (S1), 61–77.

Olivier, B. (1987). *Pharmacological Properties of DU 28853.* Internal Duphar Report, pp. 1–296.

Olivier, B., & Mos, J. (1986a). A female aggression paradigm for use in psychopharmacology: Maternal agonistic behaviour in rats. In P. F. Brain & J. M. Ramirez (Eds.), *Cross-Disciplinary Studies on Aggression.* University of Seville Press, pp. 73–111.

Olivier, B., Mos, J., & Schipper, J. (1986a). Serotonin and aggressive behaviour in the rat. *Psychopharmacology, 89,* 26.

Olivier, B., & Mos, J. (1986b). Serenics and aggression. *Stress Med, 2,* 197–209.

Olivier, B., Mos, J., Schipper, J., Tulp, M. T. M., Van der Heyden, J. A. M., Berkelmans, B., & Bevan, P. (1987). Serotonergic modulation of agonistic behaviour. In B. Olivier, J. Mos, & P. F. Brain (Eds.), *Ethopharmacological Analysis of Agonistic Behaviour* in *Animals and Humans.* Martinus Nijhoff, Dordrecht, pp. 162–186.

Olivier, B., Mos, J., & Van Oorschot, R. (1985). Maternal aggression in rats: Effects of chlordiazepoxide and fluprazine. *Psychopharmacology, 86,* 68–76.

Olivier, B., Mos, J., & Van Oorschot, R. (1986b). Maternal aggression in rats: Lack of interaction between chlordiazepoxide and fluprazine. *Psychopharmacology, 88,* 40–43.

Olivier, B., Olivier-Aardema, R. L., & Wiepkema, P. R. (1983). Effect of anterior hypothalamic and mammillary area lesions on territorial aggressive behaviour in male rats. *Behav Brain Res, 9,* 59–81.

Olivier, B., Schipper, J., & Tulp, M. T. M. (1986c). 5-hydroxytryptamine agonists: Neurochemical profile and effects on aggressive behavior. *Br J Pharmacol, 89* (suppl), 648P.

Olivier, B., Van Aken, H., Jaarsma, I., Van Oorschot, R., Zethof, T., & Bradford, L. D. (1984a). Behavioural effects of psychoactive drugs on agonistic behaviour of male territorial rats (resident-intruder paradigm). In K. A. Miczek, M. R. Kruk, & B. Olivier (Eds.), *Ethopharmacological Aggression Research.* Alan R. Liss Inc, New York, pp. 137–156.

Olivier, B., & Van Dalen, D. (1982). Social behavior in rats and mice: An ethologically based model for differentiating psychoactive drugs. *Aggr Behav, 8,* 163–168.

Olivier, B., Van Dalen, D., & Hartog, J. (1986d). A new class of psychoactive drugs: Serenics. *Drugs of the Future, 11,* 473–499.

Olivier, B., Van Oorschot, R., Boschman, T. A. C., Van der Heyden, J. A. M., Schipper, J., & Mol, F. (1984b). Mouse killing in male TMD-S3 rats: Incidence of killing and the effects of experience, castration and pharmacological manipulations. *Aggr Behav, 10,* 165–166.

Osborne, N. N. (1982). *Biology of Serotonergic Transmission.* John Wiley & Sons, Chichester, pp. 1–522.

Payne, A. P., & Swanson, H. H. (1970). Agonistic behaviour between pairs of hamsters of same and opposite sex in a neutral observation area. *Behaviour, 36,* 259–269.

Pazos, A., Cortes, R., & Palacios, J. M. (1985). Quantitative autoradiographic mapping of serotonin receptors in the rat brain. II. Serotonin-2 receptors. *Brain Res, 346,* 231–249.

Pazos, A., & Palacios, J. M. (1985). Quantitative autoradiographic mapping of serotonin receptors in rat brain. I. Serotonin-1 receptors. *Brain Res, 346,* 205–230.

Peroutka, S. J. (1986). Pharmacological differentiation and characterization of 5-HT_{1A}, 5-HT_{1B}, and 5-HT_{1C} binding sites in rat frontal cortex. *J Neurochem, 47,* 529–540.

Pert, C. B., & Snyder, S. H. (1974). Opiate receptor binding of agonists and antagonists affected differentially by sodium. *Mol Pharmacol, 10,* 868–879.

Pradhan, S. N. (1975). Aggression and central neurotransmitters. In C. C. Pfeiffer & J. M. Smythies (Eds.), *International Review of Neurobiology.* Academic Press, New York, pp. 213–262.

Richardson, B. P., & Engel, G. (1986). The pharmacology and function of 5-HT_3 receptors. *TINS,* pp. 424–428.

Rodgers, R. J. (1979). Neurochemical correlates of aggressive behaviour: Some relations to emotion and pain sensitivity. In K. Brown & S. J. Cooper (Eds.), *Chemical Influences on Behaviour.* Academic Press, New York, pp. 374–419.

Rodgers, R. J. (1981). Drugs, aggression and behavioural methods. In P. F. Brain & D. Benton (Eds.), *Multidisciplinary Approaches to Aggression Research.* Elsevier/North-Holland Biomedical Press,Amsterdam, New York, Oxford, 325–340.

Rossi, A. C. (1975). The "mouse-killing" rat: Ethological discussion on an experimental model of aggression. *Pharmacol Res Commun, 7,* 199–216.

Sbordone, R. J., Gorelick, D. A., & Elliot, M. L. (1981). An ethological analysis of drug-induced pathological aggression. In P. F. Brain & D. Benton (Eds.), *Multidisciplinary Approaches to Aggression Research.* Elsevier/North-Holland Biomedical Press—Amsterdam, New York—Oxford, pp. 369–385.

Scott, J. P. (1966). Agonistic behavior in mice and rats: A review. *Am Zool, 6,* 683–701.

Shannon, N. J., Gunnet, J. W., & Moore, K. E. (1986). A comparison of biochemical indices of 5-hydroxytryptaminergic neuronal activity following electrical stimulation of the dorsal nucleus. *J Neurochem, 47,* 958–965.

Sheard, M. H., & Davis, M. (1976). Shock-elicited fighting in rats: Importance of intershock interval upon the effect of p-chlorophenylalanine (PCPA). *Brain Res, 111,* 433–437.

Sills, M. A., Wolfe, B. B., & Frazer, A. (1984). Determination of selective and non-selective compounds for the 5-HT and 5-HT_{1B} receptor subtypes in rat frontal cortex. *J Pharmacol Exp Ther, 231,* 480–487.

Simantov, R., Childers, S. R., & Snyder, S. H. (1978). The opiate receptor binding interactions of (^{3}H) methionine enkephalin, an opioid peptide. *Eur J Pharmacol, 47,* 319–331.

Smith, D. E., King, M. B., & Hoebel, B. G. (1970). Lateral hypothalamic control of killing: Evidence for a cholinoceptive mechanism. *Science, 167,* 900–901.

Soubrié, P. (1986). Reconciling the role of central serotonin neurons in human and animal behavior. *Behav Brain Sci, 9,* 319–364.

Steinbusch, H. W. M. (1981). Distribution of serotonin-immunoreactivity in the central nervous system of the rat—Cell bodies and terminals. *Neurosci, 6,* 557–618.

Svare, B. (1977). Maternal aggression in mice: Influence of the young. *Biobehav Rev, 1,* 151–164.

Svare, B. (1981). Models of aggression employing female rodents. In P. F. Brain & D. Benton (Eds.), *The Biology of Aggression.* Sijthoff and Noordhoff, Alphen a.d. Rijn, The Netherlands, pp. 503–508.

Svare, B., & Gandelman, R. (1973). Postpartum aggression in mice: Experimental and environmental factors. *Horm Behav, 4,* 323–334.

Svare, B. B., & Mann, M. A. (1983). Hormonal influences on maternal aggression. In B. Svare (Ed.), *Hormones and Aggressive Behavior.* Plenum Press, New York and London, pp. 91–104.

Svare, B., Mann, M., & Samuels, O. (1980). Mice: Suckling stimulation but not lactation important for maternal aggression. *Behav Neural Biol, 29,* 453–462.

Takahashi, L. K., & Lore, R. K. (1982). Intermale and maternal aggression in adult rats tested at different ages. *Physiol Behav, 29,* 1013–1018.

Taylor, R. L., & Burt, D. R. (1981). Preparation of ^{3}H-[3]Me-His^2] as an improved ligand for TRH receptors. *Neuroendocrinology, 32,* 310–316.

Tedeschi, R. E., Tedeschi, D. H., Mucha, A., Cook, L., Mattis, P. A., & Fellows, E. J. (1959). Effect of various centrally acting drugs of fighting behaviour on mice. *J Pharmacol Exp Ther, 125,* 28–34.

Timmermans, P. B. M. W. N., Karamat, A. F., Kwa, H. Y., & Schoop, A. M. C. (1981). Identical antagonist selectivity of central and peripheral alpha$_1$-adrenergic receptors. *Mol Pharmacol, 20,* 295–301.

Timmermans, P. J. A. (1978). *Social Behaviour in the Rat.* PhD Thesis, University of Nijmegen.

Tran, Y. T., Chang, R. S. L., & Snyder, S. H. (1978). Histamine H$_1$ receptors identified in mammalian brain membranes with (^{3}H) mepyramine. *Proc Natl Acad Sci U.S.A., 75,* 6290–6294.

Tricklebank, M. D. (1985). The behavioral response to 5-HT receptor agonists and subtypes of the central 5-HT receptor. *Trends Pharmacol Sci*, pp. 403–407.

Ulrich, R. E., & Azrin, N. H., (1962). Reflexive fighting in response to aversive stimulation. *J Exp Anal Behav, 5*, 511–520.

U'Prichard, D. C., Greenberg, D. A., & Snyder, S. H. (1977). Binding characteristics of a radiolabelled agonist and antagonist at central nervous system alpha-noradrenergic receptors. *Mol Pharmacol, 13*, 455–473.

Valzelli, L. (1969). Aggressive behaviour induced by isolation. In S. Garattini & E. B. Sigg (Eds.), *Aggressive Behaviour.* John Wiley & Sons, New York, pp. 70–76.

Valzelli, L. (1973). The "isolation syndrome" in mice. *Psychopharmacologia, 31*, 305–320.

Valzelli, L. (1978). *Psychopharmacology of Aggression*. Basel: Karger.

Valzelli, L. (1981). Psychopharmacology of aggression: An overview. *Int Pharmacopsychiatry, 16*, 39–48.

Valzelli, L. (1984). Reflections on experimental and human pathology of aggression. *Progr Neuropsychopharmacol Biol Psychiatry, 8*, 311–325.

Valzelli, L., & Garattini, S. (1968). Behavioral changes and 5-hydroxytryptamine turnover in animals. *Adv Pharmacol, 6B*, 249–260.

Valzelli, L., Garattini, S., Bernasconi, S., & Sala, A. (1981). Neurochemical correlates of muricidal behavior in rats. *Neuropsychobiology, 7*, 172–178.

Van der Poel, A. M., Mos, J., Kruk, M. R., & Olivier, B. (1984). A motivational analysis of ambivalent actions in the agonistic behaviour of rats in tests used to study effects of drugs on aggression. In K. A. Miczek, M. R. Kruk, & B. Olivier (Eds.), *Ethopharmacological Aggression Research*. Alan R. Liss Inc, New York, pp. 115–135.

Van der Poel, A. M., Olivier, B., Mos, J., Kruk, M. R., Meelis, W., & Van Aken, J. H. M. (1982). Anti-aggressive effect of a new phenylpiperazine compound (DU 27716) on hypothalamically induced behavioral activities. *Pharmacol Biochem Behav, 17*, 147–153.

Van Dijk, A., Richards, J. G., Trzeciak, A., Gillessen, D., & Möhler, H. (1984). Cholecystokin receptors: Biochemical demonstration and autoradiographal localisation in rat brain and pancreas using (^{3}H)-cholecystokinin-8 as radioligand. *J Neurosci, 4*, 1921–1933.

Van Hooff, J. A. R. A. M. (1977). The adaptive meaning of aggressive behaviour. In P. R. Wiepkema & J. A. R. A. M. Van Hooff (Eds.), *Aggressive Behavior—Causes and Functions*. Bohn, Scheltema and Holkema, Utrecht, 5–27.

Van Oortmerssen, G. A., & Bakker, T. C. M. (1981). Artificial selection for high and low attack latencies in wild Mus musculus domesticus. *Behav Genet, 11,* 115–126.

Van Oortmerssen, G. A., Benus, I., & Dijk, D. J. (1985). Studies in wild house mice: Genotype-environment interactions for attack latency. *Neth J Zool, 35,* 155–169.

Vergnes, M., DePaulis, A., & Boehrer, A. (1986). Parachlorophenylalanine-induced serotonin depletion increases offensive but not defensive aggression in male rats. *Physiol Behav, 36,* 653–658.

Vergnes, M., & Kempf, E. (1981). Tryptophan deprivation: Effects on mouse-killing and reactivity in the rat. *Pharmacol Biochem Behav, 14,* 19–23.

Vergnes, M., & Kempf, E. (1982). Effect of hypothalamic injections of 5,7-dihydroxytryptamine on elicitation of mouse-killing in rats. *Behav Brain Res, 5,* 387–397.

Walsh, L. L. (1982). Strain and sex differences in mouse killing by rats. *J Comp Physiol Psychol, 96,* 278–283.

Wilson, E. A. (1975). *Sociobiology.* Belknap Press of Harvard University Press, Cambridge, Massachusetts.

Winslow, J. T., De Bold, J. F., & Miczek, K. A. (1987). Alcohol effects on the aggressive behavior of squirrel monkeys and mice are modulated by testosterone. In B. Olivier, J. Mos, & P. F. Brain (Eds.), *Ethopharmacology of Agonistic Behaviour in Animals and Humans.* Martinus Nijhoff, Dordrecht, pp. 223–244.

Wise, D. A. (1974). Aggression in the female golden hamster: Effects of reproductive state and social isolation. *Horm Behav, 5,* 235–250.

Yamamura, H. I., & Snyder, S. H. (1974). Muscarinic cholinergic binding in rat brain. *Proc Nat Acad Sci U.S.A., 71,* 1725–1729.

Yoshimura, H. (1987). Ethopharmacology of agonistic behaviour in male and female mice. In B. Olivier, J. Mos, P. F. Brain (Eds.), *Ethopharmacology of Agonistic Behaviour in Animals and Humans.* Martinus Nijhoff, Dordrecht, pp. 94–109.

PART III

Clinical Neurochemical Issues

6

Monoamines and Suicidal Behavior

ALEC ROY
MARKKU LINNOILA

"Chemical action must of course accompany mental activity but little is known of its exact nature."
William James, 1890

Suicide is a major health problem—almost 1 percent of all deaths are due to suicide. It is estimated that in the world about 1,000 individuals commit suicide each day. In all Western countries, suicide ranks among the first 5–10 most frequent causes of death. In the United States, there are approximately 75 suicides per day, one every 20 minutes, more than 35,000 per year.

Individuals attempting suicide also represent a major health problem. For example, in the United Kingdom there are 100,000 hospital admissions per year because of deliberate self-poisoning; this represents 2.5 percent of all admissions, 1 in 7 of all acute medical admissions. Also, in England and Wales self-poisoning is the most common diagnosis in admitted patients under 50 years of age; among women it is the most common reason for acute medical admission, while among men it is second only to heart attacks. In the United States, the lifetime prevalence of thoughts of death, wanting to die, suicidal ideation, and suicide attempts was recently examined by the NIMH Epidemiologic Catchment Area Study (Moscicki et al., 1987). Among adults, 21 percent reported that there had been a period of two weeks or

Thanks are due to Dasha Parma for secretarial services.

more at some time during their lives when they thought about their own or another's death, 7.1 percent that they "felt so low" they wanted to die, 10.2 percent that they had thought about committing suicide, and 2.9 percent that they had attempted suicide at sometime in their lives.

Suicide research began with Durkheim's observation that the suicide rates within, and between, European countries varied in relation to various demographic and social factors. This led him to conclude that "the suicide rate varies inversely with the integration of social groups of which the individual forms a part." Since then a great deal has been learned about the social and clinical characteristics of individuals who exhibit suicidal behaviors. Of particular importance have been general population studies which have demonstrated that 90 to 95 percent of suicide victims were suffering from psychiatric disorder at the time of their death (reviewed in Roy, 1985a,b, 1987a).

Over the last few years there have been a number of studies suggesting that there may be monoaminergic substrates underlying suicidal behavior. The purpose of this chapter is to review these studies. Some possible future research strategies will also be discussed.

SEROTONIN

The first study of central monoamine metabolites in patients exhibiting suicidal behaviors was by Asberg et al. (1976). They found a bimodal distribution of levels of the serotonin metabolite 5-hydroxy-indoleacetic acid (5-HIAA) in the lumbar cerebrospinal fluid (CSF) of 68 depressed patients. Van Praag and Korf (1974) had made a similar observation. Asberg et al., however, made the association that significantly more of the depressed patients in the "low" CSF 5-HIAA group had attempted suicide in comparison with those in the "high" CSF 5-HIAA group. This led to the proposal by Asberg et al. that low CSF 5-HIAA levels may be associated with suicidal behavior. (Figure 1).

Subsequently Brown et al. (1979, 1982), in two studies of personality disordered individuals, also found that patients with a history of suicidal behavior had significantly lower CSF 5-HIAA

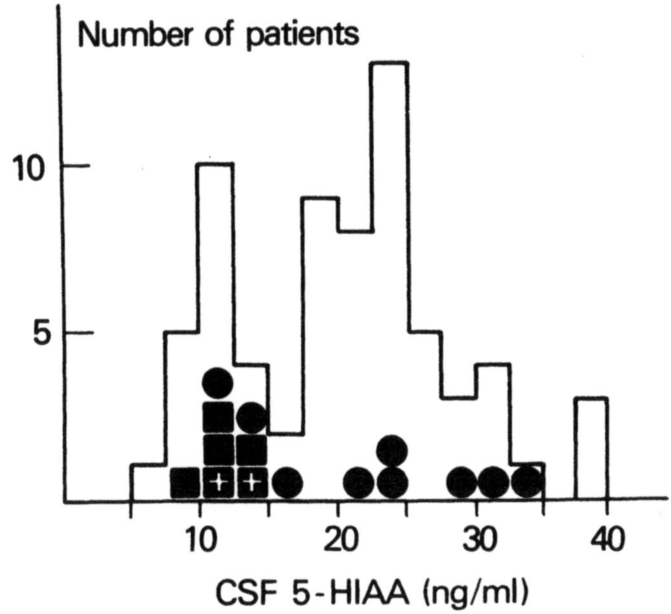

Figure 1. Suicidal acts in relation to 5-HIAA in CSF. Suicide attempts with sedative drugs (circles); attempts with other means (squares). Patients died from suicide (crosses). From Asberg, Traskman, & Thoren (1976).

levels than patients without such a history (Figure 2). Among depressed patients van Praag (1982) confirmed the observation that suicide attempts were found significantly more often among patients with low CSF 5-HIAA levels (Table 1). Other studies of CSF 5-HIAA levels in relation to suicidal behavior are shown in Tables 2 and 3. The various factors that influence CSF 5-HIAA levels have been fully discussed elsewhere by Asberg et al. (1986).

It is of note that low CSF 5-HIAA levels have been particularly associated with violent suicide attempts (Figure 3). In fact, in an early study, Traskman et al. (1981) reported that CSF 5-HIAA levels were significantly lower only among those patients who had made a violent suicide attempt (hanging, drowning, shooting, gassing, several deep cuts), and that levels were not reduced among those who had made a nonviolent suicide attempt (overdosage). More recently, Banki and Arato (1983) also

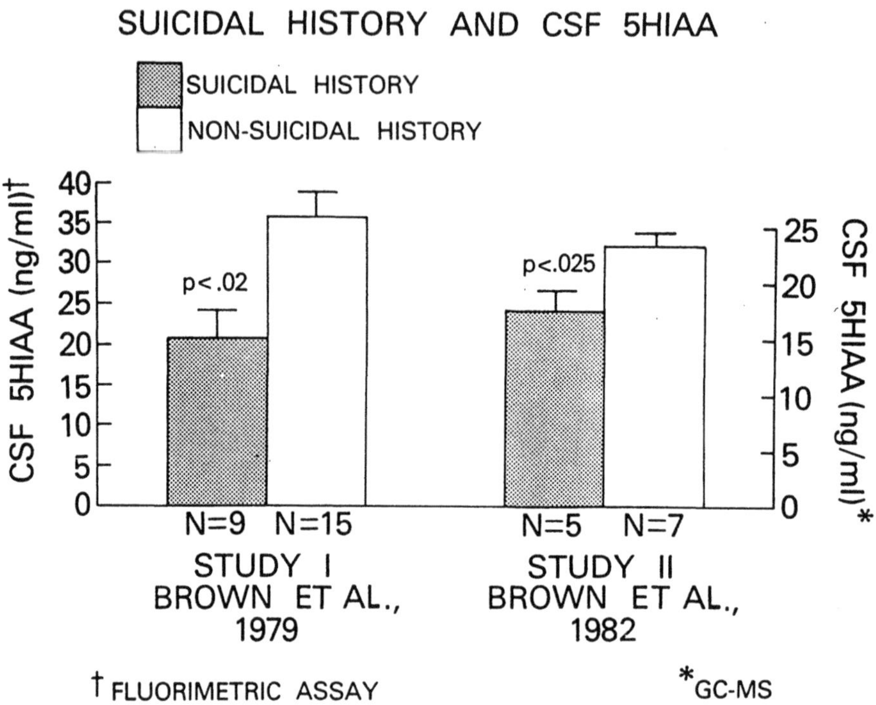

Figure 2. The relationship between suicidal history and CSF 5-HIAA levels in the two studies of Brown et al. From Brown & Goodwin (1986).

found among 141 female psychiatric patients suffering from depression, schizophrenia, alcoholism, or adjustment disorder that levels of CSF 5-HIAA were significantly lower in the violent suicide attempters in all four diagnostic categories. Other studies suggesting that low CSF 5-HIAA levels may be associated with a tendency towards impulsive violent behavior, which may manifest itself either as violence towards others or as attempts at suicide, are reviewed in the next chapter.

However, the NIMH Collaborative Study on the Psychobiology of Depression recently reported that they were unable to find a bimodal distribution of CSF 5-HIAA levels in depressed patients and that there were also no significant differences in CSF 5-HIAA levels between patients who had or had not attempted suicide (Secunda et al., 1986).

TABLE 1
Incidence of Suicide Attempts in 203 Patients Hospitalized with Depressions of Varying Symptomatology, Related to Central 5-HT Disorders

	Total	*Admitted after Suicide Attempts*	*Number of Violent Suicide Attempts*
Low CSF 5-HIAA level	51	24	4
Normal CSF 5-HIAA level	152	30	3

From van Praag (1982).

DOPAMINE

Some studies have also reported lower CSF levels of the dopamine metabolite homovanillic acid (HVA) among patients who have attempted suicide. Traskman et al. (1981) reported that both violent and nonviolent suicide attempts were associated with significantly lower levels of both CSF 5-HIAA and CSF HVA in comparison with controls (Figure 4). Their depressed suicide attempters showed the lowest CSF levels of 5-HIAA and HVA but the greatest reduction was in fact found with levels of CSF HVA, which showed a reduction of almost 50 percent when compared to controls (Figure 5). As the reduction of CSF HVA levels was significantly greater among their depressed attempters, but not among nondepressed attempters, Traskman et al. suggested that low CSF HVA levels may be more related to depression than to suicidal behavior.

Agren (1983) also reported that low CSF HVA levels were associated with the potential lethality of past suicide attempts made by depressed patients and that the contribution of CSF 5-HIAA was quite minimal in comparison to that of CSF HVA. Thus, Agren concluded that CSF HVA levels were even stronger than CSF 5-HIAA levels in explaining past suicidal behavior in depressed patients. Montgomery and Montgomery (1982) also found a highly significant relationship between CSF HVA levels and a history of attempting suicide ($p<0.001$) and that the relationship with low CSF 5-HIAA levels was less strong ($p<0.05$)

TABLE 2
Studies of CSF 5-HIAA in Relation to Suicidal Behavior

Author	*Subjects*	*Measure of Suicidality*	*Result*
Asberg et al. (1976)	68 hospitalized depressed patients	Attempted or completed suicide within index illness episode	Low 5-HIAA in the 15 attempters
Agren (1980)	33 depressed patients	SADS suicidality scale scores	Negative correlations with 5-HIAA and MHPG
Traskman et al. (1981)	30 suicide attempters (8 depressed, 22 other psychiatric disorders excluding schizophrenia and alcoholism), 45 healthy controls	Recent attempted or completed suicide	5-HIAA lower in attempters than in controls, HVA lower in depressed attempters only
Leckman et al. (1981)	132 psychiatric patients	Nurses' ratings of suicidal tendencies	Negative correlations with 5-HIAA
Brown et al. (1982)	12 patients with borderline personality disorder	Lifetime history of suicide	Lower 5-HIAA in the 5 attempters

van Praag (1982)	203 depressed patients	Recent suicide attempt	Lower CSF 5-HIAA after probenecid in the 54 suicide attempters
Palanappian et al. (1983)	40 hospitalized depressed patients	Suicide item in the Hamilton Rating Scale	Negative correlation with CSF 5-HIAA and HVA
Agren (1983)	110 depressed patients	SADS suicidality scale	Negative correlation to CSF 5-HIAA and MHPG
Roy-Byrne et al. (1983)	32 bipolar, 13 unipolar patients in different phases of illness	Lifetime history of suicide attempt	No association with 5-HIAA
Banki et al. (1983)	141 female inpatients (36 depressed, 46 schizophrenic, 35 alcoholic, 24 with adjustment disorder; 45 previously reported)	Recent suicide attempt	Negative correlation with 5-HIAA in all diagnostic groups; inconsistent relationship to HVA
Peres de los Cobos et al. (1984)	21 depressed patients	Suicide attempt, suicidal ideation rated on the Hamilton Scale and the AMDP system	More attempts and higher suicidality scores in patients with low 5-HIAA

From Asberg, Nordstrom & Traskman-Bendz (1986).

TABLE 3
Studies of CSF 5-HIAA in Relation to Suicidal Behavior in Schizophrenic Patients

Author	*Subjects*	*Measure of Suicidality*	*Result*
van Praag (1982a)	10 nondepressed who attempted suicide in response to imperative hallucinations, 10 nonsuicidal schizophrenics, 10 controls	Recent suicide attempt	Lower CSF 5-HIAA after probenecid in suicide attempters
Ninan et al. (1984)	8 suicidal, 8 nonsuicidal patients, matched for age and sex	Lifetime history of suicide attempt	Lower 5-HIAA in suicidal patients
Roy et al. (1986)	26 who had attempted compared with 26 who had not	Lifetime history of suicide attempt	No association with 5-HIAA, HVA and MHPG
Pickar et al. (1986)	13 who had attempted compared with 15 who had not	Lifetime history of suicide attempt	No association with 5-HIAA, HVA or MHPG

Violent and Non-Violent Suicidal Behavior and CSF 5HIAA

Study	Diagnosis	CSF 5HIAA Violent Suicide	CSF 5HIAA Non-Violent Suicide
1. Asberg et al., 1976 (2)	Unipolar depression	↓↓	NS
2. Oreland et al. 1981; Traskman et al., 1981	Depression and controls (anxiety; personality disorders)	↓↓	↓
3. Van Praag, 1982	Depression	↓↓	↓
4. Van Praag, 1983	Schizophrenia	↓↓	↓
5. Roy-Byrne et al., 1983	Unipolar depression Bipolar depression	NS[a] NS	NS NS
6. Banki et al. 1983 (2), 1984	Depression, schizophrenia, alcoholism, adjustment disorder	↓	NS
7. Roy et al., 1985	Schizophrenia	NS	NS

a = non-significantly lower in unipolar depressives
1 of 3 studies in which CSF HVA was examined found it lower in violent attempts;
CSF MHPG was examined in 2 studies and was lower in neither
↓ = decrease; ↓↓ = greater decrease; NS = nonsignificant change (see study for details)

Figure 3. Studies examining the relationship between violent versus nonviolent suicidal behavior and CSF 5-HIAA. From Brown & Goodwin (1986).

(Figure 5). Banki et al. (1983) found that, among depressed patients, those who had made a violent suicide attempt had significantly lower CSF HVA levels.

In a recent study, depressed patients who had attempted suicide at some time were found to have significantly lower CSF HVA levels than either depressed patients who had never attempted suicide or controls (Figure 6) (Roy et al., 1986). There were no significant differences between the groups for CSF 5-HIAA levels. Interestingly, 10 of the 19 depressed patients with a

(continued on p. 151)

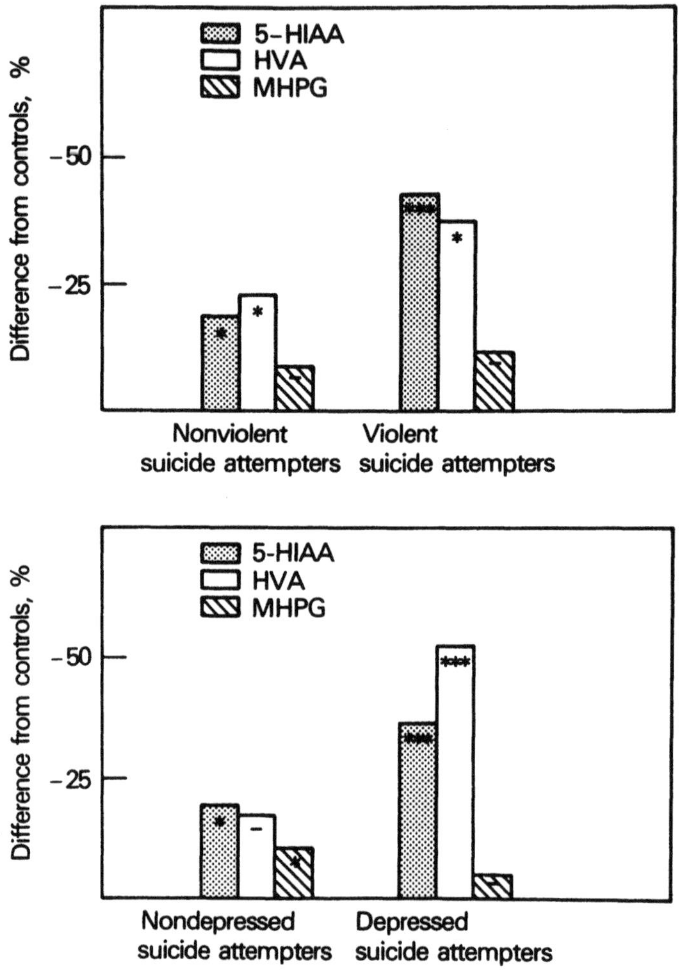

Figure 4. *Upper figure:* Differences in CSF monoamine levels (adjusted for age and height) between controls and violent and nonviolent suicide "attempters." Symbols indicate significance levels of differences from mean of controls at following levels: minus sign, $p > .05$; asterisk, $p \leq .05$; and three asterisks, $p \leq .001$. 5-HIAA indicates 5-hydroxyindoleacetic acid; HVA, homovanillic acid; and MHPG, 3-methoxy-4-hydroxyphenylglycol.

Lower figure: Differences in CSF monoamine levels (adjusted for age and height) between controls and depressed and nondepressed suicide "attempters." Symbols and abbreviations as explained above.
From Traskman, Asberg & Bertilsson et al. (1981).

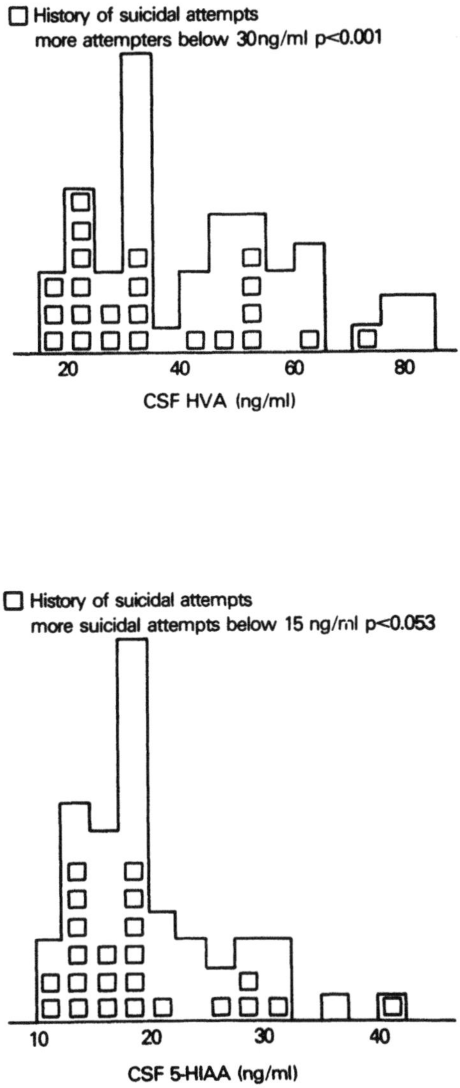

Figure 5. *Upper figure:* Distribution CSF HVA in 49 depressed patients. *Lower figure:* Distribution of CSF 5-HIAA in 49 depressed patients. From Montgomery & Montgomery (1982).

previous history of a suicide attempt had CSF HVA values below 100 pmol/L compared with 1 of 8 nonsuicidal patients and only 5 of the 41 normal controls.

However, in that study covarying for CSF 5-HIAA levels led to a loss of the significant difference for CSF HVA levels between the depressed patients who had and had not attempted suicide. This suggests that CSF 5-HIAA levels contributed to the significant differences found between the groups for CSF HVA levels. The combinations of a low CSF HVA level, or a low CSF HVA/5-HIAA ratio, and DST nonsuppression were found significantly more often among the depressed patients who had made a previous suicide attempt (Figure 7). This is of interest as Agren (1983) reported that when his depressed patients were divided into groups above and below the mean CSF HVA value, a significant positive correlation between hypercortisolism and suicidal lethality was found only among the patients with low CSF HVA levels.

NOREPINEPHRINE

There have been relatively few studies examining the noradrenergic system in relationship to suicidal behavior. Brown et al. (1979) reported that personality disordered patients who had attempted suicide at some time in their lives, when compared with those who had not, showed significantly higher CSF levels of the norepinephrine (NE) metabolite 3-methoxy-4-hydroxyphenylglycol (MHPG). Brown et al. also noted a significant positive correlation between aggression scores and CSF MHPG levels. Agren (1980), studying depressed patients, also found significant correlations between CSF MHPG levels and various aspects of suicidality.

Studies of peripheral indices of noradrenergic activity have produced conflicting results. Ostroff et al. (1985) reported that the three depressed patients who had made serious suicide attempts (two of them fatal) had significantly lower 24-hour urinary norepinephrine-to-epinephrine ratios than 19 depressed patients who had made no suicide attempts. Prasad (1985) reported similarly. The NIMH Collaborative Study (Secunda et al., 1986) found that depressed patients who had attempted suicide, when compared with those who had not, showed significantly lower plasma levels and urinary outputs of MHPG, with a similar trend with CSF MHPG levels. Another recent study-

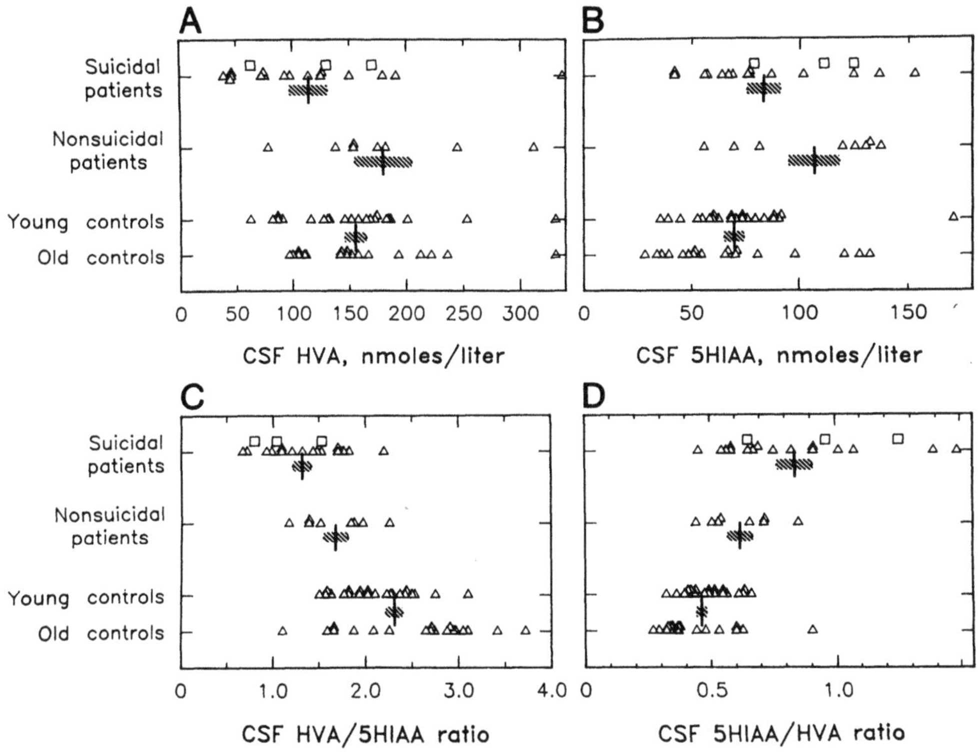

Figure 6. Individual CSF HVA and 5-HIAA levels of depressed patients who had and who had not attempted suicide and of young and old control subjects. Patients who had attempted suicide had a significantly lower mean CSF HVA level than either patients who had never attempted suicide ($p<0.05$) or the total group of control subjects ($p<0.05$). From Roy, Agren, Pickar, Linnoila, & Doran et al. (1986).

found that depressed patients who had never attempted suicide had significantly higher plasma levels of NE, urinary outputs of NM, and CSF MHPG levels than patients who had attempted suicide or normal controls (Roy et al., 1987).

Among postmortem studies, low NE levels have been reported in the putamen of suicide victims by Beskow et al. (1976). Recently Mann et al. (1987), like Zanko and Biegon (1983), found a significant increase in B-adrenergic receptor binding in the frontal cortex of suicide victims compared with controls suggesting that there may be a degree of noradrenergic dysregulation in suicide victims (Figure 8).

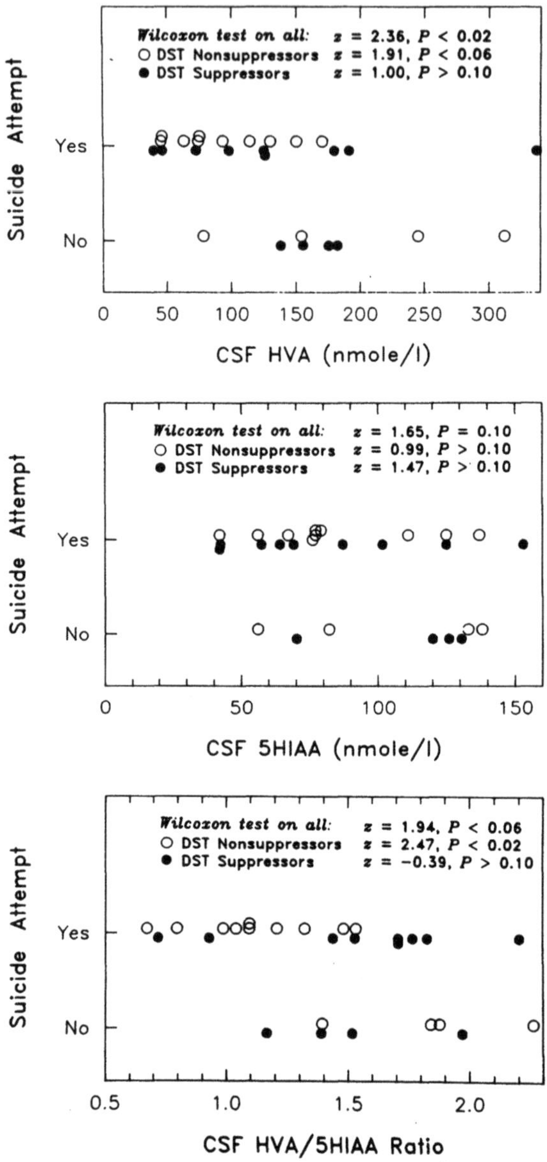

Figure 7. Individual CSF HVA and 5-HIAA levels and ratio of depressed patients who had and who had not attempted suicide, with DST nonsuppression or suppression. The combination of DST nonsuppression and low CSF HVA level ($z=1.91$, $p<0.06$) or a low HVA/5-HIAA ratio ($z=2.47$, $p<0.02$) was significantly more common among depressed patients who had attempted suicide than among those who had never attempted suicide. From Roy, Agren, Pickar, Linnoila & Doran et al. (1986).

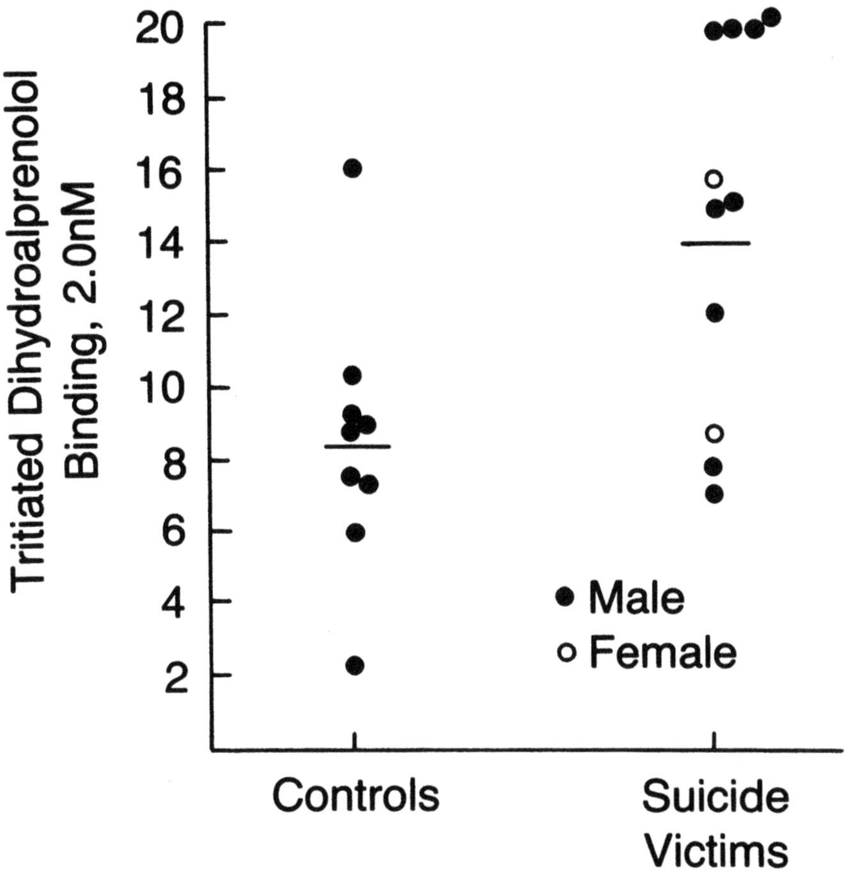

Figure 8. Postmortem β-adrenergic binding in frontal cortices of suicide victims. Binding was measured using tritiated dihydroalprenolol. Suicide group differed significantly from controls ($p<.05$) using two-tailed t test and Mann-Whitney test. From Mann, McBride & Stanley et al. (1987).

MONOAMINES AND PERSONALITY

Some investigators have reported correlations between monoamines and various measures of personality. Brown et al. (1982) noted a strong negative correlation between CSF 5-HIAA levels and lifetime aggression scores (Figure 9). This observation has

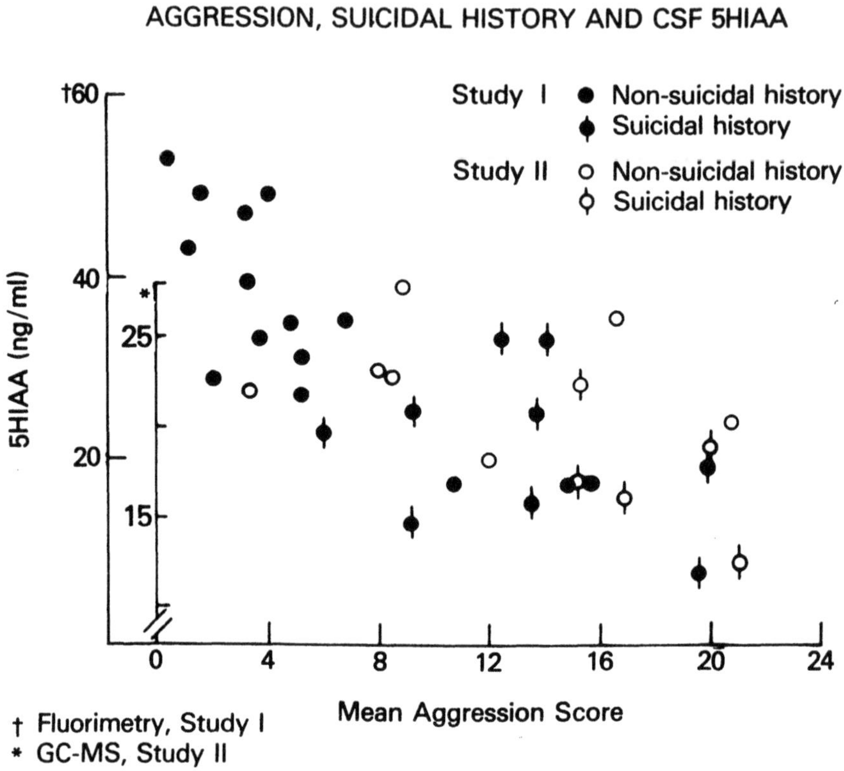

Figure 9. The trivariate relationship among aggression history, suicidal history, and CSF 5-HIAA levels in the two studies of Brown et al. From Brown & Goodwin (1986).

been recently extended to include deviant childhood behavioral variables, which also correlate negatively with CSF 5-HIAA levels (Brown et al., 1986). Van Praag (1986b) has shown that depressives with low CSF 5-HIAA levels have higher hostility scores on a variety of measures (Table 4).

Schalling et al. (1983) noted negative correlations between CSF 5-HIAA and psychoticism scores (i.e., nonconformity, aggressiveness) on the Eysenck Personality Questionnaire (EPQ) in nondepressed patients, suicide attempters, and healthy volunteers. In suicidal patients there was also a negative correlation between CSF 5-HIAA levels and EPQ neuroticism scores (i.e., emotional instability). On the Karolinska Scales of Personality

TABLE 4
Low 5-HIAA Depressives Compared to
Normal 5-HIAA Depressives

1. More suicide attempts	$p < 0.01$
2. Greater number of contacts with police	$p < 0.05$
3. Increased arguments with	
*relatives	$p < 0.05$
*spouse	$p < 0.01$
*colleagues	$p < 0.05$
*friends	$p < 0.05$
4. More hostility at interview	$p < 0.05$
5. Impaired employment history (arguments)	$p < 0.05$

From van Praag (1986a).

TABLE 5
Postmortem Neurotransmitter and
Metabolite Studies in Completed Suicides

Study	*Neurochemical Findings*
Shaw et al. (1967)	↓ Brain stem 5-HT
Bourne et al. (1968)	↓ Brain stem 5-HIAA
Pare et al. (1969)	↓ Brain stem 5-HT No change in brain stem 5-HIAA
Lloyd et al. (1974)	↓ Brain stem 5-HT No change in brain stem 5-HIAA
Gillin et al. (1986)	↓ Hypothalamus 5-HT ↓ Nucleus acumbens 5-HIAA
Korpi et al. (1986)	↓ Hypothalamus 5-HT, Lack of circadian rhythm
Beskow et al. (1976)	↓ 5-HIAA in brain stem
Owen et al. (1983)	No change in 5-HIAA levels in frontal cortex
Crow et al. (1984)	No change in 5-HIAA levels in frontal cortex
Cochran et al. (1976)	No change in brain 5-HT
Stanley et al. (1982)	No change in 5-HIAA and 5-HT levels in frontal cortex

From Stanley, Mann & Cohen (1986).

(KSP), low CSF 5-HIAA levels were associated with high scores on monotony avoidance and impulsivity and with low scores for socialization. Other groups have demonstrated significant associations between various indices of noradrenergic activity and scores on the Sensation-Seeking Scale (reviewed by Zuckerman et al., 1983).

Such observations are of interest as they suggest how biological abnormality may influence enduring behavioral patterns through an effect on personality. The extensive animal literature suggesting a role for monoamines in self-destructive animal behavior has been reviewed elsewhere (Crawley et al., 1985).

POSTMORTEM STUDIES

Over the years most postmortem brain studies among suicide victims have focused on the serotonin system. Some, but not all, neurochemical studies report modest decreases in serotonin itself, or its metabolite 5-HIAA, in either the brain stem or frontal cortex (Table 5). The few studies that have examined NE, dopamine or HVA have tended to be negative (Table 6).

There have been few postmortem studies of the enzymes involved in catecholamine metabolism. No changes in monoamine oxidase (MAO) activity have been reported (Table 7).

Four of five postmortem receptor studies, using ^{3}H imipramine as the ligand, have reported significant decreases in the presynaptic binding of this ligand to serotonin neurones in suicide victims (Table 8). Stanley and Mann (1983), using ^{3}H spiroperidol as the ligand, have also reported a significant increase in postsynaptic 5-HT_2 binding sites among suicide victims who used violent methods to end their lives.

Taken together these neurochemical and receptor studies tend to support the hypothesis that diminished central serotonin turnover as evidenced by reduced presynaptic imipramine binding, reduced levels of 5HT and 5-HIAA, and upregulation of the postsynaptic $5HT_2$ receptor, is associated with suicide. However, most of these studies do not compare suicide victims with depressed patients who have died for reasons other than suicide. Thus, the possibility exists that abnormality of central serotonin metabolism found in postmortem studies may apply to depressive illness in general. Also, Mann et al. (1986) have pointed out that a wider range of neurotransmitter systems should be examined in future postmortem studies in order to allow an examination of the neurochemical specificity of any changes associated with suicidal behavior.

POSSIBLE GENETIC FACTORS

Among psychiatric patients with different diagnoses, a family history of suicide has been found to significantly increase the risk for suicidal behavior (Roy, 1982, 1983). Linkowski et al. (1985) reported similar findings among 713 patients with affective disorder. They concluded that: "A positive family history for violent suicide should be considered as a strong predictor of active suicidal attempting behavior in major depressive illness."

Egeland and Sussex (1985) studied the suicides that had occurred during 100 years among the Amish in southeastern Pennsylvania. Almost three-quarters of the 26 suicide victims were found to cluster in four family pedigrees, each of which contained a heavy loading for affective disorder and suicide (Figure 10). The converse was not true as there were other pedigrees with heavy loadings for affective disorder but without suicides. They concluded: "Our study replicates findings that indicate an increased suicidal risk for patients with a diagnosis of major affective disorder and a strong family history of suicide."

The strongest evidence for genetic factors in suicide comes from two Danish-American adoption studies (Schulsinger et al., 1979; Wender et al., 1986). In the second study, the death registers revealed that 15 of the 407 biological relatives of the 71 adoptees who as adults suffered from an affective disorder had committed suicide compared with 1 of the 360 biological relatives of the 71 adoptee controls ($p<0.01$). It was particularly adoptee suicide victims with the diagnosis of "affective reaction" who had significantly more biological relatives who had committed suicide (Table 9). This diagnosis describes an individual who has affective symptoms accompanying a situational crisis—often an impulsive suicide attempt. These findings led Kety

TABLE 6

Postmortem Brain Levels of Catecholamines and Metabolites in Suicide Victims Versus Controls

	Brain Stem		*Frontal Cortex*			*Other Regions*		
Study	NE	DA	NE	DA	HVA	NE	DA	HVA
Bourne et al. (1968)	NC	—	—	—	—	—	—	—
Pare et al. (1969)	—	—	—	—	—	NC	NC	—
Beskow et al. (1976)	—	—	—	—	↑ 100% ↓ 75%[b]	NC or	NC	NC

[a]HVA is homovanillic acid.

[b]Putamen. Statistically nonsignificant lower levels were also found in hypothalamus (31%) and caudate (40%).

From Mann, McBride & Stanley (1986).

TABLE 7

Postmortem Studies of Biogenic Amine Synthetic and Degradative Enzymes in Suicide

Study	MAO A	MAO B	COMT[c]	Tyrosine hydroxylase	Dopamine-B- hydroxylase
Grote et al. (1974)	NC	NC	NC	NC or ↑ 219%	NC
Gottfries et al. (1975)	NC	NC	—	—	—
Mann & Stanley (1984)	NC	NC	—	—	—

[a]Assayed 28 brain regions in 4–10 brain samples/group.

[b]Assayed enzyme kinetics V_{max} and K_D.

[c]COMT is catechol-O-methyltransferase.

From Mann, McBride & Stanley (1986).

TABLE 8
Postmortem Receptor Studies of Suicide Victims

Study	*Neurochemical Findings*
Stanley et al. (1982)	↓ ^{3}H-Imipramine binding in cortex
Paul et al. (1984)	↓ ^{3}H-Imipramine binding in hypothalamus
Perry et al. (1983)	↓ ^{3}H-Imipramine binding[a] in cortex
Crow et al. (1984)	↓ ^{3}H-Imipramine binding in cortex
Meyerson et al. (1982)	↑ ^{3}H-Imipramine binding in cortex
Stanley and Mann (1983)	↑ 5-HT_2 binding in cortex
Owen et al. (1983)	↑ 5-HT_2 binding in cortex[b]
Crow et al. (1984)	No change in 5-HT_2 binding in cortex
Stanley (1984)	No change in muscarinic cholinergic receptor binding in cortex
Kaufman et al. (1984)	No change in muscarinic cholinergic receptor binding in cortex
Meyerson et al. (1982)	↑ Muscarinic cholinergic receptor binding in cortex
Zanko and Biegon (1983)	↑ Beta-receptor binding in cortex
Mann and Stanley (1987)	↑ Beta-receptor binding in cortex
Meyerson et al. (1982)	No change in beta-receptor binding in cortex

[a]Depressed patients dying of natural causes.
[b]Increased but not significantly.
From Stanley, Mann & Cohen (1986).

(1986) to suggest that a possible genetic factor in suicide may be an inability to control impulsive behavior which may have its effect independently of, or in addition to, psychiatric disorder. Psychiatric disorder, or environmental stress, may serve "as potentiating mechanisms which foster or trigger the impulsive behavior, directing it toward a suicidal outcome."

Kety also suggested the possibility that such a genetic factor for impulsivity may manifest itself through dysregulation of central serotonin systems. In this regard it is noteworthy that Buchsbaum et al. (1976) found that significantly more college students with low activity of the enzyme monoamine oxidase (MAO) in their blood platelets had a family history of suicidal behavior compared with students with high enzyme activity.

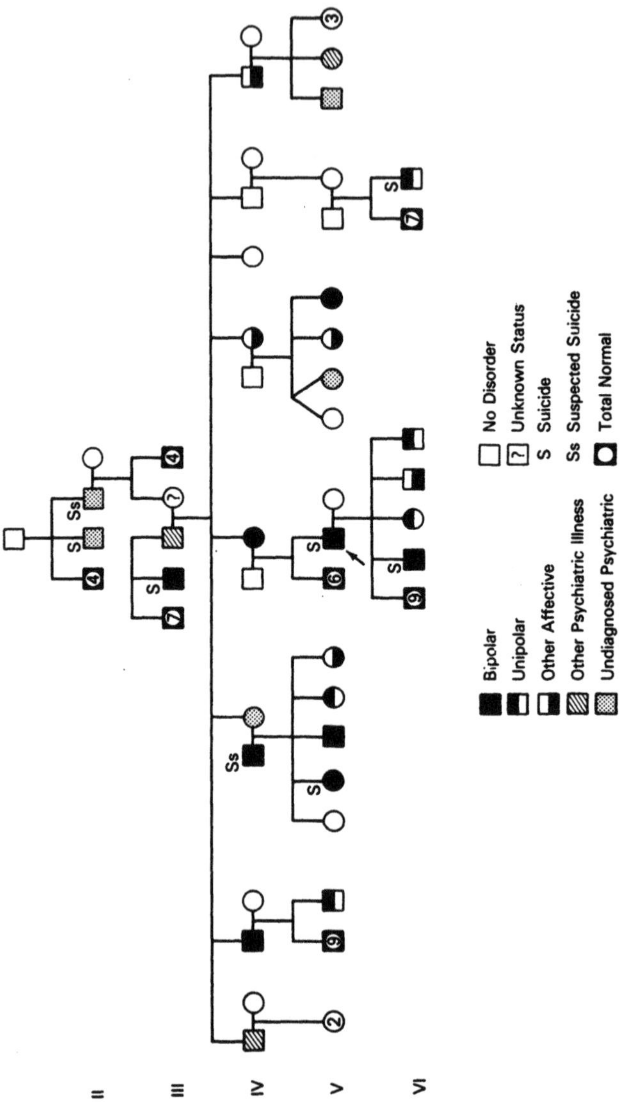

Figure 10. One of four pedigrees among the Amish with a heavy loading for affective disorder and suicide. From Egeland & Sussex (1985).

PERIPHERAL ENDOCRINE MARKERS

The first suggestion of a possible biologic marker for suicidal behavior was made by Bunney et al. (1965, 1969). Using a pe-

TABLE 9
Incidence of Suicide in the Biological Relatives of Depressive and Control Adoptees

Diagnosis in Adoptee	*Incidence of Suicide in Biological Relatives*	*p*
Affective reaction	$\frac{5}{660}$ (7.6%)	0.0004*
Neurotic depression	$\frac{3}{127}$ (2.4%)	0.056
Bipolar depression	$\frac{4}{750}$ (5.3%)	0.0036
Unipolar depression	$\frac{3}{139}$ (2.2%)	0.067
No mental illness	$\frac{1}{360}$ (0.3%)	

*Compared with biological relatives of control adoptees with no known history of mental illness.
From Kety (1986).

ripheral strategy, they observed high levels of urinary 17-hydroxcorticosteroids in suicidal depressed patients. Later, Ostroll et al. (1982, 1985) and Prasad (1985) found similar results. However, there have been recent negative reports (Koscis et al., 1987).

Several studies have examined dysregulation of the hypothalamic-pituitary-adrenal (HPA) axis as a possible peripheral endocrine marker of suicidal behavior. For example, Traskman et al. (1980) and Agren (1983) reported that hypercortisolism in depressed patients correlated positively with suicidal behavior. Targum et al. (1983) found that significantly more of 49 depressed patients who had been admitted because of a suicide attempt were DST nonsuppressors.

Meltzer et al. (1984) have demonstrated that the serum cortisol response to oral ingestion of the serotonin precursor 5-hydroxytryptophan (5-HTP) is enhanced in depressed patients and correlates significantly with suicidal ideation and behavior as recorded on rating scales. More recently, this group have reported a significant negative correlation between serum cortisol responses to 5-HTP and CSF 5-HIAA levels in depressed patients (Kayama et al., 1987). There were no significant correlations with CSF levels of other monoamine metabolites. Thus, they suggest that the enhanced cortisol response to 5-HTP may be due to heightened serotonin receptor sensitivity, secondary to diminished presynaptic serotonergic activity. They believe that this peripheral endocrine measure may be a useful marker of altered central serotonin turnover.

Other studies have examined dysregulation of the hypothalamic-thyroid-axis (HPT) and suicidal behavior. Linkowski et al. (1983, 1984) showed that among depressed women those with a history of violent suicide attempts had a reduced TSH response to TRH when compared to patients with a history of either nonviolent suicide attempts or no suicidal behavior. Roy et al. (1987b) also noted a trend for depressed patients who had attempted suicide to have lower TSH responses to TRH.

These TSH findings are of additional interest as two studies have reported significant associations between TSH responses to TRH and the serotonin system. Gold et al. (1977) found a significant negative correlation between CSF 5-HIAA levels and TSH responses to TRH in unipolar depressed patients. Roy et al. (1987b) noted that depressed patients with a blunted TSH response to TRH showed significantly decreased platelet serotonin uptake when compared with patients without a blunted TSH response.

The habituation of skin conductance responses in suicidal inpatients has been examined by Edman et al. (1986). They found that the distribution of habituation rates was bimodal. All of the violent attempters were fast habituators.

CLINICAL PREDICTION OF SUICIDAL RISK

Most suicides are probably preventable. This is because the great majority of individuals who commit suicide are suffering from a treatable psychiatric disorder. Furthermore, the possibility for prevention is often present. Many suicide victims have had past contact with physicians and psychiatrists. Also, in the months and weeks before they commit suicide, about two-thirds of suicide victims communicate their self-destructive intentions either to their physicians or to others around them (reviewed in Roy, 1985b).

Murphy (1983) drew attention to the fact that social and clinical variables, either alone or in combination, do not allow prediction of which individual in the general population will commit suicide. The best that they allow is the identification of groups with higher suicide risk. This dilemma was well demonstrated in a recent prospective study which aimed to identify which psychiatric patients would eventually commit suicide (Pokorny, 1983).

A consecutive series of 4800 patients admitted to the Houston Veterans Administration Hospital was examined and rated on a battery of instruments thought to be useful in predicting suicide. Twenty-one items were used to identify a subsample of 803 patients, about 15 percent of the total group, who were thought to be at high risk for suicide. All of the 4800 patients were followed up over an average of five years. Sixty-seven patients committed suicide during the followup period. However, only 30 of the 67 suicide victims were patients from the subsample of 803 patients thought to be at high risk. Thus, 37 of the eventual suicides—over 50 percent—were not identified earlier as being as risk, whereas 766 of the 803 patients identified as being at risk did not commit suicide.

Pokorny drew the important conclusion that:

> We are attempting to identify cases of a low-incidence disorder (suicide) with a "test" totally inadequate for that purpose, one that yields too many false-positive and false-negative results to make any clinical use feasible . . . The conclusion is inescapable that we do not possess any item of information or any combination of items that permit us to identify to a useful degree the particular persons who will commit suicide, in spite of the fact that we do have scores of items available, each of which is significantly related to suicide. (p. 256)

Cohen (1986), a statistician, reviewed the limitations of future improvements in statistical approaches to increase the predictability of suicidal behavior using psychosocial risk factors alone. He concluded: "If to the psychosocial factors now employed we can add relevant biological factors and their interactions with psychosocial factors, we may be able to develop the causal models necessary for the understanding, prediction, and prevention of suicide." (p. 44)

Single Biological Variable and Prediction

A few studies have examined one biological variable alone in relation to further suicidal behavior. For example, Coryell and Schlesser (1983) performed the DST on 243 depressed inpatients and found that all four patients who subsequently committed suicide were DST nonsuppressors. Carroll et al. (1981) have reported similar results. Linkowski et al. (1984) followed up depressed patients and found that those who subsequently committed suicide had earlier shown a blunted TSH response to TRH.

Combination of CSF and Clinical Variables in Prediction

Some recent studies have suggested that the combination of both a clinical and a biological variable may allow better prediction of increased suicide risk. The first such report was that of Traskman et al. (1981). They found that within a year of leaving hospital, 21 percent of the patients with the combination of a suicide attempt and a CSF 5-HIAA level below 90 nmoles per litre had committed suicide (Table 10).

Roy et al. (1986) found that at one-year follow up, four of 27 depressed patients had committed suicide. All four had made a

TABLE 10
Mortality from Suicide Within One Year After Admission to Hospital in Some High-Risk Groups

Patient Category	*No.*	*Suicides (%)*
Patients admitted to intensive care unit after a suicide attempt	45	2
Patients admitted to a psychiatric clinic after a suicide attempt, CSF 5-HIAA above 90 nmoles/liter	42	2
Patients admitted to a psychiatric clinic after a suicide attempt, CSF 5-HIAA below 90 nmoles/liter	34	21

From Asberg et al. (1986).

previous suicide attempt. Three of the seven patients (all melancholics) who had the combination of a previous suicide attempt and a CSF HVA level of below 75 pmol/ml had committed suicide, as had two of eight patients who had the combination of a past attempt and a CSF 5-HIAA level below 75 pmol/ml (Table 10). The combination of two biological variables and clinical variables was also examined. Three of four patients who had a previous suicide attempt, a CSF HVA level below 75 pmol/ml and DST nonsuppression had committed suicide (Table 11).

The possibility exists that these apparent biological risk factors for suicide are "markers" for severe melancholia and not suicidality per se. For example, both low CSF HVA levels and nonsuppression on the DST have been shown to be particularly associated with the depressed patient with melancholia (reviewed in Roy et al., 1986). Thus, these biological risk factors may, in fact, be markers for the depressed patient who suffers recurrent episodes of melancholia and who eventually chooses the option of suicide as a "solution" to intolerable psychological pain.

This possibility is supported by data showing that the suicide rate varies among subtypes of depressive disorder. For example, Evenson et al. (1982) recently estimated that the age-adjusted suicide rates for male patients with major affective disorder and

TABLE 11
Mortality by Suicide of Depressed Patients
at One-Year Follow-up

Category	*Total*	*N*	*%*
Total group	27	4	14.8
No past suicide attempt	8	0	0
Past suicide attempt	19	4	21.1
CSF 5-HIAA level < 75 pmol/ml	8	2	25.0
CSF HVA level < 75 pmol/ml	7	3	42.9
CSF 5-HIAA level < 75 pmol/ml and DST nonsuppressor	3	2	66.7
CSF HVA level < 75 pmol/ml and DST nonsuppressor	4	3	75.0

From Roy et al. (1986).

depressive neurosis were 400 and 190 per 100,000 respectively, while for female depressives the rates were 180 and 70 per 100,000 respectively.

Van Praag (1986a, b) and van Praag et al. (1984, 1986) have made a similar point in relation to low CSF 5-HIAA levels in depression. They found that violent suicide attempts were found significantly more often among melancholic than nonmelancholic patients, though their severity of depression was the same (Table 12). Therefore, van Praag and Plutchik concluded "that it is impossible to decide whether the biological abnormalities found in depressed, violent suicide attempters relate to autoaggressive impulses or to the melancholic syndrome as such," or to both.

Clinical studies also suggest that among depressed patients it is particularly the patient with melancholic features who is at risk for suicide. For example, Barraclough and Pallis (1975) compared the psychiatric symptoms rated at psychological autopsy among 64 depressed suicide victims with those found among 128 living depressed patients. The rank order of the frequency of the ten leading affective symptoms was the same in both groups. However, the three symptoms which differentiated

TABLE 12
Syndromal Depression Diagnosis in 31 Depressed Patients Who Had Committed Violent Suicide Attempts and in 31 Depressed Patients Who Had Committed Nonviolent Suicide Attempts

		Diagnosis	
	Number	*Major Depression (melancholic type)*	*Other Depression Types*
Violent suicide attempt	31	26	5
Nonviolent suicide attempt	31	13	18

Melancholic major depressions were found significantly more frequently in violent suicide attempters ($x^2 = 11.68$, $p < 0.001$).
From van Praag & Plutchik (1984).

the two groups were insomnia, self-neglect and impaired memory. All three symptoms were found significantly more among the depressive suicides than the living ones. Also, in the NIMH Collaborative Study the only two clinical features that strongly differentiated the 21 depressed suicide victims from the 933 living depressed patients were hopelessness and loss of pleasure, symptoms characteristic of melancholia (Fawcett et al., 1986).

Combination of Peripheral Biological and Clinical Variables in Prediction

Routine determinations of CSF monoamine metabolite levels has been difficult in most psychiatric settings. Thus, accessible peripheral markers of monoamine systems could be helpful. For example, platelet serotonin uptake has been reported to be significantly decreased among depressed patients. Also, the specific high affinity binding sites for [^{3}H]-imipramine on human platelet membranes appear to be similar to the [^{3}H]-imipramine binding sites found in human brain. There is strong evidence that the [^{3}H]-imipramine binding site is associated with the serotonin reuptake mechanism(s) in both brain and platelet membranes. Several studies have reported that the number (or density) of platelet [^{3}H]-imipramine binding sites are decreased in platelet membranes from depressed patients when compared to healthy controls (reviewed in Meltzer and Arora, 1986).

Recent studies have examined platelet measures in relation to suicidal ideation and behavior. Wagner et al. (1985) found that depressed patients who had made violent suicide attempts tended to have higher platelet [^{3}H]-imipramine binding values than nonattempters. However, Stanley et al. (1986) noted a trend for suicide attempters who had made a serious attempt to have lower Bmax values than controls. Meltzer and Arora (1986) examined six serotonergic measures in blood platelets; Km and Vmax of serotonin uptake, Kd and Bmax of [^{3}H]-imipramine binding, serotonin content, and MAO activity. Multivariate analysis showed that Km, Kd, Vmax, and MAO activity were significant predictors of Hamilton Depression Scale suicide ratings. The negative associations between the platelet measures and suicide ratings—though weak—were suggested by the au-

TABLE 13
Mortality by Suicide at One-Year Follow-up Among Depressed Patients. Relationship to a Platelet Serotonin Uptake

Patient category	*Number of Patients*	*Number (%) of Suicides*
Total group of patients	49	4(8.2)
No past suicide attempt	26	0
Past suicide attempt	23	4(17.4)
^{V}max $^{<65}$ pmol/LX 10^8 platelets/min	10	3(30.0)
Past suicide attempt and ^{V}max $^{<65}$ pmol/LX 10^8 platelets/min	6	3(50.0)
Unipolar depressed woman, past suicide attempt and ^{V}max $^{<65}$ pmol/LX 10^8 platelets/min	3	2(66.6)

^{V}max indicates maximal velocity of reaction.
All 4 patients who committed suicide were among the 49 depressed patients who had a platelet serotonin uptake V max determination.
From Roy, Everett, Pickar & Paul (1987).

thors to support the notion that there may be diminished serotonergic activity in patients with high suicide ratings.

The ability of platelet measures of the serotonin system, in combination with other variables, to identify depressed patientswho had committed suicide was recently examined (Roy et al., 1987a). Three of the six patients with the combination of both a past suicide attempt and a platelet Vmax of platelet serotonin uptake of 65 pmoles/10^8 platelets/minute or less had committed suicide (Table 13). Two of the 6 patients who had the combination of a previous suicide attempt, a platelet Bmax value of 556 fmoles/mg protein or less, and DST nonsuppression committed suicide as had both patients who in addition had a CSF HVA level below 75 pmol/ml (Table 14).

Edman et al. (1986) found no correlation between CSF 5-HIAA levels and the rate of skin conductance habituation. However, they noted that 35 % of their depressed patients with CSF 5-HIAA levels below 90 nmole/L, and 40% of those with rapid

TABLE 14
Mortality by Suicide at One-Year Follow-up Among Depressed Patients. Relationship to Platelet [^{3}H]-Imipramine Binding, Dexamethasone Suppression and CSF 5-HIAA and HVA

Patient category	*Number of patients*	*Number (%) of suicides*
Total group of patients	43	3 (7.0)
No past suicide attempt	23	0
Past suicide attempt	20	3 (15.0)
Bmax $^{<556}$ fmol/mg protein	25	3 (12.0)
Bmax $^{<556}$ fmol/mg protein and cortisol nonsuppression	15	2 (13.3)
Past suicide attempt and Bmax $^{<556}$ fmol/mg protein and cortisol nonsuppression	6	2 (33.3)
Past suicide attempt, Bmax $^{<556}$ fmol/mg protein and CSF 5-HIAA below 75 pmol ml	2	1 (50.0)
Past suicide attempt, Bmax $^{<556}$ fmol/mg protein and CSF HVA < 75 pmol/ml	3	2 (66.6)
Past suicide attempt, Bmax $^{<556}$ fmol/mg protein cortisol nonsuppression and CSF HVA < 75 pmol/ml	2	2 (100.0)

Bmax indicates platelet tritiated imipramine binding.
Only 3 of the 4 patients who committed suicide were among the 43 depressed patients who had a Bmax determination. A Bmax of 556 fmoles/mg protein was the highest value found among these 3 suicide victims.
From Roy, Everett, Pickar & Paul (1987).

skin conductance habituation, were violent suicide attempters. A combination of the two variables identified 54% of the violent suicide attempters. Furthermore, all four patients who subsequently committed suicide were fast habituators. Targum et al. (1983) found at six-month follow-up that 5 of 17 depressed patients who at admission had shown the combination of a recent suicide attempt and DST nonsuppression had committed suicide compared with none of the 32 patients who had not attempted suicide and who were DST suppressors—a significant difference.

FUTURE RESEARCH

The reports reviewed in the last two sections suggest that further studies are needed of the combination of clinical and biological variables to see if they may be useful in identifying patients at increased risk for suicidal behavior. There are three groups of patients who may be of particular interest for such further studies.

Affective Disorder

The risk of suicide is raised among psychiatric patients. Their suicide risk is from 3 to 12 times greater than the risk among nonpatients. The degree of risk varies according to age, sex, diagnosis, and in or outpatient status. After adjusting for age, male and female patients who at some time are inpatients have a suicide risk 5 and 10 times higher respectively than men and women in the general population. For male and female outpatients who are never admitted, the suicide risk is only 3 and 4 times greater than that for men and women in the general population. The higher suicide risk for patients who have been inpatients reflects that patients with more severe psychiatric disorders tend to be admitted; depressives requiring electroconvulsive therapy (ECT), for example.

Affective disorder is the psychiatric diagnosis with the highest suicide rate. This is so for both sexes. Follow-up studies of depressed patients have found that about 1 in 6 (15 percent) died by committing suicide (reviewed in Sainsbury, 1986). However, it is noteworthy that most of these studies were carried out before lithium prophylaxis was available.

A few studies have investigated which affective disorder patient has a particularly increased suicide risk. For example, in the comparison by Barraclough and Pallis (1975) of 64 depressive suicide victims and 128 living depressed patients, the striking findings were that significantly more of the depressed suicide victims had made a previous suicide attempt (41 percent versus 4 percent) and significantly more of them were unmarried and lived alone. These results suggest that among depressed patients social isolation increases a suicidal tendency (Sainsbury, 1986).

Past Suicidal Behavior

The best long range predictor of eventual suicide is a previous suicide attempt. Studies show that about 40 percent of depressed patients who commit suicide have made a previous suicide attempt. Also, about 30 percent of suicide victims in the general population have made a previous suicide attempt (Figure 11). Furthermore, follow-up studies show that approximately one percent of such individuals commit suicide during the subsequent year, approximately 10 percent over the subsequent ten years. Although subjects who have exhibited suicidal behavior in the past particularly deserve further study, it is noteworthy that their suicide risk is not uniform. The risk varies with age and sex. For example, in France it is estimated that the attempted suicide/suicide ratio for individuals between 15 and 24 years of age is 1:160 for women and 1:25 for men, whereas for individuals over 65 it is 1:3 for women and 1:1.2 for men.

Which patient who has attempted suicide is at increased risk to commit suicide was further investigated by Sainsbury (1986). He reviewed the 10 studies in which the clinical features of a group of patients who had attempted suicide were related to various measures of the medical seriousness of the attempt or of their intent to die. All the studies showed that the clinical characteristic most associated with the seriousness of the intent to die was the diagnosis of depression. Sainsbury concluded that the inference from these studies is that patients who make a serious suicide attempt resemble completed suicide victims more closely than they do individuals who attempt suicide.

Family History

Studies are needed of both suicide attempters and psychiatric patients who have a family history of suicide. This is because a family history of suicide denotes an increased risk of suicidal be-

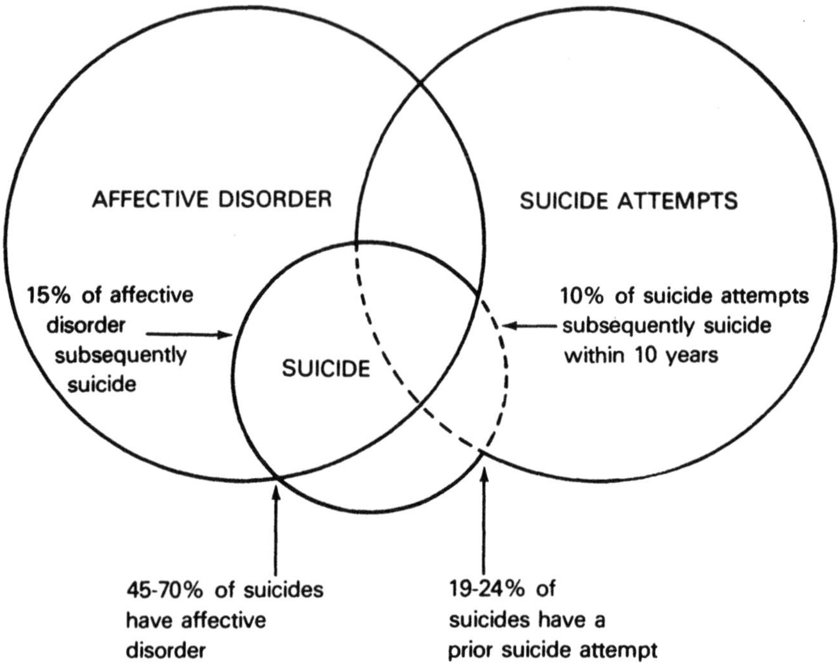

Figure 11. Venn diagram summarizing data concerning relationship between suicide attempts, affective disorder, and suicide.

havior at all stages of the life cycle (reviewed in Roy 1985c, 1986b, 1987b). Such a history may, in some families, represent a genetic factor for suicide, as discussed earlier.

Murphy and Wetzel (1982) made an important observation about which individual who attempts suicide may be at increased risk to commit suicide. They systematically interviewed a random sample of 127 suicide attempters. Fourteen percent gave a family history of suicide, 24 percent a family history of attempted suicide, and 6 percent a family history of suicide threats. Among suicide attempters with a primary diagnosis of primary affective disorder, 17 percent had a family history of suicide and 17 percent had a family history of suicide attempt. As individuals with affective disorder comprise a larger proportion of suicides than individuals with personality disorder, Murphy and Wetzel predicted that more of their patients with affective disorder could be expected to present a significant suicide risk in the future. They concluded that a "systematic family history of such behavior coupled with modern clinical diagnosis should prove useful in identifying those attempters at increased risk for suicide."

SUMMARY

Suicide is a multidetermined act. However, there is now a great deal of evidence suggesting that disturbance of monoamine regulation may play a role in suicidal behavior. Decreased serotonin turnover has been strongly implicated, particularly in relation to impulsive and violent behavior. There is a need for further studies of possible peripheral markers of suicidality. Also, the time is ripe for double-blind controlled studies to determine whether or not medications which enhance central serotonin activity, or serotonin precursors or postsynaptic receptor agonists or autoreceptor antagonists, will prevent further suicidal behavior among individuals who have already exhibited it.

REFERENCES

Agren, H. (1980). Symptom patterns in unipolar and bipolar depression correlating with monoamine metabolites in the cerebrospinal fluid: II. Suicide. *Psychiatry Research, 3,* 225–236.

Agren, H. (1983). Life at risk: Markers of suicidality in depression. *Psychiatric Developments, 1,* 87–104.

Asberg, M., Nordstrom, P., & Traskman-Bendz, L. (1986). Biological factors in suicide. In A. Roy (Ed.), *Suicide.* Williams and Wilkins, Baltimore.

Asberg, M., Traskman, L., & Thoren, P. (1976). 5-HIAA in the cerebrospinal fluid: A biochemical suicide predictor? *Archives of General Psychiatry, 33,* 1193–1197.

Banki, C. M., & Arato, M. (1983). Amine metabolites and neuroendocrine responses related to depression and suicide. *Journal of Affective Disorders, 5,* 223–232.

Barraclough, B., & Pallis, D. (1975). Depression followed by suicide: A comparison of depressed suicides with living depressives. *Psychological Medicine, 5,* 55–61.

Beskow, J., Gottfries, C., Roos, B., & Windblad, B. (1976). Determination of monoamine and monoamine metabolites in the human brain: Post mortem studies in a group of suicide and in a control group. *Acta Psychiatrica Scandinavica, 53,* 7–20.

Bourne, H., Bunney, W., Colburn, R., Davis, J., Davis, J., Shaw, D. & Coppen, A. (1968). Noradrenaline, 5-hydroxytryptamine, and 5-hydroxyindoleacetic acid in hindbrains of suicidal patients. *Lancet, II,* 805–808.

Brown, G., Ebert, M., Goyer, P., Jimerson, D., Klein, W., Bunney, W., & Goodwin, F. (1982). Aggression, suicide, and serotonin: Relationships to CSF amine metabolites. *American Journal of Psychiatry, 139,* 741.

Brown, G., Goodwin, F. (1986). Cerebrospinal fluid estimates of suicide attempts and aggression. Chapter in J. Mann & M. Stanley (Eds.) *Psychobiology of Suicidal Behavior* (Vol. 487, pp. 175–188). Annals of the New York Academy of Sciences.

Brown, G., Goodwin, F., Ballenger, J., Goyer, P., & Major, L. (1979). Aggression in humans correlates with cerebrospinal fluid metabolites. *Psychiatry Research, 1,* 131.

Brown, G., Kline, W., Goyer, P., Minichiello, M., Kreusi, M., & Goodwin, F. (1986). Relationship of childhood characteristics to cerebrospinal fluid 5-hydroxyindoleacetic acid in aggressive adults. In C. Shagass et al. (Eds.), *Proceedings of the IV World Congress of Biological Psychiatry* (pp. 177–179). Philadelphia: Elsevier.

Buchsbaum, M., Coursey, R., & Murphy, D. (1976). The biochemical high-risk paradigm: Behavioral and familial correlates of low platelet monoamine oxidase activity. *Science, 194,* 339–341.

Bunney, W., & Fawcett, J. (1965). Possibility of a biochemical test for suicide potential. *Archives of General Psychiatry, 13,* 232–239.

Bunney, W., Fawcett, J., Davis, J., & Gifford, S. (1969). Further evaluation of urinary 17-hydroxycorticosteroids in suicidal patients. *Archives of General Psychiatry, 21,* 138–150.

Carroll, B., Greden, J., & Feinberg, M. (1981). Chapter in B. Angrist (Ed.), *Recent Advances in Neuropsychopharmacology* (pp. 307–313). Pergamon Press, Oxford.

Cochran, E., Robins, E., & Grote, S. (1976). Regional serotonin levels in brain: A comparison of depressive suicides and alcoholic suicides with controls. *Biological Psychiatry, 11,* 283–294.

Cohen, J. (1986). Statistical approaches to suicidal risk factor analysis. Chapter in J. Mann & M. Stanley (Eds.), *Psychobiology of Suicidal Behaviors* (Vol. 487, pp. 34–41). Annals of the New York Academy of Sciences.

Coryell, W., & Schlesser, M. (1981). Suicide and the dexamethasone suppression test in unipolar depression. *American Journal of Psychiatry, 138,* 1120–1121.

Crawley, J., Sutton, M., & Pickar, D. (1985). Animal models of self-destructive behavior. Chapter in A. Roy (Ed.), *Symposium on Self-Destructive Behavior.* Psychiatric Clinics of North America.

Crow, T., Cross, A., Cooper, S., Deakin, J., & Ferrier, N., et al. (1984). Neurotransmitter receptors and monoamine metabolites in the brains of patients with Alzheimer-type dementia and depression and suicides. *Neuropharmacology, 23,* 1561–1569.

Edman, G., Asberg, M., Levander, S., & Schalling, D. (1986). Skin conductance habituation and cerebrospinal fluid 5-hydroxy-indoleacetic acid in suicidal patients. *Archives of General Psychiatry.*

Egeland, J., & Sussex, J. (1985). Suicide and family loading for affective disorders. *Journal of the American Medical Association, 254,* 915–918.

Evenson, R., Wood, J., Nuttall, E., & Cho, D. (1982). Suicide rates among public mental health patients. *Acta Psychiatrical Scandinavica, 66,* 254–264.

Gillin, C., Kelsoe, J., Kaufman, C., Kleinman, J., Risch, C., & Janowsky, D. (1986). Muscarinic receptor density in skin fubroblasts and autopsied brain tissue in affective disorders. Chapter in J. Mann & M. Stanley (Eds.), *Psychobiology of Suicidal Behavior* (Vol. 487, pp. 143–149). Annals of the New York Academy of Sciences.

Gold, P., Goodwin, F., Wehr, T., & Rebar, R. (1977). Pituitary thyrotropin response to thyrotropin-releasing hormone in affective illness: Relationship to spinal fluid amine metabolites. *American Journal of Psychiatry, 134,* 1028–1031.

Gottfries, C., Oreland, L., Wiberg, A., & Winblad, B. (1975). Lowered monoamine oxidase activity in brains from alcoholic suicides. *Journal of Neurochemistry, 25,* 667–673.

Grote, S., Moses, S., Robins, E., Hudgens, R., & Croninger, A. (1974). A study of selected catecholamine metabolizing enzymes: A comparison of depressive suicides and alcohol suicides with controls. *Journal of Neurochemistry, 23,* 791–802.

Kaufman, C., Gillin, J., Hill, B., O'Laughlin, T., Phillips, I., Kleinman, J., & Wyatt, R. (1984). Muscarinic binding in suicides. *Psychiatry Research, 12,* 47–55.

Kety, S. (1986). Genetic factors in suicide. Chapter 3 in A. Roy (Ed.), *Suicide.* Williams and Wilkins, Baltimore.

Korpi, E., Kleinman, J., Goodman, S., Phillips, I., DeLisi, L., Linnoila, M., & Wyatt, R. (1983). Serotonin and 5-hydroxyindoleacetic acid concentrations in different brain regions of suicide victims: Comparison in chronic schizophrenic patients with suicide as cause of death. *Archives of General Psychiatry.*

Koscis, J., Kennedy, S., Brown, R., Mann, J., & Mason, B. (1986). Neuroendocrine studies in depression: Relationship to suicidal behavior. Chapter in J. Mann & M. Stanley (Eds.), *Psychobiology of Suicidal Behavior.* Annals of the New York Academy of Sciences.

Krieger, G. (1974). The plasma level of cortisol as a predictor of suicide. *Diseases of the Nervous System, 35,* 237–240.

Koyama, T., Lowy, M., & Meltzer, H. (1987). 5-hydroxytryptophan-induced cortisol response and CSF 5-HIAA in depressed patients. *American Journal of Psychiatry, 144,* 334–337.

Leckman, J., Charney, D., Nelson, C., Heninger, G., & Bowers, M. (1981). CSF tryptophan, 5-HIAA and HVA in 132 patients characterized by diagnosis and clinical state. *Recent Advances in Neuropsychopharmacology, 31,* 289–297.

Linkowski, P., de Maertelaer, V., & Mendlewicz, J. (1985). Suicidal behavior in major depressive illness. *Acta Psychiatrica Scandinavica, 72,* 233–238.

Linkowski, P., van Wettere, J. P., Kerkhofs, M., Brauman, H., & Mendlewicz, J. (1983). Thyrotropin response to thyreostimulin in affectively ill women: Relationship to suicidal behaviour. *British Journal of Psychiatry, 143,* 401–405.

Linkowski, P., van Wettere, J., Kerkhofs, M., Gregoire, F., Brauman, H., & Mendlewicz, J. (1984). Violent suicidal behavior and the thyrotropin-releasing hormone-thyroid-stimulating hormone test: A clinical outcome study. *Neuropsychobiology, 12,* 19–22.

Lloyd, K., Farley, I., Deck, J., & Horneykiewicz, O. (1974). Serotonin and 5-hydroxyindoleacetic acid in discrete areas of the brainstem of suicide victims and control patients. In E. Costa, G. L. Gessa, & M. Sandler (Eds.), *Serotonin: New Vistas. Advances in Biochemical Psychopharmacology* (*11,* pp. 387–397). Raven Press, New York.

Mann, J., McBride, A., Stanley, M. (1986). Postmortem monoamine receptor end enzyme studies in suicide. In J. Mann & M. Stanley (Eds.), *Psychobiology of Suicidal Behavior* (Vol. 487, pp. 114–121). Annals of the New York Academy of Sciences.

Mann, J., & Stanley, M. (1984). Postmortem monoamine oxidase enzyme kinetics in the frontal cortex of suicide victims and controls. *Acta Psychiatrica Scandinavica, 69,* 135–139.

Mann, J., Stanley, M., McBride, P., & McEwen, B. (1986). Increased serotonin and beta-adrenergic receptor binding in the frontal cortices of suicide victims. *Archives of General Psychiatry, 43,* 954–959.

Meltzer, H., & Arora, R. (1986). Platelet markers of suicidality. Chapter in J. Mann & M. Stanley (Eds.), *Psychobiology of Suicidal Behavior* (Vol. 487, pp. 271–280). Annals of the New York Academy of Sciences.

Meltzer, H., Perline, R., Tricou, B. J., Lowy, M., & Robertson, A. (1984). Effect of 5-hydroxytryptophan on serum cortisol levels in major affective disorders. II. Relation to suicide, psychosis, and depressive symptoms. *Archives of General Psychiatry, 41,* 379–387.

Meyerson, L., Wennogle, L., Abel, M., Coupet, J., Lippa, A., Rauh, C., & Beer, B. (1982). Human brain receptor alterations in suicide victims. *Pharmacology, Biochemistry and Behavior, 17,* 159–163.

Montgomery, S., & Montgomery, D. (1982). Pharmacological prevention of suicidal behavior. *Journal of Affective Disorders, 4,* 291–298.

Moscicki, E., O'Carroll, P., Rae, D., Roy, A., Locke, B., & Regiere, D. (1987). Suicidal ideation and attempts: The epidemiologic catchment area study. *In preparation.*

Murphy, G. (1983). On suicide prediction and prevention. *Archives of General Psychiatry, 40,* 343–344.

Murphy, G., & Wetzel, R. (1982). Family history of suicidal behavior among suicide attempters. *Journal of Nervous and Mental Disorders, 170,* 86–90.

Ninan, P., van Kammen, D., Scheinin, M., Linnoila, M., Bunney, W., & Goodwin, F. (1984). CSF 5-hydroxyindoleacetic acid in suicidal schizophrenic patients. *American Journal of Psychiatry, 141,* 566–569.

Oreland, L., Wiberg, A., Asberg, M., Traskman, L., Sjostrand, L., Thoren, P., Bertilsson, L., & Tybring, G. (1981). Platelet MAO activity and monoamine metabolites in cerebrospinal fluid in depressed and suicidal patients and in healthy controls. *Psychiatry Research, 4,* 21–29.

Ostroff, R., Giller, E., Bonese, K., Ebersole, E., Harkness, L., & Mason, J. (1982). Neuroendocrine risk factors of suicidal behavior. *American Journal of Psychiatry, 139,* 1323–1325.

Ostroff, R., Giller, E., Harkness, L., & Mason, J. (1985). The norepinephrine-to-epinephrine ratio in patients with a history of suicide attempts. *American Journal of Psychiatry, 142,* 224–227.

Owen, F., Cross, A., Crow, T., Deakin, J., Ferrier, I., Lofthouse, R., & Poulter, M. (1983). Brain 5-HT_2 receptors and suicide. *Lancet, II,* 1256.

Palaniappan, V., Ramachandran, V., & Somasundaram, O. (1983). Suicidal ideation and biogenic amines in depression. *Indian Journal of Psychiatry, 25,* 286–292.

Pare, C., Yeung, D., Price, K., & Stacey, R. (1969). 5-Hydroxytryptamine, noradrenaline and dopamine in brainstem, hypothalamus, and caudate nucleus of controls and of patients committing suicide by coal-gas poisoning. *Lancet, II,* 133–135.

Paul, S., Rehavi, M., Skolnick, P., & Goodwin, F. (1984). High affinity binding of antidepressants to biogenic amine transport sties in human brain and platelet: Studies in depression. In R. Post & J. Ballenger (Eds.), *Neurobiology of Mood Disorders* (Vol. 1, pp. 846–853). Williams & Wilkins, Baltimore.

Perez de Los Cobos, J., Lobez-Ibor Alino, J., & Saiz Ruiz, J. (1984). Correlatos biológicos del suicidio y la agressividad en depressiones majores (con melancholia); 5-HIAA en LCR, DST, y respuesta terapeutica. Paper presented to the *First Congress of the Spanish Society for Biological Psychiatry,* Barcelona, 1984.

Perry, E., Marshall, E., Blessed, G., Tomlinson, B., & Perry, R. (1983). Decreased imipramine binding in the brains of patients with depressive illness. *British Journal of Psychiatry, 1412,* 188–192.

Pickar, D., Roy, A., Breier, A., Doran, A., Wolkowitz, O., Colison, J., & Agren, H., (1986). Suicide and aggression in schizophrenia: Neurobiologic correlates. Chapter in J. Mann & M. Stanley (Eds.), *Pychobiology of Suicidal Behavior* (Vol. 487, pp. 189–196). Annals of the New York Academy of Sciences.

Pokorny, A. (1983). Prediction of suicide in psychiatric patients. *Archives of General Psychiatry, 40,* 249–257.

Prasad, A. (1985). Neuroendocrine differences between violent and non-violent para-suicides. *Neuropsychobiology, 13,* 157–159.

Robbins, D., & Alessi, N. (1985). Suicide and the dexamethasone suppression test in adolescence. *Biological Psychiatry, 20,* 107–110.

Rose, R., Holaday, J., & Bernstein, I. (1971). Plasma testosterone, dominance rank and aggressive behavior in male rhesus monkeys. *Nature, 231,* 366–368.

Roy, A. (1982). Risk factors for suicide in psychiatric patients. *Archives of General Psychiatry, 39,* 1089–1095.

Roy, A. (1983). Family history of suicide. *Archives of General Psychiatry, 40,* 971–974.

Roy, A. (1985a). Suicide: a multidetermined act. Chapter in *Self-Destructive Behavior* (pp. 243–250). Psychiatric Clinics of North America.

Roy, A. (1985b). Suicide and psychiatric patients. Chapter in *Self-Destructive Behavior.* Psychiatric Clinics of North America.

Roy, A. (1985c). Family history of suicide in manic depressive patients. *Journal of Affective Disorders, 8,* 187–189.

Roy, A. (1986). Genetics of Suicide. Chapter in J. Mann & M. Stanley (Eds.), *Psychobiology of Suicidal Behavior* (Vol. 487, pp. 97–105). Annals of the New York Academy of Sciences.

Roy, A. (1989a). Suicide and attempted suicide. Chapter in H. Kaplan & B. Sadock (Eds.), *Comprehensive Textbook of Psychiatry* (5th Edition) (pp. 1414–1427). Williams and Wilkins, Baltimore.

Roy, A. (1989b). Genetics and suicidal behavior. *Risk Factors for Youth Suicide* (pp. 247–262). U.S. Department of Health and Human Services.

Roy, A., Agren, H., Pickar, D., Linnoila, M., Doran, A., Cutler, N., & Paul, S. (1986). Reduced cerebrospinal fluid concentrations of homovanillic acid and homovanillic acid to 5-hydroxyindoleacetic acid ration in depressed patients: relationship to suicidality and dexamethasone nonsuppression. *American Journal of Psychiatry, 143,* 1539–1545.

Roy, A., Everett, D., Pickar, D., & Paul, S. (1987a). Platelet tritiated imipramine binding and serotonin uptake in depressed patients and controls. *Archives of General Psychiatry, 44,* 320–327.

Roy, A., Karoum, F., Linnoila, M., & Pickar, D. (1987b). TRH test in unipolar depressed patients and controls: relationship to clinical and biological variables. *Acta Psychiatrica Scandinavica,* in press.

Roy, A., Ninan, P., Mazonson, A., Pickar, D., van Kammen, D., Linnoila, M., & Paul, S. M. (1985a). CSF monoamine metabolites in chronic schizophrenic patients who attempt suicide. *Psychological Medicine, 15,* 335–340.

Roy, A., Pickar, D., Linnoila, M., Doran, A., Ninan, P., & Paul, S. (1985b). Cerebrospinal fluid monoamine and monoamine metabolites in melancholia. *Psychiatric Research, 15,* 281–292.

Roy, A., Pickar, D., Roerich, L., Karoum, F., Linnoila, M. (1989). Suicidal behavior in depression: Relationship to noradrenergic function. *Biological Psychiatry, 25,* 341–350.

Roy-Byrne, P., Post, R., Rubinow, D., Linnoila, M., Savard, R., Davis, D. (1983). CSF 5-HIAA and personal and family history of suicide in affectively ill patients: A negative study. *Psychiatry Research, 10,* 263–274.

Sainsbury, P. (1986). Depression, Suicide, and Suicide Prevention. Chapter in A. Roy (Ed.), *Suicide.* Williams and Wilkins, Baltimore.

Schalling, D., Edman, G., & Asberg, M. (1983). Impulsive cognitive style and inability to tolerate boredom: Psychobiological studies of temperamental vulnerability. In M. Zuckerman (Ed.), *Biological Bases of Sensation Seeking, Impulsivity and Anxiety* (pp. 123–245). Lawrence Erlbaum Associates, Hillsdale, New Jersey.

Schulsinger, F., Kety, S., Rosenthal, D., & Wender, P. (1979). A family study of suicide. In M. Schou & E. Stromgren (Eds.), *Origin, Prevention and Treatment of Affective Disorders* (pp. 277–287). Academic Press, London.

Secunda, S., Cross, C., Koslow, S., Katz, M., Koscis, J., Maas, J., & Landis, H. (1986). Biochemistry and suicidal behavior in depressed patients. *Biological Psychiatry, 21,* 756–767.

Shaw, D., Camps, F., & Eccleston, E. (1967). 5-hydroxytryptamine in the hind-brain of depressive suicides. *British Journal of Psychiatry, 113,* 1407–1411.

Stanley, M. (1984). Cholinergic receptor binding in the frontal cortex of suicide victims. *American Journal of Psychiatry, 141,* 1432–1436.

Stanley, M., & Mann, J. (1983). Increased serotonin-2 binding sites in frontal cortex of suicide victims. *Lancet, I,* 214–216.

Stanley, M., Mann, J., & Cohen, L. (1986). Serotonin and serotonergic receptors in suicide. In J. Mann & M. Stanley (Eds.), *Psychobiology of Suicidal Behavior* (Vol. 487, 122–127). Annals of New York Academy of Sciences.

Stanley, M., Traskman-Bendy, L., & Dorovini-Zig, K. (1985). Correlations between aminergic metabolites simultaneously obtained from human CSF and brain. *Life Science, 37,* 1279–1286.

Stanley, M., Virgilio, J., & Gershon, S. (1982). Tritiated imipramine binding sites are decreased in the frontal cortex of suicides. *Science, 216,* 1337–1339.

Targum, S., Rosen, L., & Capodanno, A. (1983). The dexamethasone suppression test in suicidal patients with unipolar depression. *American Journal of Psychiatry, 140,* 877–879.

Traskman, L., Asberg, M., Bertilsson, L., & Sjostrand, L. (1981). Monoamine metabolites in CSF and suicidal behavior. *Archives of General Psychiatry, 38,* 631–636.

Traskman, L., Tybring, G., Asberg, M., Bertilsson, L., Lantto, O., & Schalling, D. (1980). Cortisol in the CSF of depressed and suicidal patients. *Archives of General Psychiatry, 37,* 761–767.

van Praag, H. M. (1982a). CSF 5-HIAA and suicide in non-depressed schizophrenics. *Lancet, I,* 977–978.

van Praag, H. M. (1982b). Depression, suicide and the metabolism of serotonin in the brain. *Journal of Affective Disorders, 4,* 275–290.

van Praag, H. M. (1986a). Affective disorders and aggression disorders. Evidence for a common biological mechanisms. In *Suicide and Life-Threatening Behavior* (pp. 103–132).

van Praag, H. M. (1986b). (auto) Aggression and CSF 5-HIAA in depression and schizophrenia. *Psychopharmacology Bulletin, 22,* 669–673.

van Praag, H. M., & Korf, J. (1971). Endogenous depressions with and without disturbances in the 5-hydroxytryptamine metabolism: a biochemical classification. *Psychopharmacologia, 19,* 148–152.

van Praag, H. M., & Plutchik, R. (1984). Depression-type and depression-severity in relation to risk of violent suicide attempt. *Psychiatry Research, 12,* 333–338.

van Praag, H. M., Plutchik, R., & Conte, H. (1986). The serotonin hypothesis of (auto) aggression. Critical appraisal of the evidence. *Annals of New York Academy Sciences* (pp. 150–167).

Vestergaard, P., Sorensen, T., & Hoppe, E., et al. (1978). Biogenic amine metabolites in cerebrospinal fluid in patients with affective disorders. *Acta Psychiatrica Scandinavica, 58,* 88–96.

Wagner, A., Aberg-Wistedt, A., Asberg, M., Ekqvist, B., Martensson, B., & Montero, D. (1985). Lower ^{3}H-imipramine binding in platelets from untreated depressed patients compared to healthy controls. *Psychiatry Research, 16,* 131–139.

Wender, P., Kety, S., & Rosenthal, D., et al. (1986). Psychiatric disorders in the biological and adoptive families of adopted individuals with affective disorders. *Archives of General Psychiatry, 43,* 923–929.

Zanko, M., & Biegon, A. (1983). Increased B adrenergic receptor binding in human frontal cortex of suicide victims. *Abstract Annual Meeting Society for Neuroscience,* Boston, Mass.

Zuckerman, M., Ballenger, J., Jimerson, D., Murphy, D., & Post, R. (1983). A correlational test in humans of the biological models of sensation seeking, impulsivity, and anxiety. In M. Zuckerman (Ed.), *Biological Bases of Sensation Seeking, Impulsivity and Anxiety* (pp. 229–248). Laurence Erlbaum Associates, Hillsdale, New Jersey.

7

Clinical Assessment of Human Aggression and Impulsivity in Relationship to Biochemical Measures

GERALD L. BROWN
MARKKU LINNOILA
FREDERICK K. GOODWIN

In 1937, Papez (1937) proposed a neuroanatomical central nervous system (CNS) mechanism for emotions, elaborated as early as 1949 by MacLean (1949, 1952), who not only continued the basic animal work, but who also proposed important analogies between animal and human emotions and behavior. In 1973, Eichelman and Thoa (1973) described applications of modern techniques of neurochemical assessment to models of aggression in animals. Though a number of neurochemical systems have been implicated in the aggressive behavior of animals, the most consistent findings have involved neurotransmitters. Though not exclusively, changes in the CNS indoleamine, viz. serotonin (5HT), and catecholamines, viz. norepinephrine (NE) and dopamine (DA), neurotransmitter systems, which largely function in inhibitory and excitatory roles, respectively, have been most associated with reproducible findings.

Beginning in 1965, neurotransmitter hypotheses for affective disorders were suggested for both indoleamines (Coppen et al., 1965; Coppen, 1967; van Praag, 1967, 1969; Lapin & Oxenkrug, 1969) and catecholamines (Schidkraut, 1965; Bunney & Davis, 1965). These hypotheses were followed by six studies from 1967 to 1976 (Shaw et al., 1967; Bourne et al., 1968; Pare et al., 1969; Lloyd et al., 1974; Beskow et al., 1976; Cochran et al., 1976) of CNS neurotransmitter levels from autopsies of suicides overwhelmingly associated with clinical psychiatric disorders, particularly affective disorders. The most consistent finding was a decrease in various parts of the CNS of the concentration of HT or its metabolite, 5-hydroxyindoleacetic acid (5HIAA); changes in catecholeamines were inconsistent. More recent autopsy studies of suicides report changes in CNS neurotransmitter receptors, particularly those for 5-HT, though mixed results have also been described for other systems (Stanley et al., 1982; Meyerson et al., 1982; Stanley & Mann, 1983; Perry et al., 1983; Stanley & Mann, 1984; Crow et al., 1984).

In 1976, Asberg et al. (1976a,b) reported the first *in vivo* study—in patients with affective disorders—in which self-destructive, specifically suicidal behavior was associated with a decreased 5-HIAA measured in the cerebrospinal fluid (CSF)—a more direct measure of brain chemistry than one might obtain from blood or urine. Brown, Goodwin et al. (1979a), not only confirmed the Asberg et al. study, but noted a strong relationship between lower CSF 5-HIAA concentration and a history of more aggressive behavior—an indication that aggressive behavior in man and animals has similar biological concomitants. In reviews of more recent clinical studies (Brown & Goodwin, 1986a, b) relating CSF 5-HIAA and aggressive and/or suicidal behavior in man, the original findings have been largely confirmed, particularly the link between 5-HT and aggression. These studies have been carried out in the U.S., several European countries, and India, all with similar results, indicating that a biological contribution to aggressive and suicidal behaviors, as well as to depression, is evident, despite significant racial and cultural differences.

AGGRESSIVE BEHAVIOR IN ANIMALS AND MAN

The extensive literature of biological findings associated with aggressive behaviors in animals has been based on a number of animal models of aggressive behavior and various measures of aggressivity. The general kinds of aggressive behavior in animals can be divided into three categories: I. Predatory (Reis, 1974; Moyer, 1968, 1971, 1976); II. Affective (Reis, 1974); and III. Other (Moyer, 1968, 1971, 1976). Predatory aggressive behaviors have been observed to be associated with little autonomic arousal, to be minimally hormonally responsive, to be related to feeding, etc. Examples are animal attacking or killing behaviors. Affective aggressive behaviors may involve intense autonomic arousal and hormonal responses, may be associated with general irritability, and their goal is not usually feeding. Examples include models such as: 1) shock-induced, 2) intruder-evoked, 3) isolation-induced, 4) surgically or pharmacologically induced aggression, etc. Other categories of animal aggressive behavior include: 1) intermale, 2) fear-induced (possibly "affective"), 3) irritable, 4) territorial, 5) maternal, 6) instrumental, etc. Much of the past, animal work has been reviewed elsewhere (Eichelman, 1979; Valzelli, 1981) (see Higley et al., Chapter 9) and Soubrié and Bizot (Chapter 10) in this volume for some current considerations).

On the other hand, human aggressive behaviors have largely been studied in association with culturally-defined "antisocial" behaviors, i.e., criminals, prisoners, etc., and, much less so, within a clinical framework (aggression or impulsivity usually being viewed as a manifestation or result of a more traditionally definable clinical disorder, e.g., psychosis). Until recently, studies attempting to link human aggressive behavior to biological findings were infrequent; some of the early attempts to relate aggressive behavior to biological or medical issues were those of Funkenstein et al. (1949), Sweet et al. (1969), and Monroe (1975). However, these early clinical investigations made little attempt to link their human findings to the literature on animal aggression. The studies reported by Brown et al. (1979a, 1981, 1982a, 1984, 1986c) were among the first to show a significant analogy between human behavioral and biochemical data and animal studies.

TRAIT AND STATE

For attempts to elucidate the relationship between aggressive behavior and biology, the concepts of "state" and "trait" are very useful in both animal and human studies. With regard to animals, examples of studies that have focused on trait characteristics include selective breeding for aggressive behavior and biochemical characteristics (Lamprecht et al., 1972; Ciaranello, et al., 1974); examples of studies that have focused on state characteristics include the induction of aggressive behavior via shock, isolation, intruder, diet, drug, and localized CNS lesions (possibly "trait") (Eichelman, 1979; Valzelli, 1981). Human studies which may elucidate a trait include those on individuals with a history of aggressive or impulsive behaviors in varied environments (Brown et al., 1979a, 1981, 1982a, 1984, 1986c) and genetic studies which indicate that antisocial behavior and suicidal behavior may be independent heritable characteristics, though often associated with psychiatric diagnoses (Schulsinger et al., 1979; Kety, 1979). Human studies of aggressive behavior which may be closely related to state conditions are those associated with menstrual cycle (Dalton, 1961, 1964), pharmacological effects (Leventhal, 1984), etc., though results of such studies may also be related to differences in genetic predisposition or vulnerability. The conceptualization of a "serotonin trait" derived from both animal and human data has been described by Depue and Spoont (1986).

AGGRESSIVE BEHAVIOR AND PSYCHIATRIC CONDITIONS

The study of behaviors as a repetitive pattern is not necessarily closely linked to the evolution of clinical psychiatric nosology for adult affective disorders (repetitive patterns are more associated with symptoms), with the notable exception of manic-depressive illness (Brown & Bunney, 1978; Goodwin & Jamison, in press). Certain childhood disorders, with a broad range of behaviors and symptoms, i.e. "hyperactivity" or Attention Deficit Disorder (ADD) and Conduct Disorder (CD) (Brown et al., 1985; Brown, 1986b), have been shown to be associated with or evolve into various behavioral disorders as children grown older (Weiss et al., 1979; Garfinkel & Klee, 1985). Suicidal behavior

(Pokorny, 1964) and, perhaps, self-directed aggressive behavior (Jones, 1982) have been associated with a spectrum of clinical disorders—particularly prominent are depressive and aggressive conditions. Suicidal behavior is somewhat more circumscribed "pathological behavior" than the concept of aggression as a "clinical entity." Suicidal behavior occasionally occurs in individuals who appear to be without psychiatric disorder, though not likely thought to be "normal." Either self-destructive or aggressive behavior, whether "pathological" or not, may be socially acceptable or even "altruistic," if thought to promote the general good; plausible counterparts have also been noted in animal behaviors (Crawley et al., 1985).

Within the specific diagnostic criteria for DSM-III (Spitzer, 1980) adult disorders, those disorders in which aggressive behavior is most prominent are among the category of personality disorders, more specifically, antisocial and borderline personality disorders. Further, there is a separate group of psychiatric disorders characterized as impulse control disorders, viz. pathological gambling, kleptomania, pyromania, and intermittent explosive disorder. A number individuals within some of the above diagnostic groups have been found to have relatively low concentrations of CSF 5-HIAA (Brown et al., 1979a; Linnoila et al., 1983; Virkkunen et al., 1987; Kreusi et al., 1985). Pharmacokinetic studies following single oral doses of tryptophan (TP) in prisoners who were characterized as "predominantly having personality disorders" (Domino, 1976; Domino & Krause, 1974) have shown significantly lower fasting plasma concentrations and slower absorption of TP compared to controls, although diet and activity were not controlled. Within the prison group, prisoners characterized as depressed vs. non-depressed on the basis of Minnesota Multiphasic Personality Inventory (MMPI) (Welsh & Dahlstrom, 1956; Lanyon, 1961) scores had significantly lower fasting TP levels. Low plasma TP/neutral amino acid ratio has been observed in alchoholics with histories of repeated aggression (Branchey et al., 1984).

In order to consider the relationship between aggression and biological factors scientifically, one has to realize that a categorical clinical diagnostic approach has certain disadvantages as opposed to a dimensional behavioral approach. Diagnoses are derived from their usefulness for communication among clinicians. They are useful for their organization of symptoms and phenomena (i.e. "syndromes"—Greek, running together), for formulation of treatment plans, for collation of responses thereto, for statistical manipulations, for epidemiological studies, for actuarial and morbidity studies, and for definition of categories for payment for the provision of health services, i.e. the Diagnostically Related Group (DRG) approach now being promulgated in U.S. medical practice.

The same diagnostic categories may or may not be useful in trying to elucidate the relationship between aggressive behavior and biology—sometimes diagnoses may provide insight and, at other times, they may becloud etiological considerations (Brown et al., 1982b). Despite the inherent heterogeneity of clinical diagnoses, Brown et al. (1979b) and Linnoila et al. (1983) did show similar findings using diagnostic groupings as a variable; the likelihood of having found similar results may have been greatly influenced by both investigators' studying individuals who were extremely aggressive and, therefore, probably less "variable" behaviorally, and, quite possibly, more uniform biochemically (see Table 1). For individuals less repeatedly aggressive, impulsive, or violent, a clinical diagnosis may simply be too non-specific meaningfully to classify aggressive behavior for biological studies. The relationship between externally directed aggressive

TABLE 1
Personality Disorder Diagnoses and CSF 5-HIAA

Personality Diagnoses	*CSF 5-HIAA*			
	Brown et al. (1979)		*Linnoila et al. (1983)*	
	N	Fluorimetry	N	HPLC
1. Explosive	4	17.6 ± 4.4	20	13.4 ± 0.8
2. Antisocial; Immature	7	23.4 ± 2.8	7	14.0 ± 0.9
3. Paranoid; Pass-Agg			9	18.4 ± 1.7
4. Pass-Agg; Pass-Dep Schizoid; Obs-Comp Inadequate	14	40.0 ± 2.7		

All CSF 5-HIAA values expressed as X ± SEM in NG/ML
ANOVA: ($p < .01$) both studies.

behavior and CSF 5-HIAA appears to be diagnostically nonspecific; however, the relationship between suicidal behavior and CSF 5-HIAA has not been found in several studies of patients with bipolar affective illness (Brown & Goodwin, 1986a).

Within the specific criteria for DSM-III adolescent and childhood disorders, ADD, with or without hyperactivity, and CD, aggressive types, are the diagnoses within which the most aggressive or impulsive behaviors are likely to be found (Brown et al., 1985; Brown, 1986b). No studies have linked CSF 5-HIAA with aggressive behavior ratings observed directly in childhood. One case report described a 13-year-old girl whose antisocial behavior was largely that of burglaries to obtain sweets; she also had a low level of CSF 5-HIAA (Kruesi et al., 1985). This report is consistent with studies that show carbohydrate ingestion to raise the level of CNS 5-HT (Fernstrom & Wurtman, 1971, 1972; Fernstrom, 1982).

One study group of young adult males with DSM-III diagnoses of borderline personality disorder who completed questionnaires describing various aspects of their childhood history (Wood et al., 1976; Wender et al., 1981; Wood & Reimherr, 1983) and subjected themselves to CSF collections showed a significant negative correlation between mean ratings of "childhood problems" and concentrations of CSF 5-HIAA (Brown et al., 1986c) (see Figure 2, p. 205). Fear of loss of control, anxiety, worrying, poor attention span, depression and sadness, and lack of friends were among items that seemed to have the greatest power to separate individuals with extreme values of CSF 5-HIAA.

Several studies of ADD, both as children (Shetty & Chase, 1976; Cohen et al., 1977; Shaywitz et al., 1977) and as young adults (those that specifically were diagnosed as not having antisocial or borderline personalities) (Reimherr et al., 1984) have reported CSF 5-HIAA levels; none, however, have been focused upon an assessment of a linkage between specific aggressive or impulsive behaviors per se and indices of CNS 5-HT metabolism. Whether children with ADD or CD, as groups, have lower levels of platelet 5-HT or whole bood 5-HT is unclear, since both low and normal levels have been reported (Coleman, 1971, 1973; Rapoport, et al., 1977; Ferguson et al., 1981). By comparison, one study has reported lower levels of platelet tritiated imipramine binding, a measure thought to be a marker of 5-HT reuptake activity, among other things, in children with CD versus a non-aggressive pediatric control group (Stoff et al., 1987).

AGGRESSIVE BEHAVIOR AND MEDICAL, NEUROPSYCHIATRIC CONDITIONS

Several medical and neuropsychiatric disorders in both adults and children may provide an interesting perspective on a possible aggression-5-HT link in humans. A review (Matthews & Barabas, 1981) has reported that populations of adult epileptics have a higher incidence of self-destructive, suicidal behaviors; they have also been shown to have increased CSF concentrations of 5-HIAA when well controlled by anticonvulsants versus untreated (Chadwick et al, 1975). Individuals with carcinoid syndrome have been shown to be more irritable and aggressive (Sjordsma et al., 1970; Major et al., 1973), particularly after parachlorophenylalanine (PCPA) has been administered (Major et al., 1973); these individuals have also been shown to have elevated peripheral blood 5-HIAA and may have lower CNS 5-HIAA before PCPA and, certainly, thereafter. Prisoners with the 47, XYY syndrome, sometimes associated with criminality and aggressive behavior (Baker, 1972; Borgaonkar & Shah, 1974; Witkin et al., 1976; Dorus, 1980; Schroeder et al, 1981), have been reported to have low base line CSF 5-HIAA and to be less responsive to probenecid loading (Bioulac et al., 1978, 1980).

Individuals with Parkinson's syndrome, who have been shown to have lower levels of CSF 5-HIAA (Johansson & Roos, 1967; Bunney et al., 1969), have also been shown to have an increased incidence of depression and suicidal behavior (Brown & Wilson, 1972; Brown et al., 1973). Furthermore, von Economo's encephalitis (childhood "Parkinson's syndrome") was described as resulting in a postencephalitic syndrome in which hyperactivity, shortened attention span, impaired fine motor coordination, and aggressive outbursts were manifest (Hohman, 1922). Individuals with disturbances in steroid metabolism, i.e. Cushing's disease, which in turn affects 5-HT metabolism, have an increased incidence of depression and suicidal behavior (Cohen, 1980; Lewis & Smith, 1983).

Studies on adult alcoholics, who may or may not be outwardly aggressive—but do have a high suicide rate—have shown mixed results with regard to concentrations of CSF 5-HIAA (Branchey et al., 1984; Takahaski et al., 1974; Major et al., 1977; Ballenger et al., 1979), despite a rise during the abstinent post-intoxication period (Ballenger et al., 1979). Lesch-Nyhan disease in children, associated with considerable self-destructive, self-mutilating behavior, has shown a favorable response to the administration of 5-hydroxytryptophan (Mizuno et al., 1975; Ciaranello et al., 1976; Anders et al., 1978; Castells et al., 1979). Gilles de la Tourette syndrome, most often first diagnosed in adolescence because of tics, uncontrollable profanity, and, frequently, aggressive behavior, has been reported to be associated with a low CSF 5-HIAA concentration (Cohen et al., 1978, 1979).

Among hospitalized patients (N = 1687) with various psychiatric and neuropsychiatric conditions, despite the problems discussed above with regard to aggressive behavior and clinical diagnoses, associations between clinical conditions and assaultive or fear-inducing behavior are much more consistent than any associations related to demographic variables (Rossi et al., 1986).

DIFFICULTIES IN MEASURING HUMAN AGGRESSION

There are certain problems with measuring aggressive and impulsive behaviors which are potential pitfalls in all human studies, but may be particularly significant in studies of patients with antisocial and criminal behavior.

Veracity, validity, and reliability come into play for subjects who purposely misrepresent data and history; inexperienced observers may not take into consideration these subject characteristics. Both factors are particularly important because of the types of individuals, i.e. antisocial and borderline personality disorders, who are likely to be included in studies assessing possible links between aggression and biology. Such subjects are also prone to be purposely deceitful and uncooperative, responding according to some personal goal unrelated, or even antagonistic, to the research goal.

By contrast, much fruitful work has been accomplished on behavioral-biological relationships in affective disorders, where patients are generally assessed by observer ratings and are assumed to have given truthful information (except, perhaps, in the case of acutely manic patients). Needless to say, such problems underscore the value of multiple observations over time in the same and different settings as well as by the same and different observers. By further corroborating observations with history from significant others who have no known interest in the outcome of the assessment, one may cautiously make assessments of aggression.

Feelings, thoughts, attitudes, and other subjective responses are clearly useful in some clinical investigational settings; however, their reliability and utility, where verifiable factual data are required, are open to question when one is evaluating a group who may be purposely deceitful or whose moods and feelings are very volatile. Even when these patients make an attempt to be cooperative in describing their feelings, they may provide information that is not reliable or accurate. For example, some extreme behaviors may appear in dissociative states of which the individual may have no recollection or, at best, a distorted one. Aside from these concerns, Rydin et al. (1982) reported that subjects with low levels of CSF 5-HIAA, who were matched for age, sex, height, and depression ratings with a comparison group with normal levels of CSF 5-HIAA, showed significantly higher levels of anxiety and hostility determined by Rorschach ratings.

Whether evaluating present behaviors or histories, gathering data within a closed setting is probably preferable (laboratory for animals; hospitals or prisons for humans) because one can more consistently maintain methodology of observation and conditions that potentially alter behavior, i.e. drug intake, diet, motor activity, social environment, etc. Physical environment cannot be ignored in view of reports of effects of season (Wirz-

Justice & Richter, 1979; Swade & Coppen, 1980; Carlsson et al., 1980; Rosenthal et al., 1984), light (Rosenthal & Sack, 1985), and, possibly, ionization of surrounding air (Krueger et al., 1968; Sulman et al., 1975). Some subjects are prone to steal food, particularly sweets (cf., Fernstrom & Wurtman, 1971, 1972; Fernstrom, 1982) in our experience, not only in the extreme example cited above (Kreusi et al., 1985) but, less dramatically so, in other individuals whom we have studied. A recent study in children (Kruesi et al., 1987), while showing no differential aggression-inducing effects from single-dose administrations of glucose, sucrose, saccharin, and aspartame, did indicate that the more aggressive children consumed more sugar and their consumption correlated with duration of aggression against property. Possibly, parents had observed aggressive behavior contiguous with consumption of sugar in children with an aggressive predisposition who were "treating" themselves, albeit unsuccessfully, and thus continued aggression.

Control subjects are obviously desirable when both the study and control or "comparison" groups have a high degree of within-group homogeneity except for the characteristic under investigation and/or the groups are clearly from different categories, depending on the nature of the study. One such "comparison" group was useful for assessing longitudinal aggressive behavior, but had the disadvantage that CSF 5-HIAA was not available (Brown et al., 1979b). If one has a well-designed observation system in a "naturalistic situation," extending over a prolonged period, observation of repetitive behaviors might well be superior to "reports" of such behaviors taken in a closed setting (see primate data reported by Higley et al. in this volume).

Some aggression-CSF studies have taken into consideration only hospital or prison behaviors (Brown et al., 1979a, 1982a; Linnoila et al., 1983; Kruesi et al., 1985; Branchey et al., 1984; Bioulac et al., 1978, 1980; Lidberg et al., 1984, 1985; Lopez-Ibor et al., 1985), but, sometimes, the interval for behavioral observation or history has been limited to two weeks (Lopez-Ibor et al., 1985). When indications of aggressive behavior are not derived from data collected over an extended interval, the findings may be more indicative of state than of trait variables. An Overt Aggression Scale (OAS) (Yudofsky et al., 1986) has a similar orientation (real events, closed setting, self or other directed aggression) to the Brown-Goodwin Questionnaire's (BGQ) use to obtain a history of aggressive behavior (AGG HX) (Brown et al., 1979a, 1979b), but the OAS does not have a historical perspective except to the degree that the inpatient observation period is prolonged. The OAS assesses: 1) verbal aggression; 2) physical aggression against objects; 3) physical aggression against self; and 4) physical aggression against other people.

Since one is more likely to be able to discern traits from data gathered over an extended interval, childhood behaviors which persist into adulthood are of keen interest (see Figure 2). To focus on the type of behavior or process (i.e. temper tantrums in the very young and difficulty getting along with peers because of angry outbursts at later ages) is obviously more useful for trait studies than to focus on the particular content of a behavior (often largely influenced by a specific set of current environmental circumstances or learned responses from previous interactions with the environment). The particular content or form that behavior or emotions may take at different ages, in different sexes, in different settings, in different cultures, all are interesting questions, but may provide little insight into relatively fixed behavioral traits. Repetitive behaviors are important in determining the reliability of any given observation.

Thus, it is the relative independence of behavior from a specific environment that may indicate the behavior to be largely internally driven (not to say that such behavior may not be "triggered" by an environmental situation, or that some "internally driven" behavior may not be emotionally or cognitively learned from previous environmental situations). Environmental issues, sometimes, might be little more than a provocation for predisposed, intermittent, unpredictable "states" (repetitive "states" and a trait could be difficult to distinguish—those that begin early in childhood may more likely "be", or "become", traits than those that begin at a later age).

Evidence for a pattern of behavior that seems to "be" identified very early in life and to continue relatively unaltered is likely to imply a more fixed biological variable, genetic or acquired; whereas, evidence for a pattern of behavior that seems to "become" or to evolve, perhaps in response to new factors, could imply either a less fixed biological variable or a trait to be subsumed under experimental learning, both cognitive and emotional. Even "experiential learning" cannot be thought of as being a set of behaviors unrelated to underlying biological substrates, as evidenced by Miller's work on the autonomic nervous system (1969) and Kandel's work on biological bases of memory and learning (1986).

HUMAN AGGRESSION AND CSF NEUROTRANSMITTER METABOLITES

This chapter does not attempt to review comprehensively the use of and results from various instruments that purport to measure human aggressive behavior. Rather, it focuses more specifically on instruments that have been used to assess a relationship between human aggression and measures thought to be indications of CNS neurotransmitter metabolism. When one is trying to determine what instrument might be most useful in a given study, common questions arise: 1) Are there standardized norms? 2) Has the instrument been widely used in similar studies? and 3) How consistent have the results been?

There are few controlled aggression studies which have quantified biochemical variables or measured drug responses, and even fewer that have made some attempt to combine both. In a controlled study of adult aggressive behavior and lithium response, the drug response was best predicted by a change in the frequency of rule breaking over time (Sheard 1971, 1975); despite the use of a number of psychological instruments, none usefully measured drug response (Marini & Sheard, 1977). One might expect the OAS to be a useful way to measure drug response in a closed setting (Yudofsky et al., 1986). In a controlled study of aggressive children (ADD and CD) and their response to d-amphetamine response, drug response was best measured by time-limited, behavioral observations in a potentially provocative setting. Though several psychological instruments were used, none were useful in measuring drug response (Amery et al., 1984).

Bioulac et al. (1980) and Montgomery et al. (1982, 1983, 1984) have reported behavioral observations related to personality disorders, CSF neurotransmitters, and drug response; the results of both groups of investigators have been unclear. Van Praag et al. (1987) have recently discussed the therapeutic implications of 5-HT altering compounds in terms of effects on behavioral dimensions as opposed to the treatment of traditional diagnostic categories.

Notwithstanding some of the results to date, and, particularly in characterizing aggressive patients, extensive use of instruments is important since the components of aggressive clinical behaviors have been less carefully characterized than some other clinical behaviors, that is, depressive behaviors and "symptoms." Historically, assessments of depression were initially primarily related to environmental variables, that is, various kinds of losses, and only gradually did instruments reflect more of an assessment of an internal state which might manifest itself in varied ways as an interaction with environmental situations. Even then, a "state" of depression seemed more acceptable than a trait (which presumably would be less controllable by both patients and physicians!). Studies indicating that internal biochemical alterations and responses to drugs known to have relatively specific biochemical effects were consistent in their relationship to various kinds of depressions (phenomenologically) under various conditions helped further the evolution of the concept of a depressive "trait".

The evolution of scientific, clinical study of human aggression lags considerably behind that of studies of affective disorders. In animal studies, the situation is somewhat the opposite. Animal models, states, and traits of depression, except, notably, those of Harlow, McKinney, Suomi et al. (Harlow, 1959, 1962; McKinney et al., 1971, 1984; Suomi et al., 1972; Suomi, 1975), seem to have been less comparable than many of the animal studies of aggression. Externally directed behaviors, for example, overt aggression, are more easily observed than much of the inwardly or self-directed behavior observed in depression—the ability of man to talk about the latter is helpful in its assessment. Human depression has been measured in more scientific, clinical studies than has been human aggression for which there is a less generally accepted definition of a "pathological" form. Aggression directed towards one's self has been thought by Freud (1976) to be expressed as suicidal behavior.

Both behavioral and biochemical data that have been so carefully documented in aggression studies in animals should be thoroughly considered when one is assessing human aggression, without losing sight of those aspects held unique to humans (there seems to be an inverse relationship between human "uniqueness of behavior and biochemistry" and the increasing knowledge of both human and animal behavior and biochemistry over time!). Valzelli (1984) and Soubrie's (1986) reviews, as well as the latter's data in Chapter 10 of this volume, describing inhibitory aspects of behavior in animals with CNS 5-HT alterations, deserve particular attention when one is considering biochemical contributions to aggressive behavior in man.

Brown et al. (1982a) reported that the Psychopathic Deviate (PD) and the Social Introversion (SI) scales of the MMPI were among those most closely and significantly related to levels of CSF 5-HIAA in humans (see Table 2). Of further interest, CSF 3-methoxy-4-hydroxyphenlygylcol (MHPG) and CSF homovanillic acid (HVA) were also measured at the same time in these subjects and no significant correlations were found between any of the MMPI scales and either of the latter two neurotransmitter metabolites. One of the validity scales, the F scale, has also been high in individuals with low CSF 5-HIAA consistent with concerns about the veracity and reliability of the clinical data provided by such subjects. Mendacious or not, on those occasions where individuals were retested with the MMPI (not in conditions where aggressive behaviors were present, but in conditions representative of the more frequent "in-between aggressive episodes" state), the same individual maintained a rather consistent profile (some individuals are also chronically untruthful!).

Other MMPI scales are also significantly related to CSF 5-HIAA (and to each other!), that is, Hypochondriasis (HS), Paranoia (PA), Psychasthenia (PT), Schizophrenia (SC) scales. These findings may reflect interrelationships among psychiatric conditions or other symptoms and states, that is, psychoses, rather than to repetitive behaviors seen in those personality disorders who are often aggressive. On the other hand, some per-

TABLE 2
Correlations of MMPI Scales with a History of Aggression and Low CSF 5-HIAA in Borderline Males

		MMPI Scales									
		HS	*D*	*HY*	*PD*	*MF*	*PA*	*PT*	*SC*	*MA*	*SI*
History of	r	+.48	+.45	+.48	+.57	+.21	+.52	+.58	+.63	+.57	+.62
Aggression	p	ns	ns	ns	.05	ns	ns	.05	.03	.05	.03
CSF	r	−.57	−.47	−.48	−.77	−.34	−.64	−.65	−.57	−.47	−.59
5-HIAA	p	.05	ns	ns	.004	ns	.03	.02	.05	ns	.04

Note: MMPI scales expressed as T scores.

sonality disorders may be more specific clinical entities than previously thought.

There is also the confounding issue that highly disturbed individuals are likely to evince their clinical disturbances variously (see Figure 1); thus, few individuals might be expected to show a deviant response on one scale only. The MMPI profile of those "borderline" subjects with lower CSF 5-HIAA, viz. an elevated "2" or Depression (D), "4" or (PD), and "8" or (SC), suggests individuals with depressive symptoms, antisocial behaviors, and transient thought process disturbances (Welsh & Dahlstrom, 1956); this profile is highly consistent with clinicians' impressions; it is also quite similar to that of the "sweets" stealing adolescent with low CSF 5-HIAA cited above (Kruesi et al, 1985).

The AGG HX (BDQ) (Brown et al., 1979a, b) probably obtained its results based upon its attempt to assess behaviors or situations where repeated "states" or episodes of aggressive behavior evident early in life and which might be repetitive at different ages, in different forms and in different environments, might indicate the possibility of a trait. Though individuals with

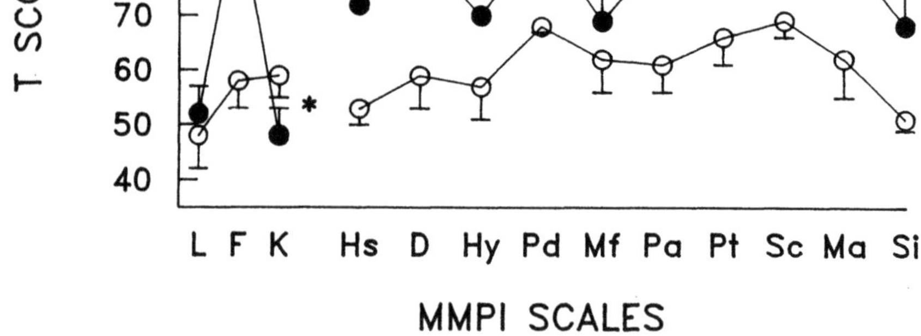

Figure 1. MMPI profiles and CSF 5-HIAA.

histories of either aggressive or suicidal behaviors are the products of more disturbed families, levels of CSF 5-HIAA per se are not directly related to measures of family disturbance, though CSF 5-HIAA remains related to target behaviors which appear to indicate difficulties in modulating or inhibiting aggressive impulses (Brown & Goodwin, unpublished data). Neither the history of a disturbed family nor a low level of CSF 5-HIAA alone is sufficient for the development of repeated aggressive behavior; but, both may be necessary, and, certainly, if both are present, the likelihood of the presence of repeated aggressive behavior is enhanced.

The Buss-Durkee Inventory (BDI), used in several psychiatric and forensic populations (Buss & Durkee, 1957; Buss et al., 1957, 1962; Buss, 1961; Morrison et al., 1975; Renson et al., 1978), by the nature of its items may relate more to acute states and environmental provocations than to traits. Only the Irritability scale, but not the total score, was significantly negatively correlated with levels of CSF 5-HIAA (Brown & Goodwin, 1984), a measure likely to indicate a trait (Asberg et al., 1978; Post et al., 1980) and likely to reflect CNS 5-HT metabolism (Goodwin et al., 1977; Stanley, in press). Some of the BDI scales, that is, Irritability, Negativism, Resentment, Suspicion, and Hostility, as well as its total score, do correlate with AGG HX; the Guilt scale showed the greatest lack of correlation with AGG HX; clinically, the subjects certainly evinced little evidence of anything more than transient guilt, if at all (see Table 3). The results from its True-False, self-report characteristics, without validity checks (as with the MMPI), may also support the idea that verbal aggression as one mode and physical aggression as another are orthogonal and relate more within mode than across mode, thus not necessarily supporting a continuum between the two (Leibowitz, 1968). Furthermore, in a prison population, the BDI measured aggressive attitude better than aggressive behavior (Gunn & Gristwood, 1975).

When 12 subjects (Brown et al., 1986c) were observed with regard to both adult and childhood instruments, one could note an increasing negatively significant correlation from the BDI, to the AGG HX (BGQ), to the childhood problems questionnaire, to the MMPI PD scales and CSF 5-HIAA (see Table 4). Of par-

TABLE 3
Correlations of Buss-Durkee Inventory (BDI) Scales with a History of Aggression and Low CSF 5-HIAA in Borderline Males

		BDI Scales								
		Assault	*Indirect*	*Irritable*	*Negative*	*Resentment*	*Suspicion*	*Verbal*	*Total*	*Guilt*
CSF	r	−.25	−.29	−.66	−.37	−.42	−.22	−.05	−.39	+.05
5-HIAA	p			.04						
History of Aggression	r	+.54	+.39	+.66	+.72	+.69	−.72	+.41	+.77	−.08
	p			.04	.02	.03	.02		.01	

ticular interest is the MMPI SI scale. The increasing positively significant correlation from the BDI, to the AGG HX, to the childhood problems questionnaire, to the MMPI PD and the MMPI SI scale is consistent with the fact that of all childhood problem items reported by the subjects, a lack of friends was the item most strongly checked by those individuals with the lowest levels of CSF 5-HIAA. The BDI Hostility scale, which correlated the most positively significantly with AGG HX, also correlated highly with the MMPI SI, which, as might be expected, also correlated with the AGG HX. Hostility is no doubt one of the factors that interferes strongly with the formation and maintenance of friendships.

When all 57 items of the childhood problem questionnaire were taken as a composite, there was a significant, inverse correlation between "childhood problems" and levels of CSF 5-HIAA measured in young adult males (see Figure 2).

Evidence for poor peer relationships, both as children and as adults, is especially interesting, since this area of function or "dysfunction," whether observed by the individual himself or by others, has been a highly focused upon area by those who have studied aggression from psychological and sociological points of view. The possibility that observations of varied interpersonal disturbances could be the dependent result of common underlying biological predispositions has been less focused upon. Most therapies for impulsive conditions have been interpersonal manipulations or environmental alterations, with the possible exception of children with ADD/CD. Though ADD/CD children are thought to be receiving pharmacological treatment for their attentional deficit, the reasons for referral are just as often related to their behavior as to their attentional deficit.

In any case, from studies of children and adolescents, it is clear that areas of behavior related to aggression, impulsivity, and social difficulty, though manifestations change with age, i.e., from the small child for whom a babysitter will "sit" only once, to the latency age child who is invited to a peer's home only once, to the adolescent who gets into a struggle with every supervisor, to the adult who forms transient relationships which predominantly are strongly, violently, and emotionally self-serving, deserve further clinical investigation from a psychobiological perspective.

TABLE 4

Adult and Child Measures of Aggression, Social Introversion, and CSF 5-HIAA

	BDI AGG	*AGG HX*	*CHD PROB*	*MMPI PD*	*CSF 5-HIAA*
BDI-AGG[a,c]					−0.39 $p = .27$
AGG-HX[b,d]	0.77 $p < .01$				−0.53 $p < .08$
CHD PROB[a,d,e]	0.68 $p < .04$	0.52 $p = .08$			−0.63 $p < .03$
MMPI-PD[a,d,e]	0.48 $p = .16$	0.57 $p = .05$	0.49 $p = .10$		−0.77 $p < .01$
MMPI-SI[a,d,e]	0.43[f] $p = .21$	0.62 $p < .04$	0.65 $p < .03$	0.74 $p < .01$	−0.59 $p < .05$

Correlations are Pearson.

a = self-rating
b = observer-rating
c = true-false
d = gradated answers
e = validity checks
f = BDI hostility and SI correlate ($r = 0.80$, $p < .01$)

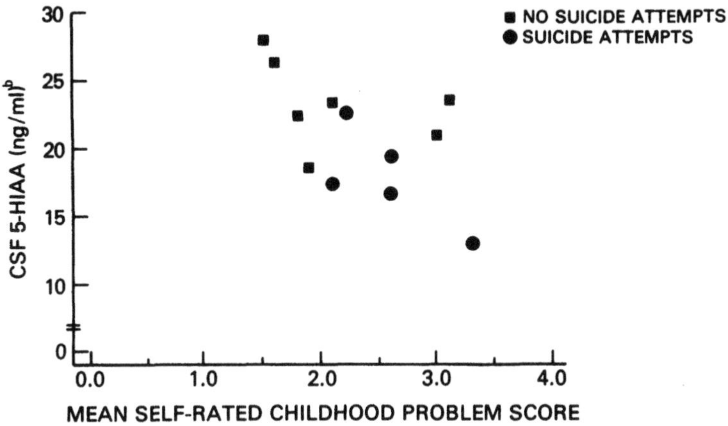

[a]THE SELF-RATED SCORES WERE NEGATIVELY CORRELATED WITH CSF 5-HIAA ($r = -0.63$, $p<0.03$)
[b]MEASURED BY GAS CHROMOTOGRAPHY - MASS SPECTROMETRY

Figure 2. Self-rated childhood problems and CSF 5-hydroxyindoleacetic acid (5-HIAA) levels of 12 young adult male patients with borderline personality disorder[a].

Though repeated episodes of aggressive or impulsive behavior may be the highly visible evidence of a trait, they may be no more reliable than the less "visible," but perhaps more consistent, evidence of a "defect" in the ability to socialize. Both could reflect, in part, an underlying biological predisposition.

REFERENCES

Amery, B., Minichiello, M. D., & Brown, G. L. (1984). Aggression in hyperactive boys: Response to d-amphetamine. *J Am Acad Child Psychiatry, 23,* 291–294.

Anders, T. F., Cann, H. M., Ciaranello, R. D., Barchas, J. D., & Berger, P. A. (1978). Further observations on the use of 5-hydroxytryptophan in a child with Lesch-Nyhan syndrome. *Neuropaediatrie, 9,* 157–166.

Asberg, M., Bertilsson, L., & Thoren, P., & Traskman, L. (1978). CSF monoamine metabolites in depressive illness. In S. Garattini (Ed), *Depressive Disorders* (pp. 292–305). New York: Friedrich-Karl Schattauer Verlag.

Asberg, M., Thoren, P., & Traskman, L. (1976a). "Serotonin depression"—A biochemical subgroup within the affective disorders? *Science, 191*, 478–480.

Asberg, M., Traskman, L., & Thoren, P. (1976b). 5-HIAA in the cerebrospinal fluid: A biochemical suicide predictor? *Arch Gen Psychiatry, 33*, 1193–1197.

Baker, D. (1972). Chromosome errors and antisocial behavior. *CRC Critical Reviews in Clinical Laboratory Sciences* (Cleveland, Ohio), *3*, 41–101.

Ballenger, J. C., Goodwin, F. K., Major, L. F., & Brown, G. L. (1979). Alcohol and central serotonin metabolism in man. *Arch Gen Psychiatry, 36*, 224–227.

Beskow, J., Gottfries, C. G., Roos, B. E, & Winblad, B. (1976). Determination of monoamine and monoamine metabolites in the human brain: post mortem studies in a group of suicides and in a control group. *Acta Psychiatr Scand, 53*, 7–20.

Bioulac, B., Benezech, M., Renaud, B., Noel, B., & Roche, D. (1980). Serotoninergic dysfunction in the 47, XYY syndrome. *Biol Psychiatry, 15*, 917–923.

Bioulac, B., Benezech, M., Renaud, B., Roche, D., & Noel, B. (1978). Biogenic amines in 47, XYY syndrome. *Neuropsychopharmacology, 4*, 366–370.

Borgaonkar, D. S., & Shah, S. A. (1974). The XYY chromosome male—or syndrome? In A. G. Steinberg, & Bearn A. C. (Eds.), *Progress in Medical Genetics* (Vol. 10, pp. 135–222). New York: Grune and Stratton.

Bourne, H. R., Bunney, W. E. Jr, Colburn, R. W., Davis, J. M., Davis, J. N., Shaw, D. M., & Coppen, A. (1968). Noradrenaline, 5-hydroxytryptamine, and 5-hydroxyindole-acetic acid in hindbrains of suicidal patients. *Lancet, II*, 805–808.

Branchey, L., Branchey, M., Shaw, S., & Lieber, C. S. (1984). Depression, suicide, and aggression in alcoholics and their relationship to plasma amino acids. *Psychiatry Res, 12*, 219–226.

Brown, G. L. (1986b). Attention Deficit Disorder. In S. S. Gellis & B. M. Kagan (Eds.), *Current Pediatric Therapy*, (Vol. 12, pp. 44–46). Philadelphia: W. B. Saunders Co.

Brown, G. L., Ballenger, J. C., Minichiello, M. D., & Goodwin, F. K. (1979b). Human aggression and its relationship to cerebrospinal fluid 5-hydroxyindoleacetic acid, 3-methoxy-4-hydroxyphenylglycol and homovanillic acid. In M. Sandler (Ed.), *Psychopharmacology of Aggression*. pp. 131–148). New York: Raven Press.

Brown, G. L., & Bunney, W. E. Jr. (1978). Affective psychosis. In G. U. Balis, L. Wurmser, E. McDaniels, R. G. Grenell (Eds.), *The*

Psychiatric Foundations of Medicine, Clinical Psychopathology (Vol. IV., pp. 177–203). Boston, London: Butterworth Publishers Inc.

Brown, G. L., Ebert, M. H., Goyer, P. F., Jimerson, D. C., Klein, W. J., Bunney, W. E. Jr., & Goodwin, F. K. (1982a). Aggression, suicide, and serotonin: Relationships to cerebrospinal fluid amine metabolites. *Am J Psychiatry, 139,* 741–746.

Brown, G. L., Ebert, M. H., & Minichiello, M. D. (1985) Biochemical and Pharmacological Aspects of Attention Deficit Disorder. In L. M. Bloomingdale (Ed.), *Attention Deficit Disorder—Identification, Course and Rationale* (pp. 93–130). New York: Spectrum Publications.

Brown, G. L., & Goodwin, F. K. (1984). Diagnostic, clinical, and personality characteristics of aggressive men with low 5-HIAA. *Clinical Neuropharmacol, 7,* 756–757.

Brown, G. L., & Goodwin, F. K. (1986a). Cerebrospinal fluid correlates of suicide attempts and aggression. In J. J. Mann & M. Stanley (Eds.). *Psychobiology of Suicide* (Vol. 487, pp. 175–188). Annals of the New York Academy of Sciences.

Brown, G. L., & Goodwin, F. K. (1986b). Human aggression: A biological perspective. In W. H. Reid, D. Dorr, J. I. Walker, & J. W. Bonner III (Eds.), *Unmasking the Psychopath: Antisocial Personality and Related Syndromes* (pp. 132–155). New York, London: W. W. Norton.

Brown, G. L., Goodwin, F. K., Ballenger, J. C., Goyer, P. F., & Major, L. F. (1979a). Aggression in humans correlates with cerebrospinal fluid amine metabolites. *Psychiatry Res, 1,* 131–139.

Brown, G. L., Goodwin, F. K., Ballenger, J. C., & Goyer P. F. (1981). Cerebrospinal fluid amine metabolites and cyclic nucleotides in human aggression. *Psychopharmacol Bull, 17,* 63–65.

Brown, G. L., Goodwin, F. K., & Bunney, W. E. Jr. (1982b). Human aggression and suicide: Their relationship to neuropsychiatric diagnoses and serotonin metabolism. In B. T. Ho, J. C. Schoolar & E. Usdin (Eds.). *Serotonin in Biological Psychiatry, Advances in Biochemical Psycopharmacology* (Vol. 34, pp. 287–307). New York: Raven Press.

Brown, G. L., Kline, W. J., Goyer, P. F., Minichiello, M. D., Kruesi, M. J. P., & Goodwin, F. K. (1986c). Relationship of childhood characteristics to cerebrospinal fluid 5-hydroxyindoleacetic acid in aggressive adults. In Shagass et al. (Eds.), *IV World Congress of Biology and Psychiatry* (pp. 177–179). Amsterdam: Elsevier Press.

Brown, G. L., & Wilson, W. P. (1972). Parkinsonism and depression. *South Med J, 64,* 540–545.

Brown, G. L., Wilson, W. P., & Green, R. L. (1973). Mental aspects of Parkinsonism and their management. In J. Siegfried (Ed.), *Parkinson's Disease: Rigidity, Akinesia, Behavior, Selected Communications on Topic* (Vol. 2, pp. 265–278). Bern, Verlag Hans Huber.

Bunney, W. E. Jr, & Davis, J. M. (1965). Norepinephrine in depressive reactions: A review. *Arch Gen Psychiatry, 13,* 483–494.

Bunney, W. E. Jr, Janowsky, D. S., Goodwin, F. K., Davis, J. M., Brodie, H. K. H., Murphy, D. L., & Chase, T. N. (1969). Effects of L-DOPA on depression. *Lancet, I,* 885–885.

Buss, A. H. (1961). *The Psychology of Aggression.* New York: John Wiley & Sons.

Buss, A. H., & Durkee, A. (1957). An inventory for assessing different kinds of hostility. *J Consult Psychol, 21,* 343–348.

Buss, A. H., Durkee, A., & Baer, M. (1957). The measurement of hostility in clinical situations. *J Abnorm Psychol, 21,* 343–348.

Buss, A. H., Fischer, H., & Simmons, A. J. (1962). Aggression and hostility in psychiatric patients. *Journal of Consulting Psychology, 26*(1), 84–89.

Carlsson, A., Svennerholm, L., & Winblad, B. (1980). Seasonal and circadian monoamine variations in human brains examined postmortem. *Acta Psychiatr Scand, 61*(suppl. 280), 75–85.

Castells, S., Chakrabarti, C., Winsberg, B. G., Hurwic, M., Perel, J. M., & Nyhan, W. L. (1979). Effects of L-5-hydroxytryptophan on monoamine and amino acids turnover in the Lesch-Nyhan syndrome. *J of Autism and Developmental Disorders, 9,* 95–103.

Chadwick, D., Jenner, P., & Reynolds, E. H. (1975). Amines, anticonvulsants, and epilepsy. *Lancet, I,* 473–476.

Ciaranello, R. D., Anders, T. F., Barchas, J. D., Berger, P. A., & Cann, H. M. (1976). The use of 5-hydroxytryptophan in a child with Lesch-Nyhan syndrome. *Child Psychiatry Hum Dev, 7,* 127–133.

Ciaranello, R. D., Lipsky, A., & Axelrod, J. (1974). Association between fighting behavior and catecholamine biosynthetic enzymes in two sublines of an inbred mouse strain. *Proc Natl Acad Sci, 71,* 3006–3008.

Cochran, E., Robins, E., & Grote, S. (1976). Regional serotonin levels in brain: A comparison of depressive suicides and alcoholic suicides with controls. *Biol Psychiatry, 11,* 283–294.

Cohen, D. J., Caparulo, B. K., Shaywitz, B. A., & Bowers, M. B. Jr. (1977). Dopamine and serotonin metabolism in neuropsychiatrically disturbed children: Cerebrospinal fluid homovanillic acid and 5-hydroxyindoleacetic acid. *Archives of General Psychiatry, 34,* 545–550.

Cohen, D. J., Shaywitz, B. A., Caparulo, B. K., Young, J. G., & Bowers, M. B. Jr. (1978). Chronic, multiple tics of Gilles de la Tourettes' disease. *Arch Gen Psychiatry, 35,* 245–250.

Cohen, D. J., Shaywitz, B. A., Young, J. G., Carbonari, C. M., Nathanson, J. A., Lieberman, D., Bowers, M. B. Jr., & Maas, J. W.

(1979). Central biogenic amine metabolism in children with the syndrome of chronic multiple tics of Gilles de la Tourette. *Journal of the American Academy of Child Psychiatry, 18,* 320–341.

Cohen, S. I. (1980). Cushing's syndrome: A psychiatric study of 29 patients. *British Journal of Psychiatry, 136,* 120–124.

Coleman, M. (1971). Serotonin concentrations in whole blood of hyperactive children. *Journal of Pediatrics, 78,* 985–990.

Coleman, M. (1973). Serotonin and central nervous system syndromes of childhood: A review. *Journal of Autism and Childhood Schizophrenia, 3,* 27–35.

Coppen, A. (1967). The biochemistry of affective disorders. *British J Psychiatry, 113,* 1237–1264.

Coppen, A., Shaw, D. M., & Malleson, A. (1965). Changes in 5-hydroxytryptophan metabolism in depression. *British J Psychiatry, 111,* 105–107.

Crawley, J. N., Sutton, M. E., & Pickar, D. (1985). Animal models of self-destructive behavior and suicide. In A. Roy (Ed.), *Symposium on Self-Destructive Behavior. Psychiatric Clinics of North America. 8*(2), 299–310. Philadelphia: W. B. Saunders Co.

Crow, T. J., Cross, A. J., Cooper S. J., Deakin J. F. W., & Ferrier, I. N. et al. (1984). Neurotransmitter receptors and monoamine metabolites in the brains of patients with Alzheimer-type dementia and depression and suicide. *Neuropharmacology, 23,* 1561–1569.

Dalton, K. (1961). Menstruation and crime. *British Med J, 3,* 1752–1753.

Dalton, K. (1964). *The Premenstrual Syndrome.* Springfield, IL: Charles C Thomas.

Depue, R. A., & Spoont, M. R. (1986). Conceptualizing a serotonin tract: A behavioral dimension of constraint. In J. J. Mann, M. Stanley (Eds.). *Psychobiology of Suicide.* (Vol. 487, pp. 47–62). Annals of the New York Academy of Sciences.

Domino, E. F. (1976). Pharmacokinetics of oral tryptophan in drug-free psychiatric patients. In L. A. Gottschalk, S. Merlis (Eds.). *Pharmacokinetics of Psychoactive Drugs: Blood Levels and Clinical Response.* (pp. 117–126). New York: Wiley.

Domino, E. J., & Krause, R. R. (1974). Plasma tryptophan tolerance curves in drug free normal controls, schizophrenic patients and prisoner volunteers. *J Psychiat Res, 10,* 247–261.

Dorus, E. (1980). Variability in the Y chromosome and variability of human behavior. *Archives of General Psychiatry, 37,* 587–594.

Eichelman, B. (1979). Role of biogenic amines in aggressive behavior. In M. Sandler (Ed.), *Psychopharmacology of Aggression.* (pp. 61–93). New York: Raven Press.

Eichelman, B., & Thoa, N. B. (1973). The aggressive monoamines. *Biol Psychiatry, 6,* 143–164.

Ferguson, H. B., Pappas, B. A., Trites, R. L., Peters, D. A. V., & Taub H. (1981). Plasma free and total tryptophan, blood serotonin, and the hyperactivity syndrome: No evidence for the serotonin deficiency hypothesis. *Biological Psychiatry, 16,* 231–238.

Fernstrom, J. D. (1982). Acute effects of tryptophan and single meals on serotonin synthesis in the rat brain. In B. T. Ho, J. C. Schoolar, & E. Usdin (Eds.). *Serotonin in Biological Psychiatry. Advances in Biochemical Psychopharmacology* (Vol. 34, pp. 85–106). New York: Raven Press.

Fernstrom, J. D. & Wurtman, R. J. (1971). Brain serotonin content: Increase following ingestion of carbohydrate diet. *Science, 174,* 1023–1025.

Fernstrom, J. D., & Wurtman, R. J. (1972). Brain serotonin content: Physiological regulation by plasma neutral amino acids. *Science, 178,* 414–416.

Freud, S. (1976). Mourning and melancholia. In J. Strachey, A. Strachey, & A. Tyson (Eds.), *Standard Edition of the Complete Psychological Works of Sigmund Freud* (Vol 14, pp. 239–258). New York: Norton.

Funkenstein, D. H., Greenblatt, M., & Solomon, H. C. (1949). Psychophysiological study of mentally ill patients. I. The Status of the peripheral autonomic nervous system as determined by the reaction to epinephrine and mecholyl. *Am J Psychiatry, 106,* 16–28.

Garfinkel, B. D., & Klee, S. H. (1985). Behavioral and personality characteristics of adolescents with a history of childhood ADD. In L. M. Bloomingdale (Ed.), *Attention Deficit Disorder—Identification, Course and Rationale* (pp. 17–31). New York: Spectrum Publications.

Goodwin, F. K., Jamison, K. (1988). *Manic Depressive Illness.* New York: Oxford University Press, in press.

Goodwin, F. K., Post, R. M. & Wehr, T. A. (1977). Clinical approaches to the evaluation of brain amine functioning in mental illness: Some conceptual issues. In M. B. H. Youdim, W. Lovenberg, D. F. Sharman, & J. R. Lagnado (Eds.), *Essays in Neurochemistry and Neuropharmacology* (Vol 2, pp. 71–104). London: Wiley.

Gunn, J., & Gristwood, J. (1975). Use of the Buss-Durkee Hostility Inventory among British prisoners. *Journal of Consulting and Clinical Psychology, 43*(4), 590.

Harlow, H. F. (1959). Love in infant monkeys. *Scientific Am, 200,* 68–74.

Harlow, H. F., & Harlow, M. K. (1962). Social deprivation in monkeys. *Scientific Am, 207*(5), 136–146.

Hohman, L. B. (1922). Post-encephalitic behavior disorders in children. *Johns Hopkins Hospital Bulletin, 380,* 372–375.

Johansson, B., & Roos, B.-E. (1967). 5-hydroxyindoleacetic acid and homovanillic acid levels in cerebrospinal fluid of healthy volunteers and patients with Parkinson's syndrome. *Life Sciences, 6,* 1449–1454.

Jones, I. H. (1982). Self-injury: Toward a biological basis. *Perspectives in Biological Medicine, 26,* 137–150.

Kandel, E. (1986). *Molecular Basis of Learning and Memory.* National Institutes of Health, Howard Hughes Memorial Lecture.

Kety, S. S. (1979). Disorders of the human brain. *Scientific American, 241*(3), 121–145.

Krueger, A. P., Andriese, P. C., & Kotaka, S. (1968). Small air ions: Their effect on blood levels of serotonin in terms of modern physical theory. *Int J Biometeor, 12*(3), 225–239.

Kruesi, M. J. P., Linnoila, M., Rapoport, J. L., Brown, G. L., & Petersen, R. (1985). Carbohydrate craving, conduct disorder and low 5-HIAA. *Psychiatry Research, 16,* 83–86.

Kruesi, M. J. P., Rapoport, J. L., Cummings, E. M., Berg, C. J., Ismond, D. R., Flament, M., Yarrow, M., & Zahn-Wexler, C. (1987). Effect of sugar and aspartame on aggression and activity in children. *American Journal of Psychiatry, 141*(11), 1487–1490.

Lamprecht, F., Eichelman, B., Thoa, N. B., Williams, R. B., & Kopin, I. J. (1972). Rat fighting behavior: Serum dopamine-B-hydroxylase and hypothalamic typrosine hydroxylase. *Science, 177,* 1214–1215.

Lanyon, R. L. (1961). *A Handbook of MMPI Group Profiles.* Minneapolis: University of Minnesota Press.

Lapin, I. P., & Oxenkrug, G. F. (1969). Intensification of the central serotonergic processes as a possible determinant of the thymoleptic effect. *Lancet, I,* 132–136.

Leibowitz, G. (1968). Comparison of self-report and behavioral techniques of assessing aggression. *Journal of Consulting and Clinical Psychology, 32*(1), 21–25.

Leventhal, B. L., (1984). The neuropharmacology of violent and aggressive behavior. In C. Keith (Ed.), *The Aggressive Adolescent: Clinical Perspectives* (pp. 299–358). New York: The Free Press.

Lewis, D. A., & Smith, R. E. (1983). Steroid-induced psychiatric syndromes: A report of 14 cases and a review of the literature. *Journal of Affective Disorders, 5,* 319–332.

Lidberg, L., Asberg, M., & Sunquist-Stensman, U. B. (1984). 5-Hydroxyindoleacetic acid levels in attempted suicides who have killed their children. *Lancet, II,* 928.

Lidberg, L., Tuck, J. R., Asberg, M., Scalia-Tomba, G. P., & Bertilsson, L. (1985). Homicide, suicide and CSF 5-HIAA. *Acta Psychiatr Scand, 71,* 230–236.

Linnoila, M., Virkkunen, M., Scheinin, M., Nuutila, A., Rimon, R., & Goodwin, F. K. (1983). Low cerebrospinal fluid 5-hydroxyindoleacetic acid concentration differentiates impulsive from nonimpulsive violent behavior. *Life Sciences, 33,* 2609–2614.

Lloyd, K. G., Farley, I. J., Deck, J. H. N., & Hornykiewicz, O. (1974). Serotonin and 5-hydroxyindoleacetic acid in discrete areas of the brainstem of suicide victims and control patients. In E. Costa, G. L. Gessa, & M. Sandler (Eds.), *Serotonin: New Vistas, Advances in Biochemical Psycopharmacology* (Vol 11, pp. 387–397). New York: Raven Press.

Lopez-Ibor, J. J., Jr., Saiz-Ruiz, J., & Perez de los Cobos, J. C. (1985). Biological correlations of suicide and aggressivity in major depressions (with melancholia): 5-hydroxyindoleacetic acid and cortisol in cerebral spinal fluid, dexamethasone suppression test and therapeutic response to 5-hydroxytryptophan. *Neuropsychobiology, 14,* 67–74.

MacLean, P. D. (1949). Psychosomatic disease and the "visceral brain." Recent developments bearing on Papez theory of emotion. *Psychosomatic Med, 11,* 338–353.

MacLean, P. D. (1952). Some psychiatric implications of physiological studies on frontotemporal portion of limbic system (visceral brain). *Electroencephalogy Clin Neurophysiol, 4,* 407–418.

Major, L. F., Ballenger, J. C., Goodwin, F. K., & Brown, G. L. (1977). Cerebrospinal fluid homovanillic acid in male alcoholics: effects of disulfiram. *Biological Psychiatry, 12,* 635–642.

Major, L. F., Brown, G. L., & Wilson, W. P. (1973). Carcinoid and psychiatric symptoms. *South Med J, 66,* 787–790.

Marini, J. L., & Sheard, M. H. (1977). Antiaggressive effect of lithium ion in man. *Acta Psychiatrica Scandinavica, 55,* 269–286.

Matthews, W. S., & Barabas, G., (1981). Suicide and epilepsy: A review of the literature. *Psychomatics, 22,* 515–524.

McKinney, W. T., Moran, E. C., & Kraemer, G. W. (1984). Separation in nonhuman primates as a model for human depression: Neurobiological implications. In R. M. Post, & J. C. Ballenger (Eds.), *Neurobiology of Mood Disorders* (pp. 393–406). Baltimore: Williams & Wilkins.

McKinney, W. T., Jr., Suomi, S. J., & Harlow, H. F. (1971). Depression in primates. *Am J Psychiatry, 127,* 1313–1320.

Meyerson, L. R., Wennogle, L. P., Abel, M. S., Coupet, J., Lippa, A. S., Rau, C. E., & Beer, B. (1982). Human brain receptor alter ations in suicide victims. *Pharmacol Biochem Behav, 17,* 159–163.

Miller, N. E. (1969). Learning of visceral and glandular responses. *Science, 163,* 434–445.

Mizuno, T., & Yugari, Y. (1975). Prophylactic effect of L-5-hydroxytryptophan on self-mutilation in the Lesch-Nyhan syndrome. *Neuropaediatrie, 6,* 13–23.

Monroe, R. R. (1975). Anticonvulsants in the treatment of aggression. *J Nerv Ment Dis, 160,* 119–126.

Montgomery, S. A., & Montgomery, D. B. (1982). Pharmacological prevention of suicidal behavior. *J Affective Dis, 4,* 291–298.

Montgomery, S. A., Roy, D., & Montgomery, D. B. (1983). The prevention of recurrent suicidal acts. *British J of Clinical Pharmacology, 15,* 1835–1885.

Montgomery, S. A., Roy, D. H., & Montgomery, D. B. (1984). HVA in the CSF: A marker for suicidal acts. In G. D. Burrows, T. R. Norman, & K. P. Maguire (Eds.), *Biological Psychiatry—New Prospects* (Vol 2., pp. 159–163). London: J. Libbey.

Morrison, S. D., Chaffin, S., & Chase, T. V. (1975). Aggression in adolescents: Use of the Buss-Durkee Inventory. *Southern Medical Journal, 68,* 431–436.

Moyer, K. E. (1968). Kinds of aggression and their pathological basis. *Communications in Behavioral Biology, (Part A), 2,* 65–87.

Moyer, K. E. (1971). The physiology of aggression and the implications for aggression control. In J. L. Singer (Ed.), *The Control of Aggression and Violence: Cognitive and Physiological Factors* (pp. 61–92). New York: Academic Press.

Moyer, K. E. (1976). *The Psychobiology of Aggression.* New York: Harper and Row.

Papez, J. W. (1937). A proposed mechanism of emotion. *Arch Neurol Psychiatry, 38,* 725–743.

Pare, C. M. B., Yeung, D. P. H., Price, K., & Stacey, R. S. (1969). 5-Hydroxytryptamine, noradrenaline and dopamine in brainstem, hypothalamus and caudate nucleus of controls and of patients committing suicide by coal-gas poisoning. *Lancet, II,* 133–135.

Perry, E. K., Marshall, E. F., Blessed, G., Tomlinson, B. E., & Perry, R. H. (1983). Decreased imipramine binding in the brains of patients with depressive illness. *British J Psychiatry, 142,* 188–192.

Pokorny, A. D. (1964). Suicide rates in various psychiatric disorders. *J Nerv Ment Dis, 139,* 499–506.

Post, R. M., Ballenger, J. C., & Goodwin, F. K. (1980). Cerebrospinal fluid studies of neurotransmitter function in manic and depressive illness. In J. H. Wood (Ed.), *Neurobiology of Cerebrospinal Fluid* (Vol 1, pp. 685–717). New York: Plenum Press.

Rapoport, J. L., Quinn, P. O., Scribanu, N., & Murphy, D. L. (1977). Platelet serotonin of hyperactive school-age boys. *British J of Psychiatry, 134,* 144–148.

Reimherr, F. W., Wender, P. H., Ebert, M. H., & Wood, D. R. (1984). Cerebrospinal fluid homovanillic acid and 5-hydroxyindoleacetic acid in adults with attention deficit disorder, residual type. *Psychiatry Research, 11,* 71–78.

Reis, O. J. (1974). Central neurotransmitters in aggression. *Research Publications, Associations for Research in Nervous and Mental Disease, 52,* 119–148.

Renson, G. J., Adams, J. E., & Tinklenberg, J. R. (1978). Buss-Durkee assessment and validation with violent versus nonviolent chronic alcohol abusers. *Journal of Consulting and Clinical Psychology, 46*(2), 360–361.

Rosenthal, N. E., & Sack, D. A. (1985). Antidepressant effects of light in seasonal affective disorder. *American Journal of Psychiatry, 142*(2), 163–170.

Rosenthal, N. E., Sack, D. A., Gillin, J. C., Lewy, A. J., Goodwin, F. K., Davenport, Y., Mueller, P. S., Newsome, D. A., & Wehr, T. A. (1984). Seasonal affective disorders—A description of the syndrome and preliminary findings with light therapy. *Archives of General Psychiatry, 41,* 72–80.

Rossi, A. M., Jacobs, M., Monteleone, M., Olsen, R., Surber, R. W., Winkler, E. L., & Wommack, A. (1986). Characteristics of psychiatric patients who engage in assaultive or other fear-inducing behaviors. *Journal of Nervous and Mental Disease, 174*(3), 154–160.

Rydin, E., Schalling, D., & Asberg, M. (1982). Rorschach ratings in depressed and suicidal patients with low levels of 5-hydroxyindoleacetic acid in cerebrospinal fluid. *Psychiatry Research, 7,* 229–243.

Schildkraut, J. J. (1965). The catecholamine hypothesis of affective disorders. A review of supporting evidence. *Am J Psychiatry, 122,* 509–522.

Schroeder, J., de la Chapelle, A., Hakola, P., & Virkkunen, M. (1981). The frequency of XYY and XXY men among criminal defenders. *Acta Psychiatrica Scandinavica, 63,* 272–276.

Schulsinger, F., Kety, S. S., Rosenthal, D., & Wender, P. H., (1979). A family study of suicide. In Schou, M., Stromgren, E. (Eds.), *Origin, Prevention and Treatment of Affective Disorders* (pp. 277–287). London: Academic Press.

Shaw, D. M., Camps, F. E., & Eccleston, E. G. (1967). 5-Hydroxytryptamine in the hindbrain of depressive suicides. *Br J Psychiatry, 113,* 1407–1411.

Shaywitz, B. A., Cohen, D. J., & Bowers, M. B., Jr. (1977). CSF monoamine metabolites in children with minimal brain dysfunction: Evidence for alteration of brain dopamine—A preliminary report. *J of Pediatrics, 90,* 67–71.

Sheard, M. (1971). Effect of lithium on human aggression. *Nature, 230,* 113–114.

Sheard, M. (1975). Lithium in the treatment of aggression. *J Nerv Mentl Dis, 100,* 108–117.

Shetty, T., & Chase, T. N. (1976). Central monoamines and hyperkinesis of childhood. *Neurology, 26,* 1000–1002.

Sjordsma, A., Lovenberg, W., Engelman, K., Carpenter, W. T., Wyatt, R. J., & Gessa, G. L. (1970). Serotonin Now. Clinical implications of inhibiting its synthesis with para-chlorophenylalanine (PCPA). Combined Clinical Staff Conference at the National Institutes of Health. *Ann Intern Med, 73,* 607–629.

Soubrie, P. (1986). Reconciling the role of central serotonin neurons in humans and animal behavior. *Behavior Brain Science, 9,* 319–364.

Spitzer, R. L. (Chr., Task Force). (1980). *Diagnostic and Statistical Manual of Mental Disorders: DSM III.* Washington D.C.: American Psychiatric Association.

Stanley, M. (in press). Postmortem findings in suicides. In *Youth Suicide,* Rockville, MD, Dept of HHS.

Stanley, M., & Mann, J. J. (1983). Increased serotonin-2 binding sites in frontal cortex of suicide victims. *Lancet, I,* 214–216.

Stanley, M., & Mann, J. J. (1984). Suicide and serotonin receptors. *Lancet, I,* 349.

Stanley, M.,Virgilio, J., & Gershon, S. (1982) Tritiated imipramine binding sites are decreased in the frontal cortex of suicides. *Science, 216,* 1337–1339.

Stoff, D. M., Pollock, L., Vitiello, B., Behar, D., & Bridger, W. H. (1987). Reduction of (3H)-Imipramine binding sites in platelets of conduct-disordered children. *Neuropsychopharmacology, 1,*(1),55-62.

Sulman, F. G., Levy, D., Pfeifer, Y., Superstine, E., & Tal, E. (1975). Effects of the Sharav and Bora on urinary neurohormone excretion in 500 weather-sensitive females. *Int J Biometeor, 19*(3), 202–209.

Suomi, S. J. (1975). Depressive behavior in adult monkeys following separation from family environment. *J Abnormal Psychology, 84,* 576–578.

Suomi, S. J., Harlow, H. F., & McKinney, W. T. (1972). Monkey psychiatrists. *Am J Psychiatry, 128,* 927–932.

Swade, C., & Coppen, A. (1980). Seasonal variation in biochemical factors related to depressive illness. *Journal of Affective Disorders, 2,* 249–255.

Sweet, W. H., Ervin, F., & Mark, V. H. (1969). The relationship of violent behaviour to focal cerebral disease. In S. Garattini & E. B. Siag, (Eds.), *Aggressive Behavior* (pp. 336–352). Amsterdam: Excerpta Medica.

Takahaski, S., Yamane, H., Kondo, H., & Tani, N. (1974). CSF monoamine metabolites in alcoholism, a comparative study with depression. *Folia Psychiatr Neurol Journal, 28,* 347–354.

Valzelli, L. (1981). *Psychobiology of Aggression and Violence.* New York: Raven Press.

Valzelli, L. (1984). Reflections on experimental and human pathology of aggression. *Prog Neuro-Psychopharmacol and Biol Psychiatry, 8,* 311–325.

van Praag, H. M. (1967). Antidepressants, catecholamines, and 5-hydroxyindoles—Trends towards a more specific research in the field of antidepressants. *Psychiat Neurochir* (Amst), *70,* 219–233.

van Praag, H. M. (1969). Monoamines and depression: The reverse of the medal. *Pharmakopsycchiatrie, Neuropsychopharmakologia, 3,* 151–160.

van Praag, H. M., Kahn, R., Asnis, G. M., Lemus, C. Z., & Brown, S. L. (1987). Therapeutic indications for serotonin-potentiating compounds: A hypothesis. *Biological Psychiatry, 22,* 205–212.

Virkkunen, M., Nuutila, A., Goodwin, F. K., & Linnoila, M. (1987). Cerebrospinal fluid monoamine metabolites levels in male arsonists. *Archives of General Psychiatry, 44,* 241–247.

Weiss, G., Hechtman, L., Perlman, T., Hopkins, J., & Wener, A. (1979). Hyperactives as young adults. *Archives of General Psychiatry, 36,* 675–682.

Welsh, G. S., & Dahlstrom, W. B., (Eds.). (1956). *Basic Readings on the MMPI in Psychology and Medicine.* Minneapolis: University of Minnesota Press.

Wender, P. H., Reimherr, F. W., & Wood, D. R. (1981). Attention Deficit Disorder ("minimal brain dysfunction") in adults: A replication. *Archives of General Psychiatry, 38,* 449–456.

Wirz-Justice, A., & Richter, R. (1979). Seasonality in biochemical determinations: A source of variance and a clue to temporal incidence of affective illness. *Psychiatry Research, 1,* 53–60.

Witkin, H. A., Mednick, S. A., Schulsinger, F., Bakkestrom, E., Christiansen, K. O., Goodenough, D. R., Hirschorn, K., Lundsteen, C., Owen, D. R., Philip, J., Rubin, D. B., & Stocking, M.

(1976). Criminality in XYY and XXY men: The elevated crime rate of XYY males is not related to aggression. It may be related to low intelligence. *Science, 193,* 547–555.

Wood, D. R., & Reimherr, F. W. (1983). Minimal brain dysfunction (Attention Deficit Disorder) in Adults. In S. Akhtar (Ed.), *New Psychiatric Syndromes—DSM III and Beyond* (pp. 109–136). New York: Jason Aronson, Inc.

Wood, D. R., Reimherr, F. W., Wender, P. H., & Johnson, G. E. (1976). Diagnosis and treatment of MBD in adults. *Archives of General Psychiatry, 33,* 1453–1460.

Yudofsky, S. C., Silver, J. M., Jackson, W., Endicott, J., & Williams, D. (1986). The overt aggression scale for the objective rating of verbal and physical aggression. *American J of Psychiatry, 143,*(1), 35–39.

8

Monoamines, Glucose Metabolism and Impulse Control

MARKKU LINNOILA
MATTI VIRKKUNEN
ALEC ROY
WILLIAM Z. POTTER

In late 1960s, work by Italian investigators implicated reduced serotonin turnover in isolation-induced aggression in male mice (Valzelli & Garattini, 1968). Ever since, the central nervous system's (CNS) serotonergic innervation has been thought to exert some control over aggressiveness. Another line of research in inbred mouse strains associated an increased length of the Y chromosome with increased intermale aggressive behavior (Selmanoff et al., 1975). In early human studies, male violent offenders were also found to exhibit a familial trait of long Y chromosomes more often than control males (De la Chapelle et al., 1963; Nielsen & Henriksen (1972).

Dutch (van Praag & Korf, 1971) and Swedish (Asberg et al., 1976) investigators reported a decade ago that depressed patients with "vital" depressions or those who attempted suicide by violent means showed a slow rate of accumulation of CSF 5-HIAA after a probenecid load or low levels of CSF 5-HIAA, respectively. In the late 1970s, Brown and Goodwin (1979, 1982) in the USA found low CSF 5-HIAA in aggressive navy men and marines being discharged from the service because of a history of exhibiting repeated and unpredictable aggressive behaviors. Furthermore, French researchers (Bioulac et al., 1980) discovered very low CSF 5-HIAA accumulation rates in six violent offenders, who had the XYY syndrome.

In the early 1980s, in a series of studies on violent offenders in Finland, Virkkunen et al. (1982a, b, 1983) showed that impulsive offenders diagnosed as having either antisocial or intermittent explosive personality disorder often became hypoglycemic during the oral glucose tolerance test. The hypoglycemias were due to increased insulin secretion. The authors also noticed that the patients who had the hypoglycemic tendency complained of severe insomnia. Japanese investigators studying CNS control of glucose metabolism demonstrated in mid 1980s that the suprachiasmatic nucleus, which is a major controller of circadian rhythms also regulates glucose metabolism (Yamamoto et al., 1984). More specifically, rats with suprachiasmatic nucleus lesions showed enhanced insulin responses to intravenous glucose administration.

In this chapter we review pertinent literature, describe our own studies in some detail, synthesize a coherent and testable hypothesis from the published but seemingly disconnected data summarized above, and describe our ongoing studies testing the hypothesis.

ANIMAL STUDIES

Aggressive Behavior and Serotonin Metabolism

Valzelli and coworkers studying isolation-induced fighting in male mice and mouse-killing behavior in rats observed an association between the emergence of these behaviors and a low 5-HIAA/serotonin ratio in whole brain homogenates obtained from the aggressive animals (1969, 1971). A low ratio is thought to reflect a low rate of serotonin turnover. Reduction of CNS serotonin by pharmacological or dietary means also leads to increased shock-induced fighting or mouse killing behavior in rats (Kantak et al., 1981; Katz, 1980). Mouse killing behavior produced by depletion of serotonin by p-chlorophenylalanine can be reduced by the serotonin reuptake inhibitor fluoxetine (Berzenyi et al., 1983). Olfactory bulbectomy, which in mice leads to increased intraspecies aggression, produces serotonin accumulation in the central nervous system. This accumulation could be indicative of reduced serotonin turnover; moreover, the time course of the serotonin accumulation and the expression of the aggressive behavior parallel each other (Garris et al., 1984).

Both isolation- and olfactory bulbectomy-induced aggression can be reduced by serotonin receptor agonists. Serotonin 1A receptor agonists such as 8-OH-DPAT are more potent than serotonin 1B receptor agonists in these animal models (Molina et al., 1986). Serotonin itself and serotonin receptor agonists show anatomical specificity in their mouse-killing reducing effects in rats. Injections into the amygdala are particularly effective (Pucilowski et al., 1985).

The monoaminergic neurone systems interact extensively in the CNS, and a certain level of activity in all of them is necessary to carry out complex behaviors. Thus, putative noradrenergic manipulations which affect mouse-killing behavior and dopaminergic changes associated with such behavior (Kozak et al., 1984; Broderick et al., 1985) could also be working indirectly through the serotonin system.

These rodent models of aggressive behavior do not permit the differentiation of aggressiveness from impulsivity. This differentiation is, however, critical if we are to extrapolate from animal to human research. Such an attempt was made by Soubrie (1986) in a recent review on the role of serotonin in human and animal behavior. He persuasively argued that serotonin serves as an endogenous inhibitor of the expression of various behaviors. Thus, reduced serotonin function might not lead to aggressive behaviors per se, but would serve a permissive role for the ready expression of aggressive impulses. According to this model, serotonin depletion leads to a primary increase in impulsivity and the resulting increment in aggressiveness is one of the more observable manifestations of the behavioral change.

In Chapter 9 of this volume, Higley and collaborators describe relevant studies in monkeys. Their findings are suggestive of an association between an age-related reduction in CSF 5-HIAA concentration and the emergence of aggressive behaviors during play. This model has not been thoroughly enough investigated to permit a confident distinction between aggressiveness or impulsivity being primarily related to reduced CSF 5-HIAA concentration.

Studies on Y Chromosome

A series of studies from the University of Connecticut have produced evidence of an association between characteristics of the Y chromosome and an increase in intermale aggressive behaviors in various inbred mouse strains (Selmanoff et al., 1977; Maxson et al., 1979, 1982; Ginsburg et al., 1981). Even though there is a relationship between the length of the Y chromosome and aggressiveness—a long Y chromosome is in certain strains associated with increased aggressiveness—interactions between the Y and other chromosomes are also important in controlling aggressive behaviors. Again, no attempt has been made to distinguish between aggressiveness and impulsivity in this model.

At the present time there are no studies on the role of the Y chromosome in controlling serotonin turnover. If both serotonin turnover and Y chromosome characteristics are important in controlling aggressiveness, or, alternatively, if both are associated with impulse control, then correlations between these two variables should be found. Specifically it could be predicted that in certain particularly aggressive mouse strains a long Y chromosome would be associated with reduced serotonin turnover in parts of the CNS which are important in controlling aggressive behaviors or impulsivity.

Studies on Glucose Metabolism

Yamamoto et al. (1984a,b,c; 1985) have demonstrated in a series of studies that lesions of the suprachiasmatic nucleus produce rats which may be vulnerable to mild hypoglycemia during their active period. These rats show hyperinsulinemic and hypoglucagonemic responses to glucose and deoxyglucose challenges, respectively. Furthermore, they do not show reactive hyperglycemia in response to central glucopenia produced by intracerebroventricular administration of deoxyglucose.

The suprachiasmatic nucleus projects to the ventromedial nucleus of the hypothalamus. This hypothalamic area, together with the lateral hypothalamus which is also connected to the suprachiasmatic nucleus (Swanson & Cowan, 1977; Kita et al., 1982) participates in the control of feeding and satiety, particularly in regard to carbohydrate intake. Interestingly, the suprachiasmatic nucleus is thought to be the major endogenous circadian pacemaker in the central nervous system (Moore & Eichler, 1972), and it receives a serotonergic input from the brain stem raphe nuclei (Falkovits et al., 1977). Thus, this nucleus provides an anatomic link between serotonergic functions, regulation of circadian rhythms such as the sleep wake cycle, and regulation of glucose metabolism.

The lesions done by Yamamoto et al. (1986) were produced by electrolysis. Thus, the actual nature of the neurochemical changes was not characterized, and further experiments are necessary to link the changes in glucose metabolism to the serotonin system.

HUMAN STUDIES CSF 5-HIAA AND HVA

Depression

In 1971, van Praag and Korf discovered that 5-HIAA concentrations in the CSF of depressed patients quantified after a probenecid load were bimodally distributed. Patients with low concentrations were characterized by having a particularly severe form of the illness which the authors called "vital" depression.

In 1976, Asberg et al. reported an increased risk of violent suicide attempts among depressed patients with a low CSF 5-HIAA concentration. Furthermore, these authors have emphasized in various presentations that the suicide attempts among the patients with low CSF 5-HIAA were characterized by being unexpected by the therapists. The latter phenomenon may to a certain extent be reflective of an impulsive nature of the acts. The finding of Asberg et al. has been replicated by many investigators as reviewed elsewhere in this volume by Roy and Linnoila (Chapter 6). Certain issues require special comment. First, the relationship is in general stronger between CSF 5-HIAA concentration and actual suicidal behavior rather than ideation. Second, the relationship does not hold in patients with bipolar depression; as a group, these patients are at a high risk of committing suicide (Agren, 1983; Berrettini et al., 1985). Unfortunately, the current knowledge of biological correlates of suicidal behavior is most rudimentary in this diagnostic group which has a very high lifetime risk of committing suicide.

There are only a few apparently well-designed studies on patients with unipolar depression which have not been found an association between low CSF 5-HIAA concentration and suicide attempts. One such study by Roy-Byrne et al. (1983) is illustrative of caveats affecting research in this field. Patients studied were housed on an NIMH research ward in the NIH Clinical Center. Because they participated in research protocols requiring drug-free washout periods of some weeks duration, patients with current severe and active suicidal behavior were excluded. Thus, the sample was biased against finding biochemical correlates of suicidal behaviors. Furthermore, the unipolar subsample analyzed separately contained only 13 patients, a number low enough to be conducive of a type 2 statistical error. This type of error is particularly likely because low CSF 5-HIAA concentrations are found in subgroups of both normals and depressed patients. In spite of these issues, the authors found a strong statistical trend towards lower CSF 5-HIAA concentrations among the subjects with unipolar depression who had a history of suicide attempts.

Some authors have reported a significantly lower mean HVA rather than 5-HIAA concentration in their suicidal patients (Agren, 1980; Montgomery & Montgomery, 1982; Roy et al., 1986a). In a large-scale clinical and animal study, Agren et al. (1986) elucidated the nature of the relationship of CSF 5-HIAA and HVA concentrations. Statistically, a sigmoid "dose-response curve"-like relationship from 5-HIAA to HVA described the data better than a straight regression line. Together with the animal data, the results were interpreted to reflect serotonergic control of dopamine turnover in regions of the CNS contributing a bulk of the HVA in lumbar CSF. Further support for this inference is provided by the finding of Roy and Linnoila (this volume) who lost a significant CSF HVA concentration difference between depressed suicide attempters and nonattempters after covarying out the influence of 5-HIAA. Therefore, either a low 5-HIAA or HVA concentration can under certain circumstances be indicative of a reduced CNS serotonergic activity.

IMPLICATIONS OF CSF HVA/5-HIAA CONCENTRATION RATIO FOR PSYCHOBIOLOGICAL RESEARCH

Rather than providing grist for the argument as to which one is more important as a possible determinant of suicidal behavior—a low CSF 5-HIAA or HVA concentration—the ratio of CSF HVA and 5-HIAA concentrations may provide information that goes beyond consideration of the concentrations themselves. On the assumption that there is an unidirectional influence of serotonin on dopamine turnover, a model for interpreting the HVA/5-HIAA ratio can be constructed. This model includes dopamine synthesized and metabolized in norepinephrine neurons.

Terms are defined as follows:

HVA	= concentration of HVA in CSF (moles/ml)
f_1	= proportion of dopamine metabolized to HVA
DA_I	= rate of formation of dopamine independent of serotonin influence (moles/min)
DA_s	= rate of formation of dopamine dependent on serotonin influence (moles/min)
Cl_1	= clearance of HVA from CSF (ml/min)
R	= function relating serotonin turnover and release to dopamine turnover
5-HIAA	= concentration of 5-HIAA in CSF (moles/ml)
f_2	= proportion of serotonin metabolized to 5-HIAA
5-HT	= rate of formation of serotonin (moles/min)
Cl_2	= clearance of 5-HIAA from CSF (ml/min)

Only three terms require special comment. The first is "DAs" which allows for a certain proportion of dopamine synthesis to be under serotonergic control. "DA_I" is the synthesis rate of dopamine dependent on all other influences. The "R" term is intentionally left vague since the linkage between the turnover of serotonin and its release at sites where it could act on dopamine or norepinephrine neurons to stimulate the synthesis and/or turnover of dopamine remains to be established. For instance, under certain situations it has been shown that the turnover of serotonin as reflected in 5-HIAA concentrations has no discernible link to serotonergic function (Commissiong, 1985). Thus, we must allow for complex relationships between serotonin turnover and any target function, alteration of dopamine turnover being the one under consideration here.

With these definitions in mind, the following equations can be derived: first, relating the concentration of HVA to the synthesis rate of dopamine:

$$1)\quad [\mathrm{HVA}] = \frac{f_1(\mathrm{DA_I} + \mathrm{DA_s})\mathrm{moles/min}}{\mathrm{Cl_1 ml/min}} = \mathrm{moles/ml}$$

Second, relating the concentration of 5-HIAA to the synthesis rate of serotonin:

$$2)\quad [\text{5-HIAA}] = \frac{f_2(\text{5-HT})}{\mathrm{Cl_2}}$$

Third, relating dopamine synthesis which is dependent on some concentration with serotonin synthesis:

$$3)\quad \mathrm{DA_s} = \mathrm{R}(\text{5-HT})$$

The ratio of HVA/5-HIAA then becomes,

$$4)\quad \frac{[\mathrm{HVA}]}{[\text{5-HIAA}]} = \frac{f_1}{f_2}\frac{\mathrm{Cl_2}}{\mathrm{Cl_1}}\frac{\mathrm{DA_I} + \mathrm{R}(\text{5-HT})}{(\text{5-HT})}$$

Under conditions in which the fractional conversion rates of the parent amines to their metabolites (f_1 and f_2) are similar or covary, the term f_1/f_2 will be close to one or a constant. Likewise, the clearance rates of 5-HIAA and HVA from the CSF (Cl_2 and Cl_1) may be very similar or covary across individuals in which case Cl_2/Cl_1 will be close to one or another constant. If these conditions hold then leaving out the constant terms yields:

$$5)\quad \frac{[\mathrm{HVA}]}{[\text{5-HIAA}]} = \frac{(\mathrm{DA_I})}{(\text{5-HT})} + \mathrm{R}$$

According to Equation 5, if the "R" term is negligible (i.e. there is, in fact, little or no functional link between serotonin and dopamine turnover), the ratio approaches or bears a constant relationship to the turnover of dopamine and serotonin. In such an instance, the ratio applied to group data would serve to get rid of the "noise" introduced by absolute interindividual differences in fractional metabolism to metabolites or their clearance from CSF. This is true only if the assumption that metabolism and clearance covaries across individuals is valid. Since the same or related forms of monoamine oxidase are probably responsible for the deamination of DA and 5-HT in the human CNS (Murphy, 1978) and since HVA and 5-HIAA are both weak organic acids which are transported by the same probenecid-inhibited pump, an assumption of covariance of the process seems responsible.

The more interesting application of Equation 5 is that if the "R" term is large (as suggested by the high correlation coefficient of HVA vs 5-HIAA in most CSF studies), then the value of the ratio is substantially influenced by the degree of linkage between serotonin and dopamine as well as by their actual rates of synthesis. A subpopulation of high or low ratios might be comprised of individuals who have an abnormality in the linkage between the two neurotransmitter systems. The ratio would thus provide a tool for exploring the extent of a neurotransmitter interaction rather than simply relative turnover rates.

Using the ratio allows an investigator to go beyond the formulation of "low serotonin" or "low dopamine" and focus on the degree of intactness of the interaction. This approach has never been applied to compare patients with problems of impulse control or aggression to appropriate controls. For meaningful statistics to compare differences in the ratio, relatively large population samples are necessary unless major differences are expected.

Personality Disorders

Brown et al. (1979, 1982) found a negative .78 correlation between CSF 5-HIAA concentration and an index of severity and number of aggressive acts in young Navy men and Marines being evaluated for discharge from service due to a pattern of recurrent aggressive and impulsive behaviors. A similar correlation (-.77) was found between CSF 5-HIAA and scores on the MMPI psychopathic deviate scale. In a recent report (Brown et al., 1986) the authors describe a negative .63 correlation between CSF 5-HIAA concentration and history of aggressive behaviors in childhood in the same men.

The relationships between MMPI scores and CSF 5-HIAA, and aggressiveness during childhood and CSF 5-HIAA are suggestive of low CSF 5-HIAA in these patients being an indicator of a trait rather than a state. The emphasis in the writings of the Karolinska and NIMH groups has been to associate the low CSF 5-HIAA trait primarily with either aggressiveness or violence.

A noteworthy void in research on CSF 5-HIAA is in the area of women with borderline personality disorder. These patients at a high risk of acting out by harming themselves have not been systematically studied.

Alcoholism

CSF 5-HIAA concentrations in alcoholics have been studied in Japan, USA and Hungary. Takahashi et al. (1974), investigating 30 alcoholics, found that only patients with severe withdrawal symptoms had lower 5-HIAA concentrations than controls. Major et al. (1977) reported a lower mean CSF HVA concentration in alcoholics during withdrawal compared to controls. Ballenger et al. (1979) performed two LPs on a group of alcoholics, the first one within 48 hours of consumption of the last drink and the other after four weeks of supervised abstinence. CSF 5-HIAA concentrations were significantly reduced from the first to the second LP. Furthermore, the average concentration in the second sample was significantly lower than mean CSF 5-HIAA in the controls, who had personality disorders. Based on their findings and previous animal research, the authors postulated that alcoholics as a group have a central serotonin deficit, and that alcohol functionally remedies such a deficit by releasing serotonin. Alcoholics studied by Ballenger et al. were relatively young Navy men (mean age 28.8 years).

Banki (1981) investigating women alcoholics in Hungary found, similar to Ballenger, a negative correlation between the number of days abstinent prior to LP and CSF 5-HIAA concentration. Branchey et al. (1984) found a low ratio of plasma tryptophan to other neutral amino-acid concentration in a subgroup of alcoholics who had histories of depressed mood and aggressive behavior. The ratio is thought to regulate the rate of entry of tryptophan, the amino acid precursor of serotonin into the brain. Because tryptophan hydroxylase, the rate limiting enzyme in serotonin synthesis, is not saturated in the brain, tryptophan's rate of entry may be the actual rate limiting step for the synthesis of this transmitter. Thus, by implication Branchey et al.'s patients may have had low CSF 5-HIAA concentrations. This interpretation warrants some caution, however, because Hagenfelt et al. (1984) found very low correlations between precursor amino acid and neurotransmitter metabolite concentrations in human CSF.

Roy et al. (1986a) pointed out the high suicide rate in alcoholics. Whether this finding is associated with a low CSF 5-HIAA concentration has not been investigated.

Relatives of Alcoholics

Rosenthal et al. (1980), investigating depressed relatives of alcoholics, found that they had a lower mean CSF 5-HIAA concentration than depressed patients without a family history of alcoholism. This relatively small-scale study raises a potentially important issue because the results suggest that not only may a low CSF 5-HIAA concentration be a trait but it may be a familial trait. Moreover, the results are compatible with Winokur's (1979) hypothesis of "depression spectrum" disorder, characterized by the coexistence of depression, sociopathy and alcoholism in the family, being different from pure depressive disorder. Whether depressed patients with a family history compatible with the definition of "depression spectrum" disorder are as a group more likely to have a lower CSF 5-HIAA concentration than patients with pure depressive disorder would require a prospective large scale test of the hypothesis.

Familial antisocial personality disorder has by Cloninger et al. (1981) been associated with "type 2" or male-limited alcoholism. Roy et al. (1987) have speculated that this subgroup of alcoholics, who represent roughly a quarter of all male alcoholics, may be biochemically characterized by low CSF 5-HIAA concentrations.

This hypothesis has not been prospectively tested as yet, but the results of Ballenger et al. are compatible with the hypothesis. They compared young male alcoholics, who as a group are most likely to have a high prevalence of "type 2" alcoholism, to controls, and they found a more than 30% difference in mean CSF 5-HIAA concentrations between alcoholics and controls.

Violent Offenders

To further elucidate associations between specific behaviors and CNS serotonin metabolism we studied 36 violent offenders (Linnoila et al., 1983). The idea was to have two equally violent groups and classify them according to the impulsiveness of their behavior. The hypothesis was that impulsive violent offenders would have a lower mean CSF 5-HIAA concentration than nonimpulsive offenders independent of the degree of violence. All patients were undergoing court ordered forensic psychiatry examinations in the Department of Psychiatry, University of Helsinki. Impulsiveness was defined by characteristics of the index crime. Patients with a clear premeditation of their act were classified as nonimpulsive while patients without established premeditation (attacking without provocation and not knowing the victim) were classified as impulsive. The source of the information was the police report concerning the index crime. Using this method, nine patients were classified as nonimpulsive and 27 as impulsive.

Diagnoses were made according to DSM-III criteria (American Psychiatric Assn., 1980) by a forensic research psychiatrist, who was not blind to the criminal records of the patients. The impulsive patients had either intermittent explosive or antisocial personality disorder, whereas the nonimpulsive patients had either paranoid or passive aggressive personality disorder. All patients fulfilled criteria for alcohol abuse. Seventeen of the 25 impulsive patients had a past history of suicide attempts. The impulsive patients had a significantly lower mean CSF 5-HIAA concentration than the nonimpulsive patients. Moreover, patients with a history of suicide attempts had the lowest mean CSF 5-HIAA. There was no difference in CSF free testosterone concentrations between the groups (Roy et al., 1986b). This is of interest because high testosterone concentrations in animal experiments have been associated with aggressiveness (Selmanoff et al., 1977).

Lidberg et al. (1984, 1985) found a low CSF 5-HIAA concentration in murderers killing their children or lovers, but not in alcoholic murderers. They did not, however, stratify their violent subjects according to their degree of impulsivity.

Arsonists

Impulsive firesetters are known to show very little interpersonal aggressive behavior. Therefore, to investigate further whether low CSF 5-HIAA concentration in humans is primarily associated with impulsiveness or aggressiveness we studied 20 impulsive arsonists (Virkkunen et al., 1987). Impulsiveness in these patients was defined as a sudden uncontrollable urge to set a fire. Subjects setting fires for economic gain such as insurance fraud were excluded from the sample. The arsonists were compared to 20 age- and sex-matched violent offenders and 10 controls. The arsonists were found to have the lowest mean CSF 5-HIAA concentration, followed by the violent offenders, who had a lower concentration than the healthy volunteers. Interestingly, mean CSF HVA concentrations were practically identical in the three groups, but CSF MHPG concentrations paralleled CSF 5-HIAA concentrations. Thus, both low mean CSF 5-HIAA and MHPG concentrations were relatively specifically associated with impulsivity rather than violence in these samples of violent offenders and impulsive fire setters.

Patients with Frontal Lobe Lesions

Patients who have suffered brain damage to the frontotemporal regions are often recognized to have frequent uncontrollable bursts of anger and to show "emotional lability." In one Dutch study (van Woerkom et al., 1977), 11 patients, who had sustained frontotemporal brain insults and who had an LP within one to nine days of the insult, had significantly lower CSF 5-

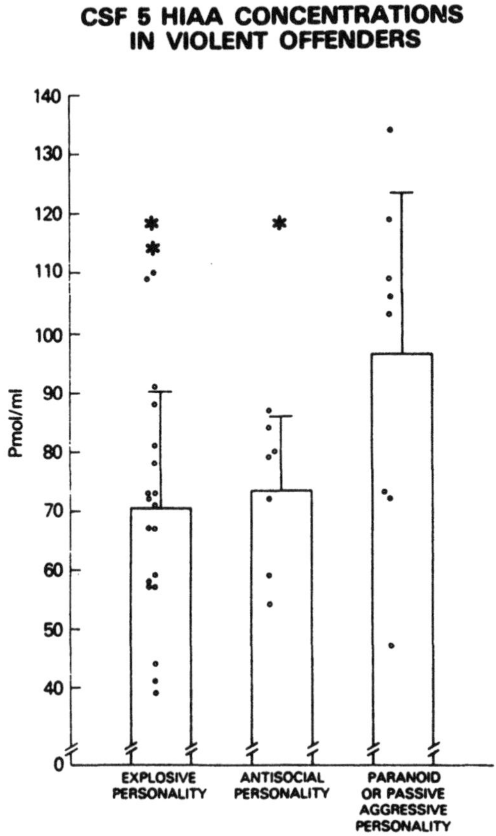

Figure 1. CSF 5-HIAA concentrations in 36 violent offenders. Violent offenders with intermittent explosive and antisocial personality disorders had been a priori, independent of diagnosis, classified as impulsive and the others as nonimpulsive offenders. ⋆ = $p<.05$, ⋆⋆ = $p<.01$, t-test for independent samples, two tailed probability. For abbreviations see text.

HIAA concentrations than 30 patients with diffuse brain injuries or 10 nonspecified controls.

Because the behavioral disturbances observed in patients with frontotemporal lesions can be construed as indicative of impaired impulse control, further studies on CSF 5-HIAA concentration are needed in this patient population. It is particularly important

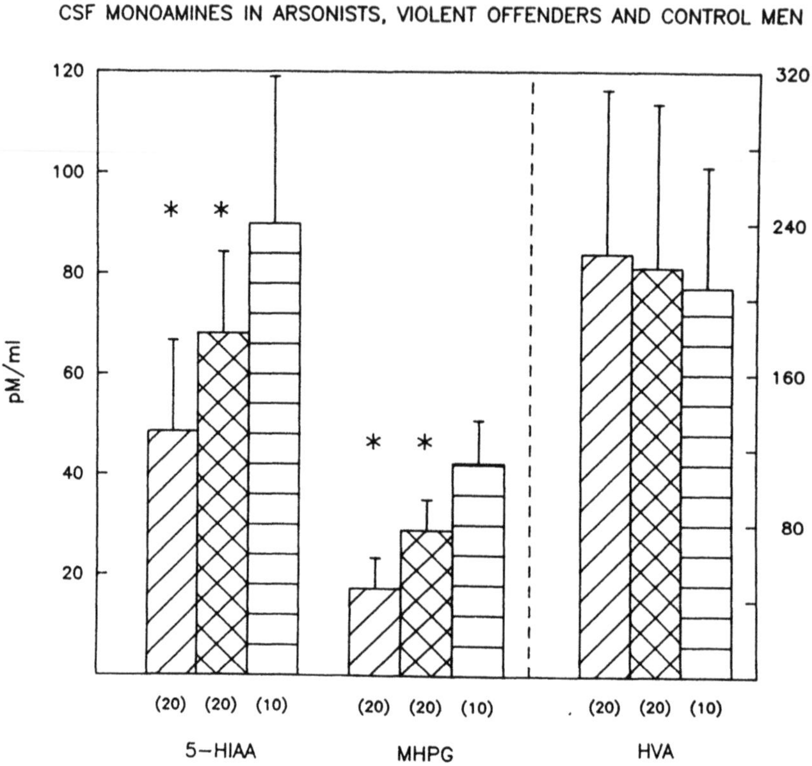

Figure 2. CSF 5-HIAA, MHPG and HVA concentrations in 20 arsonists, violent offenders and 10 healthy volunteers. Arsonists are on the left, violent offenders in the middle and healthy volunteers on the right in each cluster of bars. The violent offenders were age matched to the arsonists. The group includes both impulsive and nonimpulsive offenders. For symbols see Figure 1.

to investigate patients who have a stable condition months or years after the insult.

Pathological Gamblers

DSM-III classifies pathological gambling as an impulse control disorder. Furthermore, the criteria specify that patients with an antisocial personality disorder are excluded. We studied psychopathology and biology in 19 men fulfilling the DSM-III criteria for pathological gambling. Behaviorally, the patients were not particularly impulsive in other aspects of life. Analogous with "Type 1" alcoholics in the Cloninger classification, who are often characterized by an inability to stop drinking, one of the pathological gamblers' problems was inability to stop gambling once they had started. Biochemically, the patients had a mean CSF 5-HIAA concentration similar to 20 control men, but their mean CSF MHPG concentration was somewhat higher (Roy et al., 1988). We hypothesize that this finding may be associated with an abnormality in the biological arousal and reward system of these patients.

STUDIES ON TREATMENTS OF VIOLENT BEHAVIORS IN HUMANS

Tryptophan and lithium (Morand et al., 1983; Sherd et al., 1976) have in controlled studies shown efficacy in reducing violent outbursts in aggressive schizophrenics and prisoners, respectively. Propranolol has in a controlled study reduced assaultive behaviors in patients with organic brain diseases (Greendyke et al., 1986).

In uncontrolled clinical reports, propranolol, metoprolol, nadolol, and a combination of trazodone and tryptophan have been alleged to be efficacious in the treatment of violent behaviors in patients with schizophrenia and mental retardation due to various causes (Sorgi et al., 1986; Mattes, 1985; O'Neil et al., 1986).

All these treatments have serotonergic effects. Lithium and propranolol enhance presynaptic serotonergic functioning by different mechanisms (Hotta et al., 1986; Sprouse & Aghajanian, 1986) and tryptophan is the precursor aminoacid for serotonin synthesis.

GLUCOSE METABOLISM

Depression

Glucose tolerance has been extensively studied in depression. The major findings have been that patients with unipolar depression become hyperglycemic and hyperinsulinemic shortly after an oral or intravenous glucose load (Pryce, 1958a, b). Patients with bipolar depression are not different from normals and are significantly different from patients with unipolar depression (Pryce, 1958b). Successful treatment of depression reverses the abnormal glucose tolerance (van Praag & Leijnse, 1965). Furthermore, Heninger et al. (1975) found that in patients with psychotic unipolar depression suicidality was weakly but significantly associated with reduced disappearance of glucose and hyperinsulinemia.

The results of these early studies are difficult to interpret because the patients were reported to be actually hyper- rather than hypoglycemic. They were, however, followed only for an hour after administration of glucose. Because they were also hyperinsulinemic, they may well have become hypoglycemic later on, similar to some adult-onset diabetics, had they been followed for 5 to 6 hours. Be this as it may, the difference between uni- and bipolar depressives is intriguing because it parallels the reported difference in the relationship between CSF 5-HIAA and suicidality in these patient groups.

There is a need for studies on CSF 5-HIAA and oral glucose tolerance with 5- to 6-hour follow up in patients with major unipolar depression.

Violent Offenders

Virkkunen and collaborators (1982a,b, 1983, 1984, 1986a,b) have demonstrated that impulsive violent offenders often become hypoglycemic and hyperinsulinemic after an oral glucose load. There is an interesting difference in the time course of events in that patients with intermittent explosive personality disorder show a more rapid onset and recovery of the hypoglycemia than patients with antisocial personality disorder. Intuitively, these time course differences are of interest because they phenomenologically parallel characteristics of disturbed behaviors in these two patient groups.

Similar to the patients with a low CSF 5-HIAA concentration studied by Brown and Goodwin, the patients in Virkkunen's studies, who have clinically significant hypoglycemic responses, have a life-long history of aggressive, violent and antisocial behaviors. Moreover, they are also more likely to have fathers with histories of antisocial and criminal behaviors. Thus, both a low CSF 5-HIAA concentration and the tendency to become hypoglycemic after an oral glucose load may be familial traits. Whether they coexist in most impulsive patients remains to be established in further studies.

Arsonists

In the study by Virkkunen (1984), 11 out of 20 arsonists became hypoglycemic in the oral glucose tolerance test. They also had low CSF 5-HIAA concentrations, but correlation between the two measures was not statistically significant. In a larger sample of 59 arsonists, Virkkunen found mild hypoglycemia during the oral glucose tolerance test in 27 patients.

Healthy Volunteers

Benton and Kumari (1982), in a study on 24 healthy male volunteers, found significant correlations between the degree of hypoglycemia during an oral glucose tolerance test and scores on two psychological tests of hostility and frustration tolerance administered during the glucose tolerance test. Subjects with low blood glucose concentrations showed more hostility and lower frustration tolerance.

CONCLUSIONS

A large body of literature on aggressive, violent and impulsive behaviors and their biochemical correlates has been reviewed above. Further studies are clearly needed to elucidate possible interrelationships between such behaviors and serotonin and glucose metabolism, Y chromosome markers and alcohol abuse. Such studies should be pursued in human population samples and in animal models.

The existing results are consistent enough to permit prospective studies on the predictive value of biochemical variables such as CSF 5-HIAA and HVA in evaluating the risk of suicide or recurrent impulsive violent behavior. Furthermore, new highly specific serotonergic drugs should be investigated in preventing various forms of impulsive and violent behaviors and in maintaining sobriety in alcoholics.

REFERENCES

Agren, H. (1980). Symptom patterns in unipolar and bipolar depression correlating with monoamine metabolites in the cerebrospinal fluid, II: Suicide. *Psychiatry Res, 3,* 225–236.

Agren, H. (1983). Life at risk: Markers of suicidality in depression. *Psychiatr Dev, 1,* 87–104.

Agren, H., Mefford, I. N., Rudorfer, M. V., Linnoila, M., & Potter, W. Z. (1986). Interacting neurotransmitter systems. A nonexperimental approach to the 5-HIAA-HVA correlation in human CSF. *J Psychiat Res, 20,* 175–193.

American Psychiatric Association: *Diagnostic and Statistical Manual, Third Edition*. Washington, DC, American Psychiatric Association, 1980.

Asberg, M., Traskman, L., & Thoren, P. (1976). 5-HIAA in the cerebrospinal fluid—a biochemical suicide predictor? *Arch Gen Psychiatry, 33,* 1193–1197.

Ballenger, J., Goodwin, F., Major, L., & Brown, G. (1979). Alcohol and central serotonin metabolism in man. *Arch Gen Psychiatry, 36,* 224–227.

Banki, C. (1981). Factors influencing monoamine metabolites and tryptophan in patients with alcohol dependence. *J Neur Trans, 50,* 1193–1197.

Benton, D., & Kumari, N. (1982). Mild hypoglycemia and questionnaire measures of aggression. *Biol Psychol, 14,* 129–135.

Berrettini, W. H., Nurnberger, J. I. Scheinin, M., Seppala, T., Linnoila, M., Simmons-Alling, S., & Gershon, E. (1985). Cerebrospinal fluid and plasma monoamines and their metabolites in euthymic bipolar patients. *Biol Psychiatry, 20,* 257–269.

Berzenyi, P., Galateo, E., & Valzelli, L. (1983). Fluoxetine activity on muricidal aggression induced in rats by p-chlorophenylalanine. *Aggr Behav, 9,* 333–338.

Bioulac, B., Benezich, M., Renaud, B., Noel, B., & Roche, D. (1980). Serotonergic functions in the 47, XYY syndrome. *Biol Psychiatry, 15,* 917–9023.

Branchey, L., Branchey, M., Shaw, S., & Lieber, C. S. (1984). Depression, suicide, and aggression in alcoholics and their relationship to plasma amino acids. *Psychiatry Res, 12,* 219–226.

Broderick, P. A., Barr, G. A., Sharpless, N. S., & Bridger, W. H. (1985). Biogenic amine alterations in limbic brain regions of muricidal rats. *Res Comm Chem Path Pharmacol, 48,* 3–15.

Brown, G. L., Ebert, M. H., Goyer, D. C., Jimerson, D. C., Klein, W. J., Bunney, W. E., & Goodwin, F. K. (1982). Aggression, suicide and serotonin: Relationships to CSF amine metabolites. *Am J Psychiatry, 139,* 741–746.

Brown, G. L., Goodwin, F. K., Ballenger, J. C., Goyer, P. F., & Major, L. F. (1979). Aggression in humans correlates with cerebrospinal fluid metabolites. *Psychiatry Res, 1,* 131–139.

Brown, G. L., Kline, W. J., Goyer, P. F., Minichiello, M. D., Kruesi, M. J. P., & Goodwin, F. K. (1986). Relationship of childhood characteristics to cerebrospinal fluid 5-hydroxyindoleacetic acid in aggressive adults. In C. Chagass (Ed.), *Biological Psychiatry 1985* (pp. 177–179). New York: Elsevier.

Cloninger, C., Bohman, M., & Sigvardsson, S. (1981). Inheritance of alcohol abuse: Cross-functioning analysis of adopted men. *Arch Gen Psychiary, 38,* 861–868.

Commissiong, J. W. (1985). Monoamine metabolites: Their relationship and lack of relationship to monoaminergic neuronal activity. *Biochem Pharmacol, 34,* 1127–1131.

De la Chapelle, A., Hortling, H., Edgren, J., & Kaariainen, R. (1963). Evidence for the existence of heritable large Y chromosomes unassociated with a developmental disorder. A cytogenetical and clinical study of 4 males with hypogonadism, one with mongolism, and their relatives. *Hereditas, 50,* 351–360.

Garris, D. R., Chamberlain, J. K. & DaVanzo, J. P. (1984). Histofluorescent identification of indoleamine-concentrating brain loci associated with intraspecies, reflexive biting and locomotor behavior in olfactory-bulbectomized mice. *Brain Res, 294,* 385–389.

Ginsburg, B. E., Vigue, L. E., Larsom, W. A., & Maxson, S. C. (1981). Y-chromosome length in sublines of two mouse strains. *Behav Gen, 11,* 359–368.

Greendyke, R. M., Kanter, D. R., Schuster, D. B., Verstreate, S., & Wootton, J. (1986). Propranolol treatment of assaultive patients with organic brain disease. *J Nerv Ment Dis, 174,* 290–294.

Hagenfelt, L., Bjerkenstedt, G., Edman, G., Sedvall, G., & Wiesel, F. A. (1984). Amino acids in plasma and CSF and monoamine metabolites in CSF: Interrelationship in healthy subjects. *J Neurochem, 42,* 833–837.

Heninger, G. R., Mueller, P. S., & Davis, L. S. (1975). Depressive symptoms and the glucose tolerance test and insulin tolerance test. *J Nerv Ment Dis, 161,* 421–431.

Hotta, I., Yamawaki, S., & Segawa, T. (1986). Long-term lithium treatment causes serotonin receptor down-regulation via serotonergic presynapses in rat brain. *Neuropsychobiology, 16,* 19–26.

Kantak, K. M., Hegstrand, L. R., & Eichelman, B. (1981). Facilitation of shock-induced fighting following intraventricular 5,7 di-hydroxytryptamine and 6-hydroxy DOPA. *Psychopharmacology, 74,* 157–160.

Katz, R. J. (1980). Role of serotonergic mechanisms in animal models of predation. *Progr Neuro-Psychopharmacol, 4,* 219–231.

Kita, H., Shibata, S., Domura, Y., & Ohki, K. (1982). Excitatory effects of the suprachiasmatic nucleus on the ventromedial nucleus in the rat hypothalamic slice. *Brain Res, 235,* 137–141.

Kozak, W., Valzelli, L., & Garattini, S. (1984). Anxiolytic activity on locus coeruleus-mediated suppression of muricidal aggression. *Eur J Pharmacol, 105,* 323–326.

Lidberg, L., Asberg, M., & Sundqvist-Stensman, U. B. (1984). 5-Hydroxyindoleacetic acid levels in attempted suicides who have killed their children. *Lancet, II,* 928.

Lidberg, L., Tuck, J. R., Asberg, M., Scalia-Tomba, G. P., & Bertilsson, L. (1985). Homicide, suicide and CSF 5-HIAA. *Acta Psychiatr Scand, 71,* 230–236.

Linnoila, M., Virkkunen, M., Scheinin, M., Nuutila, A., Rimon, R., & Goodwin, F. K. (1983). Low cerebrospinal fluid 5-hydroxyindoleacetic acid concentration differentiates impulsive from non-impulsive violent behavior. *Life Sci, 33,* 2609–2614.

Major, L., Ballenger, J., Goodwin, F., & Brown, G. (1977). Cerebrospinal fluid homovanillic acid in male alcoholics: Effect of disulfiram. *Biol Psychiatry, 12,* 635–642.

Mattes, J. A. (1985). Metoprolol for intermittent explosive disorder. *Am J Psychiatry, 142,* 1108–1109.

Maxson, S. C., Ginsburg, B. E., & Trattner, A. (1979). Interaction of Y-chromosomal and autosomal gene(s) in the development of inter-male aggression in mice. *Behav Gen, 9,* 219–369.

Maxson, S. C., Platt, T., Shrenker, P., & Tratner, A. (1982). The influence of the Y-chromosome of Rb/1Bg mice on agnostic behaviors. *Aggr Behav, 8,* 285–291.

Molina, V. A., Gobaille, S., & Mandel, P. (1986). Effects of serotonin-mimetic drugs on mouse-killing behavior. *Aggr Behav, 12,* 201–211.

Montgomery, S., & Montgomery, D. (1982). Pharmacological prevention of suicidal behavior. *J Affective Disord, 4,* 291–298.

Moore, R. Y., & Eichler, V. B. (1972). Loss of a circadian adrenal corticosterone rhythm following suprachiasmatic lesions in the rat. *Brain Res, 42,* 201–206.

Morand, C., Young, S. N., & Ervin, F. R. (1983). Clinical response of aggressive schizophrenics to oral tryptophan. *Biol Psychiatry, 18,* 575–578.

Murphy, D. L. (1978). Substrate selective monoamine oxidase inhibitor, tissue, species and functional differences. *Biochem Pharmacol, 27,* 1889–1893.

Nielsen, J., & Henriksen, F. (1972). Incidence of chromosome aberrations among males in a Danish youth prison. *Acta Psychiat Scand, 48,* 87–102.

O'Neil, M., Page, N., Adkins, W. N., & Eichelman, B. (1986). Tryptophan-trazodone treatment of aggressive behaviour. *Lancet, II,* 859-860.

Palkovits, M., Saavedra, J. M., Jacobovits, D. M., Kizer, J. S., Zaborsky, L., & Brownstein, M. J. (1977). Serotonergic innervation of the forebrain: effect of lesions on serotonin and tryptophan hydroxylase levels. *Brain Res, 130,* 121–134.

Pryce, I. G. (1958a). Melancholia, glucose tolerance, and body weight. *J Ment Sci, 104,* 421–427.

Pryce, I. G. (1958b). The relationship between glucose tolerance, body weight, and clinical state in melancholia. *J Ment Sci, 104,* 1079–1092.

Pucilowski, O., Plaznik, A., & Kostowski, W. (1985). Aggressive behavior inhibition by serotonin and quipazine injected into the amygdala in the rat. *Behav Neur Biol, 43,* 58–68.

Rosenthal, N., Davenport, Y., Cowdry, R., Webster, M. & Goodwin, F. (1980). Monoamine metabolites in cerebrospinal fluid of depressive subgroups. *Psychiatry Res, 2,* 113–119.

Roy, A., Adinoff, B., Roehrich, L., Lamparski, D., Custer, R., Lorenz, V., Barbaccia, M., Guidotti, A., Costa, E., Linnoila, M. (1988). Pathological Gambling: A psychological study. *Arch Gen Psychiatry, 45,* 369–373.

Roy, A., Agren, H., Pickar, D., Linnoila, M., Doran, A. R., Cutler, N. R., & Paul, S. (1986a). Reduced CSF concentrations of homovanillic acid and homovanillic acid to 5-hydroxyindoleacetic acid ratios in depressed patients: Relationship to suicidal behavior and dexamethasone nonsuppression. *Am J Psychiatry, 143,* 1539–1545.

Roy, A., Virkkunen, M., Guthrie, S., Poland, R., & Linnoila, M. (1986b). Monoamines, glucose metabolism and aggressive behaviors. *Psychopharmacol Bull, 22,* 661–665.

Roy, A., Virkkunen, M., & Linnoila, M. (1987). Reduced central serotonin turnover in a subgroup of alcoholics? *Progr Neuropsychopharmacol Biol Psychiatry, 11,* 173–177.

Roy-Byrne, P., Post, R. M. Rubinow, D. R., Linnoila, M., Savard, R., & Davis, D. (1983). CSF 5-HIAA and personal and family history of suicide in affectively ill patients: A negative study. *Psychiatry Res, 10,* 263–274.

Selmanoff, M. K., Abreu, E., Goldman, B. D., & Ginsburg, B. E. (1977). Manipulation of aggressive behavior in adult DBA/2/Bg and c57BL/10/Bg male mice implanted with testosterone in silastic tubing. *Hormon Behav, 8,* 377–390.

Selmanoff, M. K., Goldman, B. D., Maxson, S. C., & Ginsburg, B. E. (1977). Correlated effects of the Y-chromosome of mice on developmental changes in testosterone levels and intermale aggression. *Life Sci, 20,* 359–366.

Selmanoff, M. K., Jumonville, J. E., Maxson, S. C., & Ginsburg, B. E. (1975). Evidence for a Y chromosomal contribution to an aggressive phenotype in inbred mice. *Nature, 253,* 529–530.

Sherd, M. H., Marini, J. L., Bridges, C. I., & Wagner, E. (1976). The effect of lithium on impulsive aggressive behavior in man. *Am J Psychiatry, 133,* 1409–1413.

Sorgi, P. J., Ratey, J. J., & Polakoff, S. (1986). B-adrenergic blockers for the control of aggressive behaviors in patients with chronic schizophrenia. *Am J Psychiatry, 143,* 775–776.

Soubrie, P. (1986). Reconciling the role of central serotonin neurons in human and animal behavior. *Behav Brain Sci, 9,* 319–364.

Sprouse, J. S., & Aghajanian, G. K. (1986). (-)-propranolol blocks the inhibition of serotonergic dorsal raphe cell firing by 5-HT 1A selective agonists. *Europ J Pharmacol, 128,* 295–298.

Swanson, L. W., & Cowan, W. M. (1977). The efferent projections of the suprachiasmatic nucleus of the hypothalamus. *J Comp Neurol, 160,* 1–12.

Takahashi, S., Yamane, H., Kondo, H., & Tani, N. (1974). CSF monoamine metabolites in alcoholism, a comparative study with depression. *Folia Psychiatr Neurol Jap, 28,* 347–354.

Valzelli, L. (1969). Aggressive behavior induced by isolation. In S. Garattini & E. B. Sigg (Eds.), pp 70–76, Amsterdam: Excerpta Medica.

Valzelli, L. (1971). Further aspects of the exploratory behavior in aggressive mice. *Psychopharmacologia, 19,* 91–94.

Valzelli, L., & Garattini, S. (1968). Behavioral changes and 5-hydroxytryptamine turnover in animals. *Adv Pharmacol, 68,* 249–260.

van Praag, H. M., & Korf, J. (1971). Endogenous depressions with and without disturbances in the 5-hydroxytryptamine metabolism: A biochemical classification. *Psychopharmacol, 19,* 148–152.

van Praag, H. M. & Leijnse, B. (1965). Depression, glucose tolerance, peripheral glucose uptake and their alterations under the influence of anti-depressive drugs of the hydrazine type. *Psychopharmacologia, 8,* 67–78.

van Woerkom, T. C. A. M., Teelken, A. W., & Minderhoud, J. M. (1977). Difference in neurotransmitter metabolism in fronto-temporal-lobe contusion and diffuse cerebral contusion. *Lancet, I,* 812–813.

Virkkunen, M. (1982a). Reactive hypoglycemic tendency among habitually violent offenders. *Neuropsychobiology, 8,* 35–40.

Virkkunen, M. (1983). Insulin secretion during the glucose tolerance test in antisocial personality. *Brit J Psychiatry, 142,* 598–604.

Virkkunen, M. (1984). Reactive hypoglycemic tendency among arsonists. *Acta Psychiatr Scand, 69,* 445–452.

Virkkunen, M. (1986a). Insulin secretion during the glucose tolerance test among habitually violent and impulsive offenders. *Aggr Behav, 12,* 303–310.

Virkkunen, M. (1986b). Reactive hypoglycemic tendency among habitually violent offenders. *Nutr Rev, Suppl,* 94–103.

Virkkunen, M., & Huttunen, M. O. (1982b). Evidence for abnormal glucose tolerance test among violent offenders. *Neuropsychobiology, 8,* 30–34.

Virkkunen, M., Nuutila, A., Goodwin, F. K., & Linnoila, M. (1987). CSF monoamine metabolites in male arsonists. *Arch Gen Psychiatry, 44,* 241–247.

Winokur, G. (1979). Unipolar depression. Is it divisible in autonomous subtypes? *Arch Gen Psychiatry, 36,* 47–52.

Yamamoto, H., Nagai, K., & Nakagava, H. (1984). Bilateral lesions of the suprachiasmatic nucleus enhance glucose tolerance in rats. *Biomed Res, 5,* 47–54.

Yamamoto, H., Nagai, K., & Nakagava, H. (1984a). Role of the suprachiasmatic nucleus in glucose homeostasis. *Biomed Res, 5,* 55–60.

Yamamoto, H., Nagai, K., & Nakagava, H. (1984b). Bilateral lesions of the SCN abolish lipolytic and hyperphagic responses to 2DG. *Physiol Behav, 32,* 1017–1020.

Yamamoto, H., Nagai, K., & Nakagava, H. (1984c). Additional evidence that the suprachiasmatic nucleus is the center for regulation of insulin secretion and glucose homeostasis. *Brain Res, 304,* 237–241.

Yamamoto, H., Nagai, K., & Nakagava, H. (1985). Lesions involving the suprachiasmatic nucleus eliminate the glucagon response to intracranial injection of 2-deoxy-D-glucose. *Endocrinology, 117,* 468–473.

PART IV

Animal Neurochemical Studies

9

Parallels in Aggression and Serotonin: Consideration of Development, Rearing History, and Sex Differences

J. D. HIGLEY
STEPHEN J. SUOMI
MARKKU LINNOILA

Aggression in primates has been the focus of several empirical studies. A major difficulty in interpreting the results of these studies is that different definitions of aggression are used by different investigators. For the purposes of this study with rhesus monkeys, we define aggression as follows: *behaviors directed at another conspecific for purposes of causing physical or psychological harm.* Included within this definition are behaviors such as hitting, biting, hostile chasing, and open mouth threats directed at other conspecifics.

Numerous studies have indicated that within primate species, levels of aggression are not uniform across age or sex. In general, these studies have shown that aggression first emerges in the animals' behavioral repertoires in late infancy (albeit at low levels), increases throughout the juvenile period, peaks in early adolescence, and then declines or remains constant through early and middle adulthood (Bernstein, Williams & Ramsay, 1983; Cross & Harlow, 1965). While this general trend exists for both sexes, levels of aggression are generally higher for males than for females, albeit with major individual differences and considerable overlap across sexes (Bernstein, Williams, & Ramsay, 1983; Coelho & Bramblett, 1981; Cross & Harlow, 1965).

Levels of aggression are also affected by the type of rearing background. For example, animals reared for their first few months in impoverished environments, such as social isolation, typically show higher levels of aggression towards conspecifics than those reared by their mothers (Mitchell, 1968; Mitchell & Clark, 1968). Often, the previously isolated animals display aggression towards inappropriate targets. For example, instead of decreasing aggression as they become familiar with age-mates with whom they have lived, isolates' levels of aggression may increase across episodes of cohabitation (Mitchell & Clark, 1968). Moreover, they fail to inhibit their aggression appropriately in order to prevent severe injury to their familiar age-mates (Mason, 1963). As further examples of inappropriate expression of aggressive behavior, small preadolescent isolates may show aggression towards a full-grown adult male (Harlow & Harlow, 1969; Mitchell, 1968; Suomi, 1982); they may direct unprovoked aggression towards unrelated infants (Mitchell, 1968), or in the case of adult female isolates abuse their own infants (e.g., see Ruppenthal, Arling, Harlow, Sackett, & Suomi [1976] for a review of these studies).

The converse is also true: Certain rearing conditions can decrease levels of aggressive behavior in monkeys. For example, one rearing condition producing low levels of aggression is the so called peer-only condition. These subjects are deprived of adult exposure, but are given constant exposure to age-mates from birth. Studies on these subjects have shown that relative to subjects reared by their mother, they demonstrate high levels of anxiety and low levels of aggression (Chamove, Rosenblum, & Harlow, 1973; Harlow & Harlow, 1969). Other similar conditions, such as deprivation from adults but a 2–4 hour daily exposure to peers, also produce low levels of aggression (Coelho & Bramblett, 1981).

There are many possible explanations for the causes of differing levels of aggression. One explanation is biochemical, which focuses on relationship between aggression and serotonin. Serotonin (5-HT), an inhibitory neurotransmitter, has been postulated to reduce the expression of aggressive behaviors. Hence, subjects with reduced 5-HT function might be expected to exhibit more aggression. Studies investigating the relationship have indeed demonstrated an association between behavioral indices of impulsivity, aggression, depression, suicide, and biochemical measures of reduced serotonin functioning (e.g., see Mann & Stanley, 1986 for a review of these studies).

Studies that have examined the development of the indolamine system in nonhuman primates are few in number and cross-sectional in design. To our knowledge, no studies to date have assessed the development of the indolamine system in nonhuman primates in longitudinal fashion, nor have there been studies that linked developmental changes in the indolamine systems with developmental changes in the expression of aggression. The purpose of the present study was to describe longitudinally developmental changes in the serotonergic system as characterized by cerebrospinal fluid (CSF) 5-HIAA concentration and the development of aggressive behaviors during the first two years of life for both male and female rhesus monkeys who had been reared under carefully controlled conditions in our laboratory. Additional subjects were also examined cross-sectionally in order to describe changes that occur as subjects grow older. Based on general developmental trends in the expression of aggression described above, we hypothesized the following. First, since levels of aggression increase with age, 5-HIAA levels should decrease with age. Second, because males show more aggression than females, 5-HIAA should be lower in males than females. Finally, because subjects reared in a peer-only condition show lower levels of aggression, peer-only reared subjects should show higher levels of 5-HIAA.

METHODS

Subjects

The subjects were a total of 45 rhesus macaque monkeys *(Macaca mulatta)* studied longitudinally since birth. Using comparable procedures, data were obtained at three age points: In Analysis 1, subjects were all 6 months of age; in Analysis 2, subjects were studied at 6 and 18 months of age, and in Analysis 3, 50-month-old subjects were compared to the same 18-month-old subjects (See Figures 1–4 below).

In the first analysis, data were obtained on 37 subjects when they were 6 months of age (9 male and 9 female mother-reared subjects, 9 male and 10 female peer-only reared subjects). In the second analysis, data were obtained on 20 of these same subjects one year later; thus, the same measures were obtained from these subjects at 6 and again at 18 months of age (5 male and 7 female mother-reared subjects, 4 male and 4 female peer-only reared subjects). The third analysis was a cross-sectional comparison of the twenty 19-month-olds with 8 different 50-month-old subjects. These 8 additional subjects (4 mother reared and 4 peer-only reared), were reared and separated under conditions similar to the 18-month-aged animals.

Rhesus macaques were chosen as subjects because of their biological similarities to humans as fellow primates and because they show relatively more aggression than many other nonhuman primate species (Bernstein et al., 1983). Furthermore, aggression, a relatively infrequent behavior, has been more widely described in this species than in other nonhuman primates. In addition, rhesus macaques offer an excellent opportunity to obtain neurochemical measures during manipulations which cannot be performed on humans.

Rearing Background

Subjects were reared for their first 6 months in one of two different rearing conditions: with their mother in a single-caged mother-infant dyad (MI), or without any adults present in a peer-only (PO) condition. PO rearing was chosen because monkeys subjected to it have been shown to be emotionally labile and anxious, and to exhibit low levels of aggression (Higley, Hopkins, Yuill, Suomi, Linnoila, Kraemer, & Bush, 1986; Higley Suomi, Hopkins, & Bush, 1986; Bush, Steffen, Higley, & Suomi, 1987). When the subjects were 6 months of age, they underwent a series of 4-day social separations followed by 3-day reunions. Subsequent to these 6-month separation-reunions, MI subjects were removed from their mother and placed with the PO subjects. Thus, from the seventh month of life, subjects received identical treatment. This paper describes the results of 5-HIAA measures obtained from the cisterna magna during the social separations at 6, 18, and 50 months of age.

Separation Procedure

When animals were approximately 6 and 18 months of age, they were subjected to the same basic social separation paradigm. In both years, all subjects received 4 consecutive 4-day separations which were each followed by 3 days of reunion. During all separations, subjects were separated from their cage-mates and placed into single cages. They could hear the other separated subjects but were unable to see or touch them.

Removal of Cerebrospinal Fluid

Three weeks prior to separation, and on day 4 of the first and fourth separations, between 11:50 and 14:00 hours, subjects were removed from their respective home and separation cages, given general anesthesia (ketamine hydrochloride .15 mg/kg), and CSF was removed from their cisterna magna. The sample volume was two milliliters in subjects over 6 months of age and 1 milliliter in the 6-month-olds. The samples were analyzed for the major metabolites of norepinephrine: 3-methoxy-4-hydroxyphenylglycol (MHPG), dopamine: homovanillic acid (HVA), and serotonin: 5-hydroxyindoleacetic acid (5-HIAA), using liquid chromatography with electrochemical detection. Intra and interassay variabilities for all analyses were less than 10%.

Data Analysis

Three different analyses were used to describe the data. Mixed design analyses of variance (ANOVA) were used to detect significant overall effects, and post hoc Duncan New Multiple Range tests were used to analyze differences between individual means. The first analyses was computed on the 6-month separations. A 3-way mixed design ANOVA was used with 2 between-group factors: (a) rearing group (MI/PO), and (b) sex, and a within-group factor time of the CSF removal (preseparation, and week 1 or 4 of separation). The second analysis was a comparison of the 6- and 18-month data. A 4-way mixed design ANOVA was used with 2 between-group factors: (a) rearing group and (b) sex, and two within-group factors: (a) age (6 versus 18 month), and (b) time of the CSF removal (preseparation, and week 1 or 4 of separation). The third analysis was a cross-sectional comparison of the 20 subjects from the 18-month separations with the 8 subjects who were 50 months of age. A 3-way mixed design ANOVA was performed with 2 between-group factors: (a) rearing group (MI/PO) and (b) age (18 and 50 months), and a within-group factor, time of the CSF removal (preseparation and week 1 of separation). For the comparison using the 50-month-olds, the sex factor could not be analyzed because the sample size for females was too small.

RESULTS

The results of the ANOVA for the 6-month data indicated that there was a significant interaction ($p.<.05$) for the rearing condition and sex ($F=4.1$, *df* 1/32). Duncan tests indicated that the MI reared females had significantly higher levels of 5-HIAA than any other group ($p<.05$—see Figure 1).

There were also significant interactions for the 6- vs. 18-month analyses. Specifically, a rearing group by sex interaction ($F=4.48$, *df* 1/16), and a rearing group by year interaction ($F=5.65$, *df* 1/16) were significant. The rearing by sex interaction was largely due to male PO-reared subjects having significantly higher levels than the MI-reared males ($p<.05$); however, similar to the 6-month old subjects, MI-reared females showed a trend for higher levels than MI-reared males (see Figure 2). For the rearing group by year interaction, there was a significant decline from the 6- to 18-month separations, with PO reared subjects demonstrating less of a decline ($p<.01$—see Figure 3).

For the cross-sectional comparison, there was a significant main effect for age ($F=13.5$, *df* 1/24), with the 50-month-old

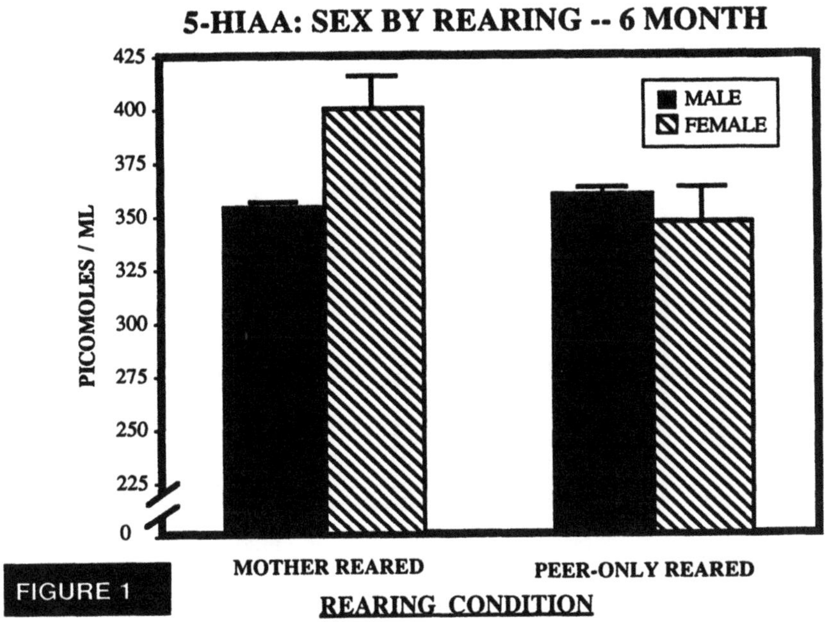

Figure 1. Levels of 5-HIAA in cisternal CSF (picomoles/ml) taken during the fourth day of social separation for 6-month-old subjects reared either in mother-infant dyads or peer-only groups. Male subjects are denoted by solid bars, and females are denoted by the hatch pattern.

subjects having a significantly lower level of CSF 5-HIAA ($p<.05$). Group differences in 5-HIAA had largely disappeared by 50 months (see Figure 4).

DISCUSSION

In general, the results supported our original hypotheses: As aggression increased, either as a result of age, sex, or rearing condition, CSF 5-HIAA concentration decreased. Overall, the age effect was clearest: All 3 analyses demonstrated a significant age-related decline in 5-HIAA. The decline with age was similar to human studies, which have found the highest lumbar CSF 5-

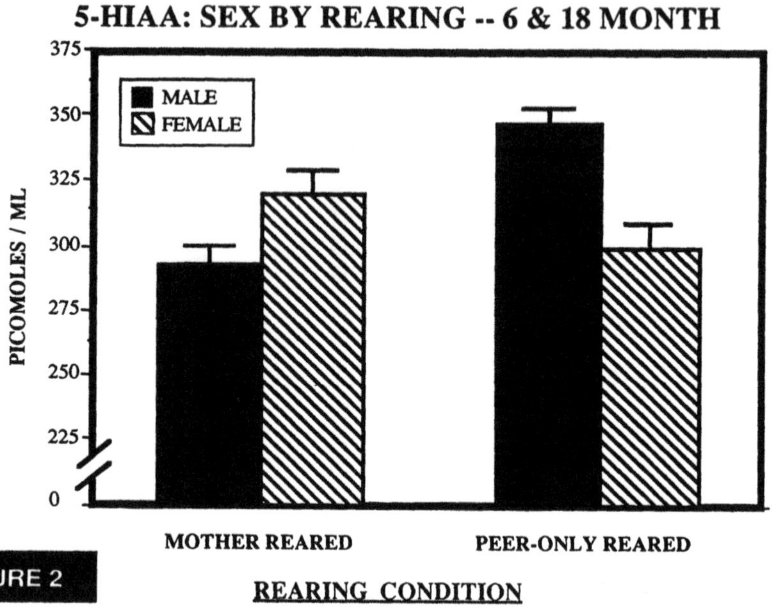

FIGURE 2

Figure 2. Levels of 5-HIAA in cisternal CSF (picomoles/ml) taken during the fourth day of social separation for 6- and 18-month-old subjects reared either in mother-infant dyads or peer-only groups. Male subjects are denoted by solid bars, and females are denoted by the hatch pattern.

HIAA levels in infancy and an age-related decline thereafter (Andersson & Roos, 1969; Rogers & Dubowitz, 1970; Silverstein, Johnston, Hutchinson, & Edwards, 1985).

The sex differences also demonstrated the hypothesized inverse relationship between aggression and serotonin metabolism with females, who show lower levels of aggression, having higher CSF 5-HIAA concentrations. Specifically, among the mother-reared subjects, 6-month-old females showed significantly higher levels than males, and similarly, the 6-month-old females showed a trend towards higher levels than the 18-month-old males.

The group differences demonstrated that the PO-reared subjects had higher levels of 5-HIAA than the MI-reared subjects. However, PO rearing produced higher CSF 5-HIAA concentra-

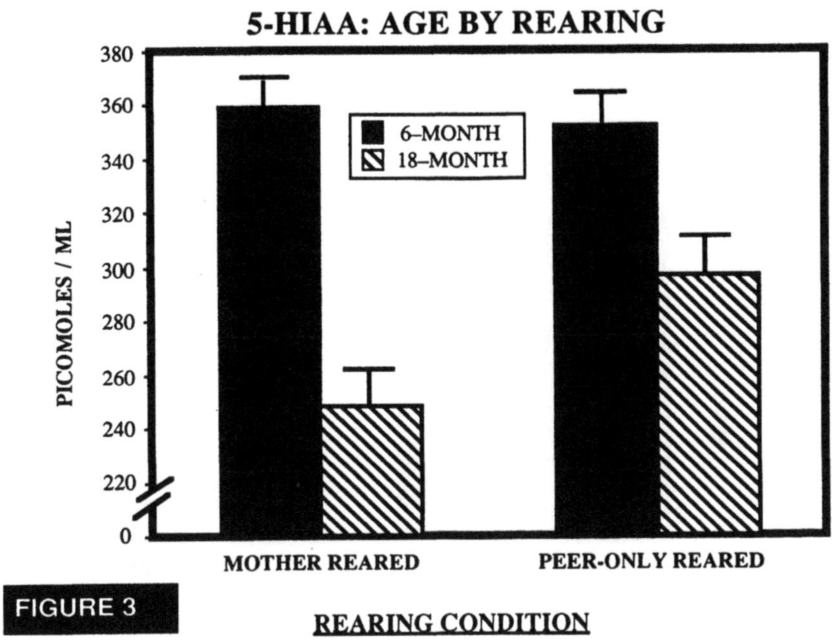

Figure 3. Levels of 5-HIAA in cisternal CSF (picomoles/ml) taken during the fourth day of social separation for 6- and 18-month-old subjects reared either in mother-infant dyads or peer-only groups. The solid bars denote 6-month values, and the hatched bars represent the 18 month values.

tion only in males. While PO females seemed relatively unaffected by this rearing condition, PO males demonstrated very high levels of 5-HIAA. The immediate reason for this is unclear, but it is noteworthy that in human depressives negative life events are associated with increased CSF 5-HIAA concentrations (Roy et al., 1986). Future studies should investigate whether sex differences remain as these subjects reach adulthood and whether the sex differences are influenced by rearing conditions.

Behaviorally, it is clear that the sex differences in expressing aggression become increasingly marked by puberty. Interestingly, like the aggression data, there is evidence that 5-HIAA shows a larger sex difference at puberty. While we were unable to perform a statistical analysis for sex differences on our data

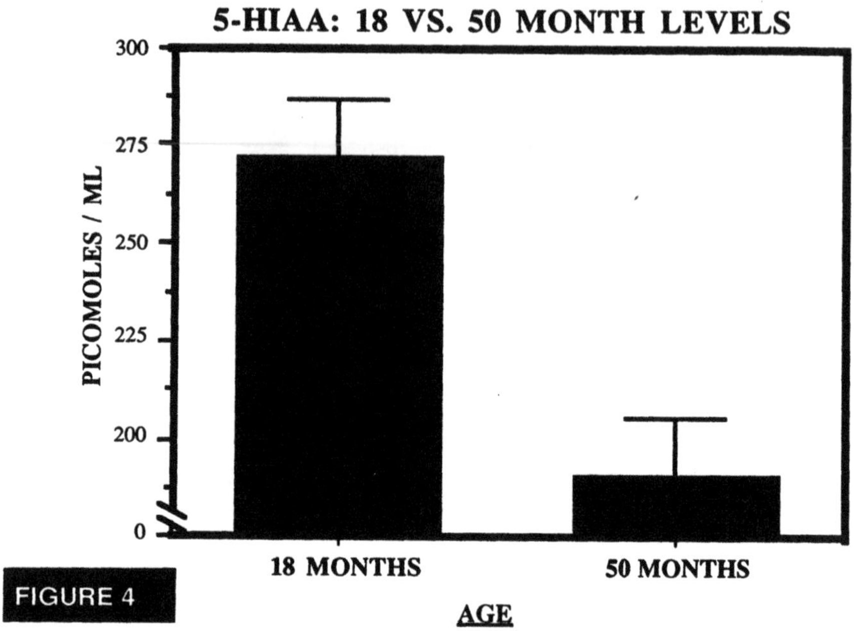

Figure 4. Levels of 5-HIAA in cisternal CSF (picomoles/ml) taken during the fourth day of social separation for 18- and 50-month-old subjects reared either in mother-infant dyads or peer-only groups.

for the 50-month-old animals, when type of rearing and timing of the CSF removal were controlled for, 5 of the 6 lower concentrations of CSF 5-HIAA in the 50-month-old animals were in males.

In our study we have established an association between developmental trends for CSF 5-HIAA concentration and aggression. As subjects grow older and aggression increases, our data indicate that the levels of 5-HIAA decrease. Under normal conditions, male subjects, who show more aggression, demonstrate lower levels of CSF 5-HIAA. Finally, peer-only rearing, a condition that reduces aggression, reduces CSF 5-HIAA concentration.

It should be noted that the relationships we have described are correlative in nature and that statements regarding possible causation remain purely speculative at this time. Pharmacological manipulations or lesions of serotonin systems performed at various ages and under different rearing conditions should be performed to establish how the two are linked. We are currently performing studies with subjects whose levels of 5-HIAA have been previously established, under conditions where aggression is likely to occur, such as stranger introduction and group reformation, in an attempt to link established individual differences in levels of 5-HIAA with individual differences in levels of aggression. We are also assessing the long-term stability of individual differences in behavior and serotonin metabolism.

REFERENCES

Andersson, H., & Roos, B. E. (1969). 5-Hydroxindoleacetic acid in cerebrospinal fluid of hydrocephalic children. *Acta Paediatrica Scandinavica, 58,* 601–608.

Bernstein, I., Williams, L., & Ramsay, M. (1983). The expression of aggression in old world monkeys. *International Journal of Primatology, 4,* 113–124.

Bush, D. S., Steffen, S. L., Higley, J. D., & Suomi, S. J. (1987). *Continuity of behavior in rhesus macaques* (Macaca mulatta) *during social separation.* Paper presented at the American Society of Primatologists, Madison, WI.

Chamove, A. S., Rosenblum, L. A., & Harlow, H. F. (1973). Monkeys *(Macaca mulatta)* raised only with peers. A pilot study. *Animal Behavior, 21,* 316–325.

Coelho, A. M., & Bramblett, C. A. (1981). Effects of rearing on aggression and subordination in papio monkeys. *American Journal of Primatology, 1,* 401–412.

Cross, H.A., & Harlow, H. F. (1965). Prolonged and progressive effects of partial isolation on the behavior of macaque monkeys. *Journal of Experimental Research in Personality, 1,* 39–49.

Harlow, H. F., & Harlow, M. K. (1969). Effects of various mother-infant relationships on rhesus monkey behaviors. In B. M. Foss (Ed.), *Determinants of Infant Behavior* (Vol. 4., pp. 15–295). London: Methuen & Co.

Higley, J. D., Hopkins, W. J., Yuill, E. A., Suomi, S. J., Linnoila, M., Kraemer, G. W., & Bush, D. S. (1986). *Early roots of affective disorders: Central amine correlates of separation-induced anxiety and despair in rhesus monkeys.* Paper presented at the American Society of Primatologists, Austin, TX.

Higley, J. D., Suomi, S. J., Hopkins, W. J., & Bush, D. S. (1986). *Early peer-only rearing deficits in rhesus monkeys that last into late childhood.* Paper presented at the American Society of Primatologists, Austin, TX.

Langlais, P. J., Walsh, F. X., Bird, E. D., & Levy, H. L. (1985). Cerebrospinal fluid neurotransmitter metabolites in neurologically normal infants and children. *Pediatrics, 75,* 580–586.

Mann, J. J., & Stanley, M. (Eds.) (1986). Psychobiology of suicidal behavior (Special Issue). *Annals of the New York Academy of Sciences, 487.*

Mason, W. A. (1963). The effects of environmental restriction on the social development of rhesus monkeys. In C. H. Southwick (Ed.), *Primate Social Behavior* (pp. 161–173). New York: Van Nostrand.

Mitchell, G. D. (1968). Persistent behavior pathology in rhesus monkeys following early social isolation. *Folia Primatoligica, 8,* 132–147.

Mitchell, G. D., & Clark, D. L. (1968). Long-term effects of social isolation in nonsocially adapted rhesus monkeys. *The Journal of Genetic Psychology, 113,* 117–128.

Rogers, J. J., & Dubowitz, V. (1970). 5-Hydroxindoles in hydrocephalus: A comparative study of cerebrospinal fluid and blood levels. *Developmental Medicine and Child Neurology, 12,* 461–466.

Roy, A., Pickar, D., Linnoila, M., Doran, A. R., & Paul, S. M. (1986). Cerebrospinal fluid monamine and monoamine metabolite levels and the dexamethasone suppression test in depression. *Archives of General Psychiatry, 43,* 356–360.

Ruppenthal, G. C., Arling, G. L., Harlow, H. F., Sackett, G. P., & Suomi, S. J. (1976). A 10-year perspective of motherless-mother monkey behavior. *Journal of Abnormal Psychology, 85,* 341–349.

Silverstein, F. S., Johnston, M. V., Hutchinson, R. J., & Edwards, N. L. (1985). Lesch-nyhan syndrome: CSF neurotransmitter abnormalities. *Neurology, 35,* 907–911.

Suomi, S. J. (1982). Abnormal behavior in nonhuman primates. In J. Forbes & F. King (Eds.), *Primate Behavior* (pp. 171–215). New York: Academic Press.

10

Monoamineric Control of Waiting Capacity (Impulsivity) in Animals

P. SOUBRIÉ and J. C. BIZOT

When one is scrutinizing many animal testing procedures and more particularly animal models used for investigating experimental anxiety and antianxiety agents, ability to wait appears as a potential confounding variable. For instance, in standard punishment procedures, withholding bar pressing prevents the animal from being exposed to contingent electric shock (punishment), but also delays to the "safe period" the possibility of obtaining food reward and thus requires a certain ability to wait. Likewise, with reinforcement schedules in which laboratory animals are required to let a specified time elapse between successive responses to gain reward, the level of performance might not only relate to the animal's sensitivity to "frustrative" nonreward in case of premature responses but also to the animal's ability to wait. (See the reviews by Gray (1982), Soubrié (1986) and Thiébot (1986) for more detailed procedural and interpretational considerations).

Since, according to Herrnstein (1981), "in impulsiveness versus self control time is always of the essence" (p.3), one can wonder whether, even in animals, waiting ability cannot be subsumed into the more inclusive dimension, impulse control. Considerable research activity has been developed in the field of psychobiology of human impulsivity (Brown, Goodwin & Bunney, 1982; Zuckerman, 1984; van Praag, 1986). In animals, however, the paucity of relevant models and theories in this field is conflicting to a disturbing degree. Indeed, if one excepts the intensive investigation concerning aggressive behaviors, not to mention that much of this investigation has been performed without any clear reference to "impulse control" (but see Valzelli, 1985), very few data can be found which may serve as guidelines for future research in such a direction. Moreover, no drugs are sufficiently specific of impulsivity (pro or anti) to be considered as relevant tools for a pharmacological validation of such-needed animal models of impulse control.

In this context and in spite of the limitations and difficulties inherent in such an approach, we decided to design animal testing procedures aimed at investigating various aspects of impulse control, special attention being devoted to waiting capacity or tolerance to delay of reward. Then, experiments were conducted to investigate the sensitivity of these dimensions to selected psychotropic drugs in order to gain insight into the neurobiochemical correlates of impulse control. Hence, it will emerge that not only serotonergic but also noradrenergic systems are involved, probably in an interactive way, in the animal's ability to wait. These points will constitute the first part of the present review. In light of the results obtained in our models, and those reported in the scientific literature concerning a selected number of human and animals studies, attempts will be made to sort out a specific working principle for the action of serotonergic neurons. Thus, in the second part of this study it will be tentatively proposed that these systems are implicated in a dual process: control of information processing and of response emission that allows the organism to tolerate and/or arrange a delay before acting.

I: ANIMAL MODELS OF WAITING CAPACITY AND SEROTONERGIC TRANSMISSION

The first model consists of subjecting hungry rats to a choice, in a T-maze, between delayed access to a large quantity of food, and immediate access to a small quantity of food. After training in this experimental procedure, the amount of preference for the arm associated with small reward is directly related to the waiting time fixed in the arm leading to the large reward. With a 15-sec waiting period, control rats choose the arm allowing an immediate access to small reward in 20–30 percent of their runs. When a 25-sec delay is imposed in the arm leading to the large reward goal box, rats choose the other arm in 60–70 percent of their runs. Interestingly, we found that rats' choices were not substantially affected by food deprivation level (24 or 48 h fasting). Moreover, that the delay is introduced before the access to the food and its consumption seems to be of crucial importance since up to an 8-min waiting period in the goal box after the consumption of the large reward fails to alter the preference of the rats for this large-reward goal box. With an imposed 25-sec delay we found that serotonin uptake blockers such as citalopram, clomipramine, indalpine and zimelidine all shifted rats' preference towards the large-but-delayed reward. Conversely, with an imposed 15-sec delay, many drugs assumed to reduce serotonergic transmission such as benzodiazepines, methysergide, buspirone or TVXQ 7821 reliably reduced waiting capacity in the T-maze (Table 1). The inefficacy of ritanserin in this paradigm could suggest that a reduced serotonergic transmission at 5HT2 receptors is not critical in ability to wait. (Thiébot et al., 1985; Thiébot et al., 1986; and personal unpublished results).

In order to minimize the forced aspect of the T-maze, a second model has been designed. In this model, rats were subjected to a fixed ratio 48 (FR 48) schedule of food reinforcement but after completion of a series of 48 presses, and in case of no further press, free pellets were delivered according to fixed, increasing intervals (from 5 to 80 sec). Pressing during the "free sequence" stopped the sequence and required of the rat to complete 48 presses to be reinforced and to reinitiate the "free sequence." For each rat, a mean waiting time tolerated between free pellets was calculated by recording the delay between free pellets before lever pressing (interruption of the sequence). Interestingly, important and reproducible interindividual differences (perhaps more marked than in the T-maze situation) were observed concerning waiting capacity: some animals stop the free sequence when the delay between rewards was reaching 10/15 sec, whereas some others were able to tolerate more than a 30-sec delay between pellets. We were unable to find any significant relationship be-

TABLE 1
Effects of Drugs Affecting Serotonergic and Noradrenergic Transmission on Rats' Waiting Capacity

	Tolerance to Delay of Reward
Drugs enhancing serotonin transmission (5-HT uptake blockers)	enhanced
Drugs reducing serotonin transmission (5-HT1A agonists, benzodiazepines)	reduced
Drugs enhancing noradrenergic transmission (NA uptake blockers, beta stimulant)	enhanced
Drugs reducing noradrenergic transmission (Low doses of clonidine)	unchanged

This table summarizes the main pharmacological data obtained by using the T-maze procedure and the FR 48 + free pellets procedure.

tween waiting capacity and various parameters of rats' conditioning history such as the speed of learning, baseline level of responding, number of pellets earned by session. In addition, we found (Figure 1) that waiting time between free rewards was lengthened by serotonin uptake blockers such as clomipramine, indalpine, or zimelidine (Thiébot et al., 1986, and unpublished results).

Taken together, these findings strengthen the hypothesis of a critical involvement of serotonergic neurons in the ability of the animals to wait for reward and agree with current experiments suggesting that rats whose serotonergic neurons have been destroyed by an injection of the neurotoxin 5,7-dihydroxytryptamine into the raphe area are less prone than controls to tolerate a delay before reaching food reward (Thiébot, 1986).

A number of points however remain to be elucidated.

In the T-maze paradigm, 5-HT 1A agonists such as 8-OH-DPAT or gepirone, as distinct from buspirone or TVXQ 7821, were found not to reduce significantly waiting capacity.

We do not know what could be the specific serotonergic pathways (i.e., their raphe nucleus of origin and their areas of projection: extrapyramidal, limbic or cortical structures) most intimately involved in waiting capacity. Although of impor-

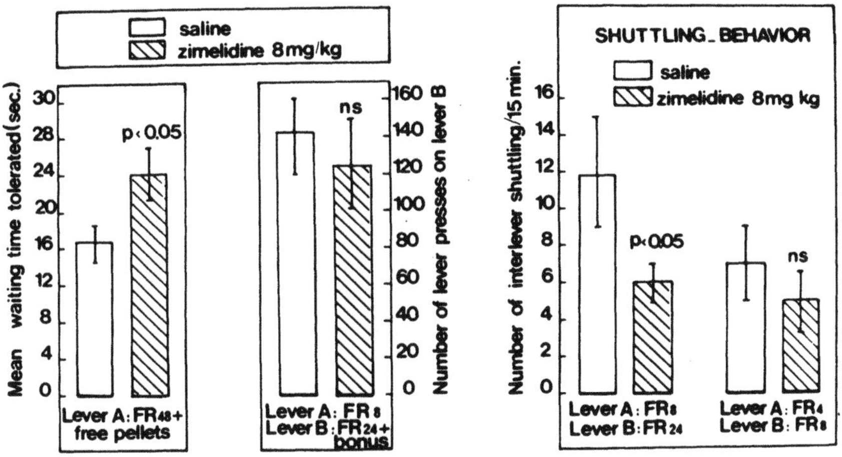

Figure 1. Effects of zimelidine on different parameters of impulse control in rats subjected to 15 min daily session of lever pressing for food; Zimelidine was injected i.p. 1 h before testing.

tance, these points have not been investigated further in order to focus our experiments on two additional issues. The first one dealt with the possibility that other behavioral aspects of impulse control could be influenced by manipulations affecting the activity of serotonergic systems. The second one dealt with the possible role of additional neurotransmitter systems (namely, noradrenergic neurons) in the control of waiting capacity.

II: ADDITIONAL INVESTIGATION ON IMPULSE CONTROL

Behavior can be termed impulsive when it privileges short- rather than long-range consequences of acting or responding. At first look, it can be speculated that, in the T-maze paradigm, rats choose the smaller reinforcement first because the larger one is later. A model was therefore designed to test more specifically such a dimension. Rats were subjected to a 2-levers schedule of food delivery under which pressing on lever A was reinforced according to a Fixed ratio 8 (FR8) schedule and pressing on lever

B, according to a FR24 schedule. Pressing on the B lever, however, was associated with a "bonus" of 12 additional food rewards delivered in one-third of the completed FR24 series. It appeared that only one-fourth of the presses were performed on the lever B but with marked interindividual differences. Twenty-five percent of the rats were working on the FR8 lever almost exclusively, whereas an identical percentage of animals were working on the FR24 lever. Zimelidine, at doses able to enhance waiting capacity in the aforementioned tests was found not to be effective in facilitating responding on lever B, the FR8/FR24 presses ratio being unaffected by the drug (Figure 1).

A second set of experiments was aimed at studying further the extent to which short-range outcomes are controlling rat operant behavior and whether such a control can be mediated by serotonergic neurons. Rats were subjected to a 2-levers schedule of food delivery, with levers A and B associated with FR8 and FR24 schedule, respectively. The schedules in effect on the levers, however, were constantly interchanged after any reward delivery. This procedure resulted in a considerable number of rats' alternations from one lever to the other. We observed that zimelidine decreased by 50 percent such a "shuttling" behavior (Figure 1). However, in testing procedures under which there is no advantage to adopt such a shuttling behavior (lever A: FR4 and lever B: FR8, randomly alternating after 50 percent of the reward delivery), the number of rats' alternations was low, and zimelidine did not affect shuttling behavior (Figure 1).

Although additional testing procedures and drug challenges are required to draw definite conclusions, these observations suggest that serotonergic neurons might not be in a position to control all the various components of impulsivity. Serotonergic systems seem to be more critical when an overt conflict emerges between reward densities or delays. Hence, it cannot be excluded that serotonergic neurons play a more crucial role in the tolerance of frustrative events than on impulse control per se (cf the effects of zimelidine in the T-maze paradigm versus the situation dealing with lever pressing for bonus). In addition, it cannot be ruled out that serotonergic neurons are brought into play whenever behavioral inhibition is required, and competes with making response contingencies. This is the case under the schedule with free pellets delivery, but certainly less so under the FR4 vs FR8 procedure in which pressing for food on the FR8 level allows the animal to express its "acting out" tendencies with minimal detrimental consequence on reward access. It might be worth adding that an increased waiting capacity was observed in rats with opportunities available in their environment to display adjunctive or displacement activities (Table 2). These activities may in fact enable the animal to express its impulsiveness outside the critical situational conflict (responding or not on the lever). Finally another important dimension might be the duration of the exposure of the animal to the critical factors of the situation before being drugged. Precipitation of active behavior may only occur when the animal's strategy is not fully established.

III: NORADRENERGIC MEDIATION OF WAITING CAPACITY

The fact that serotonergic uptake inhibitors reportedly exert antidepressant activity in humans prompted us to study the effects of additional drugs of this class, including compounds with preferential impact on noradrenergic processes.

We found that in the T-maze paradigm as well as in the operant schedule with increasingly delayed free rewards, drugs such as nialamide, desipramine, maprotiline and an agonist of beta-adrenergic receptors, clenbuterol, enhanced waiting capacity. Indeed, these agents increased the selections of the large-but-delayed reward and the time tolerated between free pellets (Table 1). Clonidine at low doses assumed to reduce noradrenergic transmission through a stimulation of autoreceptors, however, did not reduce the number of choices of the delayed reward in the T-maze.

In agreement with the numerous anatomical and functional relationships that have been described between noradrenergic and serotonergic neurons, taken together these findings militate in favor of a dual noradrenergic/serotonergic mediation of waiting capacity.

TABLE 2
Effects of Opportunities Made in the Environment to Display Adjunctive Drinking on Rats' Waiting Capacity

	Waiting Time Tolerated Between Free Pellets *Mean ± SEM*	*Total Time Spent Drinking During the Free Sequences* *Mean ± SEM*
Baseline (no water in the chamber)	17.2±2.1	—
After 6 daily sessions with water in the chamber[1]	22.3±2.2	42 ± 9
After 12 daily sessions with water in the chamber[1]	28.5±1.8*	188 ± 50
After 6 daily sessions following water removal	16.8±1.5	—

Waiting time was estimated in the paradigm in the course of which omission of lever pressing allowed the rats to receive free pellets according to a fixed sequence of increasing intervals (5, 10, 15, 20, 30 sec). Any lever press stopped the "free sequence" and required the rat to emit 47 presses to be reinforced and to reinitiate the "free sequence."

[1]Rats were not water deprived and water was available in a drinking bottle located in a corner of the operant chamber.

*$p < 0.05$ as compared with baseline.

This may offer a plausible explanation to the fact that the effects of 5-HT 1A agonists were somewhat weaker or less consistent than those of benzodiazepines or those that could be expected from the data obtained with drugs assumed to enhance serotonin transmission. The following hypothesis can tentatively be proposed: If 5-HT 1A agonists release noradrenergic neurons from serotonergic inhibitory control (as shown for some of these compounds—Sanghera, McMillen & German, 1983), this would result in competing noradrenergic/serotonergic influences on waiting behavior.

That all antidepressant drugs studied enhanced waiting capacity is consonant with previous reports showing that a large variety of antidepressants improve DRL performance (O'Donnell & Seiden, 1983). This would suggest that these drugs, at least when given acutely, may improve impulse control. Although such possibility is hardly tenable when considering only the suicide-promoting effects of these agents in depressed individuals (Feuerstein & Jackisch, 1986), this same possibility would be compatible with the observation that antidepressants ameliorate pathologies characterized, among other clinical dimensions, by an impulse-control deficiency. They include mainly bulimia and obsessive-compulsive symptomatology, with reports suggesting that amelioration of these disorders could be either dependent on or independent of an antidepressant "halo" effect (Pope et al., 1985; Mavissakalian et al., 1985; Jenike, Armentano & Baer, 1987).

IV: TOWARDS A WORKING PRINCIPLE FOR SEROTONERGIC NEURONS

This rapid survey indicates that waiting might be a basic dimension for the involvement of monoaminergic systems, perhaps more significantly for serotonergic neurons, and thus open up new vistas concerning the functional roles of these systems.

Serotonin-containing neurons can be viewed as processes implicated in the control of response emission and information processing, enabling the organism to arrange or tolerate a delay before acting, so that a motor response might not be triggered on the sole basis of the saliency of the information sampled but also on the basis of its relevance or significance. This implies that serotonergic neurons do not directly govern a single behavior nor even a set of behaviors, but that, in contrast, they govern any kind of behavior (aggression, exploration, pressing for food, approach or avoidance) when that behavior enters into the waiting dimension. In other words, serotonergic neurons are probably not involved in the control of specific acts as such, but in the way in which they are carried out. Although such a contention requires further substantiation, it is compatible with the wide range of animal behaviors that are reportedly affected by serotonergic manipulation (Soubrié, 1986), and in particular certain forms of aggressivity and aversion-related behaviors (Copenhaver, Schalock & Carver, 1978; Katz, 1980; Schütz, De Aquiar & Graeff, 1985).

Such contention may also account for the many contradictions or inconsistencies that can be noticed throughout the scientific literature concerning serotonergic systems and their putative role in controlling fear or anxiety-related conducts in animals.

V: THE SEROTONIN HYPOTHESIS OF ANXIETY

Since Brodie and Shore (1957) hypothesized that behavioral arousal is a joint function of serotonergic inhibition and catecholaminergic excitation, the general idea has gradually emerged that 5-HT neurons play a role in fear- or anxiety-mediated behavioral suppression. Decreased serotonin transmission has been linked to reduced anxiety and proposed as the mechanism in the anxiolytic activity of benzodiazepines.

Much of the supportive evidence for this hypothesis that has been obtained by using the classical paradigm of punishment-induced suppression can be summarized as follows.

Experiments conducted with the serotonin depletor, parachlorophenylalanine (pCPA), or serotonin receptors blockers (methysergide, cinanserin, mianserin), as well as lesion studies with specific neurotoxins such as 5,7-dihydroxytryptamine have led to the conclusion that a depressed serotonin transmission produces, as benzodiazepines do, a significant attenuation of punishment-induced inhibition (Iversen, 1984; Gardner, 1986; Johnston & File, 1986; Thiébot, 1986).

The involvement of serotonergic neurons seems further substantiated by the fact that the administration of lysergic acid diethylamide (Schoenfeld, 1976) or the application of serotonin to the raphe area (Thiébot et al., 1982), manipulations known to cause suppression of the firing rate of raphe cells as well as diminished release of the indoleamine in terminal areas, attenuate the behavioral inhibition elicited by punishment or a signal paired with punishment. Likewise, intra raphe micro-injection of chlordiazepoxide, which also depresses raphe neuronal activity, produces an antipunishment effect. This effect is abolished when serotonergic neurons of the dorsal raphe are first destroyed by local infusion of 5,7-dihydroxytryptamine (Thiébot et al., 1982).

Moreover, antipunishment effects have been reported with drugs assumed to specifically bind to 5-HT2 or 5-HT1A sites (ritanserine, 8-OH-DPAT, buspirone, etc.) Although these effects require the integrity of serotonergic pathways to be observed, they are generally observed in only a narrow dose-range, fail to reach the magnitude of those produced by benzodiazepines and greatly depend on the testing procedure used (Gardner, 1986; Merlo-Pich and Samanin, 1986; Colpaert et al., 1985).

The serotonin hypothesis of anxiety, however, is flawed by two sets of observations:

Firstly, most of the additional behavioral procedures that have been investigated as potential animal models of anxiety, including novelty- or frustration-related behaviors, though sensitive to benzodiazepines, are poorly sensitive to manipulations (lesions or drugs) affecting serotonin transmission (Soubrié, 1986).

Secondly, few animal data support the notion that the anti-anxiety effects of benzodiazepines, even those observed in punishment paradigm, derive from their ability to depress serotonin transmission.

The doses of benzodiazepine required to modify serotonergic transmission are generally higher than those necessary to influence punished behavior. Moreover, changes in serotonin turnover do not closely parallel the efficacy of benzodiazepines in releasing punished behavior under acute (Sepinwall & Cook, 1980) or chronic (Lister & File, 1983) treatment conditions.

Tye, Everitt & Iversen (1977) reported that a lesion of ascending serotonergic pathways blocked the action of parenteral chlordiazepoxide in a conflict paradigm. However, other studies clearly show that destruction or inactivation or serotonergic neurons or serotonergic receptor blockade fails to impair the release of punished behavior induced by peripheral administration of benzodiazepines (Shephard, Buxton & Broadhurst, 1982; Thiébot et al., 1984; Green & Hodges, 1986). Finally, direct stimulation of serotonergic receptors or enhanced serotonin availability did not antagonize, and even may potentiate, the anticonflict effect of benzodiazepines (Kilts et al., 1982; Shephard and Broadhurst, 1982).

It is time now to come back to the notion mentioned in the introduction that, in punishment models of anxiety, during the course of which animals are required to stop responding for reward to avoid punishment, we are probably studying anxiety but also ability to wait for reward. Hence, it is conceivable that serotonergic neurons would exert a control over punished behavior not by affecting anxiety per se but by altering waiting ability and thus changing those responses (behavioral suppression) which are commonly taken as measures of animal anxiety. This alternative would be consonant with the fact that destruction of serotonergic innervation of brain structures, the substantia nigra for instance, assumed to be more concerned with the performance of behaviors than with the control of emotions, released behavioral suppression in two models of punishment (Thiébot et al., 1983). Moreover, it can be asked whether the presence or the absence of a waiting dimension, especially waiting for food reward, in a presumed model of anxiety is not critical for the apparent antianxiety effect of reducing serotonin transmission to be ovserved.

CONCLUSIONS

The hypothesis of a significant interplay between serotonergic neurons and waiting dimensions does not postulate any kind of human/animal behavioral isomorphism, and seems to be amongst those most compatible with findings from biological psychiatry or psychology. Indeed, although serious methodological criticism can be levelled against these studies, a large degree of unanimity emerges to suggest a privileged connection between indexes of reduced serotonin transmission (low 5-HIAA in CSF, 3H-imipramine binding) and impulsive conduct (Brown et al., 1982; Linnoila et al., 1983; Rydin et al., 1982; Stanley et al., 1982; Van Praag, 1986). It is worthy of mention that no such a relationship can be found with any classical nosographic entity. The hypothesis based on our data on animals that noradrenergic neurons may also be involved in waiting ability is compatible with human studies which have pointed to an association between suicide attempts and noradrenergic dysfunction, including abnormal results on the dexamethasone suppression test, low CSF MHPG levels, or urinary norepinephrine/epinephrine ratios. (Agren, 1980; Ostroff et al., 1985).

Finally, one can inquire whether the inhibitory influence exerted by benzodiazepines on serotonin transmission may parallel their ability to shift behavior toward such paradoxical or aberrant reactions in an "acting out" behavioral style (see Feldman, 1986). Hence, one can ask whether these drugs are the most appropriate ones when given at non-incapacitating dosages to patients who lack impulsive control or have low CSF 5-HIAA levels.

REFERENCES

Agren, H. (1980). Symptom patterns in unipolar and bipolar depression correlating with monoamine metabolites in the cerebrospinal fluid. 2. *Suicide. Psychiatry Research, 3,* 225–236.

Brodie, B. B., & Shore, P. (1957). A concept for a role of serotonin and norepinephrine as chemical mediators in the brain. *Annals of the New York Academy of Sciences, 66,* 631–642.

Brown, G. L., Goodwin, F. K., & Bunney, W. E. (1982). Human aggression and suicide: Their relationship to neuropsychiatric diagnoses and serotonin metabolism. In B. T. Ho et al. (Eds.), *Advances in Bio-*

chemical Psychopharmacology, Vol. 34: Serotonin in Biological Psychiatry (pp. 287–306). New York: Raven Press.

Colpaert, F. C., Meert, T. F., Niemegeers, C. J. E., & Janssen, P. A. J. (1985). Behavioral and 5-HT antagonistic effects of ritanserin: A pure and selective antagonist of LSD discrimination in rat. *Psychopharmacology, 86,* 45–54.

Copenhaver, J. H., Schalock, R. L., & Carver, M. J. (1978). Parachloro-D,1-phenylalanine induced filicidal behavior in the female rat. *Pharmac. Biochem. Behav., 8,* 263–270.

Feldman, M. D. (1986). Paradoxical effects of benzodiazepines. *N. C. Med. J., 47,* 311–312.

Feuerstein, T. J. & Jackisch, R. (1986). Why do some antidepressants promote suicide? *Psychopharmacology, 90,* 422.

Gardner, C. R. (1986). Recent developments in 5-HT related pharmacology of animal model of anxiety. *Pharmac. Biochem. Behav., 24,* 1479–1485.

Gray, J. A. (1982). Précis of the neuropsychobiology of anxiety: An enquiry into the functions of the septo-hippocampal system. *Behav. Brain Sci., 5,* 469–534.

Green, S., & Hodges, H. (1986). Differential effects of dorsal raphe lesions and intraraphe GABA and benzodiazepines on conflict behavior in rats. *Behav. Neur. Biol., 46,* 13–25.

Herrnstein, R. J. (1981). Self control as response strength. In C. M. Bradshaw, E. Szabadi, & C. F. Lowe (Eds.), *Quantification of Steady-State Operant Behavior.* Elsevier, North-Holland Biomedical Press.

Iversen, S. D. (1984). 5-HT and anxiety. *Neuropharmacology, 23,* 1553–1560.

Jenike, M. A., Armentano, M. E., & Baer L. (1987). Disabling obsessive thoughts responsive to antidepressants. *J. Clin. Psychopharmacol., 7,* 33–35.

Johnston, A. L., & File, S. E. (1986). 5-HT and anxiety: Promises and pitfalls. *Pharmac. Biochem. Behav., 24,* 1467–1470.

Katz, R. J. (1980). Role of serotonergic mechanisms in animal models of predation. *Prog. Neuro-Psychopharmacol., 4,* 219–231.

Kilts, C. D., Sommisaris, R. L., Cordon, J. J. & Tech, R. H. (1982). Lack of central 5-hydroxytryptamine influence on the anticonflict activity of diazepam. *Psychopharmacology, 78,* 156–164.

Linnoila, M., Virkkunen, M., Scheinin, M., Nuutila, A., Rimon, R., & Goodwin, F. K. (1983). Low cerebrospinal fluid 5-hydroxyindoleacetic acid concentration differentiates impulsive from nonimpulsive violent behavior. *Life Sci., 33,* 2609–2614.

Lister, R. G., & File, S. E. (1983). Changes in regional concentrations in the rat brain of 5-hydroxytryptamine and 5-Hydroxyindoleacetic acid during the development of tolerance to the sedative action of chlordiazepoxide. *J. Pharm. Pharmacol.*, *35*, 601–603.

Mavissakalian, M., Turner, S. M., Michelson, L., & Jacob, R. (1985). Tricyclic antidepressants in obsessive-compulsive disorder: Antiobsessional and antidepressant agents? II. *Am. J. Psychiatry*, *142*, 5.

Merlo-Pich, E., & Samanin, R. (1986). Dishinibitory effects of buspirone and low doses of sulpiride and haloperidol in two experimental anxiety models in rats: Possible role of dopamine. *Psychopharmacology*, *89*, 125–130.

O'Donnell, J. M., & Seiden, L. S. (1983). Differential-reinforcement-of-low-rate 72-seconds schedule: Selective effects of antidepressant drugs. *J. Pharmacol. Exp. Ther.*, *224*, 80–88.

Ostroff, R. B., Giller, E., Harkness, L., & Mason, J. (1985). The norepinephrine-to-epinephrine ratio in patients with a history of suicide attempts. *Am. J. Psychiatry*, *142*, 224–227.

Pope, H. G., Hudson, J. I., Jonas, J. M., & Yugerlun-Tood, D. (1985). Antidepressant treatment of bulimia: A two-year follow-up study. *J. Clin. Psychopharm.*, *5*, 320–327.

Rydin, E., Schalling, D., & Asberg, M. (1982). Rorschach ratings in depressed and suicidal patients with low levels of 5-hydroxyindoleacetic acid in cerebrospinal fluid. *Psychiatry Research*, 7, 229–243.

Sanghera, M. J., McMillen, B. A. & German, D. C. (1983). Buspirone, a nonbenzodiazepine anxiolytic, increases locus coeruleus noradrenergic neuronal activity. *Eur. J. Pharmacol.*, *86*, 107–110.

Schoenfeld, R. I. (1976). Lysergic acid diethylamide- and mescaline-induced attenuation of the effect of punishment in the rat. *Science*, *192*, 801–803.

Schütz, M. T. B., De Aguiar, J. C., & Graeff, F. G. (1985). Anti-aversive role of serotonin in the dorsal periaqueductal grey matter. *Psychopharmacology*, *85*, 340–345.

Sepinwall, J., & Cook, L. (1980). Mechanism of action of the benzodiazepines: Behavioral aspect. *Fed. Proc.*, *39*, 3024–3031.

Shephard, R. A. & Broadhurst, P. L. (1982). Effects of diazepam and of serotonin agonists on hyponeophagia in rats. *Neuropharmacology*, *21*, 337–340.

Shephard, R. A., Buxton, D. A., & Broadhurst, P. L. (1982). Drug interactions do not support reduction in serotonin turnover as the mechanism of action of benzodiazepines. *Neuropharmacology*, *21*, 1027–1032.

Soubrié, P. (1986). Reconciling the role of central serotonin neurons in human and animal behavior. *Behavioral and Brain Sci., 9,* 319–364.

Stanley, M., Virgilio, J., & Gherson, S. (1982). Tritiated imipramine binding sites are decreased in the frontal cortex of suicides. *Science, 216,* 1337–1339.

Thiébot, M. H. (1986). Are serotonergic neurons involved in the control of anxiety and in the anxiolytic activity of benzodiazepines? *Pharmacol. Biochem. Behav., 24,* 1471–1477.

Thiébot, N. C., Le Bihan, C., Soubrié, P., & Simon P. (1985). Benzodiazepines reduce the tolerance to reward delay in rats. *Psychopharmacology, 86,* 147–152.

Thiébot, M. H., Bizot, J. C., Le Bihan, C., Soubrié, P., & Simon, P. (1986). Waiting as a behavioral dimension sensitive to benzodiazepines (BZP) and antidepressants (ADs). *Psychopharmacology, 89,* S36, abs. 120.

Thiébot, M. H., Harmon, M., & Soubrié, P. (1982). Attenuation of induced-anxiety in rats by chlordiazepoxide: Role of raphe dorsalis benzodiazepine binding sites and serotonergic neurons. *Neurosci.*, 7, 2287–2294.

Thiébot, M. H., Harmon, M., & Soubrié, P. (1983). The involvement of nigral serotonin innervation in the control of punishment-induced behavior in rats. *Pharmacol. Biochem. Behav., 19,* 225–229.

Tye, N. C., Everitt, B. J., & Iversen, S. D. (1977). 5-Hydroxytryptamine and punishment. *Nature (Lond.), 268,* 741–743.

Valzelli, L. (1985). Animal models of behavioral pathology and violent aggression. *Meth. and Find. Exptl. Clin. Pharmacol.*, 7, 189–193.

van Praag, H. M. (1986). Biological suicide research: outcome and limitations. *Biol. Psychiatry, 21,* 1305–1323.

Zuckerman, M. (1984). Sensation seeking: A comparative approach to human trait. *Behav. and Brain Sci.*, 7, 413–471.

PART V

Basic Neuroreceptor Functions

11

Functional Correlates of Central 5-HT Receptors

STEPHEN J. PEROUTKA

In the 30 years since the differentiation of M and D receptors (Gaddum and Picarelli, 1957), it has become clear that multiple 5-hydroxytryptamine (5-HT) receptors exist. The heterogeneity of 5-HT receptors has become even more apparent in the past decade. To a significant degree, the appreciation of this fact is a direct result of the development of radioligand binding techniques (Snyder, 1983). At the present time, at least five 5-HT binding site subtypes have been differentiated by radioligand techniques in brain homogenates (Fillion, 1983; Leysen, 1983; Fuller, 1984; Hamon et al., 1984; Peroutka, 1987). Anatomic studies using autoradiographic techniques have also confirmed that a variety of serotonergic recognition sites, with distinct regional localizations, exist in the central nervous system (Biegon et al., 1982; Pazos and Palacios, 1985; Pazos et al., 1985a; Hoyer et al., 1986a; 1986b). The identification and characterization of these 5-HT receptor subtypes has, and will continue to have, multiple clinical implications. For example, neuropsychiatric disorders such as anxiety, depression and hallucinosis have been specifically linked to specific 5-HT receptor subtypes in the central nervous system. As evidenced by this publication, 5-HT has also been linked to the regulation of aggression and impulse control. This review will summarize data concerning the pharma-

This work was supported in part by the John A. and George L. Hartford Foundation, the McKnight Foundation, the Alfred P. Sloan Foundation and NIH Grants NS12151-12 and NS 23560-01.

cological characteristics and possible functional correlates of 5-HT receptors.

RADIOLIGAND BINDING STUDIES OF 5-HT RECEPTORS

Preliminary Binding Studies

Bennett and Aghajanian (1974) were the first investigators to successfully radiolabel 5-HT receptors. The binding of ^{3}H-d-lysergic acid diethylamide (d-LSD) was saturable, reversible, stereoselective and displayed high affinity (K_D = 7.5 nM) for its membrane recognition site. The binding sites also displayed appropriate regional variations since brain regions with the highest density of receptors were areas known to receive a dense projection of 5-HT neuronal terminals. These findings were soon extended and confirmed by other laboratories (Bennett and Snyder, 1975; Lovell and Freedman, 1976).

The second radioligand used to label 5-HT receptors was ^{3}H-5-HT (Bennett and Snyder, 1976; Fillion et al., 1978; Nelson et al., 1978). Like ^{3}H-LSD binding, ^{3}H-5-HT binding was saturable, stereoselective and displayed appropriate regional variations. However, important discrepancies were noted between the binding of ^{3}H-LSD and ^{3}H-5-HT. At the time, Bennett and Snyder (1976) suggested that ^{3}H-5-HT and ^{3}H-LSD did not label the same membrane recognition site but rather two different "states" of the same receptor.

Radioligand analysis of 5-HT receptors was considerably advanced by the finding that ^{3}H-spiperone could also be used to label presumed 5-HT recognition sites (Leysen et al., 1978). Previously, ^{3}H-spiperone had been considered a pure dopaminergic ligand. However, in the rat frontal cortex, where dopamine receptors are sparse, ^{3}H-spiperone was found to label a receptor that appeared to be "serotonergic" in the sense that 5-HT antagonists were the most potent displacers of the ligand. However, 5-HT and related tryptamines were extremely weak displacers of ^{3}H-spiperone.

Differentiation of 5-HT$_1$ and 5-HT$_2$ Receptors

Thus, marked differences were noted between the binding characteristics of ^{3}H-5-HT, ^{3}H-LSD and ^{3}H-spiperone (Peroutka and Snyder, 1979). If each ligand labeled the same membrane recognition site, then unlabeled drugs should be equipotent in displacing ^{3}H-5-HT, ^{3}H-LSD and ^{3}H-spiperone. This pattern is observed with d-LSD displacement of the three ligands. A K_i value of approximately 10 nM is observed with d-LSD competition studies against each of these three ligands. The K_i value is a measure of the potency of the drug. In marked contrast, 5-HT is approximately three orders of magnitude more potent in displacing ^{3}H-5-HT (3.8 nM) than ^{3}H-spiperone (2,700 nM). Its apparent K_i for ^{3}H-LSD binding is 110 nM, a value which is intermediate between its affinity for ^{3}H-5-HT and ^{3}H-spiperone labeled sites. The converse pattern is observed with spiperone displacement of the three radioligands. For example, spiperone is extremely potent against ^{3}H-spiperone binding (0.51 nM) yet has 1400 fold less affinity for total ^{3}H-5-HT labeled sites (730 nM). In addition, its apparent K_i for ^{3}H-LSD binding is 18 nM but the displacement curve is biphasic with a "plateau" occurring between 10 and 30 nM spiperone.

Given the results outlined above and the fact that no correlation exists between drug potencies for ^{3}H-5-HT and ^{3}H-spiperone labeled "serotonergic" receptors, Peroutka and Snyder (1979) concluded that at least two distinct 5-HT membrane recognition sites are present in the central nervous system. The sites labeled by ^{3}H-5-HT were designated "5-HT$_1$ receptors" and those labeled by ^{3}H-spiperone were designated "5-HT$_2$ receptors." Since ^{3}H-LSD had equal affinity for both sites, it was proposed that this ligand could be used to label both 5-HT$_1$ and 5-HT$_2$ receptors.

Characterization of 5-HT$_1$ Binding Site Subtypes

However, 5-HT$_1$ binding sites labeled by ^{3}H-5-HT were soon shown to be heterogeneous. Non-sigmoidal displacement of ^{3}H-5-HT by spiperone led to the suggestion that sites with high affinity (K_i = 2 - 13 nM) for spiperone should be designated

$5\text{-}HT_{1A}$ sites while sites with relatively low affinity for spiperone (K_i = 35 uM) should be designated $5\text{-}HT_{1B}$ sites (Pedigo et al., 1981). These two subtypes have different regional localizations and have been identified in many species (Schnellmann et al., 1984). A third subtype of the $5\text{-}HT_1$ class of recognition sites (the $5\text{-}HT_{1C}$ site) has been identified in the choroid plexus and cortex of various species (Pazos et al., 1984a; 1984b; Yagaloff and Hartig, 1985; Peroutka, 1986). Most recently, a fourth subtype site labeled by ^{3}H-5-HT, the $5\text{-}HT_{1D}$ site, has been identified in bovine brain (Heuring and Peroutka, 1987). In the past three years, the availability of selective and novel agents has greatly facilitated the analysis of $5\text{-}HT_1$ binding site subtypes. A summary of the currently accepted 5-HT receptor classification system based on radioligand data is presented in Table 1. A summary of drug potencies at each of the five known 5-HT binding site subtypes in the central nervous system is provided in Table 2. These data are discussed in greater detail in the following section.

$5\text{-}HT_{1A}$ Binding Sites

The $5\text{-}HT_{1A}$ binding site was first identified by Nelson and colleagues and was defined as ^{3}H-5-HT binding which was sensitive to nanomolar concentrations of spiperone (Pedigo et al., 1981; Schnellmann et al., 1984). Subsequently, the $5\text{-}HT_{1A}$ binding site has been more directly labeled with ^{3}H-8-hydroxy-2-(di-n-propyl-amino)tetralin (8-OH-DPAT) (Gozlan et al., 1983; Hall et al., 1985; Peroutka, 1985; Hoyer et al., 1985b), ^{3}H-ipsapirone (formerly called TVX Q 7821) (Dompert et al., 1985), ^{3}H-buspirone (Moon and Taylor, 1985), ^{3}H-1-(2-(4-amino-phenyl)ethyl)-4-(3-trifluromethyl-phenyl)piperazine (PAAP) (Ransom et al., 1986) and ^{3}H-spiroxatrine (Nelson et al., 1987). In addition, ^{3}H-WB 4101, previously considered a selective alpha$_1$-adrenergic radioligand, has been demonstrated to label the $5\text{-}HT_{1A}$ site (Norman et al., 1985). Regardless of the ^{3}H-ligand used to label the site, it displays high and selective affinity for 8-OH-DPAT, 5-methoxydimethyl-tryptamine, ipsapirone and buspirone. The $5\text{-}HT_{1A}$ site is densely present in the CA1 region and dentate gyrus of the hippocampus and in the

TABLE 1
Characteristics of 5-HT_{1A}, 5-HT_{1B}, 5-HT_{1C}, 5-HT_{1D}, and 5-HT_2 Binding Sites

	5-HT_{1A}	*5-HT_{1B}*	*5-HT_{1C}*	*5-HT_{1D}*	*5-HT_2*
Radiolabeled by	^{3}H-5-HT ^{3}H-8-OH-DPAT ^{3}H-Ipsapirone ^{3}H-WB 4101 ^{3}H-Buspirone ^{3}H-PAPP ^{3}H-Spiroxatrine	^{3}H-5-HT ^{125}I-CYP (Rat and Mouse only)	^{3}H-5-HT ^{3}H-Mesulergine ^{125}I-LSD	^{3}H-5-HT	^{3}H-Spiperone ^{3}H-Mesulergine ^{125}I-LSD ^{3}H-Ketanserin ^{3}H-Mianserin ^{125}I-Methyl-LSD ^{3}H-DOB
High Density Regions	Raphe nuclei	Substantia Nigra	Choroid Plexus	Basal Ganglia	Layer IV Cortex
	Hippocampus	Globus Pallidus			

TABLE 2
Drug Affinities for 5-HT_{1A}, 5-HT_{1B}, 5-HT_{1C}, 5-HT_{1D}, and 5-HT_2 Receptors

Drug Potencies (K_i, nM)	*5-HT_{1A}*	*5-HT_{1B}*	*5-HT_{1C}*	*5-HT_{1D}*	*5-HT_2*
< 10 nM	5-CT 8-OH-DPATq. 5-HT RU 24969 d-LSD	RU 24969 5-CT 5-HT	Mesulergine Metergoline Methysergide	5-CT 5-HT Metergoline	Spiperone Mesulergine Methysergide Metergoline Mianserin
10–1000 nM	Metergoline Methysergide Spiperone Mesulergine	Metergoline Methysergide d-LSD	Mianserin 5-HT RU 24969 5-CT d-LSD	Methysergide Mianserin 8-OH-DPAT d-LSD RU 24969	d-LSD
> 1000 nM	Mianserin	Mianserin Spiperone Mesulergine 8-OH-DPAT	Spiperone 8-OH-DPAT	Mesulergine Spiperone	RU 24969 5-HT 8-OH-DPAT

Data given are derived from Peroutka and Snyder (1979), Peroutka (1986), Hoyer et al. (1985b), Heuring and Peroutka (1986) and unpublished observations.

raphe nuclei (Deshmukh et al., 1983; Marcinkiewicz et al., 1984; Pazos and Palacios, 1985; Glaser et al., 1985; Hoyer et al., 1986a).

In addition, the fact that 5,7-dihydroxytryptamine-induced lesions of the raphe system cause a loss of ^{3}H-8-OH-DPAT binding in the striatum but not hippocampus has led Hamon and colleagues to hypothesize that ^{3}H-8-OH-DPAT also labels a presynaptic 5-HT autoreceptor (Gozlan et al., 1983; Hall et al., 1985; 1986). ^{3}H-8-OH-DPAT has also been reported to label the "5-HT transporter" (Schoemaker and Langer, 1986). Importantly, in the absence of ascorbate, ^{3}H-8-OH-DPAT also labels glass fiber filter paper (Peroutka and Demopulos, 1986; Demopulos and Peroutka, 1987). The 5-HT$_{1A}$ binding site is the only site that has been labeled by ^{3}H-8-OH-DPAT in the presence of ascorbate (Peroutka, 1985; 1986; Hoyer et al., 1985b).

5-HT-Sensitive Adenylate Cyclase

Because of the large number of agents which display potent and selective affinity for the 5-HT$_{1A}$ site, correlations have been established between the pharmacologic characteristics of this binding site and specific physiological effects. For example, serotonergic modulation of adenylate cyclase has been linked to the 5-HT$_{1A}$ site. Thus, GTP and GDP, but not GMP, inhibit the binding of ^{3}H-8-OH-DPAT to brain membranes (Hall et al., 1985; Schlegel and Peroutka, 1986). In addition, guanine nucleotides significantly reduce agonist potencies for ^{3}H-8-OH-DPAT binding sites whereas antagonist potencies are not affected by nucleotides.

In studies using both rat (Markstein et al., 1986) and guinea pig (Shenker et al., 1985) hippocampal membranes, a 5-HT-sensitive adenylate cyclase could be stimulated by nanomolar concentrations of 5-HT$_{1A}$ selective agents such as 5-carboxyamido-tryptamine (5-CT) and 8-OH-DPAT. In addition, 5-HT can inhibit forskolin-stimulated adenylate cyclase in rat and guinea pig hippocampal membranes (De Vivo and Maayani, 1986). In pharmacologic data derived from this system appears to be consistent with a single, homogeneous population of receptors. 8-OH-DPAT, d-LSD and buspirone are similar to 5-HT in their ability to inhibit cyclase activity. By contrast, spiperone is a competitive antagonist at this receptor whereas ketanserin has no effect on 5-HT-induced inhibition of the cyclase activity. The 5-HT_{1A} receptor also appears to mediate inhibition of VIP-stimulated cyclic AMP formation in purified striatal and cortical cultured neurons (Weiss et al., 1986). Thus, the 5-HT_{1A} receptor appears to modulate adenylate cyclase activity in certain brain regions.

Neurophysiological Studies

Neurophysiological analyses have also benefited from the recent development and characterization of 5-HT_{1A} selective agents. For example, neurophysiological studies have clearly demonstrated that the 5-HT_{1A} receptor mediates inhibition of raphe nuclei. VanderMaelen and Wilderman (1984) first showed that buspirone, a 5-HT_{1A} selective agent, caused complete inhibition of dorsal raphe neuronal firing in the rat. Buspirone also has identical effects in mouse brain slices (Trulson and Arasteh, 1986). The ability of other 5-HT_{1A} selective agents to produce this effect was soon demonstrated by multiple laboratories. For example, ipsapirone, 8-OH-DPAT and 5-CT were also found to mimic the effect of 5-HT on raphe cell firing (Sinton and Fallon, 1986; VanderMaelen et al., 1986). By contrast, (-)propranolol, a beta-adrenergic agent which also displays high affinity for the 5-HT_{1A} receptor (Hiner et al., 1986), was shown to reversibly block the inhibitory effects of ipsapirone and 8-OH-DPAT on raphe cell inhibition (Sprouse and Aghajanian 1987).

The hippocampus is a second anatomical structure containing a high concentration of 5-HT_{1A} sites which has been used to study 5-HT_{1A} receptor function (Deshmukh et al., 1983; Pazos and Palacios, 1985). Preliminary studies suggested that 5-HT_{1A} selective drugs may directly inhibit CA1 pyramidal cells (Beck et al., 1985; Andrade and Nicoll, 1985). However, more detailed analysis suggests that 5-HT_{1A} selective agents also have effects on hippocampal activity that are not mediated by direct inhibition of CA1 pyramidal cells (Peroutka et al., 1987; Mauk et al., 1987). Putative 5-HT_{1A} selective agents such as 8-OH-DPAT, buspirone and ipsapirone cause pre-synaptic fiber inhibition which cannot be mimicked or antagonized by 5-HT (Mauk et al., 1987).

Other Systems

5-HT-induced contractions of the canine basilar artery have been proposed to be a functional correlate of the 5-HT_{1A} receptor (Taylor et al., 1986; Peroutka et al., 1986). Specific components of the 5-HT behavioral syndrome have also been linked to activation of 5-HT_{1A} receptors (Tricklebank, 1985; Smith and Peroutka, 1986). In addition, studies in male rats have shown that 5-HT_{1A} selective agonists facilitate seminal emissions and/or ejaculations (Kwong et al., 1986). The hypotensive potencies of 8-OH-DPAT and RU 24969 in pentobarbitone-anesthesized rats suggest that the 5-HT_{1A} site may mediate these effects (Doods et al., 1985). Finally, the thermoregulatory effects of 8-OH-DPAT and RU 24969 also appear to be mediated by the 5-HT_{1A} receptor (Tricklebank et al., 1986; Gudelsky et al., 1986).

5-HT_{1B} Binding Sites

The putative 5-HT_{1B} site has been more difficult to characterize. Sills et al. (1984) defined 5-HT_{1B} binding as specific ^{3}H-5-HT binding in the presence of 1 nM GTP and 2000 nM spiperone. They concluded that RU 24969 and TFMPP were selective 5-HT_{1B} agents. The 5-HT_{1B} site has been more directly labeled in rat brain with ^{125}I-cyanopindolol (Pazos et al., 1985b; Hoyer et al., 1985a; 1985b). The ^{125}I-cyanopindolol site has high affinity for 5-HT and RU 24969 and relatively low affinity for d-LSD and 8-OH-DPAT. The highest densities of 5-HT_{1B} sites in rat brain are found in the globus pallidus, dorsal subiculum and substantia nigra (Pazos and Palacios, 1985). Recent data has demonstrated that this site can also be labeled with ^{3}H-5-HT in rat frontal cortex (Peroutka, 1986; Blurton and Wood, 1986).

Interestingly, the 5-HT_{1B} site, as defined by radioligand binding studies, appears to be species specific. The 5-HT_{1B} site is present in rat and mouse brain membranes, but not in guinea pig, cow, chicken, turtle, frog or human brain membranes

(Heuring et al., 1986; Hoyer et al., 1986a). In rat brains, the 5-HT_{1B} site is most dense in the substantia nigra and globus pallidus (Pazos and Palacios, 1985).

To date, functional correlates of this site have been limited to studies of the serotonin "autoreceptor." Briefly, 5-HT autoreceptors are studied in synaptosomal or slice preparations in which depolarization-evoked release of stored ^{3}H-5-HT is measured by superperfusion techniques. The release of ^{3}H-5HT can be inhibited by 5-HT and related agonists, presumably through a presynaptic "autoreceptor." Engel et al. (1986) have convincingly demonstrated that in rat brain synaptosomes, the effects of 5-HT and other agents are mediated by the 5-HT_{1B} receptor. No significant correlation was observed between drug potencies at the 5-HT "autoreceptor" and drug affinities for 5-HT_{1C} or 5-HT_2 binding sites. However, a significant correlation was obtained between drug affinities for 5-HT_{1B} sites and the rat 5-HT "autoreceptor." As a result, the 5-HT_{1B} binding site appears to be the receptor which mediates release of 5-HT from nerve terminals in rat brains.

A similar conclusion was reached from an analysis of 5-HT and related drug effects on the release of ^{3}H-5-HT induced by depolarization of rat cerebellum synaptosomes (Raiteri et al., 1986). By contrast, the 5-HT heteroreceptor mediating release of endogenous glutamate induced by depolarization of rat cerebellum synaptosomes did not conform to the previously described pharmacological characteristics of 5-HT_{1A}, 5-HT_{1B}, 5-HT_{1C} and 5-HT_2 binding sites.

5-HT_{1C} Binding Sites

The 5-HT_{1C} site was first discovered as a result of the autoradiographic analysis of 5-HT binding site subtypes. The 5-HT_{1C} site was characterized initially in membranes from pig choroid plexus and cortex (Pazos et al., 1984a; 1984b; Hoyer et al., 1985b). The site was labeled by both ^{3}H-5-HT and ^{3}H-mesulergine. Independently, Yagaloff and Hartig (1985) labeled the site with ^{125}I-LSD in the rat choroid plexus. The 5-HT_{1C} site has high affinity for 5-HT, methysergide and mianserin and relatively low affinity for RU 24969. These pharmacological characteristics are also shared with the putative 5-HT_{1C} site identified in rat cortex (Hoyer et al., 1985b; Peroutka, 1986).

The recent work of Sanders-Bush and colleagues has convincingly demonstrated that 5-HT stimulation of phosphatidylinositol hydrolysis is mediated by the 5-HT_{1C} site in choroid plexus membranes (Conn et al., 1986). Drug effects on 5-HT-stimulated phosphatidylinositol hydrolysis in choroid plexus were compared to drug potencies at ^{125}I-LSD binding sites in the same tissue. Mianserin and ketanserin were potent antagonists of 5-HT-induced changes whereas spiperone was more than an order of magnitude less potent in this system. The authors concluded that the 5-HT_{1C} site in choroid plexus is functionally linked to the phosphatidylinositol second messenger system.

5-HT_{1D} Binding Sites

Recently, a fourth subtype of 5-HT_1 site labeled by ^{3}H-5-HT has been identified in bovine brain membranes (Heuring and Peroutka, 1987). The addition of either the 5-HT_{1A} selective drug 8-OH-DPAT (100 nM) or the 5-HT_{1C} selective drug mesulergine (100 nM) to the radioligand binding assay results in a 5–10% decrease in specific ^{3}H-5-HT binding. Scatchard analysis reveals that the simultaneous addition of both drugs decrease the B_{max} of ^{3}H-5-HT binding by 10–15% without affecting the K_D value (1.8 ± 0.3 nM) of ^{3}H-5-HT. Competition studies using a series of pharmacologic agents reveal that the sites labeled by ^{3}H-5-HT in bovine caudate in the presence of 100 nM 8-OH-DPAT and 100 nM mesulergine appear to be homogeneous. 5-HT_{1A} selective agents such as 8-OH-DPAT, ipsapirone and buspirone display micromolar affinities for these sites. RU 24969 and (-)pindolol are approximately two orders of magnitude less potent at these sites than at 5-HT_{1B} sites which have been identified in rat brain. Agents which display nanomolar potencies for 5-HT_{1C} sites such as mianserin and mesulergine are two to three orders of magnitude less potent at the ^{3}H-5-HT binding sites in bovine caudate. In addition, both

$5\text{-}HT_2$ and $5\text{-}HT_3$ selective agents are essentially inactive at these binding sites. These ^3H-5-HT sites display nanomolar affinity for 5-carboxyamidotryptamine (5-CT), 5-methoxytryptamine, metergoline and 5-HT. Apparent K_i values of 10–100 nM are obtained for d-LSD, RU 24969, methiothepin, tryptamine, methysergide and yohimbine whereas l-LSD and corynanthine are significantly less potent. Regional studies demonstrate that this class of sites is most dense in the basal ganglia but exists in all regions of bovine brain.

These data therefore demonstrate the presence of a homogeneous class of $5\text{-}HT_1$ binding sites in bovine caudate which is pharmacologically distinct from previously defined $5\text{-}HT_{1A}$, $5\text{-}HT_{1B}$, $5\text{-}HT_{1C}$ and $5\text{-}HT_2$ binding site subtypes. We suggested that this class of sites be designated the $5\text{-}HT_{1D}$ subtype of binding site labeled by ^3H-5-HT (Heuring and Peroutka, 1987). A specific physiological effect of 5-HT has not yet been correlated with the $5\text{-}HT_{1D}$ binding site. However, the site shares many pharmacological similarities to the inhibitory prejunctional "$5\text{-}HT_1$-like" receptor in the isolated perfused rat kidney (Charlton et al., 1986) and the receptor mediating 5-HT-induced contractions of the rat stomach fundus (Leysen and Tollenaere, 1981; Clineschmidt et al., 1985; Cohen and Wittenauer, 1986).

$5\text{-}HT_2$ Binding Sites

Because of the availability of a large number of potent and selective antagonists, the $5\text{-}HT_2$ class of binding sites has been extensively analyzed. ^3H-spiperone, ^3H-LSD, ^3H-mianserin, ^3H-ketanserin, ^3H-mesulergine, ^{125}I-LSD and N_1-methyl-2-^{125}I-LSD can be used to label the $5\text{-}HT_2$ binding site (Leysen, 1981; Leysen et al., 1978; 1982; Peroutka and Snyder, 1981; Hartig et al., 1983; Closse, 1983; Pazos et al., 1984a; Engel et al., 1984b; Hoffman et al., 1987). Serotonergic antagonists have high affinity for this site while 5-HT and related tryptamines are markedly less potent. The number of $5\text{-}HT_2$, but not $5\text{-}HT_1$, binding sites can be decreased by chronic treatment with antidepressant drugs (Peroutka and Snyder, 1980a,b). The highest level of $5\text{-}HT_2$ binding is in the cerebral cortex and caudate with all other brainregions having substantially fewer binding sites (Schotte et al., 1983; Pazos et al., 1985; Hoyer et al., 1986b).

In addition, the putative hallucinogen ^{3}H-DOB has been reported to label an apparent 5-HT$_2$ recognition site (Lyon et al., 1987). Since the pharmacological characteristics of this site are distinct from the characteristics of 5-HT$_2$ sites labeled by ^{3}H-antagonists, Titeler and colleagues (Lyon et al., 1987) have suggested that the site labeled by ^{3}H-DOB is a high affinity form of the 5-HT$_2$ receptor. This finding may be significant since Glennon and associates have hypothesized that hallucinogens act as agonists at the 5-HT$_2$ receptor in the central nervous system (Glennon, 1985). This theory is based largely on the observation that d-LSD and other hallucinogens produce similar stimulus effects in drug discrimination studies (Glennon et al., 1983) and that specific 5-HT$_2$ antagonists are able to block these discriminative cue effects (Colpaert and Janssen, 1983; Colpaert et al., 1985). Moreover, hallucinogenic discriminative cue effects correlate with known hallucinogenic potencies (Glennon et al., 1983; 1986; Glennon, 1985). However, 2,5-dimethoxy-4-ethylamphetamine (DOET), lisuride, fenfluramine and yohimbine also generalize to hallucinogens in discriminative cue studies, yet these agents are not hallucinogenic in man (Snyder et al., 1971; Colpaert, 1984; Glennon et al., 1986). Studies are in progress to determine more clearly the possible relevance of this site to 5-HT$_2$ sites labeled by ^{3}H-antagonists (Wang and Peroutka, 1987).

Phosphatidylinositol Turnover

Besides adenylate cyclase, phosphatidylinositol hydrolysis is believed to be a common "second messenger" in the transduction of neurotransmitter signals to the cell interior. The hydrolysis of phosphoinositides may modulate a number of intracellular processes including calcium flux, increased arachidonate metabolism, increased cyclic GMP production and protein kinase C activation. 5-HT has been shown to increase phosphoinositide turnover in the mammalian central nervous system (Brown et al., 1984; Conn and Sanders-Bush, 1984; 1985; Kendall and Nahorski, 1985).

5-HT-induced phosphoinositide hydrolysis in rat cerebral cortex (Kendall and Nahorski, 1985; Conn and Sanders-Bush, 1985) appears to occur as a result of 5-HT_2 receptor activation. 5-HT stimulates phosphoinositide turnover with an EC_{50} of 1 uM. The response to 5-HT is blocked by nanomolar concentrations of ketanserin and phosphoinositide turnover is not affected by 8-OH-DPAT. Furthermore, tricyclic antidepressants decrease both 5-HT_2 binding sites and 5-HT-induced phosphoinositide turnover (Conn and Sanders-Bush, 1986). The rat thoracic aorta (Roth et al., 1984), cultured bovine aortic smooth muscle cells (Coughlin et al., 1984) and platelets (de Chaffoy de Courcelles et al., 1985) are three additional systems in which 5-HT appears to modulate phosphoinositide turnover via a receptor which is similar to the 5-HT_2 binding site.

Neurophysiological Studies

At the present time, two specific neurophysiological effects of 5-HT have been attributed to activation of the 5-HT_2 receptor. Extracellular studies have indicated that 5-HT facilitates excitation of facial motor neurons. This effect of 5-HT is antagonized by selective 5-HT_2 antagonists such as methysergide, cyproheptadine and cinanserin (McCall and Aghajanian, 1980). Similar data were derived from intracellular studies of this brainstem nucleus. Thus, 5-HT caused a slow depolarization of facial motor neuron membranes which remained subthreshold. The membrane effects of 5-HT could be blocked by methysergide (VanderMaelen and Aghajanian, 1980). These data suggest that 5-HT_2 receptors mediate 5-HT-induced excitation of facial motor neurons.

More recently, Davies et al. (1987) demonstrated that 5-HT caused a slow depolarization of 68% of cortical neurons, which was associated with a decreased conductance. The response displayed some voltage dependency and was easily desensitized by repeated 5-HT applications. The selective 5-HT_2 receptor antagonists ritanserin and cinanserin blocked the depolarizing effects of 5-HT. Therefore, the effects of 5-HT on cortical pyramidal neurons share many similarities to the depolarizing effects of 5-

HT in the facial motor nucleus and also appear to be mediated by 5-HT_2 receptors.

Other Systems

In contrast to 5-HT-induced contractions of the canine basilar artery, 5-HT-induced contractions of many other vascular tissues are mediated by 5-HT_2 receptors (Peroutka, 1984). A number of behavioral effects of 5-HT have also been attributed to 5-HT_2 receptors. For example, drug antagonism of the "head-shake" or "head-twitch component" of the 5-HT behavioral syndrome has clearly been related to a blockade of 5-HT_2 receptors (Peroutka et al., 1981; Leysen et al., 1984). Likewise, tryptamine induced seizure activity can be prevented by selective 5-HT_2 antagonists (Leysen et al., 1978). Behavioral studies of the discriminative cue properties of 5-HT agonists have concluded that this behavioral response may be mediated by 5-HT_2 receptors (Glennon et al., 1983).

Antagonism of 5-HT induced forepaw edema in that rat by 22 antagonists correlates with drug affinity for 5-HT_2 sites labeled by ^{3}H-spiperone (Ortmann et al., 1982). Similarly, drug antagonism of tracheal smooth muscle contraction, *in vivo* bronchoconstriction and contraction of guinea pig ileum is consistent with mediation by 5-HT_2 sites (Leysen et al., 1984). 5-HT_2 receptors have also been implicated in the regulation of aldosterone production (Matsuoka et al., 1985). 5-HT induction of platelet shape changes and aggregation may also be mediated by 5-HT_2 receptors (Leysen et al., 1984).

5-HT_3 RECEPTORS

Finally, 5-HT has a number of potent effects outside of the central nervous system. At the present time, this site has not been labeled in either peripheral or central nervous system tissues. Because these receptors have an extremely distinct pharmacology, they have been designated 5-HT_3 receptors. They have been defined as peripheral 5-HT receptors which do not coincide with any of the 5-HT binding site subtypes which have been identified in the central nervous system (Bradley et al., 1986; Richardson and Engel, 1986).

In general, 5-HT effects in the peripheral nervous system are not affected by 5-HT_1 and/or 5-HT_2 selective drugs such as 8-OH-DPAT and ketanserin. However, unlike central 5-HT effects, 5-HT effects in the periphery can often be blocked with drugs such as MDL 72222, (-)cocaine, metoclopramide and ICS 205-930 (Fozard, 1984; Richardson et al., 1985; Richardson and Engel, 1986). It is also clear that heterogeneity exists within the 5-HT_3 class of receptors. Significant differences exist between the potency of selective 5-HT_3 antagonists in various physiological systems. For example, MDL 72222 has a $_pA_2$ of 9.1 against 5-HT-induced effects on postganglionic sympathetic and parasympathetic neurons in the rabbit heart but is inactive against putative 5-HT_3 receptors in the guinea pig ileum (Richardson and Engel, 1986). The development of more selective and varied pharmacological agents should further define the pharmacological characteristics and functional correlates of 5-HT_3 receptors and their probable subtypes.

FUTURE TRENDS

In this report, evidence has been provided from a variety of biochemical, physiological and behavioral studies to suggest that multiple 5-HT receptors exist. At the present time, the differentiation of 5-HT receptors into 5-HT_{1A}, 5-HT_{1B}, 5-HT_{1C}, 5-HT_{1D}, 5-HT_2, and 5-HT_3 subtypes appears to be the most relevant classification system. Indeed, a number of functional correlates of these "5-HT binding sites" have been proposed (Table 3). In many of these systems, significant correlations have been documented between physiological drug potencies and drug affinities for specific binding site subtypes.

The development of selective 5-HT_1 agonists such as 8-OH-DPAT (Middlemiss and Fozard, 1983) and RU 24969 has greatly facilitated research into the analysis of 5-HT_1 binding site sub-

TABLE 3
Proposed Functional Correlates of
5-HT Receptor Subtypes

5-HT_{1A}	Adenylate Cyclase Modulation Raphe Cell and CA1 Hippocampal Cell Inhibition Canine Basilar Artery Contractions Forepaw Treading, Tremor, Head-Weaving Facilitation of Ejaculation and/or Seminal Emissions Thermoregulation Hypotensive Effects
5-HT_{1B}	"Autoreceptor"
5-HT_{1C}	Phosphatidylinositol Turnover
5-HT_{1D}	? Rat Kidney Perfusion ? Rat Stomach Fundus
5-HT_2	Phosphatidylinositol Turnover Contraction of Vascular Smooth Muscle 5-Hydroxytryptophan or Mescaline Induced Head Twitches Tryptamine Induced Seizures Rat Forepaw Edema Discriminative Cue Properties Contraction of Bronchial Smooth Muscle Platelet Shape Changes and Aggregation Smooth Muscle Prostacyclin Synthesis
5-HT_3	Depolarization of Postganglionic Autonomic Neurons Contraction of Ileal Smooth Muscle Pain, Wheal and Flare Reaction

types. To a significant degree, the recent advancements in the analysis of 5-HT receptor subtypes are a direct result of radioligand binding studies using these novel compounds. Although binding techniques have been criticized in terms of their relevance to functional receptor sites, the current data strongly support an association between the majority of serotonergic binding sites defined in radioligand studies and distinct functional responses.

Further advancements in the understanding of the physiologic effects of 5-HT would have important implications. To the basic scientist, characterization of all specific 5-HT receptors would greatly clarify the role of 5-HT in the central nervous system. Clinically, 5-HT has been implicated in a number of human disorders such as anxiety, depression, migraine, vasospasm, epilepsy, aggression and impulse control. Analysis of 5-HT receptor subtypes and their functional role in the nervous system should greatly elucidate the pathophysiological basis of many of these human diseases.

REFERENCES

Andrade, R., & Nicoll, R. A. (1985). The novel anxiolytic buspirone elicits a small hyperpolarization and reduces serotonin responses at putative 5-HT_1 receptors on hippocampal CA1 pyramidal cells. *Soc. Neurosci. Abs., 11,* 597.

Beck, S. G., Clarke, W. P., & Goldfarb, J. (1985). Spiperone differentiates multiple 5-hydroxytryptamine responses in rat hippocampal slices in vitro. *Eur. J. Pharmacol., 116,* 195–197.

Bennett, J. L., & Aghajanian, G. K. (1974). D-LSD binding to brain homogenates: Possible relationship to serotonin receptors. *Life Sci., 15,* 1935–1944.

Bennett, J. P., Jr., & Snyder, S. H. (1975). Stereospecific binding of d-lysergic acid diethylamide (LSD) to brain membranes: Relationship to serotonin receptors. *Brain Res., 94,* 523–544.

Bennett, J. P., Jr., & Snyder, S. H. (1976). Serotonin and lysergic acid diethylamide binding in rat brain membranes: Relationship to postsynaptic serotonin receptors. *Mol. Pharmacol., 12,* 373–389.

Biegon, A., Rainbow, T. C., & McEwen, B. S. (1982). Quantitative autoradiography of serotonin receptors in the rat brain. *Brain Research, 242,* 197–204.

Blurton, P. A., & Wood, M. D. (1986). Identification of multiple binding sites for [^{3}H]5-hydroxytryptamine in the rat CNS. *J. Neurochem., 46,* 1392–1398.

Bradley, P. B., Engel, G., Feniuk, W., Fozard, J. R., Humphrey, P. P. A., Middlemiss, D. N., Mylecharane, E. J., Richardson, B. P., & Saxena, P. R. (1986). Proposals for the classification and nomenclature of functional receptors for 5-hydroxytryptamine. *Neuropharmacol., 25,* 563–576.

Brown, E., Kendall, D. A., & Nahorski, S. R. (1984). Inositol phospholipid hydrolysis in rat cerebral cortical slices: I. receptor characterization. *J. Neurochem., 42,* 1379–1387.

Charlton, K. G., Bond, R. A., & Clarke, D. E. (1986). An inhibitory prejunctional 5-HT_1-like receptor in the isolated perfused rat kidney. *Naunyn-Schmiedeberg's Arch. Pharmacol., 332,* 8–15.

Clineschmidt, B. V., Reiss, D. R., Pettibone, J., & Robinson, J. L. (1986). Characterization of 5-hydroxytryptamine receptors in rat stomach fundus. *J. Pharmacol. Exp. Ther. 235,* 696–708.

Closse, A. (1983). [^{3}H]Mesulergine, a selective ligand for serotonin-2 receptors. *Life Sci., 32,* 2485–2495.

Cohen, M. L., & Wittenauer, L. A. (1986). Further evidence that the serotonin receptor in the rat stomach fundus is not 5-HT_{1A} or 5-HT_{1B}. *Life Sci., 38.* 1–5.

Colpaert, F. C. (1984). Cross generalization of LSD with yohimbine in the rat. *Eur. J. Pharmacol., 102,* 541–544.

Colpaert, F. C., & Janssen, P. A. J. (1983). The head-twitch response to intraperitoneal injection of 5-hydroxytryptophan in the rat: Antagonist effects of purported 5-hydroxytryptamine antagonists and of pirenperone, and LSD antagonist. *Neuropharmacol, 22,* 993–1000.

Colpaert, F. C., Meert, T. F., Niemegeers, C. J. E., & Janssen, P. A. J. (1985). Behavioral and 5-HT antagonist effects of ritanserin: A pure and selective antagonist of LSD discrimination in the rat. *Psychopharmacol, 86,* 45–54.

Conn, P. J., & Sanders-Bush, E. (1984). Selective 5-HT-2 antagonists inhibit serotonin stimulated phosphatidylinositol metabolism in cerebral cortex. *Neuropharmacol, 8,* 993–996.

Conn, P. J., & Sanders-Bush, E. (1985). Serotonin-stimulated phosphoinositide turnover: Mediation by the S_2 binding site in rat cerebral cortex but not in subcortical regions. *J. Pharmacol. Exp. Ther., 234,* 195–203.

Conn, P. J., & Sanders-Bush, E. (1986). Regulation of serotonin-stimulated phosphoinositide turnover: Relation to the 5-HT-2 binding site. *J. Neurosci., 6,* 3369–3379.

Conn, P. J., & Sanders-Bush, E., Hoffman, B. J., & Hartig, P. R. (1986). A unique serotonin receptor in choroid plexus is linked to phosphatidylinositol turnover. *Proc. Natl. Acad. Sci., 83,* 4086–4088.

Coughlin, S. R., Moskowitz, M. A., Antoniades, H. N., & Levine, L. (1981). Serotonin receptor-mediated stimulation of bovine smooth muscle cell prostacyclin synthesis and its modulation by platelet-derived growth factor. *Proc. Natl. Acad. Sci. USA, 78,* 7134–7138.

Davies, M. F., Deisz, R. A., Prince, D. A., & Peroutka, S. J. (1987). Two distinct effects of 5-hydroxytryptamine on cortical neurons. *Brain Res., 423,* 347–352.

de Chaffoy de Courcelles, D., Leysen, J. E., De Clerck, F., Van Belle, H., & Janssen, P. A. (1985). Evidence that phospholipid turnover is the signal transducing system coupled to serotonin-S_2 receptor sites. *J. Biol. Chem., 260,* 7603–7608.

Deshmukh, P. P., Yamamura, H. I., Woods, L., & Nelson, D. L. (1983). Computer-assisted autoradiographic localization of subtypes of serotonin$_1$ receptors in rat brain. *Brain Research, 288,* 338–343.

Demopulos, C. M., & Peroutka, S. J. (1987). "Specific" ^{3}H-8-OH-DPAT binding to glass fiber filter paper: Implications for the analysis of serotonin binding site subtypes. *Neurochem. Int., 10,* 371–376.

De Vivo, M., & Maayani, S. (1986). Characterization of the 5-hydroxytryptamine$_{1A}$ receptor-mediated inhibition of forskolin-stimulated adenylate cyclase activity in guinea pig and rat hippocampal membranes. *J. Pharmacol. Exp. Ther., 238,* 248–253.

Dompert, W. U., Glaser, T., & Traber, J. (1985). ^{3}H-TVX Q 7821: Identification of 5-HT$_1$ binding sites as target for a novel putative anxiolytic. *Naunyn-Schmiedeberg's Arch. Pharmacol., 328,* 467–470.

Doods, H. N., Kalkman, H. O., De Jonge, A., Thoolen, M., Wilffert, B., Timmermans, P., & Van Zwieten, P. A. (1985). Differential selectivities of RU 24969 and 8-OH-DPAT for the purported 5-HT$_{1A}$ and 5-HT$_{1B}$ binding sites. Correlation between 5-HT$_{1A}$ affinity and hypotensive activity. *Eur. J. Pharmacol., 112,* 363–370.

Engel, G., Gothert, M., Hoyer, K., Schlicker, D., & Hillenbrand, E. (1986). Identity of inhibitory presynaptic 5-hydroxytryptamine (5-HT) autoreceptors in the rat brain cortex with 5-HT$_{1B}$ binding sites. *Naunyn-Schmiedeberg's Arch. Pharmacol., 357,* 1–7.

Engel, G., Muller-Schweinitzer, E., & Palacios, J. M. (1984b). 2-[^{125}Iodo] LSD, a new ligand for the characterization and localisation of 5HT$_2$ receptors. *Naunyn-Schmiedeberg's Arch. Pharmacol., 325,* 328–336.

Fillion, G. (1983). 5-Hydroxytryptamine receptors in brain. *Handbook Psychopharmacol., 17,* 139–166.

Fillion, G. M. B., Rousselle, J., Fillion, M., Beaudoin, D. M., Goiny, M. R., Deniau, J., & Jacob, J. J. (1978). High-affinity binding of [^{3}H]5-Hydroxytryptamine to brain synaptosomal membranes: Comparison with [^{3}H]lysergic acid diethylamide binding. *Mol. Pharmacol., 14,* 50–59.

Fozard, J. R. (1984). Neuronal 5-HT receptors in the periphery. *Neuropharmacol., 23,* 1473–1486.

Fuller, R. W. (1984). Serotonin receptors. *Monogr. Neural Sci., 10,* 158–181.

Gaddum, J. H., & Picarelli, Z. P. (1957). Two kinds of tryptamine receptor. *Br. J. Pharmacol. Chemother., 12,* 323–328.

Glaser, T., Rath, M., Traber, J., Zilles, K., & Schleicher, A. (1985). Autoradiographic identification and topographical analyses of high affinity serotonin receptor subtypes as a target for the novel putative anxiolytic TVX Q 7821. *Brain Research, 358,* 129–136.

Glennon, R. A. (1985). Involvement of serotonin in the action of hallucinogenic agents. In A. R. Green (Ed.), *Neuropharmacology of Serotonin.* Oxford: Oxford University Press.

Glennon, R. A., McKenney, J. D., Lyon, R. A., & Titeler, M. (1986). 5-HT_1 and 5-HT_2 binding characteristics of 1-(2,5-dimethoxy-4-bromophenyl)-2-aminopropane analogues. *J. Med. Chem., 29,* 194–199.

Glennon, R. A., Young, R., & Rosecrans, J. A. (1983). Antagonism of the effects of the hallucinogen DOM and the purported 5-HT agonist quipazine by 5-HT_2 antagonists. *Eur. J. Pharmacol., 91,* 189–196.

Gozlan, H., El Mestikawy, S., Pichat, L., Glowinski, J., & Hamon, M. (1983). Identification of presynaptic serotonin autoreceptors using a new ligand: ^{3}H-PAT. *Nature, 305,* 140–142.

Gudelsky, G. A., Koenig, J. I., & Meltzer, H. Y. (1986). Thermoregulatory responses to serotonin (5-HT) receptor stimulation in the rat. *Neuropharmacol., 25,* 1307–1313.

Hall, M. D., El Mestikawy, S., Emerit, M. B., Pichat, L., Hamon, M., & Gozlan, H. (1985). [^{3}H]8-hydroxy-2-(Di-n-Propylamino)tetralin binding to pre- and postsynaptic 5-hydroxytryptamine sites in various regions of the rat brain. *J. Neurochem., 44,* 1685–1696.

Hall, M. D., Gozlan, H., Emerit, M. B., El Mestikawy, S., Pichat, L., & Hamon, M. (1986). Differentiation of pre- and postsynaptic high affinity serotonin receptor binding sites using physico-chemical parameters and modifying agents. *Neurochem. Res., 11,* 891–912.

Hamon, M., Bourgoin, S., El Mestikawy, S., & Goetz, C. (1984). Central serotonin receptors. In H. Lajtha (Ed.), *Handbook of Neurochemistry—2nd Edition* (Vol. 6, pp. 107–143). New York: Plenum Press.

Hartig, P. R., Kadan, M. J., Evans, J. J., & Krohn, A. M. (1983). ^{125}I-LSD: A high sensitivity ligand for serotonin receptors. *Eur. J. Pharmacol., 89,* 321–322.

Heuring, R. E., & Peroutka, S. J. (1987). Characterization of a novel ^{3}H-5-HT binding site subtype in bovine brain membranes. *J. Neurosci.*, 7, 894–903.

Heuring, R. E., Schlegel, J. R., & Peroutka, S. J. (1986). Species variations in 5-HT_{1B} and 5-HT_{1C} binding sites defined by RU 24969 competition studies. *Eur. J. Pharmacol, 122,* 279–282.

Hiner, B. C., Roth, H. L., & Peroutka, S. J. (1986). Antimigraine drug interactions with 5-hydroxytryptamine$_{1A}$ receptors. *Ann. Neurol., 19,* 511–513.

Hoffman, B. J., Scheffel, U., Lever, J. R., Karpa, M. D., & Hartig, P. R. (1987). N_1-methyl-2-I^{125} LSD (I^{125}MIL), a preferred ligand for in vitro and in vivo characterization of serotonin receptors. *J. Neurochem., 48,* 115–124.

Hoyer, D., Engel, G., & Kalkman, H. O. (1985a). Characterization of the 5-HT_{1B} recognition site in rat brain: Binding studies with (-) [^{125}I] iodocyanopindolol. *Eur. J. Pharmacol., 118,* 1–12.

Hoyer, D., Engel, G., & Kalkman, H. O. (1985b). Molecular pharmacology of 5-HT_1 and 5-HT_2 recognition sites in rat and pig brain membranes: radioligand binding studies with [^{3}H]5-HT, [^{3}H]8-OH-DPAT, (-)[^{125}I]iodocyanopindolol, [^{3}H]mesulergine and [^{3}H]ketanserin. *Eur. J. Pharmacol., 118,* 13–23.

Hoyer, D., Pazos, A., Probst, A., & Palacios, J. M. (1986a). Serotonin receptors in the human brain: I. Characterization and autoradiographic localization of 5-HT_{1A} recognition sites. Apparent absence of 5-HT_{1B} recognition sites. *Brain Research, 376,* 85–96.

Hoyer, D., Pazos, A., Probst, A., & Palacios, J. M. (1986b). Serotonin receptors in the human brain: II. Characterization and autoradiographic localization of 5-HT_{1C} and 5-HT_2 recognition sites. *Brain Research, 376,* 97–107.

Kendall, D. A., & Nahorski, S. R. (1985). 5-hydroxytryptamine-stimulated inositol phospholipid hydrolysis in rat cerebral cortex slices: Pharmacological characterization and effects of antidepressants. *J. Pharmacol. Exp. Ther., 233,* 473–479.

Kwong, L. L., Smith, E. R., Davidson, J. M., & Peroutka, S. J. (1986). Differential interactions of "prosexual" drugs with 5-hydroxytryptamine$_{1A}$ and alpha$_2$-adrenergic receptors. *Behavioral Neuroscience, 100,* 664–668.

Leysen, J. E. (1981). Serotonergic receptors in brain tissue: Properties and identification of various ^{3}H-ligand binding studies in vitro. *J. Physiol. (Paris),* 77, 351–362.

Leysen, J. E. (1983). Serotonin receptor binding sites: Is there pharmacological and clinical significance? *Med. Biol., 61,* 139–143.

Leysen, J. E., de Chaffoy de Courcelles, D. C., De Clerck, F., Niemegeers, J. E., & Van Nueten, J. M. (1984). Serotonin-S_2 receptor binding sites and functional correlates. *Neuropharmacol., 23,* 1493–1501.

Leysen, J. E., Niemegeers, C. J. E., Tollenaere, J. P., & Laduron, P. M. (1978). Serotonergic component of neuroleptic receptors. *Nature, 272,* 163–166.

Leysen, J. E., Niemegeers, C. J. E., Van Nueten, J. M., & Laduron, P. M. (1982). ^{3}H-Ketanserin (R 41 468), a selective ^{3}H-ligand for receptor binding sites. *Mol. Pharmacol., 21,* 301–314.

Leysen, J. E., & Tollenaere, J. P. (1982). Biochemical models for serotonin receptors. *Ann. Rev. Med. Chem., 17,* 1–10.

Lovell, R. A., & Freedman, D. X. (1976). Stereospecific receptor sites for d-lysergic diethylamide in rat brain: Effects of neurotransmitters, amine antagonists, and other psychotropic drugs. *Mol. Pharmacol., 12,* 620–630.

Lyon, R. A., Davis, K. H., & Titeler, M. (1987). ^{3}H-DOB (4-bromo-2,5-dimethoxyphenylisopropylamine) labels a guanyl nucleotide-sensitive state of cortical 5-HT_2 receptors. *Mol. Pharmacol. 31,* 194–199.

Marcinkiewicz, M., Verge, D., Gozlan, H., Pichat, L., & Hamon, M. (1984). Autoradiographic evidence for the heterogeneity of 5-HT_1 sites in the rat brain. *Brain Research, 291,* 159–163.

Markstein, R., Hoyer, D., & Engel, G. (1986). 5-HT_{1A} receptors mediate stimulation of adenylate cyclase in rat hippocampus. *Nauyn-Schmiedeberg's Arch. Pharmacol., 333,* 335–341.

Matsuoka, H., Ishii, M., Goto, A., & Sugimoto, T. (1985). Role of serotonin type 2 receptors in regulation of aldosterone production. *Am. Physiol. Soc., 234,* 0193–1849.

Mauk, M. D., Peroutka, S. J., & Kocsis, J. D. (1988). Buspirone attenuates synaptic transmission of hippocampal pyramidal cells. *J. Neurosci., 8,* 1–11.

McCall, R. B., & Aghajanian, G. K. (1980). Pharmacological characterization of serotonin receptors in the facial motor nucleus: A microiontophoretic study. *Eur. J. Pharmacol., 65,* 175–183.

Middlemiss, D. N., & Fozard, J. R. (1983). 8-hydroxy-2-(di-n-Propylamino)-tetralin discriminates between subtypes of the 5-HT_1 recognition site. *Eur. J. Pharmacol., 90,* 151–153.

Moon, S. L., & Taylor, D. P. (1985). *In vitro* autoradiography of ^{3}H-buspirone and ^{3}H-2-deoxyglucose after buspirone administration. *Soc. Neurosci. Abs., 11,* 114.

Nelson, D. L., Herbet, A., Bourgoin, S., Glowinski, J., & Hamon, M. (1978). Characteristics of central 5-HT receptors and their adaptive changes following intracerebral 5,7-dihydroxytryptamine administration in the rat. *Mol. Pharmacol., 14,* 983–995.

Nelson, D. L., Monroe, P. J., Lambrit, G. & Yamamura, H. I. (1987). ^{3}H-Spiroxatrine labels a serotonin 1A-like site in the rat hippocampus. *Life Sciences, 41,* 1567–1576.

Norman, A. B., Battaglia, G., Morrow, A. L., & Creese, I. (1985). [^{3}H]WB4101 labels S_1 serotonin receptors in rat cerebral cortex. *Eur. J. Pharmacol., 106,* 461–462.

Ortmann, R., Bischoff, S., Radeke, E., Buech, O., & Delini-Stula, A. (1982). Correlations between different measures of anti-serotonin activity of drugs. *Naunyn-Schmiedeberg's Arch. Pharmacol., 321,* 265–270.

Pazos, A., Cortes, R., & Palacios, J. M. (1985a). Quantitative autoradiographic mapping of serotonin receptors in the rat brain. II. Serotonin-2 receptors. *Brain Research, 346,* 231–249.

Pazos, A., Engel, G., & Palacios, J. M. (1985b). Beta-adrenoceptor blocking agents recognize a subpopulation of serotonin receptors in brain. *Brain Research, 343,* 403–408.

Pazos, A., Hoyer, D., & Palacios, J. M. (1984a). Mesulergine, a selective serotonin-2 ligand in the rat cortex, does not label these receptors in porcine and human cortex: Evidence for species differences in brain serotonin-2 receptors. *Eur. J. Pharmacol., 106,* 531–538.

Pazos, A., Hoyer, D., & Palacios, J. M. (1984b). The binding of serotonergic ligands to the porcine choroid plexus: characterization of a new type of serotonin recognition site. *Eur. J. Pharmacol., 106,* 539–546.

Pazos, A., & Palacios, J. M. (1985). Quantitative autoradiographic mapping of serotonin receptors in the rat brain. I. Serotonin-1 receptors. *Brain Research, 346,* 205–230.

Pedigo, N. W., Yamamura, H. I., & Nelson, D. L. (1981). Discrimination of multiple [^{3}H]5-hydroxytryptamine binding sites by the neuroleptic spiperone in rat brain. *J. Neurochem., 36,* 220–226.

Peroutka, S. J. (1984). Vascular serotonin receptors: Correlation with 5-HT_1 and 5-HT_2 binding sites. *Biochem. Pharmacol., 33,* 2349–2353.

Peroutka, S. J. (1985). Selective labeling of 5-HT_{1A} and 5-HT_{1B} binding sites in bovine brain. *Brain Research, 344,* 167–171.

Peroutka, S. J. (1986). Pharmacological differentiation and characterization of 5-HT_{1A}, 5-HT_{1B}, and 5-HT_{1C} binding sites in rat frontal cortex. *J. Neurochem., 47,* 529–540.

Peroutka, S. J. (1988). 5-Hydroxytryptamine receptor subtypes. *Ann. Rev. Neurosci., 11,* 45–60.

Peroutka, S. J., & Demopulos, C. M. (1986). ^{3}H-8-OH-DPAT "specifically" labels glass fiber filter paper. *Eur. J. Pharmacol., 129,* 199–200.

Peroutka, S. J., Huang, S., & Allen, G. S. (1986). Canine basilar artery contractions mediated by 5-hydroxytryptamine$_{1A}$ receptors. *J. Pharmacol. Exp. Ther., 237,* 901–906.

Peroutka, S. J., Lebovitz, R. M., & Snyder, S. H. (1981). Two distinct central serotonin receptors with different physiological functions. *Science, 212,* 827–829.

Peroutka, S. J., Mauk, M. D., & Kocsis, J. D. (1987). Modulation of hippocampal neuronal activity by 5-hydroxytryptamine and 5-hydroxytryptamine$_{1A}$ selective drugs. *Neuropharmacol., 26,* 139–146

Peroutka, S. J., & Snyder, S. H. (1979). Multiple serotonin receptors: Differential binding of ^{3}H-serotonin, ^{3}H-lysergic acid diethylamide and ^{3}H-spiroperidol. *Mol. Pharmacol., 16,* 687–699.

Peroutka, S. J., & Snyder, S. H. (1980a). Long-term antidepressant treatment decreases spiroperidol-labeled serotonin receptor binding. *Science, 210,* 88–90.

Peroutka, S. J., & Snyder, S. H. (1980b). Regulation of serotonin$_2$ (5-HT$_2$) receptors labeled with ^{3}H-spiroperidol by chronic treatment with the antidepressant amitriptyline. *J. Pharmacol. Exp. Ther., 215,* 582–587.

Peroutka, S. J., & Snyder, S. H. (1981). ^{3}H-Mianserin: Differential labeling of serotonin$_2$ and histamine$_1$ receptors in rat brain. *J. Pharmacol. Exp. Ther., 216,* 142–148.

Raiteri, M., Maura, G., Bonanno, G., & Pittaluga, A. (1986). Differential pharmacology and function of two 5-HT$_1$ receptors modulating transmitter release in cerebellum. *J. Pharmacol. Exp. Ther., 237,* 644–648.

Ransom, R. W., Asarch, K. B., & Shih, J. C. (1986). [^{3}H]-1-[2-(4-Aminophenyl)ethyl]-4-(3-trifluoromethylphenyl)piperazine: A selective radioligand for 5-HT$_{1A}$ receptors in rat brain. *J. Neurochem., 46,* 68–75.

Richardson, B. P., & Engel, G. (1986). The pharmacology and function of 5-HT$_3$ receptors. *Trends Neurosci., 7,* 424–428.

Richardson, B. P., Engel, G., Donatsch, P., & Stadler, P. A. (1985). Identification of serotonin M-receptor subtypes and their specific blockade by a new class of drugs. *Nature, 336,* 126–131.

Roth, B. L., Nakaki, T., Chuang, D. M., & Costa, E. (1984). Aortic recognition sites for serotonin (5-HT) are coupled to phospholipase C and modulate phosphatidylinositol turnover. *Neuropharmacol., 23,* 1223–1225.

Schlegel, J. R., & Peroutka, S. J. (1986). Nucleotide interactions with 5-HT_{1A} binding sites directly labeled by [^{3}H]-8-hydroxy-2-(DI-n-propylamino)tetralin ([^{3}H]-8-OH-DPAT) *Biochem. Pharmacol., 35,* 1943–1949.

Schnellmann, R. G., Waters, S. J., & Nelson, D. L. (1984). [^{3}H]5-hydroxytryptamine binding sites: Species and tissue variation. *J. Neurochem., 42,* 65–70.

Schoemaker, H., & Langer, S. Z., (1986). [^{3}H]8-OH-DPAT labels the serotonin transporter in the rat striatum. *Eur. J. Pharmacol., 124,* 371–373.

Schotte, A., Maloteaux, J. M., & Laduron, P. M. (1983). Characterization and regional distribution of serotonin S_2-receptors in human brain. *Brain Research, 276,* 231–235.

Shenker, A., Maayani, S., Weinstein, H., & Green, J. P. (1985). Two 5-HT receptors linked to adenylate cyclase in guinea pig hippocampus are discriminated by 5-carboxamidotryptamine and spiperone. *Eur. J. Pharmacol., 109,* 427–429.

Sills, M. A., Wolfe, B. B., & Frazer, A. (1984). Determination of selective and nonselective compounds for the 5-HT_{1A} and 5-HT_{1B} receptor subtypes in rat frontal cortex. *J. Pharmacol. Exp. Ther., 231,* 480–487.

Sinton, C. M., & Fallon, S. L. (1986). Differences in the response of dorsal and median raphe serotonergic neurons to 5-HT_1 receptor ligands. *Soc. Neurosci. Abs., 12,* 1239.

Smith, L. M., & Peroutka, S. J. (1986). Differential effects of 5-$\text{hydroxytryptamine}_{1A}$ selective drugs on the 5-HT behavioral syndrome. *Pharmacol. Biochem. Behav., 24,* 1513–1519.

Snyder, S. H. (1983). Molecular aspects of neurotransmitter receptors: An overview. *Handbook Psychopharmacol., 17,* 1–12.

Snyder, S. H., Weingartner, H., & Faillace, L. A. (1971). DOET (2,5-dimethoxy-4-ethylamphetamine), a new psychotropic drug. *Arch. Gen. Psychiat., 24,* 50–55.

Sprouse, J. S., & Aghajanian, G. K. (1987). Electrophysiological responses of serotonergic dorsal raphe neurons to 5-HT_{1A} and 5-HT_{1B} agonists. *Synapse, 1,* 3–9.

Taylor, E. W., Duckles, S. P., & Nelson, D. L. (1986). Dissociation constants of serotonin agonists in the canine basilar artery correlate to K_i values at the 5-HT_{1A} binding site. *J. Pharmacol. Exp. Ther., 236,* 118–125.

Tricklebank, M. D. (1985). The behavioral response to 5-HT receptor agonists and subtypes of the central 5-HT receptor. *Trends Pharmacol. Sci., 6,* 403–407.

Tricklebank, M. D., Middlemiss, D. N., & Neill, J. (1986). Pharmacological analysis of the behavioral and thermoregulatory effects of the putative 5-HT_1 receptor agonist, RU 24969, in the rat. *Neuropharmacol., 25,* 877–886.

Trulson, M. E., & Arasteh, K. (1986). Buspirone decreases the activity of 5-hydroxytryptamine-containing dorsal raphe neurons in-vitro. *J. Pharm. Pharmacol., 38,* 380–382.

VanderMaelen, C. P., & Aghajanian, G. K. (1980). Intracellular studies showing modulation of facial motoneurone excitability by serotonin. *Nature, 287,* 346–347.

VanderMaelen, C. P., Gehlbach, G., Yocca, F. D., & Mattson, R. J. (1986). Inhibition of serotonergic dorsal raphe neurons in rat brain slice by the 5-HT_1 agonist 5-carboxyamidotryptamine. *Soc. Neurosci. Abs., 12,* 1239.

VanderMaelen, C. P., & Wilderman, R. C. (1984). Buspirone, a non-benzodiazepine anxiolytic drug, causes inhibition of serotonergic dorsal raphe neurons in the rat. *Soc. Neurosci. Abs., 10,* 259.

Wang, S. S. H., Mathis, C. A. & Peroutka, S. J. (1988). R(-)-2,5-dimethoxy-4-^{77} bromo amphetamine [^{77}Br-R(-)DOB]: a novel radioligand which labels a 5-HT binding site subtype. *Psychopharmacol., 14,* 431–432.

Weiss, S., Sebben, M., Kemp, D., & Bockaert, J. (1986). Serotonin 5-HT_1 receptors mediate inhibition of cyclic AMP production in neurons. *Eur. J. Pharmacol., 120,* 227–230.

Yagaloff, K. A., & Hartig, P. R. (1985). ^{125}I-LSD binds to a novel serotonergic site on rat choroid plexus epithelial cells. *J. Neurosci., 5,* 3178–3183.

Yap, C. Y., & Taylor, D. A. (1983). Involvement of 5-HT_2 receptors in the wet-dog shake behaviour induced by 5-hydroxytryptophan in the rat. *Neuropharmacol., 22,* 801–804.

12

Functional Significance of Central Dopamine Receptors

NORTON H. NEFF
MARIA HADJICONSTANTINOU

The most useful classification of dopamine receptors was suggested by Kebabian and Calne in 1979. This classification is based primarily on the biochemical characteristics of dopamine receptors, such as, ligand binding and adenylate cyclase activity. The most studied biochemical property of the receptor is the ability of dopamine to either activate (Kebabian et al., 1972; Brown & Makman, 1972) or inhibit (Onali et al., 1985; Weiss et al., 1985; Stoof & Kebabian, 1981) adenylate cyclase activity. In 1979, there were few selective dopaminergic drugs; thus, it was difficult to assess the functional role of the receptors in the whole animal. There are now a variety of selective dopaminergic receptor agonist and antagonists (Table 1) that can be used to evaluate dopaminergic receptor function. In this presentation we will attempt to correlate function with receptor classification. We have not attempted to relate responsiveness to autoreceptors or postsynaptic receptors as the origin in the central nervous system of most functional responses is controversial or unknown.

DOPAMINE RECEPTOR NOMENCLATURE

In the central nervous system there are two types of dopamine receptors and they are termed D-1 and D-2 (Table 1). This

TABLE 1
Classification of Dopamine Receptors

	D-1	*D-2*
Prototype Location	Parathyroid Gland	Anterior and Intermediate Lobes
Adenylate Cyclase	Stimulatory	Inhibitory or Unlinked
Nucleotide Regulatory Protein	N_s	N_i
Agonists	Dopamine (uM) SKF38393	Dopamine (nM) LY171555 (Quinpirole) Bromocryptine Pergolide
Antagonists	SCH-23390	Sulpiride [– > +] Domperidone Spiperone Butaclamol [+ >>> –]

Adapted from Kebabian and Calne (1979).

terminology is in contrast to the nomenclature that is used for peripheral vascular dopamine receptors where the classification is based on the location of the receptor (Goldberg & Kohli, 1983). These receptors are abbreviated differently to distinguish them from the receptors in the central nervous system. Peripheral dopamine DA-1 receptors are located on vascular smooth muscle and their activation leads to direct myorelaxation. DA-2 receptors are located on sympathetic nerve endings and their activation decreases the release of norepinephrine. There is experimental evidence that DA-1 and DA-2 receptors have biochemical properties similar to the D-1 and D-2 receptors of brain, respectively (Missale et al., 1985).

RECEPTOR STRUCTURE

Dopamine receptor adenylate cyclase systems are composed of three units: the recognition site, a nucleotide regulatory protein, and a catalytic unit (Gilman, 1984). The recognition or binding sites for D-1 and D-2 receptors recognize different ligands and either stimulate or inhibit the production of cyclic-AMP by adenylate cyclase, respectively. D-2 receptors may not always be coupled to adenylate cyclase activity (Kebabian & Calne, 1979). The nucleotide regulatory protein, sometimes called G or N protein (Gilman, 1984), is composed of three subunits (alpha, beta, and gamma) of different molecular weights. The subunit composition of the G protein varies depending on whether it stimulates or inhibits cyclase activity. The alpha unit of the stimulatory G protein (Gs) differs from the alpha unit of the inhibitory G protein (Gi) while the beta and gamma units appear similar for both G proteins. The role of the gamma subunit is unknown. When the dopamine receptor is activated the alpha unit dissociates from the beta unit and there is hydrolysis of GTP by the alpha unit. The alpha unit then interacts with the catalytic unit to either stimulate or inhibit cyclic-AMP production depending on whether the alpha unit originates from Gs or Gi. Reassociation of the alpha and beta units terminates catalytic activity. Cyclic-AMP activates protein kinase leading to phosphorylation of substrate proteins which changes ion channels, enzyme activities, etc. (Nestler & Greengard, 1983). Thus, the content of cyclic-AMP in a neuron profoundly effects its activity and ultimately the response of the biological system.

DOPAMINERGIC DRUGS

There are several relatively selective dopaminergic drugs that are being used to differentiate the functional activity of dopamine receptors in the whole animal. Table 1 presents a number of these drugs. This is not a complete list. However, these are the drugs that have been used most often to evaluate functional activity experimentally. It should be emphasized that these drugs are selective for dopaminergic receptors and are not specific, that is, they may act at other neurotransmitter receptors.

Schizophrenia is currently thought to be caused by excessive activation of dopamine receptors on mesocortical and mesolimbic structures (Snyder, 1981). This hypothesis is the consequence of the following clinical observations: 1. Drugs that are used to treat schizophrenia block dopamine receptors; 2. Repeated administration of amphetamine, which releases dopamine from neuronal stores, results in a psychotic state that may be indistinguishable from paranoid psychosis; 3. A psychotic state can result from the administration of L-DOPA, the precursor of dopamine.

In contrast, Parkinson's disease is associated with the loss of nigrostriatal dopaminergic neurons. This was originally determined from postmortem human brain studies (Hornykiewicz, 1966) and has recently been confirmed in studies of humans that self administered illicit narcotics containing the neurotoxin MPTP (1-methyl-4-phenyl-1,2,3,6-tetrahydropyridine) (Davis et al., 1979; Langston et al., 1983). Administration of L-DOPA or dopamine receptor agonists to correct the dopamine deficiency in parkinsonism ameliorates the symptoms of the disease. For schizophrenia and Parkinson's disease, D-2 receptors blockade or activation, respectively, is associated with successful therapy (Snyder, 1981). Moreover, it is clear that side effects associated with aggressive therapy for Parkinson's disease or for schizophrenia can result in the appearance of symptoms that resemble the other disease. This is not surprising as the diseases are associated with different regions of brain, while the drugs are distributed to all regions of the brain.

With the availability of selective dopaminergic drugs, it is now possible to evaluate the functional activity associated with D-1 and D-2 receptors in animals. Differentiation of receptor function, however, is not simple. It appears that D-1 and D-2 receptors can have independent actions, opposing actions or synergistic actions depending on the function studied. Moreover, for some receptor responses it appears that functional dopaminergic neurons are required (Breese & Mueller, 1985).

For full expression of some functions, activation of both D-1 and D-2 receptors are required (Waddington, 1986; Walters et al., 1987; Carlson et al., 1987). Thus, the ratio of D-1 and D-2 receptors may be an important consideration for understanding the etiology of a central nervous system disorder. For example,

TABLE 2
Provisional Assignment of Functional Activity with Dopamine Receptor Subtype

D-1	*D-2*
Grooming	Repetitive Head Movements
Self-Mutilation Behavior	Hyperactivity
Oral Dyskinesia;	Inhibition of Oral Activity
Tongue Protrusion	
Oral Movements	
Chewing	
Stimulation of Prolactin Release	Inhibition of Prolactin Release
L-Aromatic Amino Acid Decarboxylase	Tyrosine Hydroxylase
Firing of Nigrostriatal Neurons	Firing of Somatosensory Cortical Neurons
	DA Release Induced by K+
	Acetylcholine Release From Striatum
	DA Turnover
	Feeding Behavior
	Yawning
	Emesis
	Anti-Parkinson Activity
	Antipsychotic Activity
	Tardive Dyskinesia

Note: For some functions, both receptors must be activated for full expression of the response (see text).

it was recently reported that there is a dopamine receptor subtype imbalance in schizophrenia (Hess et al., 1987). There was an increase of D-2 receptors and a reduction of D-1 receptors resulting in a highly significant difference of D-2/D-1 ratio between control and schizophrenic subjects. It should also be understood that some behaviors are the consequence of complex neuronal interactions thus it is possible that several neurotransmitter systems participate in a behavior. Table 2 lists some of the activities thought to be modulated by D-1 and D-2 receptors. This is a provisional listing as dopamine receptor function is currently under intensive study by many laboratories.

FUNCTIONAL ACTIVITY ASSOCIATED WITH D-1 RECEPTORS

By combining a D-2 antagonist with a D-1 agonist, the functional activity associated with activation of the D-1 receptor can be unmasked, especially when D-2 receptor functions predominate (Onali et al., 1985; Rosengarten et al., 1983). In the rat, D-1 activities include oral dyskinesias such as tongue protrusion and chewing movements and grooming activity. There is a recent report that oral movements in rats can be inhibited by administering the selective D-2 agonist quinpirole (Johansson et al., 1987). The oral movements may be related to the oral movements of tardive dyskinesia. Indeed, if oral movements are modulated by opposing dopamine receptors, there may be better therapeutic procedures for treating or preventing tardive dyskinesia in the future.

There is experimental evidence that D-1 receptors can modulate the firing rate of nigrostriatal neurons while having only modest effects on dopamine synthesis (Onali et al., 1985). Dopamine synthesis is apparently modulated by D-2 receptors via control of tyrosine hydroxylase activity. In the rat retina we have found that D-1 dopamine receptors modulate the activity of L-aromatic amino acid decarboxylase (commonly known as DOPA decarboxylase) (Rossetti et al., 1986). This was surprising as most textbooks state that this enzyme is not modulated. These observations could mean that both receptors play a role in the modulation of the release of dopamine and its rate of formation.

In the pituitary gland, activation of D-1 receptors may stimulate the release of prolactin (Saller & Salama, 1986). This is in contrast to activation of pituitary D-2 receptors which are known to inhibit the release of prolactin (Swennen & Denef, 1982).

The stage of development of the nervous system and, particularly, dopaminergic neurons appears to be important for the behavioral response to dopamine receptor activation (Henry et al., 1986). The administration of L-DOPA or apomorphine to neonatal and adult 6-hydroxydopamine (6-OHDA)-treated rats results in different behavioral responses depending on the age when the dopaminergic neurons were destroyed (Breese et al., 1984; Breese et al., 1986). When neonatal 6-OHDA-treated rats were tested as adults, they exhibited marked stereotypies, self-biting and self-mutilation behavior (SMB) when given dopamine agonists. Cis-flupentixol, a selective D-1 antagonist, blocks SMB and self-biting behavior. Adult 6-OHDA-treated rats do not exhibit SMB or self-biting but they display paw treading and head nodding after dopamine agonists. These studies are significant as they may provide an explanation for the different symptomatologies associated with Lesch-Nyhan and Parkinson's disease. Both disorders are characterized by reduced striatal dopamine content. Lesch-Nyhan children show choreoathetoid movements and SMB symptomatology both of which are not found in Parkinson's disease patients.

FUNCTIONAL ACTIVITY ASSOCIATED WITH D-2 RECEPTORS

The administration of drugs that release endogenous dopamine, such as amphetamine, or selective D-2 receptor agonists, results in hyperactivity and stereotypic behavior in rats that can be attenuated with selective D-2 receptor antagonists (Starr & Starr, 1986). In Parkinson's disease, dopamine agonists and dopamine formed following the administration of L-DOPA apparently alleviate the clinical symptomatology by activating D-2 receptors. Neuroleptic drugs are thought to be beneficial for the treatment of schizophrenia because they block D-2 receptors. Vomiting is often controlled by administering selective D-2 antagonists. Thus, activation or blockade of D-2 receptors is associated with most of the clinically useful dopaminergic drugs (Stoff & Kebabian, 1984).

A number of electrophysiological observations have been made in animals that could be related to the therapeutic actions of dopaminergic drugs. Microelectrophoresis of dopaminergic agents onto somatosensory cortex has revealed that D-2 receptors are involved in mediating an excitatory response to dopamine (Bradshaw et al., 1985). D-1 receptors appear not to be involved in the response. In a slice preparation of the nucleusaccumbens from the guinea pig studied with intracellular recording, dopamine caused hyperpolarization by activation of D-1 receptors which was associated with an increase of potassium conductance. In contrast, dopamine depolarization was generated by activation of D-2 receptors which was accompanied by a decrease of potassium conductance (Uchimura et al., 1986).

Dopamine inhibits the potassium-evoked release of radioactive acetylcholine from rat striatal slices (Scatton, 1982; Boireau et al., 1986). Compounds that selectively block D-2 receptors increase the release of radioactive acetylcholine. In Parkinson's disease there is a loss of nigrostriatal dopaminergic neurons; thus, presumably less dopamine reaches receptors in the striatum and it would be expected that more acetylcholine would be released from cholinergic neurons intrinsic to the striatum. Such a mechanism would explain why anticholinergic drugs are often useful for treating early Parkinson's disease.

Dopamine agonists have anticonvulsant activity when tested in rodent models of epilepsy (Loscher & Czuczwar, 1986). D-2 receptors apparently mediate anticonvulsant effects. The threshold for seizures induced by pentylenetetrazol in mice is increased by D-2 agonists. Also selective D-2 antagonists increase the threshold for maximal electroshock seizures induced by L-DOPA. D-1 receptors seem not to be involved.

Feeding behavior in rats is apparently modulated by dopamine receptors (Schneider et al., 1986). Blockade of D-2 receptors reduces the intake of pellets and of a sweet solution by intact, food-deprived rats and reduces the sham intake of sucrose solutions by food-deprived rats with an open chronic gastric fistula.

SYNERGISTIC ACTIONS OF D-1 AND D-2 RECEPTORS

There is now increasing evidence that D-1 and D-2 receptors act in concert to produce a full response or for some responses selective blockade of either receptor subtype blocks a response.

For example, small doses of a D-2 agonist that produces weak threshold stereotype behavior when combined with a D-1 agonist, at a dose that is inactive, produce a full array of compulsive stereotypic behavior (Mashurano & Waddington, 1986; Arnt et al., 1987). Indeed, it appears that D-1 dopaminergic-activity promotes the expression of behaviors initiated through D-2 receptor stimulation (Braun & Chase, 1986; Barone et al., 1986). Moreover, in rats with unilateral 6-OHDA lesions of the substantia nigra, D-1 receptor agonists at doses that do not induce turning behavior significantly increase the contralateral rotation observed following a low dose of a D-2 agonist (Robertson & Robertson, 1986).

The two dopamine receptor subtypes appear to interact in a synergistic way to affect basal ganglion output (Weick & Walters, 1987). The globus pallidus receives a major input from the striatum thus activity in the globus palladus is likely to reflect changes of striatal dopamine receptor stimulation (Walters et al., 1987). The selective D-2 agonist quinpirole induces dose-dependent increases of pallidal neuronal activity that is significantly less than the activity found after administering the nonselective agonist apomorphine. When quinpirole and a selective D-1 agonist are administered together, activity is similar to that found after apomorphine alone. Depletion of endogenous dopamine by blocking its synthesis with alpha-methyltyrosine reduces the response to quinpirole. Behavior studies of the effects of selective D-1 and D-2 receptor stimulation have yielded comparable changes in locomotor behavior. Thus, it appears that some behaviors require that dopamine receptor subtypes act synergistically to produce a full response.

D-2 antagonists increase dopamine metabolites in the striatum. Selective D-1 agonists enhance the ability of D-2 antagonists to increase dopamine metabolism suggesting a possible functional interaction of the two receptors (Saller & Salama, 1985, 1986a,b).

The administration of small doses of apomorphine and other dopamine receptor agonists produces repeated episodes of yawning in rats and in humans. Experimental evidence (Serra et al., 1987) suggests that the dopamine receptors that mediate the yawning response are of the D-2 type and that these receptors are connected with D-1 receptors in such a way that blockade of the latter results in the functional inactivation of the response. Moreover, methamphetamine releases dopamine and the response can be blocked by either D-1 or D-2 antagonists (Sonsalla et al., 1986).

CONCLUSIONS

The nomenclature proposed by Kebabian and Calne (1979) has had a significant impact on our ability to describe and evaluate dopamine receptors and the functions they modulate. Dopaminergic neurons are found throughout the brain thus it is not surprising that a variety of responses are elicited by administering agonist or antagonist drugs. The development of selective D-1 and D-2 dopaminergic drugs has revealed that some responses may be modulated by a single receptor subtype, others may be modulated reciprocally by the two receptors, and still others may require activation of both receptors for full expression of the response. Table 2 is a first attempt to order function with receptor subtype. We fully recognize that this table will change as future studies unmask the relationships between receptor subtype and function. A better understanding of receptor function may be of significant value for treating central nervous system disorders and for preventing the side effects associated with dopaminergic drug therapy.

REFERENCES

Arnt, J., Hyttel, J., & Perregaard, J. (1987). Dopamine D-1 receptor agonists combined with the selective D-2 agonist quinpirole facilitate the expression of oral stereotyped behavior in rats. *Eur. J. Pharmacol.*, *133*, 137–145.

Barone, P., Davis, T. A., Braun, A. R., & Chase, T. N. (1986). Dopaminergic mechanisms and motor function: Characterization of D-1 and D-2 dopamine receptor interactions. *Eur. J. Pharmacol.*, *123*, 109–114.

Boireau, A., Chambry, J., Dubedat, P., Farges, G., Carruette, A. M., Zundel, J. L., & Blanchard, J. C. (1986). Enhancing effect of dopamine blockers on evoked acetylcholine release in rat striatal slices: A classical D-2 antagonist response? *Eur. J. Pharmacol., 128,* 93–98.

Bradshaw, C. M., Sheridan, R. D., & Szabadi, E. (1985). Excitatory neuronal responses to dopamine in the cerebral cortex: Involvement of D-2 but not D-1 dopamine receptors. *Br. J. Pharmac., 86,* 483–490.

Braun, A. R., & Chase, T. N. (1986). Obligatory D-1/D-2 receptors interaction in the generation of dopamine agonist related behaviors. *Eur. J. Pharmacol., 131,* 301–306.

Breese, G. R., Baumeister, A. A., McCown, T. J., Emerick, S. G., Frye, G. D., Crotty, K., & Mueller, R. A. (1984). Behavioral differences between neonatal and adult 6-hydroxydopamine-treated rats to dopamine agonists: Relevance to neurological symptoms in clinical syndromes with reduced brain dopamine. *J. Pharmacol. Exptl. Therap., 231,* 343–354.

Breese, G. R., Duncan, G. E., Napier, T. E., Bondy, S. C., Iorio, L. C., & Mueller, R. A. (1986). 6-Hydroxydopamine treatments enhance behavioral responses to intracerebral microinjection of D1 and D2-Dopamine agonists into nucleus accumbens and striatum without changing dopamine antagonist binding. *J. Pharmacol. Exptl. Therap., 240,* 167–176.

Breese, G. R., & Mueller, R. A. (1985). SCH-23390 antagonism of a D-2 dopamine agonist depends upon catecholaminergic neurons. *Eur. J. Pharmacol., 113,* 109–114.

Brown, J. H., & Makman, M. H. (1972). Stimulation by dopamine of adenylate cyclase in retinal homogenates and of adenosine-3′: 5′-cyclic monophosphate formation in intact retina. *Proc. Nat. Acad. Sci. USA, 69,* 539–543.

Carlson, J. H., Bergstrom, D. A., & Walters, J. R. (1987). Stimulation of both D1 and D2 dopamine receptors appears necessary for full expression of postsynaptic effects of dopamine agonists: A neurophysiological study. *Brain Res., 400,* 205–218.

Davis, G. C., Williams, A. C., Markey, S. P., Ebert, M. H., Caine, E. D., Reichert, C. M., & Kopin, I. J. (1979). Chronic Parkinsonism secondary to intravenous injection of meperidine analogues. *Psychiat. Res., 1,* 249.

Gilman, A. G. (1984). G Proteins and dual control of adenylate cyclase. *Cell, 36,* 577–579.

Goldberg, L. I., & Kohli, J. D. (1983). Peripheral dopamine receptors: A classification based on potency series and specific antagonism. *Trends Pharmacol. Sci., 4,* 64–66.

Henry, J. M., Filburn, C. R., Joseph, J. A., & Roth, G. S. (1986). Effect of aging on striatal dopamine receptor subtypes in Wistar rats. *Neurobiol. Aging, 7,* 357–361.

Hess, E. J., Bracha, H. S., Kleinman, J. E., & Creese, I. (1987). Dopamine receptor subtype imbalance in schizophrenia. *Life Sci., 40,* 1487–1497.

Hornykiewicz, O. (1966). Metabolism of brain dopamine in human Parkinsonism: Neurochemical and clinical aspects. In E. Costa, L. J. CoTé, and M. D. Yahr (Eds.), *Biochemistry and Pharmacology of the Basal Ganglia* (pp. 171–185). New York: Raven Press.

Johansson, P., Levin, E., Gunne, L., & Ellison G. (1987). Opposite effects of a D1 and a D2 agonist on oral movements in rats. *Eur. J. Pharmacol., 134,* 83–88.

Kebabian, J. W., & Calne, D. B. (1979). Multiple receptors for dopamine. *Nature, 277,* 93–96.

Kebabian, J. W., Petzold, G. L., & Greengard P. (1972). Dopamine-sensitive adenylate cyclase in caudate nucleus of rat brain, and its similarity to the "Dopamine Receptor." *Proc. Nat. Acad. Sci. USA, 69,* 2145–2149.

Langston, J. W., Ballard, P., Tetrud, J. W., & Irwin, I. (1983). Chronic Parkinsonism in humans due to a product of meperidine-analog synthesis. *Science, 219,* 979–980.

Loscher, W., & Czuczwar, S. J. (1986). Studies on the involvement of dopamine D-1 and D-2 receptors in the anticonvulsant effect of dopamine agonists in various rodent models of epilepsy. *Eur. J. Pharmacol., 128,* 55–65.

Mashurano, M., & Waddington, J. L. (1986). Stereotyped behavior in response to the selective D-2 dopamine receptor agonist RU-24213 is enhanced by pretreatment with the selective D-1 agonist SKF 38393. *Neuropharmacol., 25,* 947–949.

Missale, C., Pizzi, M., Memo, M., Picotti, G. B., Carruba, M. O., & Spano, P. F. (1985). Postsynaptic D1 and D2 dopamine receptors are present in rabbit renal and mesenteric arteries. *Neurosci. Lett., 61,* 207–211.

Nestler, E. J., & Greengard, P. (1983). Protein phosphorylation in the brain. *Nature, 305,* 583–588.

Onali, P., Mereu, G., Olianas, M. C., Bunse, B., Rossetti, Z., & Gessa, G. L. (1985). SCH 23390, a selective D1 dopamine receptor blocker, enhances the firing rate of nigral dopaminergic neurons but fails to activate striatal tyrosine hydroxylase. *Brain Res., 340,* 1–7.

Onali, P., Olianas, M. C., & Gessa, G. L. (1985). Characterization of dopamine receptors mediating inhibition of adenylate cyclase activity in rat striatum. *Mol. Pharmacol., 28,* 138–145.

Robertson, G. S., & Robertson, H. A. (1986). Synergic effects of D1 and D2 dopamine agonists on turning behavior in rats. *Br. Res., 384,* 387–390.

Rosengarten, H., Schweitzer, J. W., & Friedhoff, A. J. (1983). Induction of oral dyskinesias in naive rats by D1 stimulation. *Life Sci., 33,* 2479–2482.

Rossetti, Z., Neff, N. H., & Hadjiconstantinou, M. (1986). Aromatic L-amino acid decarboxylase activity is modulated by D1 dopamine receptors in rat retina. *The Pharmacologist, 28,* 134.

Saller, C. F., & Salama, A. I. (1985). Dopamine receptor subtypes: In vivo biochemical evidence for functional interaction. *Eur. J. Pharmacol., 109,* 297–300.

Saller, C. F., & Salama, A. I. (1986a). D-1 dopamine receptor stimulation elevates plasma prolactin levels. *Eur. J. Pharmacol., 122,* 139–142.

Saller, C. F., & Salama, A. I. (1986b). D-1 and D-2 dopamine receptor blockade: Interactive effects in vitro and in vivo. *J. Pharmacol. Expt. Therap., 236,* 714–720.

Schneider, L. H., Gibbs, J., & Smith, G. P. (1986). D-2 selective receptor antagonists suppress sucrose sham feeding in the rat. *Brain Res. Bull., 17,* 605–611.

Seatton, B. (1982). Further evidence for the involvement of D-2, but not D-1 dopamine receptors in dopaminergic control of striatal cholinergic transmission. *Life Sci., 31,* 2883–2890.

Serra, G., Collu, M., & Gessa, G. L. (1987). Yawning is elicited by D2 dopamine agonists but is blocked by the D1 antagonist, SCH-23390. *Psychopharmacol., 91,* 330–333.

Snyder, S. H. (1981). Dopamine receptors, neuroleptics and schizophrenia. *Am. J. Psychiat., 138,* 1811–1814.

Sonsalla, P. K., Gibb, J. W., & Hanson, G. R. (1986). Roles of D1 and D2 dopamine receptor subtypes in mediating the methamphetamine-induced changes in monoamine systems. *J. Pharmacol. Exptl. Therap., 238,* 932–937.

Starr, B. S., & Starr, M. S. (1986). Differential effects of dopamine D-2 and D-2 agonists and antagonists on velocity of movement, rearing and grooming in the mouse: Implications for the roles of D-2 and D-2 receptors. *Neuropharmacol., 25,* 455–463.

Stoof, J. C., & Kebabian, J. W. (1981). Opposing roles for D-1 and D-2 dopamine receptors in efflux of cyclic AMP from rat neostriatum. *Nature, 294,* 366–368.

Stoof, J. C., & Kebabian, J. W. (1984). Two dopamine receptors: Biochemistry, physiology and pharmacology. *Life Sci., 35,* 2281–2290.

Swennen, L., & Denef, C. (1982). Physiological concentrations of dopamine decrease adenosine 3′,5′-monophosphate levels in cultured rat anterior pituitary cells and enriched population of lactotrophs: Evidence for a causal relationship to inhibition of prolactin release. *Endocrinology, 111,* 398–403.

Uchimura, N., Higashi, H., & Nishi, S. (1986). Hyperpolarizing and depolarizing actions of dopamine via D-1 and D-2 receptors on nucleus accumbens neurons. *Brain Res., 375,* 368–372.

Waddington, J. L. (1986). Behavioral correlates of the action of selective D-1 dopamine receptor antagonists. *Biochem. Pharmacol., 35,* 3661–3667.

Walters, J. R., Bergstrom, D. A., Carlson, J. H., Chase, T. N., & Braun, A. R. (1987). D1 Dopamine receptor activation required for postsynaptic expression of D2 agonist effects. *Science, 236,* 719–722.

Weick, B. G., & Walters, J. R. (1987). Effects of D1 and D2 dopamine receptor stimulation on the activity of substantia nigra pars reticulata neurons in 6-hydroxydopamine lesioned rats: D1/D2 coactivation induces potentiated responses. *Br. Res., 405,* 234–246.

Weiss, S., Sebben, M., Garcia-Sainz, A., & Beckaert, J. (1985). D-2 Dopamine receptor-mediated inhibition of cyclic AMP formation in striatal neurons in primary culture. *Mol. Pharmacol., 27,* 595–599.

13

Dopamine Agonist Induced Dyskinesias, Including Self-Biting Behavior in Monkeys with Supersensitive Dopamine Receptors

MENEK GOLDSTEIN

Animal models which mimic a specific disorder are useful tools for elucidation of the biochemical and pathological abnormalities. Furthermore, animal models are used for evaluation of the therapeutic drug actions and their propensities to produce undesirable side effects. In the last decade we have extensively investigated an animal model in nonhuman primates which replicates certain features of Parkinson's disease (Goldstein et al., 1973, 1980). This model is produced by placing a surgical unilateral lesion in the ventromedial tegmental (VMT) area of the brain stem in monkeys (Poirier & Sourkes, 1965). In Table 1 the deficits in human parkinsonism are compared with those in monkeys with unilateral VMT lesions of the brain stem. Among the various neurological deficits in Parkinson's disease, only tremor and hypokinesia of the extremities contralateral to the lesion are manifested in these monkeys. Moreover, the administration of levodopa or of various centrally acting dopamine (DA) agonists produces responses similar to those observed in parkinsonian patients (Goldstein et al., 1973, 1980).

We have therefore used this animal model to evaluate the antitremor action and the propensity to produce abnormal involuntary movements (AIM's) by various classes of DA agonists. Since in some monkeys DA agonists induce self-biting behavior

TABLE 1
A Comparison of Deficits in Parkinson's Disease and in Monkeys with Unilateral VMT Lesions of the Brain Stem

Parkinson's Disease	*Monkeys with VMT Lesions*
Degeneration of the nigrostriatal DA neurons, lesions in other pigmental brainstem nuclei (locus ceruleus, lew bodies)	Degeneration of the nigrostriatal and mesolimbic DA neurons
Tremor, rigidity, akinesia, gait disturbance	Hypokinesia, tremor
Decreased levels of nigrostriatal DA and of DA synthesizing enzymes	Decreased levels of nigrostriatal mesolimbic DA and of DA synthesizing enzymes
Supersensitivity of postsynaptic DA receptors	Supersensitivity of postsynaptic DA receptors

(SBB) (Goldstein, Kuga et al., 1986) we have investigated the mechanisms which might be responsible for this behavior. Thus, in this presentation we review our studies concerning the antitremor activities of various classes of DA agonists and induction of AIM's with specific emphasis on the occurrence of SBB in monkeys with supersensitive central DA receptors rendered by a unilateral surgical lesion in the VMT area of the brain stem.

TREMOR

In order to evaluate whether the antitremor activity of DA agonists is associated with stimulation of central D-1 or D-2 DA receptors, we have tested a number of DA agonists which stimulate one or both DA receptor subtypes. The results presented in Table 2 show that administration of compounds which stimulate both D-1 and D-2 central DA receptors, such as levodopa, apomorphine and pergolide, effectively relieves tremor. The administration of compounds which stimulate D-2 DA receptors selectively also results in an effective relief of tremor. The extent and duration of the relief is dose-dependent and varies for different DA agonists. However, the administration of the selective D-1 DA agonist SKF 38393 does not produce relief. Several DA agonists which selectively stimulate presynaptic DA receptors (autoreceptors) also effectively relieve tremor in these monkeys. Thus, administration of the selective presynaptic DA agonist EMD 23-448 or of ciladopa results in a complete relief of tremor and the duration is also dose-dependent.

AIMS

In order to evaluate whether the DA agonist-induced AIMs are associated with the stimulation of a specific DA receptor subtype, we have compared the effects of various selective and non-selective agonists. The results presented in Table 3 show that the mixed D-1/D-2 DA agonists (e.g. DA formed from dopa, apomorphine, pergolide), as well as the selective D-2 agonists (e.g. bromocriptine, quinpirole [LY 171555], etc.), produce AIMs in monkeys with unilateral VMT lesions of the brain stem. The duration and severity of the AIMs differ among various DA agonists and parallel with the duration of the relief of tremor. All the tested mixed D-1/D-2 and selective D-2 DA agonists produce AIMs classified as Type I and Type II (see Table 3), while the selective D-1 DA agonist SKF 38393 produces AIMs only of Type I. It is noteworthy that the selective presynaptic DA agonists also produce the less severe AIMs of Type I.

SBB

In the course of our study, we have observed that DA agonists induce SBB in some monkeys with unilateral VMT lesions of the brain stem which postsurgically do not exhibit tremor of the contralateral extremities. To assess whether SBB is associated with stimulation of a specific DA receptor subtype, we have tested the effects of various DA agonists and antagonists on this behavior. It is evident from the results presented in Table 4 that mixed DA agonists, such as DA formed from L-dopa, apomorphine, abeorphine 201-678, produce SBB. The selective D-2 DA agonist quinpirole (LY 171555) or the selective D-1 DA agonist SKF 38393 does not produce this behavior. However, the combined administration of quinpirole and SKF 38393 results in the occurrence of SBB. To determine whether blockade of a DA receptor subtype prevents the DA agonist-induced SBB, the monkeys were pretreated with D-1 or D-2 DA antagonists. Pretreatment with the D-2 DA antagonist (±) sulpiride did not prevent the occurrence of SBB, while pretreatment with the mixed D-1/D-2 DA antagonist fluphenazine or with the selective D-1 antagonist SCH 23390 prevented the L-dopa- or abeorphine 201-678-induced SBB.

TABLE 2
Effect of Different Types of DA Agonists on Tremor in Monkeys with Unilateral VMT Lesions of the Brain Stem

DA Agonist (dose mg/kg)	*Type*	*Tremor*	*Duration of Relief (hrs)*
None	—	Sustained	
DL-Dopa (30)	mixed D-1/D-2	Complete relief	0.5–1
Apomorphine (0.5)	mixed D-1/D-2	Complete relief	0.5–1
Pergolide (0.2)	mixed D-1/D-2	Complete relief	5–8
Bromocriptine (8.0)	D-2	Complete relief	4–6
Quinpirole (0.2)	D-2	Complete relief	4–6
SKF 38393 (3.0)	D-1	No effect	—
Ciladopa (3.0)	Partial agonist (presynaptic)	Complete relief	2–3
EMD 23-448	Partial agonist (presynaptic)	Complete relief	2–3

TABLE 3
Effect of Different Types of DA Agonists on Occurrence of AIMs in Monkeys with Unilateral VMT Lesions of the Brain Stem

DA Agonist		*AIMs*[a]	
(Dose mg/kg)	*Type*	*Type*	*Duration (hrs)*
DL-Dopa (30)	mixed D-1/D-2	I, II	0.5–1
Apomorphine (0.5)	mixed D-1/D-2	I, II	0.5–1
Pergolide (0.2)	mixed D-1/D-2	I, II	5–8
Bromocriptine (8.0)	D-2	I, II	4–5
Quinpirole (0.2)	D-2	I, II	4–5
SKF 38393 (3.0)	D-1	I	0.5
Ciladopa (3.0)	partial agonist (presynaptic)	I	2–3
EMD 23-448	partial agonist (presynaptic)	I	2–3

[a]*AIM I:* Restlessness, slight oral dyskinesia and stereotyped movements.
AIM II: Intensive stereotyped movements, chorea-like movements, biting of the surrounding cage.

DISCUSSION

The existence of two distinct central DA receptor subtypes, D-1 and D-2 (Schwarcz et al., 1978) prompted us to examine whether one or both of them are involved in the mediation of parkinsonian-like tremor in monkeys with unilateral VMT lesions of the brain stem. The results of our study indicate that the relief of tremor is associated with stimulation of central D-2 DA receptors. Furthermore, the selective D-2 DA agonists induce AIMs of Type I and Type II and we conclude that these behaviors are primarily mediated by the central D-2 DA receptors. However, some of the oral dyskinesias and restlessness is also induced by the D-1 DA agonist SKF 38393-A and these components of the abnormal behavior might be attributable to the stimulation of the D-1 DA receptors.

The findings that mixed D-1/D-2 DA agonists produce SBB in some monkeys with unilateral VMT lesions of the brain stem and that SBB is abolished by the administration of the selective D-1 DA antagonist SCH 23390 indicate that this behavior is mediated by D-1 DA receptors (Goldstein, Kuga et al., 1986). Although the selective D-1 agonist SKF 38393 or the selective D-2 agonist quinpirole by itself does not produce SBB, the combined administration of the two agonists produces SBB for a short period. These results suggest that the combined stimulation of D-1 and D-2 DA receptors produces a synergistic response. Since this effect is short-lasting and since the action of SKF 38393, but not of quinpirole, is short-acting, one may also interpret that SBB is mainly associated with stimulation of the D-1 DA receptors.

It is noteworthy that even prolonged treatment with DA agonists in parkinsonian patients does not produce SBB. The absence of this behavior in parkinsonian patients, whose pathology is associated with degeneration of the nigro-striatal DA neurons, suggests that either the patients are treated with lower doses of DA agonists than those required to produce SBB in monkeys or that the DA neuronal degeneration in monkey brain differs from the parkinsonian brain. To examine the latter possibility we have studied the anatomical correlates of DA agonist-induced SBB in the primate. (Goldstein, Deutsch et al., 1986). The preliminary results indicate that in an animal which exhibited agonist-

TABLE 4
The Effect of Different Types of DA Agonists on the Occurrence of SBB in Some Monkeys with Unilateral VMT Lesions of the Brain Stem

DA Agonist (dose mg/kg)	*Type*	*Severity of SBB*	*Duration of SBB (hrs)*
DL-Dopa (30)	mixed D-1/D-2	mild	0.5–1
Apomorphine (0.5)	mixed D-1/D-2	mild	0.5–1
Abeorphine 201-678 (0.1)	mixed D-1/D-2	severe	2–3
Pergolide* (0.2)	mixed D-1/D-2	none	2–3
Quinpirole (0.2)	D-2	none	2–3
SKF 38393 (3.0)	D-1	none	2–3
Quinpirole (0.2) + SKF 38393 (3.0)		mild	0.5

*Pergolide is predominantly a D-2 DA agonist.

induced SBB the surgically induced lesion occupied the dorsolateral VMT. Tyrosine hydroxylase (TH) immunohistochemistry revealed that DA neurons in the lesion area were lost, as were most DA neurons in the substantia nigra (A_9 cell group) and retrorubral field (A_8 cell group). Surviving DA neurons in the ventral substantia nigra were greatly hypertrophied. The loss of TH fibers in the putamen was virtually complete, whereas only a slight decrease in the caudate innervation was observed. The caudate loss was restricted to the diffuse DA innervation, and the dotted innervation was spared. In addition to lesion-induced loss of midbrain DA neurons, there was a partial loss of neurons in the A_7 cell group of the pons and in the medullary C1 adrenergic cell group. The density of substance P fibers in the substantia nigra rostral to the lesion was also decreased. Based on these results we conclude that denervation supersensitivity of mesolimbic and mesocortical sites as well as striatal areas may be central to the development of SBB. Furthermore other monoaminergic systems, such as the C1 adrenergic neurons and the A_7 noradrenergic neurons, may be important in agonist-induced SBB and Lesch-Nyhan disease.

The question whether the DA agonist-induced SBB in monkeys with unilateral VMT lesions of the brain stem represents a valid model of the Lesch-Nyhan syndrome in man deserves some comment. The levels of DA and its metabolites were found to be reduced in the postmortem striatum of Lesch-Nyhan patients (Lloyd et al., 1981) and its relation to the deficiency of hypoxanthine-guanine phosphoribosyltransferase (HPRT) (Wilson et al., 1983) in this disease is not known. Our recent findings that HPRT is localized on intrastriatal neurons which contain D-1 and D-2 DA receptors suggest that in these neurons the DA receptor might be regulated by nucleotide levels arising from the salvage pathway. The abnormal regulation of the affinity states of the DA receptors by the guanine nucleotides might be involved in the pathology of Lesch-Nyhan disease. Since GTP serves as a precursor for the pteridine cofactor which is required for the activity of TH, the rate-limiting enzyme in the biosynthesis of DA, it is conceivable that reduced HPRT levels result in a reduction of DA formation. The decreased formation of DA could explain the low levels of this neurotransmitter in the postmortem brain of Lesch-Nyhan patients and the development of DA receptor supersensitivity. It is noteworthy that automutilation occurs not only in Lesch-Nyhan syndrome but also in some autistic children, as well as in some children with mental retardation. The possible link between the manifestations of automutilation in these disorders and a dysfunction of DA neurons deserves further investigation.

REFERENCES

Goldstein, M., Battista, A. H., Ohmoto, T., Anagnoste, B. & Fuxe, K. (1973). *Science, 179,* 816–817.

Goldstein, M., Deutch, A. Y., Shimizu, Y., Fuxe, K., & Roth, R. H. (1986). *Soc. Neurosci.,* Abstr. 26814.

Goldstein, M., Kuga, S., Kusano, N., Meller, E., Dancis, J., & Schwarcz, R. (1986). *Brain Res., 367,* 114–120.

Goldstein, M., Lieberman, A., Lew, J. Y., Asano, T., Rosenfeld, M. R., & Makman, M. H. (1980). *Proc. Natl. Acad. Sci. U.S.A., 77,* 3725–3728.

Lloyd, K. G., Hornykiewicz, O., Davidson, L., Shannak, K., Farley, I., Goldstein, M., Shibuya, M., Kelley, W. N., & Fox, I. H. (1981). *N. Engl. J. Med., 305,* 1106–1111.

Poirier, L. J., & Sourkes, T. L. (1965). *Brain, 88,* 181–192.

Schwarcz, R., Creese, I., Coyle, J. T., & Snyder, S. H. (1978). *Nature (London), 271,* 766–768.

Wilson, J. M., Young, A. B., & Kelley, W. N. (1983). *N. Engl. J. Med., 309,* 900–910.

Name Index

Subject Index

www.ingramcontent.com/pod-product-compliance
Ingram Content Group UK Ltd.
Pitfield, Milton Keynes, MK11 3LW, UK
UKHW022004180926
475701UK00003B/184
* 9 7 8 1 1 3 8 8 8 4 4 3 4 *